Computer Based Learning and Information Technology

Computer Based Learning and Information Technology

Edited by **Stanley Harmon**

New York

Published by Willford Press,
118-35 Queens Blvd., Suite 400,
Forest Hills, NY 11375, USA
www.willfordpress.com

Computer Based Learning and Information Technology
Edited by Stanley Harmon

International Standard Book Number: 978-1-68285-326-9 (Hardback)

Printed in the United States of America.

Contents

Preface

As the presence of computers is impacting all areas of our lives; education is no exception. Technological advances have constantly aided sectors such as e-learning. This exclusive book is a compilation of researches and case studies contributed by eminent scholars from across the globe. It brings forth some revolutionary studies in the field of computer-assisted learning and cognition. It presents human-centric computing in a new light. This book will be an asset for students, scholars and professionals engaged in this field.

Various studies have approached the subject by analyzing it with a single perspective, but the present book provides diverse methodologies and techniques to address this field. This book contains theories and applications needed for understanding the subject from different perspectives. The aim is to keep the readers informed about the progress in the field; therefore, the contributions were carefully examined to compile novel researches by specialists from across the globe.

Indeed, the job of the editor is the most crucial and challenging in compiling all chapters into a single book. In the end, I would extend my sincere thanks to the chapter authors for their profound work. I am also thankful for the support provided by my family and colleagues during the compilation of this book.

Editor

Publishing and discovering context-dependent services

Naseem Ibrahim[1]*, Mubarak Mohammad[2] and Vangalur Alagar[2]

*Correspondence:
naseem.ibrahim@asurams.edu
[1] Department of Mathematics and
Computer Science, Albany State
University, Georgia, USA
Full list of author information is
available at the end of the article

Abstract

In service oriented computing, service providers and service requesters are main interacting entities. A service provider *publishes* the services it wishes to make public using service registries. A service requester initiates a *discovery* process to find the service that meets its requirements using the service registries. Current approaches for the publication and discovery do not realize the essential relationship between the service contract and the conditions in which the service can guarantee its contract. Moreover, they do not use any formal methods for specifying services, contracts, and compositions. Without a formal basis it is not possible to justify through a rigorous verification the correctness conditions for service compositions and the satisfaction of contractual obligations in service provisions. In our recent works, we have identified the role of contextual information, trustworthiness information and legal rules in service provision. This paper focuses on the publication and discovery of trustworthy context-dependent services as supported by the novel framework *FrSeC*. It introduces a novel ranking algorithm that ranks trustworthy context-dependent services according to the degree they match service requesters requirements. Finally, this paper introduces a prototype implementation for the matching and ranking of services as supported by *FrSeC*.

Keywords: Service publication, Service discovery, Service ranking, Context-awareness, Trustworthy service provision

Introduction

In traditional Service-oriented Architecture (SOA) interactions, the three main interacting elements are the *service provider*, the *service requester* and the *service registry*. The service provider defines a service and publishes it through the service registry. The service registry acts as a data center that holds the services published by the different service providers. The service requester accesses the registry to get information about available services. It will then use this information to select a specific service that meets its requirements and will interact with the service provider of the selected service.

Hence, the main activities in SOA are *service publication*, *service discovery* and *service provision*. *Service publication* refers to the process of defining service contracts by service providers and publishing them through available service registries. *Service discovery* is the process of finding services that have been previously published and that meet the requirements of a service requester [1]. Typically, service discovery includes *service query, service matching,* and *service ranking.* Service requesters define their require-ments as service queries. Service matching refers to the process of matching the service requester requirements, as defined in the service query, with the published services. Ser-vice ranking is the process of ordering the matched services according to the degree they meet the requester requirements. The ranking will enable the service requester to select a specific or a most relevant service from the list of candidate services. *Ser-vice provision* refers to the process of executing a selected service. The execution may include some form of an interaction between the service requester and the service provider.

In practice, before publishing services a service provider defines the contract that can be guaranteed by a service. This contract includes the functionalities and quality of services guarantees that the provider can make. But such guarantees are not absolute. A service cannot guarantee its contract in all situations. It can only guarantee its contract in a predefined set of conditions. These conditions are usually related to the *context* of the service provider and requester. Context information has been defined as any infor-mation used to characterize the situation of an entity, such as location, time and purpose [2]. Legal rules also play a crucial role in constraining the publication and discovery of services. For example, a wireless phone provider may include in the service contract a guarantee of excellent quality, but this guarantee is not absolute. It may have a constrain-ing condition stating that in order to ensure excellent quality, the consumer should be located within 1000 meters from cell phone stations. This constraint is related to the con-textual information of the service consumer. In addition, local legal rules may black-out wireless service in secure-critical locations. Such legal rules should be an essential part of every contract.

It is necessary to distinguish between legal rules and nonfunctional requirements. If a nonfunctional property is "a soft" requirement it may be ignored. However ignoring a legal rule is equivalent to a "legal violation", which might land in legal disputes and even lead to loss of entire business. In essence, not enforcing a legal rule prevents the execution of a contract. Almost all current approaches use only functional and nonfunctional prop-erties to enable the publication, discovery and provision of services. In [3], no distinction is made between legal rules and nonfunctional properties. Failure to include contextual information and legal rules will only mislead the consumer to believe in the advertised excellent quality of wireless service, regardless of where the consumer is domiciled which is not true.

To remedy the drawbacks of available service provision frameworks we have introduced two main concepts [4-6]. The first is a formal service model, which is called *Config-uredService.* In this model, service and contract are packaged together. The service part includes functional and nonfunctional aspects of service, and the data parameters and attributes that are essential to define the functional and nonfunctional aspects. The con-tract part includes business rules, legal aspects, and context information. The second concepts is the *Formal Framework for Providing Context-dependent Services (FrSeC)* in which *ConfiguredServices* and their compositions are formally embedded. Service publi-cation, service discovery, service selection and ranking, and service delivery are rigorously defined. The significance here is the way context information is defined for each stage, and is used in the interactions between the different components of the architecture elements in order to sustain the trustworthiness properties at all stages.

Motivation and contribution

In *FrSeC*, we have introduced contextual information, trustworthiness properties and legal rules as first class elements in both service publication and discovery. The introduction of contextual information and legal rules in service contracts introduces many challenges in service adaptation during service rediscovery process. The main goal of this paper is to address these challenges, and offer novel approaches for service publication, discovery and ranking, taking into consideration contextual information and legal rules.

This paper is structured as follows. First, we provide an overview of our formal framework for providing context dependent services *FrSeC* [4-6]. *FrSeC* supports the provision of services with context dependent services. Second, we focus on the publication and discovery of context-dependent services. We provide a novel formal notation for service publication. The three issues that we emphasize are *context*, *legal rules*, and *adaptability*. In *FrSeC*, service providers publish only *ConfiguredServices* in the service registry. A *ConfiguredService* is a structure that bundles together service functionality, service contract, and provision context. Service requesters query the service registry to find available *ConfiguredServices*. Often there is a semantic gap between the service query and the services in the registry. To deal with this, we introduced in the third part of this paper three novel query types for service discovery, and a ranking algorithm. Fourth, we discuses adaptability in *FrSeC*. Fifth, we introduce a prototype implementation of the ranking and matching supported by *FrSeC*. Finally, we briefly compare our work with the related work and provide concluding remarks.

An overview of FrSeC

This section briefly introduce the formal framework for providing context-dependent services *FrSeC*. The introduction of the main elements of *FrSeC* is essential to understand the contribution of this paper, namely the publication, discovery and ranking of services supported by *FrSeC*.

FrSeC was motivated by the need for a framework that supports the publication, discovery and provision of services with context-dependent contracts. The main elements of *FrSeC* are shown in Figure 1. A complete formal definition of *FrSeC* is presented in the two recent papers [4,6]. Below is a brief summary of *FrSeC* elements.

Service Provider (SP)

It is the entity that provides an implementation of a service specification. The service specification is published by the SP using SRe.

Service Registry (SRe)

It is a central repository for services, in which Service Providers publish their services and PU discovers services. It includes semantic definitions for domain specific concepts.

Context Gathering Unit (CGU)

FrSeC contains at least three context gathering units. One unit collects contextual information to assist SR in formulating their service queries. Another unit collects contextual information relevant to SP. The third unit collects contextual information to assist EU and

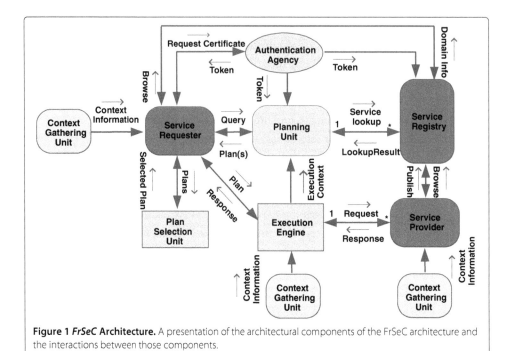

Figure 1 *FrSeC* **Architecture.** A presentation of the architectural components of the FrSeC architecture and the interactions between those components.

PU in dynamic planning activities. A central context manager may be added to monitor and trigger the adaptive context-aware behavior of the framework.

Service Requester (SR)

It is the entity requiring a certain functionality to be satisfied. It represents the client side of the interaction. It can be an application or another service. SR defines its requirements in a service query.

The Authentication Agency (AU)

It is the entity responsible for ensuring trustworthy access to SRe. It provides requesters with certificates (tokens) that allow them to access SRe. The certificate type depends on the legal and contextual information of the requester.

Planning Unit (PU)

It is responsible for managing the service discovery process by interacting with SR, SRe and AU. It also defines service composition. The composition includes defining the *plans* that can satisfy a query requirement. A plan defines the execution logic of a service or multiple services that collectively achieve the functional, nonfunctional and trustworthiness requirements of the requester. A complete formal composition theory is defined in [5]. This theory considers the functional, nonfunctional, legal and contextual parts of the service when defining the composition result.

Plan Selection Unit (PSU)

It is responsible for helping SR to select one or more plans from the set of plans received from PU. For each plan received, it requests additional information, such as data parameters, from SR and verifies that the information in the plan is complete with respect to the request. If it finds the information incomplete the chosen plan is ignored, otherwise the plan is selected for SR.

Execution Unit (EU)

It is responsible for managing the provision of services. It executes the selected plan. The execution process will include communicating with the service providers involved in the plan by sending service *requests* and obtaining service *responses*.

Service publication

Service providers publish service contracts through the Service Registry (introduced above) in order to make them available for discovery. In current approaches (discussed in the Related Work Section), the service contract includes only the functional and nonfunctional requirements together with any semantic information the service provider wishes to make public. But in *FrSeC* the service definition is much richer. It includes the service contract together with the related contextual conditions. Hence, we introduced the concept *ConfiguredService*, which is a structure in which service functionality, service contract, and service provision context are bundled together. SP publishes the two main elements, namely the *contract* and *context*, in the *ConfiguredService*.

The contract includes *function, nonfunctional properties* and *legal issues*. The context part of the *ConfiguredService* includes the main parts *context info* and *context rules*. The *context info* defines the contextual information of the *ConfiguredService*. The *context rules* define the contextual information related to SR that should be true for SP to guarantee its *ConfiguredService* contract.

Example 1. *Table 1 shows a ConfiguredService of a Car Repair Shop. The repair shop charges 60$ per hour and requires a deposit of 300$ with the condition that the car owner is a member of the* Canadian Automotive Association (CAA).

In [5], we introduced the novel service model *ConfiguredService*. *ConfiguredService* is formally defined using a model-based approach. The formal model is built from set theory and logic. Below is a formal presentation of *ConfiguredService*.

Constraints

A constraint is a logical expression, defined over data parameters and attributes in first order predicate logic. If $\mathbb{C}$ denotes the set of all such logical expressions, $X \in \mathbb{C}$ is a constraint. The following notation is used in our definition:

- $\mathbb{T}$ denotes the set of all data types, including abstract data types and $Dt \in \mathbb{T}$ means Dt is a datatype.
- $v : Dt$ denotes that v is either constant or variable of type Dt.
- X_v is a constraint on v. If v is a constant then X_v is true.
- V_q denotes the set of values of data type q.
- $x : \Delta$ denotes a logical expression $x \in \mathbb{C}$ defined over the set of parameters Δ.

Parameters

A parameter is a 3-tuple, defining a data type, a variable of that type, and a constraint on the values assumed by the variable. We denote the set of data parameters as $\Lambda = \{\lambda = (Dt, v, X_v) | Dt \in \mathbb{T}, v : Dt, X_v \in \mathbb{C}\}$.

Table 1 RepairShop *ConfiguredService* description

ConfiguredService	Function		NonFunctional	Legal	ContextRule	ContextInfo
RepairShop	**Name:**ReserveRS **Pre:**CarBroken==T **Post:**HasAppointment==T **Address:** XXX	**InputParameters:** CarBroken:bool deposit:double CarType:string failureType:string	**ResultName:**ResultRS **OutputParameters:** HasAppointment:bool numberOfHours:int	Price==60$/h	deposit==300$ **PriceCondition:** CarType=toyota	membership==CAA	(location,montreal)

A description of the RepairShop *ConfiguredService* containing the contract and context information.

Attributes

An attribute has a name and type, and is used to define some semantic information associated with the name. The set of attributes is $\alpha = \{(Dt, v_\alpha) | Dt \in \mathbb{T}, v_\alpha : Dt\}$.

Context

A context is formalized as a 2-tuple $\beta = \langle r, c \rangle$, where $r \in \mathbb{C}$, built over the contextual information c. Context information is formalized using the notation in [7]: Let $\tau : DIM \rightarrow I$, where $DIM = \{X_1, X_2, \ldots, X_n\}$ is a finite set of dimensions and $I = \{a_1, a_2, \ldots, a_n\}$ is a set of types. The function τ associates a dimension to a type. Let $\tau(X_i) = a_i$, $a_i \in I$. We write c as an aggregation of ordered pairs (X_j, v_j), where $X_j \in DIM$, and $v_j \in \tau(X_j)$.

Example 2. *Using the context notation, the contextual information of ConfiguredService RepairShop(rs) presented in Table 1, is written as $\beta_{rs} = \langle r_{rs}, c_{rs} \rangle$, where $r_{rs} = \{(membership == caa)\}$ is the context rule and $c_{rs} = \{(Location, Montreal)\}$ is the contextual information of the service provider.*

Contract

A contract is a 3-tuple $\sigma = \langle f, \kappa, l \rangle$, where the service function f, the set of nonfunctional properties κ and the set l of legal issues that bind the service contract are defined below.

Example 3. *Using this formalism the RepairShop contract presented in Table 1, is written as $\sigma_{rs} = \langle f_{rs}, \kappa_{rs}, l_{rs} \rangle$.*

- ***Service function:*** A service function is a 4-tuple $f = \langle g, i, pr, po \rangle$, where g is the function signature, i is the function result, pr is the precondition, and po is the postcondition. A signature is a 3-tuple $g = \langle n, d, u \rangle$, where n is the function identification name, d is the set of function parameters and u is the function address, the physical address on a network that can be used to call a function. The result is defined as $i = \langle m, q \rangle$, where m is the result identification name and q is the set of parameters resulting from executing the *ConfiguredService*. The precondition pr and the postcondition po are data constraints.

  Example 4. *The RepairShop contract functionality presented in Table 1, is formally written as $f_{rs} = \langle g_{rs}, i_{rs}, pr_{rs}, po_{rs} \rangle$, where*

    - *$g_{rs} = \langle n_{rs}, d_{rs}, u_{rs} \rangle$, where $n_{rs} = (ReserveRS)$, $d_{rs} = \{(CarBroken, bool), (deposit, double), (CarType, string), (failureType, string)\}$, and $u_{rs} = (XXX)$.*
    - *$i_{rs} = \langle m_{rs}, q_{rs} \rangle$, where $m_{rs} = (ResultRS)$ and $q_{rs} = \{(HasAppointment, bool), (numberOfHours, int)\}$.*
    - *$pr_{rs} = \{(CarBroken == true)\}$ and $po_{rs} = \{(HasAppointment == true)\}$.*

- ***Nonfunctional property:*** Defined as a 6-tuple $\kappa = \langle \rho, \epsilon, \psi, \eta, p, tr \rangle$. The safety guarantee ρ includes time guarantee ρ_t and data guarantee ρ_d. The time guarantee is defined as the time the service takes to provide its function. The data guarantee refers to the accuracy of data. The security guarantee ϵ defines the set of security protocols that the Service Provider has followed to guarantee confidentiality and integrity constraints. The reliability guarantee ψ refers to the guaranteed maximum time between failures. The availability guarantee η refers to the guaranteed maximum time for repairs. The price is defined as a 3-tuple $p = \langle a, cu, un \rangle$, where a is the price amount defined as a non negative double, cu is currency tied to a currency type $cType$, and un is the pricing unit. Provider Trust is defined as a 3-tuple $tr = \langle ce, pg, re \rangle$. Lowest price guarantee pg is represented by a Boolean flag that is true when a *ConfiguredService* can guarantee its price to be lower than the price of any other *ConfiguredService* providing the same functionality. Client recommendations ce and recommendations from independent organizations re can be defined as sets of ordered pairs representing the clients or organization and associated recommendation.

Example 5. *The nonfunctional property in the RepairShop contract presented in Table 1, is formalized as $\kappa_{rs} = \langle p_{rs} \rangle$, $p_{rs} = \langle a_{rs}, cu_{rs}, un_{rs} \rangle$, where $a_{rs} = (60)$ is the cost, $cu_{rs} = (dollar)$ is the currency, and $un_{rs} = (hour)$ is the pricing unit.*

- ***Legal issues:*** A legal issue is a rule, expressed as a logical expression in $\mathbb{C}$. A rule may imply another rule, however no two rules may conflict each other. We write $l = \{y | y \in \mathbb{C}\}$ to represent the set of legal rules. The legal aspect of the RepairShop contract presented in Table 1, is formally written as $l_{rs} = \{(deposit = 300), (CarType == toyota)\}$.

Putting the above definitions together we arrive at a formal definition for *ConfiguredService*.

Definition 1. *A ConfiguredService is a 4-tuple $s = \langle \Lambda, \alpha, \beta, \sigma \rangle$, where Λ is a set of parameters, α is a set of attributes, β is a context, and σ is a contract.*

Service discovery

To be able to select and invoke a service that meets its requirements, a service requester should initiate a discovery process. The discovery process includes *service query, service matching,* and *service ranking.* First, SR defines his requirements in the service query. Second, the query is matched with available *ConfiguredServices* by PU. Third, PU ranks available candidate *ConfiguredServices*. Fourth, SR with the help of PSU, selects a *ConfiguredService* from the set of ranked *ConfiguredServices*. The novelty of the discovery process supported by *FrSeC* is two-fold. First, the discovery process takes into consideration legal requirements and context conditions together with functional and nonfunctional requirements. Second, depending on the requirements of the service requester, *FrSeC* supports the two types of queries *traditional style* and *buffet style.* The rest of this section discusses service query and matching. Service ranking is discussed separately in the next section.

Traditional style

In traditional style discovery, the requester has a clear idea about the requirements. But, the semantic information necessary to define the query is missing. Hence, SR accesses SRe to get the domain knowledge which will help in defining the query. The query process can be defined in the following steps:

1. SR sends a request to the AU for a certificate to access SRe.
2. AU provides the certificate depending on the legal and contextual information of SR.

3. SR, with the help of the certificate, browses SRe to gain domain knowledge.
4. SRe provides SR with domain knowledge, such as available domains and their associated functionalities.
5. SR uses this domain knowledge to construct the query and sends it to PU.
6. PU defines and sends service lookups to SRe.
7. The service lookup result is then used by PU to perform matching between the query and available services.
8. PU defines the query result (plan) and sends it to SR with any feedback if necessary.

Traditional style discovery can be either *exact-match* discovery or *weighted-match* discovery as discussed below.

Exact-match

In exact-match discovery, the requester requires an exact match to the requirements. The candidate *ConfiguredServices* should be able to guarantee all the requirements. The exact-match query, as shown in Figure 2, consists of the five main parts *required function, required nonfunctional properties, required legal issues, consumer contextual information,* and *authentication certificate*. The query also contains the set of parameters that it can understand. This set is a subset of the parameters associated with the functionality it chose when accessing SRe. The required nonfunctional properties are a subset of the nonfunctional properties associated with the functionality defined in SRe. The three following definitions formalize an exact-match query.

Definition 2. *An exact-match query q_e is defined as $q_e = \langle \hat{f}, \hat{\kappa}, \hat{c}, \hat{l}, E, \hat{\Lambda} \rangle$, where $\hat{f}$ is a query required function, $\hat{\kappa}$ is the nonfunctional requirement, $\hat{l}$ is the legal rules requirements, $\hat{c}$ is the contextual information of the service consumer, E is the authentication certificate and $\hat{\Lambda}$ is the set of parameters SR can provide or understand. The formal definitions of context information, legal rules and parameters are identical to the definitions in the previous section.*

Definition 3. *The required function is defined as $\hat{f} = \langle \hat{pr}, \hat{po}, \hat{D}, \hat{SF} \rangle$, where $\hat{pr}$ is the set of preconditions of the required function, $\hat{po}$ is the set of postconditions of the required*

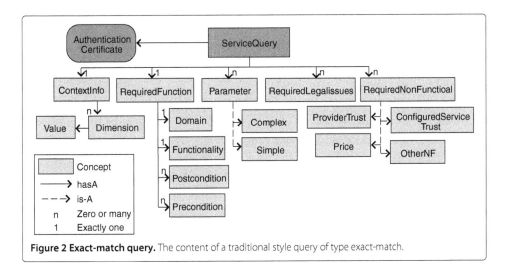

Figure 2 Exact-match query. The content of a traditional style query of type exact-match.

function, $\hat{D} = (x : x|string)$ is the associated domain as defined in SRe and $\hat{SF} = (x : x|string)$ is the functionality as defined in SRE. The formal definition of precondition and postcondition is identical to the one in the previous section.

Definition 4. *The required nonfunctional property is defined as $\hat{\kappa} = \langle \hat{\rho}, \hat{\epsilon}, \hat{\psi}, \hat{\eta}, \hat{p}, \hat{tr} \rangle$, where $\hat{\rho}$ is the required safety guarantee, $\hat{\epsilon}$ is the required security guarantee, $\hat{\psi}$ is the required availability guarantee, $\hat{\eta}$ is required the reliability guarantee, $\hat{p}$ is the maximum price required and $\hat{tr}$ is the required provider trust guarantee. The formal definition of each of those nonfunctional properties is identical to the definition in the previous section.*

Example 6. *If a service requester is attempting an exact-match query for the repair shop functionality defined in Table 1, the query could be defined as $q_e = \langle \hat{f}, \hat{\kappa}, \hat{c}, \hat{l}, E, \hat{\Lambda} \rangle$ where:*

- *$\hat{f} = \langle \hat{pr}, \hat{po}, \hat{D}, \hat{SF} \rangle$, where $\hat{pr} = \{(CarBroken == true)\}$, $\hat{po} = \{(HasAppointment == true)\}$, $\hat{D} = (CarDomain)$, and $\hat{SF} = (RepairShopFunctionality)$.*
- *$\hat{\kappa} = \langle \hat{p} \rangle$, where $\hat{p} = \langle \hat{a}, \hat{cu}, \hat{un} \rangle$, $\hat{a} = (50)$, $\hat{cu} = (dollar)$ and $\hat{un} = (hour)$.*
- *$\hat{l} = \{(deposit = 500)\}$.*
- *$\hat{c} = \{(membership == caa)\}$.*
- *$\hat{\Lambda} = \{(CarBroken, bool), (deposit, double), (CarType, string), (failureType, string)\}$*

After receiving the lookup result from SRe, PU will match available *ConfiguredServices* with the service query. In exact-match the matching process will result in a *ServiceType* which is a list of candidate *ConfiguredServices*. All *ConfiguredServices* in the *ServiceType* provide the exact match to all the requirements defined in the service query. For each *ConfiguredService* in the lookup result the matching will:

1. compare the query functionality with the *ConfiguredService* functionality,
2. compare the query nonfunctional requirements with the *ConfiguredService* nonfunctional properties,
3. compare the query legal issues with the *ConfiguredService* legal rules, and
4. use the query contextual information to make sure the *ConfiguredService* context rules are met.

Weighted-match

The formal definition of the weighted-match query is very close to the exact-match query. The only difference is the inclusion of the weights. In weighted-match discovery, the requester knows the requirements, however unsure about them. SR states the requirements in a query with the expectation that the best matched services, that might not be exact matches, will be given. That is, the *ConfiguredServices* received by the service requester do not have to match all the stated requirements. When stating the query the requester assigns a weight, representing the priority, with every property requirement. A higher weight indicates a higher priority. SR can also state *exact* property to indicate that an exact match is necessary for this particular property. Stating the weight is valid for the elements of the required function, nonfunctional requirements and the required legal rules. With respect to contextual information, SR can state more than one possible set of contextual information. As an example, the context information for service delivery can be either the service be delivered at home or at office. Each contextual information will be assigned a weight to indicate the preference of the requester. In our further discussion we assume that the assigned weights belong to the set *{Low, BelowAverage, Average, AboveAverage, High, Exact}*, in which the values are listed in strictly decreasing order of priority.

Definition 5. *A weighted-match query is defined as* $q_w = \langle \hat{f}, \hat{\kappa}, \hat{c}, \hat{l}, E, \hat{\Lambda}, \Xi \rangle$, *where* $\hat{f}$, $\hat{\kappa}$, $\hat{l}$, $\hat{c}$, E *and* $\hat{\Lambda}$ *are defined as in the traditional query, and* $\Xi : (x \in \{Low, BelowAverage, Average, AboveAverage, High, Exact\}) \to (y \in \{\hat{pr}, \hat{po}, \hat{\rho}, \hat{\epsilon}, \hat{\psi}, \hat{\eta}, \hat{p}, \hat{tr}, \hat{l}, \hat{c}\}$ *is a function that assign weights to the elements of the weighted-match query.*

Example 7. *Adding weights to the query defined in Example 6 the weighted-match style query will be defined as* $q_w = \langle \hat{f}, \hat{\kappa}, \hat{c}, \hat{l}, E, \hat{\Lambda}, \Xi \rangle$ *where* $\hat{f}$, $\hat{\kappa}$, $\hat{c}$, $\hat{l}$, E *and* $\hat{\Lambda}$ *are defined as in Example 6, and* $\Xi = \{((CarBroken == true), \textbf{Exact}), ((HasAppointment == true), \textbf{Exact}), (\hat{p}, \textbf{High}), ((deposit = 500), \textbf{Average})\}$.

The matching process in weighted-match discovery considers all possible *Configured-Services* even if some properties are not satisfied. All candidate *ConfiguredServices* will be included in the matching result *ServiceType*, with the exception of the *ConfiguredServices* that do not provide a match for a requirement with *Exact* weight.

Buffet style

The main difference between traditional style and buffet style is that in traditional style the requester is more or less clear about the requirements in order to be able to define the query in terms of these requirements, whereas in buffet style the requester is not at all clear about the requirements. Hence, the SRe is browsed for available *ConfiguredServices* and a query is defined only in terms of existing *ConfiguredServices*. The buffet style query process can be defined in the following steps:

1. SR sends a request to the AU for a certificate to access SRe.
2. AU provides the certificate depending on the legal and contextual information of SR.
3. SR, with the help of the certificate, browses SRe for available *ConfiguredServices*.
4. SRe provides SR with high level information about the set of available *ConfiguredServices*.
5. SR defines the query in terms of specific *ConfiguredServices* and sends it to PU.
6. PU will access the SRe to get the complete information about the required *ConfiguredServices*.
7. SRe will verify that SR has the required authentication to use the required *ConfiguredServices*.
8. PU defines the query result (plan) to include the complete *ConfiguredServices* information and sends it to SR with any feedback if necessary.

No matching process is necessary in buffet style, because the service requester is querying only *ConfiguredServices*. As a consequence, the definition of buffet style query, shown in Figure 3, consists of the three main parts *required ConfiguredService, consumer*

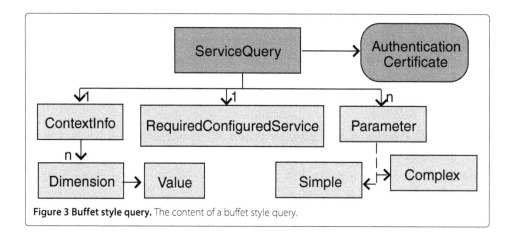

Figure 3 Buffet style query. The content of a buffet style query.

contextual information, and *authentication certificate.* The following two definitions formalize a buffet style query.

Definition 6. *A buffet style query is defined as $q_b = \langle \hat{cs}, \hat{c}, E, \hat{\Lambda} \rangle$, where $\hat{cs}$ is the required ConfiguredService defined as in Section 2, $\hat{c}$ is the contextual information of the service consumer defined as in Section 2, E is the authentication certificate and $\hat{\Lambda}$ is the set of parameters SR can provide or understand, all defined as in Section 2.*

Example 8. *If SR is attempting a buffet style query for the Configured-Service RepairShop defined in Table 1, the query will be defined as $q_b = \langle \hat{cs}, \hat{c}, E, \hat{\Lambda} \rangle$, where $\hat{cs} = s_{rs}$. $\hat{c} = \{(membership == caa)\}$, and $\hat{\Lambda} = \{(CarBroken, bool), (deposit, double), (CarType, string), (failureType, string)\}$.*

Service ranking

In buffet-style the service requester queries for a concrete *ConfiguredService,* and hence no ranking is necessary. Service ranking is necessary for weighted-match service queries, for the following reasons. In exact matching, the only difference between the *Configured-Services* in the *ServiceType* is the *order* they were discovered. A *ConfiguredService A* that was discovered before *ConfiguredService B* will precede it in the *ServiceType* list. This is because all services provide an exact match to the requirements, which is *not* the case in weighted-match. For a weighted-match, the position of a service in a *ServiceType* should indicate the degree to which the requester requirements are met. That is, in weighted-match search a service that appears first in a *ServiceType* should have the best match with the stated requirements than a service that appears later in the *ServiceType* list. These considerations have motivated us to discover a ranking method.

In *FrSeC,* the ranking process is performed by PU. The process takes as inputs the weighted-match query and the *ServiceType,* and generates as output an ordered *Service-Type.* The ranking process can be defined in the following 3 steps.

Form weight vector

In formulating a weighted-match query the requester assigns a weight to each property that is relevant for him. PU extracts these weights and constructs the weight vector, as in Equation 1, where Q_w is the weighted-match query weight vector and w_i is the weight of property i as defined by the service requester. Property i can be a precondition, a postcondition, a nonfunctional requirement or a legal requirement. The number of properties n depends on the weighted-match query defined by the service requester.

$$Q_w = [w_1, w_2, w_3, .., w_n] \tag{1}$$

We have mentioned earlier that the weight can be *{Low, BelowAverage, Average, AboveAverage, High, Exact}*. *ConfiguredServices* that do not satisfy *Exact* values are filtered when doing the weighted-match matching. So the possible weight values are *{Low, BelowAverage, Average, AboveAverage, High}*. We assume in further discussion that weight values are whole numbers in the range $1 \ldots 5$, where 1 denotes *Low* and 5 denotes *High*.

Construct weight matrix

By using the weight vectors constructed in Step 1, the weight matrix for the *ConfiguredServices* in the *ServiceType* is constructed. This is shown in Equation 2, where n is the number of properties defined in Equation 1 and m is the number of *ConfiguredServices* in the *ServiceType*. Each column represents the weights of the properties in a single *ConfiguredService*. Each row represents the weights of a single property in the different *ConfiguredServices*.

$$CS_w = \begin{bmatrix} w_{1,1} & w_{2,1} & .. & w_{m,1} \\ w_{1,2} & w_{2,2} & .. & w_{m,2} \\ .. & .. & .. & .. \\ w_{1,n} & w_{2,n} & .. & w_{m,n} \end{bmatrix} \tag{2}$$

The value of the *ConfiguredService* property weight depends on the property type. If a property j is a precondition, postcondition, legal rule (without values) or a security property, a weight $w_{i,j}$ is equal to 1, if *ConfiguredService* i satisfies property j and is equal to 0 otherwise. If property j is price, legal rule (with values), availability or time-safety, $w_{i,j}$ is calculated according to Equation 3, where z is the required property value as defined in the weighted-match query and x is the actual property value specified in *ConfiguredService*.

$$w_{i,j} = \begin{cases} 1 & \text{if } x \leq z \\ 1 - \left(\frac{x-z}{2z-z}\right) = 2 - \frac{x}{z} & \text{if } z < x < 2z \\ 0 & \text{if } x \geq 2z \end{cases} \tag{3}$$

Equation 3 assumes that actual value that is more than double the required value will be given a weight of 0. Anything that is less than the required value will be given 1. And an actual value between the required value and double the required value will be given a weight that depends on how close the actual value is to the required value. For example, if the required price as defined in the service query is 50, an actual *ConfiguredService* price of 55 should be given a better weight than a price of 80.

If property j is reliability, $w_{i,j}$ is calculated according to Equation 4, where z is the required reliability value as defined in the weighted-match query and x is the *ConfiguredService* actual reliability value.

$$w_{i,j} = \begin{cases} 1 & \text{if } x \geq z \\ 1 - \left(\frac{z-x}{z-\frac{z}{2}}\right) = \frac{2x}{z} - 1 & \text{if } \frac{z}{2} < x < z \\ 0 & \text{if } x \leq \frac{z}{2} \end{cases} \tag{4}$$

Equation 4 assumes that actual values that is less than half the required value will be given a weight of 0. A value that is more than the required value will be given a weight of 1. And an actual value between the required value and half the required value will be given a weight that depends on how close the actual value is to the required value. The main difference between reliability and other properties is that reliability values represent a minimum while other properties represent a maximum.

Calculate weights for ranking

A single weight value for each *ConfiguredService* is computed, and the services are ranked based on these weights. Equation 5 uses the results of steps one and two to calculate the raking weight vector.

$$W = Q_w \times CS_w \qquad\qquad (5)$$

The ranking weight vector W contains the weights of the different *ConfiguredServices*. These weights are used to rank the *ConfiguredServices*. The *ConfiguredService* with the highest weight value is placed first in the *ServiceType*. The *ConfiguredService* with the second highest weight value is placed second in the *ServiceType* and so on for the rest of the *ConfiguredServices*.

Example 9. *Two ConfiguredServices RepairShopA and ReapirShopB provide the functionality required in Example 7. They don't provide an exact match to the nonfunctional and legal requirements, but rather a partial match. The list of properties will include: {RequiredPrecondition, RequiredPostcondition, RequiredPrice, RequiredDeposit}. The RequiredPrecondition and the RequiredPostcondition will be filtered out because they require an exact match. So we are left with RequiredPrice and RequiredDeposit. Hence, the weighted-match query weight vector is $Q_w = \begin{bmatrix} High & Average \end{bmatrix}$. In numbers, $Q_w = \begin{bmatrix} 5 & 3 \end{bmatrix}$. ConfiguredService RepairShopA (rsA) has a cost of $rsA_c = 40\$/hour$ and requires a deposit of $rsA_d = 600\$$. ConfiguredService RepairShopB (rsB) has a cost of $rsB_c = 70\$/hour$ and requires a deposit of $rsB_d = 400\$$. Hence, the ConfiguredServices weight matrix is defined, using Equations 2 and 3, as:*

$$CS_w = \begin{bmatrix} w_{rsA,c} & w_{rsB,c} \\ w_{rsA,d} & w_{rsB,d} \end{bmatrix}$$

where, $w_{rsA,c} = 1$, $w_{rsB,d} = 1$ and:

$$w_{rsA,d} = 2 - \frac{600}{500} = 0.8$$

$$w_{rsB,c} = 2 - \frac{70}{50} = 0.6$$

The ranking weight vector will then be defined using Equation 5 as:

$$W = \begin{bmatrix} 5 & 3 \end{bmatrix} \begin{bmatrix} 1 & 0.6 \\ 0.8 & 1 \end{bmatrix} = \begin{bmatrix} 7.4 & 6 \end{bmatrix}$$

Hence, ConfiguredService RepairShopA scores 7.4 and ranked first, while ConfiguredService RepairShopB scores 6 and ranked second.

FrSeC adaptability

One of the main features of *FrSeC* is its ability to adapt to situations that trigger a need for a rediscovery or re-ranking process. Below is a discussion of the most important triggers and how they are handled in *FrSeC*.

Context change

The discovery process uses the contextual information of the service requester at service discovery time. But during service execution, the contextual information of the service requester might have changed. As a consequence, the contextual rules of the discovered service(s) might be violated, other services may be more suitable. In order to deal with the dynamic change in context we introduce an adaptable discovery mechanism. In *FrSeC*, this mechanism includes the following steps:

1. CGU senses the new context information and informs SR.
2. SR generates a new query with the new context information.
3. The context change may result in a change to the security level. So SR contacts AU with the new context information.
4. AU sends a new token to SR.
5. SR sends the new query to the PU which will initiate a new discovery process.
6. PU will send a new plan with the set of new ordered *ConfiguredServices*.
7. EU will migrate from the old *ConfiguredService* to the new *ConfiguredService*.

Failure in service availability

During service execution, the executing service might fail or become unavailable. For example, the wireless router might fail. *FrSeC* is designed to adapt to service failures. In our design, PU uses *ServiceType*, and not specific *ConfiguredServices* when defining query result. The list *ServiceType* contains ordered *ConfiguredServices* that can meet the requirements of a specific query. These *ServiceTypes* will be part of the plan sent to EU. During run time, if a *ConfiguredService* fails or becomes unavailable, the EU will select the next *ConfiguredService* in the *ServiceType*. The worst case is that an equivalence class has only one *ConfiguredService* and it fails. The feedback loop in *FrSeC* will restart the discovery process in this case.

New alternative services

Service executions may be performed over days, or even months. But service selection and binding are usually performed only the first time the requester uses the service. This might not be practical because new services might be available during this long execution time. The new alternative services might be new services or old services with new modified contracts. A new contract might include a lower price or a better quality. For example, a wireless provider with cheaper price and same quality guarantees might become available. In order to adapt to new alternative services during run time, SR registers with PU. This registration will guarantee that PU will inform SR in case of a new *ConfiguredService* that provides the requester the required functionality becomes available. Thus, SR can initiate a new discovery process.

New contract rules

Contracts bound to *ConfiguredServices* may be either *strict* or *flexible*. In a strict contract, the life-time of contract is made explicit. Providers and requesters are bound by this timeline. In a flexible contract, there is no life-time specification, which allows providers to change the contract terms at any point of time. For example, the service provider might increase the price of his wireless Internet connection. Providers might not be aware of the identity of their clients. This design decision was made to enshrine privacy issues. In *FrSeC*, providers inform EU of changes to service contract. At the time of service delivery, EU informs SR of changes to the contract and delivers the service only upon receiving the acceptance of new contract terms from SR. In order not to deny service, requesters are allowed to initiate a rediscovery process in accordance with the new contract terms.

New requester requirements

Some service executions might be too long and during this service time the requirements of the requester might change. To deal with new requirements, the requester has the choice of a rediscovery process or a re-ranking process. In the rediscovery process the requester will define a new query and go through all steps of service discovery. In a re-ranking process, the requester will ask PU to re-rank the *ConfiguredServices* in the *ServiceType* taking into consideration the new assigned weights to the elements in the modified query.

Evaluation and experiments

To evaluate the contributions presented in this paper, a Java based application has been implemented to represent the Planning Unit. This application takes as input the set of *ConfiguredService* that provide a specific functionality as returned from the Service Registry, and the service query. The application will then match between the service query and the candidate *ConfiguredServices* taking into consideration the functional, nonfunctional, legal, and contextual information. Two types of matching has been implemented 1) exact match and 2) weighted-match. The ranking algorithm has also been implemented. Figure 4 shows a snap shot of the Planning Unit application.

The application was tested on a standard PC using an Intel Centrino processor with 4GB of memory and running Windows 7 Professional. The average matching and ranking time was in in milliseconds for each *ConfiguredService* which eliminate the concerns of scalability issues.

The tool was tested on multiple case studies including the Automotive Emergency Case Study. Table 2 shows the set of *ConfiguredServices* that are matched and ranked according to the service requester query presented in Table 3. The matching and ranking result of these *ConfiguredServices* are:

- *ConfiguredService* RepairShop5 is matched by 100.0%
- *ConfiguredService* RepairShop4 is matched by 88.19%
- *ConfiguredService* RepairShop1 is matched by 83.33%
- *ConfiguredService* RepairShop2 is matched by 80.56%
- *ConfiguredService* RepairShop3 is matched by 78.12%

Related work

Related work can be divided into related publication approaches and related service discovery approaches.

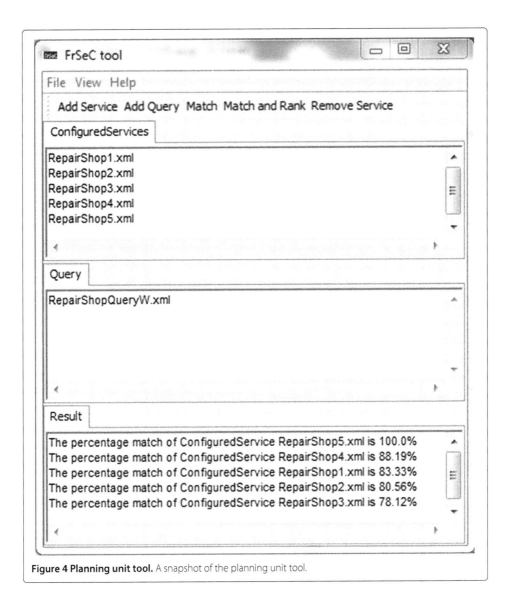

Figure 4 Planning unit tool. A snapshot of the planning unit tool.

The most notable publication approaches are UML-based such as [8,9], WSDL [10], OWL-S [11], WSMO [12], SOADL [13], SRML [14], and (SOFM) [15]. These approaches are compared and the result of comparison is presented in Table 4. It is clear that all approaches support the modeling of the functional behavior. Nonfunctional and trustworthiness properties are only supported in a simple manner by few approaches. Contextual information is not represented by any approach, hence the relationship between contract and context is totally ignored. A couple of approaches, which have ignored the modeling of nonfunctional and trustworthiness properties, have used formal methods and conducted formal verification. Except for UML and Web services languages most of the approaches provide a minimum amount of tools to support the modeling using their service models.

The most notable service discovery approaches are SeGSeC [16], eFlow [17], SELF-SERV [18], SHOP2 [19], SWORD [20], Argos [21], FUSION [22], Proteus [23], SPACE [24], StarWSCoP [25], METEOR-S [26], SeCSE [27], DynamiCoS [28] and TSCN [29]. These approaches have been compared with respect to the following criteria.

Table 2 Multiple RepairShop ConfiguredServices descriptions

ConfiguredService	Function	NonFunctional	Legal	ContextRule	ContextInfo
RepairShop1	**Name**:ReserveRS **Pre**:CarBroken==T **Post**:HasAppointment==T **Address**: XXX · **InputParameters**: CarBroken:bool deposit:double CarType:string failureType:string · **ResultName**:ResultRS **OutputParameters**: **HasAppointment**:bool **numberOfHours**:int	Price = 60$/h Client Rec.=5	deposit=300$ Warranty= 3 **PriceCondition**: CarType=toyota	membership==CAA	(location,montreal)
RepairShop2	**Name**:ReserveRS **Pre**:CarBroken==T **Post**:HasAppointment==T **Address**: XXX · **InputParameters**: CarBroken:bool deposit:double CarType:string failureType:string · **ResultName**:ResultRS **OutputParameters**: HasAppointment:bool numberOfHours:int	Price=50$/h Client Rec.=4 Recommended by CAA	deposit=400$ Warranty= 2 **PriceCondition**: CarType=toyota	membership==CAA	(location,montreal)
RepairShop3	**Name**:ReserveRS **Pre**:CarBroken==T **Post**:HasAppointment==T **Address**: XXX · **InputParameters**: CarBroken:bool deposit:double CarType:string failureType:string · **ResultName**:ResultRS **OutputParameters**: HasAppointment:bool numberOfHours:int	Price=40$/h Client Rec.=3 Recommended by CAA	deposit=500$ Warranty= 1 **PriceCondition**: CarType=toyota	membership==CAA	(location,montreal)
RepairShop4	**Name**:ReserveRS **Pre**:CarBroken==T **Post**:HasAppointment==T **Address**: XXX · **InputParameters**: CarBroken:bool deposit:double CarType:string failureType:string · **ResultName**:ResultRS **OutputParameters**: HasAppointment:bool numberOfHours:int	Price=70$/h Client Rec.=5 Recommended by CAA	deposit=300$ Warranty= 4 **PriceCondition**: CarType=toyota	membership==CAA	(location,montreal)
RepairShop5	**Name**:ReserveRS **Pre**:CarBroken==T **Post**:HasAppointment==T **Address**: XXX · **InputParameters**: CarBroken:bool deposit:double CarType:string failureType:string · **ResultName**:ResultRS **OutputParameters**: HasAppointment:bool numberOfHours:int	Price=40$/h Client Rec.=5 Recommended by CAA	deposit=250$ Warranty= 4 **PriceCondition**: CarType=toyota	membership==CAA	(location,montreal)

A descriptions of 5 ConfiguredServices providing the same RepairShop functionality.

Table 3 Service query description

Service query	Function		NonFunctional	Legal	ContextInfo
Repair Shop Query	**RequiredPre**: CarBroken==T Weight=6 **RequiredPost**: HasAppointment==T Weight =6	**Parameters**: CarBroken:bool deposit:double CarType:string failure Type:string	Price = 45$/h Weight = 3 Client Rec. = 4 Weight = 3 Recommended by CAA Weight = 3	deposit = 280$ Weight = 4 Warranty= 3 Weight = 5 **PriceConditione**: CarType=toyota Weight = 6	membership==CAA (location,montreal)

A description of the service query content.

- *Dynamic selection:* The service provision framework should be designed to allow service requesters specify the requirements with the full knowledge that some service bindings may occur only at run time.
- *Dynamic composition:* With the increased number of services and the increased composition complexity, it is difficult to have all service compositions predefined in a static manner.
- *Context support:* Contextual information is essential at service publication, service query, service selection and planting, and service execution.
- *Semantic support:* Semantic information is essential at service specification, service query, and service composition.
- *Formal:* Formalism is necessary to 1) verify the interaction between services by making sure there are no incompatible behaviors between services in a composition, 2) achieve correct automatic composition by verifying that the composition satisfies the requirements of the requester, and 3) check the conformance of requester requirements and the contracts of the services being provided.
- *Negotiation support:* Each service requester has his own set of requirements. In many cases, none of the available services may fully match these requirements. The service provision framework should provide a mechanism to support the negotiation between service requesters and providers.
- *Nonfunctional and trust:* The consideration of nonfunctional and trustworthiness properties in service publication, discovery and ranking is essential.
- *Replanning support:* At run time, the contextual information of the service consumer and requester might change. The service provision framework should support a replanning process to generate a new plan that best satisfies the requirements in the new context.
- *Fault-tolerance:* If a service fails or becomes unavailable at run time, the service provision framework should recover from this failure by selecting alternative services.

Table 4 Related service publication

	Functional	Nonfunctional and trust	Legal rules	Context	Formal	Verification support	Tool support
UML-based	YES	SOME	SOME	NO	NO	NO	YES
SRML	YES	NO	SOME	NO	YES	YES	YES
SOADL	YES	SOME	NO	NO	YES	YES	YES
SOFM	YES	SOME	NO	NO	YES	YES	NO
WSDL	YES	NO	NO	NO	NO	NO	YES
OWL-S WSMO	YES	SOME	NO	NO	NO	NO	YES

A list of related service publication approaches.

Table 5 Related service discovery

	Dynamic selection	Dynamic composition	Context support	Semantic support	Formal	Negotiation support	Nonfunctional & trust	Replanning support	Fault-tolerance
SeGSeC	YES	YES	YES	YES	NO	NO	NO	YES	YES
eflow	YES	No	NO	SOME	NO	NO	NO	NO	YES
Self-serv	YES	NO	NO	NO	NO	NO	NO	NO	NO
SHOP2	YES	YES	SOME	YES	NO	NO	NO	NO	NO
SWORD	NO	YES	NO	SOME	NO	NO	NO	NO	NO
Argos	NO	YES	YES	YES	NO	NO	NO	NO	-
Composer	YES	NO	YES	YES	NO	NO	SOME	NO	-
FUSION	YES	YES	NO	NO	NO	NO	NO	YES	-
Protus	YES	YES	NO	NO	NO	NO	SOME	YES	YES
SPACE	YES	NO	NO	NO	YES	NO	NO	YES	YES
StarWSCop	YES	YES	NO	YES	NO	NO	YES	YES	YES
Meteor-s	YES	NO	NO	YES	NO	NO	YES	YES	-
SeCSE	YES	NO	NO	NO	NO	NO	YES	YES	YES
DynamiCos	YES	YES	NO	YES	YES	NO	NO	NO	NO
TSCN	YES	NO	NO	NO	YES	NO	NO	NO	NO

A list of related service discovery approaches.

The result of this comparison is presented in Table 5 and it shows the following:

1. With the exception of SWORD and Argos, all approaches support dynamic selection.
2. Dynamic composition is considered by almost half of the approaches. In most of these approaches AI planning techniques are used.
3. Contextual information is used by very few approaches. In these approaches, context is used to filter the services, but not to constrain the service contract. Hence, the relationship between the contract and context is not considered.
4. Semantic information using ontology is supported by almost half of the approaches. The use of ontology restrains the semantic support due to the complexity and difficulty of composing ontologies.
5. With the exception of three approaches, all remaining approaches are not formally based. This will limit their verification support.
6. None of the investigated approaches supports negotiation.
7. The support of nonfunctional and trustworthiness properties is very simple and limited.
8. Replanning is supported by almost half of the approaches. With the exception of protus, approaches that support replanning do not support dynamic composition and hence the replanning is manually performed.
9. Fault-tolerance is supported by only few approaches. A number of approaches such as Argos, Composer, FUSION and Meteor-s do not mention fault-tolerance. Hence, by default we consider that they do not support fault tolerance.

Conclusion and future work

We have presented *FrSeC* that supports the publication, discovery, and provision of services with context-dependent contracts. *FrSeC* is formally based and considers legal rules and contextual conditions during service provision. It also supports an adaptive rediscovery and reranking operations. We are currently working on a detailed service architecture extended with flexible contracts and trustworthiness guarantees. We are developing a set of tools and a process model in order to provide a platform in which service-oriented applications within the confines of *FrSeC* can be developed.

Competing interests
The authors declare that they have no competing interests.

Authors' contributions
The main contributions of NI are defining the *ConfiguredService* structure for service publication, defining the query structures for service discovery, and defining the service ranking algorithm. The major contribution of MM includes defining a service oriented architecture which influenced the formal framework *FrSeC*. VA has contributed to the formalization of the framework and issues related to adaptability. All authors participated in drafting and approving the paper manuscript.

Author details
[1]Department of Mathematics and Computer Science, Albany State University, Georgia, USA. [2]Department of Computer Science and Software Engineering, Concordia University, Montreal, Canada.

References
1. Papazoglou MP (2008) Web services: principles and technology, First edition. Prentice Hall, England, UK
2. Dey AK (2001) Understanding and using context. Perso Ubiquitous Comput 5: 4–7
3. OSullivan J (2007) Towards a precise understanding of service properties. Phd thesis, Queensland University of Technology, Brisbane, Australia

4.   Ibrahim N, Alagar VS, Mohammad M (2011) Managing and Delivering Trustworthy Context-Dependent Services. In: proceedings of the 2011 IEEE 8th International Conference on e-Business Engineering (ICEBE), Beijing China, pp 358–363

5.   Ibrahim N, Alagar V, Mohammad M (2011) Specification and verification of context-dependent services. In: Kovács L, Pugliese R, Tiezzi F (eds) Proceedings of the 7th International Workshop on Automated Specification and Verification of Web Systems, Reykjavik Iceland. Volume 61 of EPTCS, pp 17–33

6.   Ibrahim N, Mohammad M, Alagar V (2011) An architecture for managing and delivering trustworthy context-dependent services. In: Proceeding of the 8th IEEE International Conference on Services Computing, Washington, DC, USA, pp 737–738

7.   Wan K (2006) Lucx: Lucid enriched with context. Phd thesis, Concordia University, Montreal, Canada

8.   Mayer P, Schroeder A, Koch N (2008) MDD4SOA: Model-Driven Service Orchestration. In: EDOC '08: Proceedings of the 2008 12th International IEEE Enterprise Distributed Object Computing Conference. IEEE Computer Society 2008, Washington, DC, USA, pp 203–212

9.   Service oriented architecture Modeling Language (SOAML) (2008) Specification for the UML Profile and Metamodel for Services (UPMS). OMG Submission document: ad/2008-11-01. Available at http://www.omgwiki.org/SoaML/doku.php?id=specification

10. WSDL (2001) Web Services Description Language 1.1. W3C Note. March, http://www.w3.org/TR/wsdl

11. Martin D, Paolucci M, McIlraith S, Mark McDermott D, McGuinness D, Parsia B, Payne T, Sabou M, Solanki M, Srinivasan N, Sycara K (2004) Bringing Semantics to Web Services: The OWL-S Approach. In: First International Workshop on Semantic Web Services and Web Process Composition (SWSWPC 2004), San Diego, California, USA, pp 243–277

12. Zaremba M, kerrigan M, Mocan A, Moran M (2006) Web services modeling ontology. In: Cardoso J, Sheth AP(eds) Semantic Web Services, Processes and Applications. Springer, pp 63–87

13. Jia X, Ying S, Zhang T, Cao H, Xie D (2007) A new architecture description language for service-oriented architecture. In: Sixth International Conference on Grid and Cooperative Computing (GCC 2007), Urumchi, Xinjiang, China, pp 96–103

14. Marino J, Rowley M (2009) Understanding SCA (Service Component Architecture). Person Education, Inc., Boston, MA, USA

15. Cao XX, Miao HK, Xu QG (2008) Modeling and refining the service-oriented requirement. In: TASE '08: Proceedings of the 2008 2nd IFIP/IEEE International Symposium on Theoretical Aspects of Software Engineering. IEEE Computer Society, Washington, DC, USA, pp 159–165

16. Fujii K, Suda T (2009) Semantics-based context-aware dynamic service composition. ACM Trans Autonomous Adaptive Syst 4(2): 1–31

17. Casati F, Ilnicki S, Jin Lj, Krishnamoorthy V, Shan MC (2000) Adaptive and dynamic service composition in eFlow. In: Proceedings of the 12th Int'l Conference on Advanced Info. Systems Engineering. Springer-Verlag, pp 13–31

18. Sheng QZ, Benatallah B, Dumas M, Mak EOY (2002) SELF-SERV: a platform for rapid composition of web services in a peer-to-peer environment. In: Proceedings of the 28th international conference on Very Large Data Bases, VLDB Endowment, Hong Kong, China, pp 1051–1054

19. Wu D, Parsia B, Sirin E, Hendler J, Nau D, Nau D (2003) Automating DAML-S web services composition using SHOP2. In: Proceedings of 2nd International Semantic Web Conference, Sanibel Island, Florida, USA, pp 195–210

20. Ponnekanti SR, Fox A (2002) SWORD: A developer toolkit for web service composition. In: Proceedings of the 11th International WWW Conference, Honolulu, Hawaii, USA. http://www2002.org/CDROM/alternate/786/index.html

21. Ambite JL, Weathers M (2005) Automatic composition of aggregation workflows for transportation modeling. In: Proceedings of the 2005 national conference on Digital government research, Digital Government Society of North America, Atlanta, GA, USA, pp 41–49

22. VanderMeer D, Datta A, Dutta K, Thomas H, Ramamritham K, Navathe SB (2003) FUSION: A system allowing dynamic web service composition and automatic execution. In: Proceedings of the IEEE Int. Conference on E-Commerce Technology, IEEE Computer Society, p 399

23. Ghandeharizadeh S, Knoblock C, Papadopoulos C, Shahabi C, Alwagait E, Ambite JL, Cai M, Chen CC, Pol P, Schmidt R, Song S, Thakkar S, Zhou R (2003) Proteus: A system for dynamically composing and intelligently executing web services. In: Proceedings of the 1st International Conference on Web Services, Las Vegas, NV, USA, pp 17–21

24. Jin C, Wu M, Ying J (2009) A Structure-based approach for dynamic services composition. J Software 4(8): 891–898

25. Sun H, Wang X, Zhou B, Zou1 P (2003) Research and implementation of dynamic web services composition. In: Zhou X, Jahnichen S, Xu M, Cao J (eds) Advanced Parallel Processing Technologies, 5th International Workshop, APPT 2003, Volume 2834 of Lecture Notes in Computer Science. Springer-Verlag, pp 457–466

26. Verma K, Gomadam K, Sheth AP, Miller JA, Wu Z (2005) The METEOR-S Approach for configuring and executing dynamic web processes. Technical report, LSDIS Lab, University of Georgia, Athens, Georgia

27. Penta MD, Bastida L, Sillitti A, Baresi L, Maiden N, Melideo M, Tilly M, Spanoudakis G, Cruz JG, Hutchinson J, Ripa G (2009) SeCSE–Service centric system engineering: An overview. In: Nitto ED, Sassen AM, Traverso P, Zwegers A (eds) At Your Service: Service-Oriented Computing from an EU Perspective. The MIT Press, Cambridge, Massachusetts, USA, pp 241–272

28. Silva E, Pires LF, van Sinderen M (2009) Supporting dynamic service composition at runtime based on end-user requirements. In: Proceedings of the 1st Workshop on User-generated Services (UGS2009) at the 7th International Joint Conference on Service Oriented Computing, (ICSOC 2009), Stockholm, Sweden, pp 20–30

29. Fan G, Yu H, Chen L, Liu D (2009) An approach to analyzing dynamic trustworthy service composition. In: Gómez-Pérez A, Yu Y, Ding Y (eds) The Semantic Web, Fourth Asian Conference, ASWC 2009, Shanghai, China, December 6-9, 2009. Proceedings, Volume 5926 of Lecture Notes in Computer Science. Springer, pp 261–275

2

Incremental development & revolutions of E-learning software systems in education sector: a case study approach

Varun Gupta[1*], Durg Singh Chauhan[1] and Kamlesh Dutta[2]

* Correspondence:
varun13_cse@yahoo.co.in
[1]Uttarakhand Technical University,
Dehradun, Uttarakhand, India
Full list of author information is
available at the end of the article

Abstract

Advancement in the area of software engineering, mobile computing together with web technologies have paved way for myriad range of applications, including good quality E-learning software's, delivering online classes in real time to unlimited number of students across the world, on a personalized E-learning space for every student. These E-learning software systems have virtually made the whole world as a single campus education hub. However, development of these software's has been a challenge for industry, as the requirement of various stakeholders—learner, educator, institutional management, accreditation bodies, has to be handled in the software effectively. Software systems developed for E-learning applications should implement all the requirements of its diverse stakeholders and must be delivered well in time. Delays, incomplete software and faulty modules could be a big failure for educational institute. To be able to deliver the software within deadline, software's are delivered in increments. In order to support incremental delivery, paper proposes a new requirement prioritization method that selects those requirements for implementation that are essentially required by stakeholders and has a lower regression count associated with them, thereby reducing regression testing effort. This paper reports the advantages reaped from E-learning software project of "Virtual Classroom" employed in teaching "Multimedia Technologies" course to undergraduate students of sixth semester. Total 50 students, enrolled under both distance education and full time education (25 in each category), were asked a set of questions. Results indicate that E-learning system would bring revolution in the field of education, whether study program is full time, part time or a distance education program. Students found augmenting classroom teaching with the use of E-learning software systems as an enriching experience.

Keywords: E-learning software system, Virtual classroom, Requirement prioritization, Regression testing, Analytical Hierarchical Process (AHP)

Introduction

Research in the area of software engineering had been focussed on improving quality of developed software. The software solves problem of the particular application area like medicine, education, engineering etc. Numerous software's finds their application in almost all areas (eg. Microsoft office) and are generic in nature. Others are specific for a given domain (eg. Moodle in education sector, and NS2 for network simulation). Higher quality software will improve quality and efficiency of work to be carried out in particular application area. Adoption of software engineering practices during the software development phases can improve the quality of the software, eventually improving the acceptability of software by the users. This paper focuses on the applicability of web 2.0 software applications in education sectors, reports advantages of the introduction of E-learning software, based on authors' teaching experience and presents the solution to various problems that tend to occur during the development of software for education sector.

Education sector requires software in minimum possible time. Delays in delivery of software might not be acceptable to various education organizations. Moreover, misinterpreted, missing or incomplete requirements elicited during the requirement engineering process might result in all activities of education institutes ending up with errors and disorders. For example, if a software development organization delays delivery of software by one year, then it means that client educational institute might be deprived of the benefits of the software for the whole academic year. Another scenario of virtual classroom where one of the requirement in present "copy-paste" environment is "Software must be able to detect the percentage of plagiarism and must report the details" is required essentially by the institute. If software developer is unable to implement this requirement, then all implemented requirements might be at stake, since teacher might wish to evaluate students at various stages in academic year by detecting plagiarism.

In order to avoid delays, software developers try to develop software incrementally by implementing requirements of highest priority. Highest priority requirements are such that they are preferred most by all the stakeholders, and stakeholders will get maximum benefits with the implementation of a highest priority subset of set of thousands of requirements. Effective prioritization of requirements will depend on the quality of stakeholders involved and effectiveness in creating win-win situation among them. Thus, for the education sector, to take advantages of various software's, the software should be of high quality delivered, well in time implementing highest priority requirements.

Once the software with highest priority requirements are delivered and new version or increment requirements are added in existing source code, ripple effects are likely to exist in other code parts. It means that other requirements that were working perfectly well before the additions to the code would now malfunction. Regression testing is the only option to not only check the newly added code but also to check already test code. This calls for investing of more efforts, thereby enhancing cost of software and delaying its delivery to its educational organizations. As discussed earlier, such delays could prove to be very detrimental for such organizations. In order to reduce regression testing, prioritization process could be altered in such a manner that maximum requirements dependent on each other are implemented during the same the same increment. Thus, implementation of next increment would have less chance of creating ripple effects. As a heuristic, requirements with highest regression count and lesser customer satisfaction value could be ignored to achieve more optimizations in regression testing effort. Customer satisfaction is the most important aspect during prioritization. E-learning educational software would find its great acceptability among teachers, students etc., if and only if the needs of these stakeholders are satisfied.

Since, not all of the gathered requirements are equally required by stakeholders, incremental development is possible for E-learning software. Some set of requirements are not mandatory in nature and does not affect the academic work. For example, if delivery deadline is very tight, requirements like video conferencing, searching using multiple inputs etc., that require huge implementation efforts could be dropped. Academic work will not suffer due to dropping of these requirements, since all basic requirements related to uploading; downloading of lecture notes and assignments, online tests, automatic generation of results etc. would be implemented in the first release.

E-learning software systems are beneficial not only for students registered as full time programme, but also to those who undertake the course under the category of distance education. In most populated developing country like India, where educating masses is quite challenging and important for having all round development and strong economy, distance education could play a vital role. Distance education in India was adopted as a result of recommendations of the Planning Commission of India (1960) (Third Five Year Plan) and Education Commission, also known as Kothari commission (1964–66) [1]. Some policies like National Policy on Education (1968) were formulated on the basis of recommendations of above commissions. Today, the distance education imparted by numerous universities had been able to cater to the needs of large number of Indian population.

The paper is structured as follows: The need for timely delivery of high quality software to be used in the educational domain for both full time and distance education programmes is highlighted in the introductory section. The existing work related to E-learning and the relevance of requirement prioritization and regression testing is reported in the "related work" section. Efforts are made to get an insight into the area of E-learning tools, techniques and status in countries like India. To improve the quality of such systems, requirement prioritization and regression testing approaches are analyzed, since timely deliveries of high quality E-learning systems can be obtained by following incremental development model. Section "E-Learning Software Systems" describes E-learning software systems from an implementation point of view. Next section "Web 2.0 Applications in Educational Sector" gives the applicability of such systems in educational institutions. It highlights the transformation of implementation model given in the previous section into a set of services offered to the institutes. Section "Survey of Applicability of E-Learning Software In Education Sector: A Case Study" gives the survey conducted by means of questionnaire administered to students registered in full time and distance education mode as experimental subjects. The results are analyzed and discussed in detail in "Result Analysis" section. Section "Proposed Prioritization Model: Development of E-learning software system" gives the proposal for a new requirement prioritization model termed as "CCR" technique where First C stands for Customer satisfaction, second C stands for cost and R stand for Regression count. This model stresses on selection of those requirements that provides maximum customer satisfaction to its intended users (one of the important criteria for educational sector software success) and lowest cost and highest regression count value. The final section "Conclusion and Future Work" summarizes conclusions and highlights future direction.

Related work

Survey of various E-learning tools and technologies is presented in [2]. Few of the IT organizations involved in building E-learning projects like SAP and Tata Interactive Systems (TIS), are also reported in [2].

The use of software agents to enhance the effectiveness of E-learning systems is proposed in [3]. The agents include Personalization agents, Evaluation agents, Query management agents, Feedback agents etc. The agents based E-learning software system was also implemented in the Java Agent Development Environment (JADE) and employed for OOPS training. The agents interact with each other to make E-learning as interactive as possible.

Paper [4] reported current status of E-learning based educational programmes in India. Authors reported that there is a huge increase in the number of educational institutes, Indian universities and the number of students enrolled in various programmes in these educational universities or institutes. These numbers are expected to increase in the near future and thus resulting in burden on existing available resources. E-learning will provide a good solution to the problem of an increase in the number under resource constrained environments, with reputed institutes like Indian Institute of Management Ahmadabad (IIMA), Symbiosis Center for Health Care (SCHC) and AMRITA already started offering some of educational programmes through E-learning.

Web based framework supported by requirement prioritization method that considers the preferences of multiple stakeholders, was proposed in [5]. The proposed prioritization technique is based on the idea of identification of "prioritization required factors" and "reducing factors". Cost and penalty were identified as reducing factors while Benefits, value, Risk, Time to Market and dependencies are categorized as prioritization required factors. Values allotted by each stakeholder for each requirement against each one, among five decision aspects were populated in Prioritization matrix. Each requirement is considered individually one by one decision aspect wise, where preference values are multiplied by weight of stakeholders that had allotted the value and finally added to the product of weight and preference of another stakeholder. Values allotted to each "prioritization required factors" were divided by those allotted to each "reducing factors". The computed value represents final priority value. This technique finds its greatest usage in globally distributed software development environments due to the proposed web based frameworks and such frameworks overcomes global distances that exists between the different software development site teams [6].

Paper [7] reported direct influence of decision aspect prioritization on requirement prioritization and hence on regression testing. In order to analyze the impacts, regression testing technique as proposed in [8] was slightly modified into two versions. First version involves all the algorithmic steps of original version excluding clustering, while later version employs all steps of the proposed algorithm. The two versions were executed on unsuccessful and successful project of the payroll management system. This project was experimental unit. Requirement prioritization and regression testing were experimental variables. To report the dependency between these experimental variables, decision aspect prioritization technique as proposed in [9] and requirement prioritization process as proposed in [5] were employed on the experimental unit. The main findings of the paper were that effectiveness in decision aspect prioritization will bring improvement in a requirement prioritization process, which reduces the number of regression test cases, without decreasing the fault detection capability.

In the present paper, we focus on the advantages and the revolution that could be brought in the education sector, as a result of the introduction of E-learning system.

The quality of such software systems is of prime importance, since quality of the software determines quality of the imparted and derived knowledge, thereby influencing future of both students and country.

E-learning software systems

E-learning is defined as an instruction, delivered via a computer that is intended to promote learning [10]. In other words, educational material in the form of multimedia documents (combination of audio, video and text) is delivered with the help of internet, intranet, CD-ROM etc. to various learners. A very good example is of "National Programme on Technology Enhanced Learning (NPTEL)" an Initiative of Ministry of Human resource and development (MHRD) for enhancing the quality of engineering education in the country by providing free online courseware (http://www.nptel.iitm.ac.in). NPTEL provides students and teachers lecture notes of renowned professors of institutes like IIT's and IISC in both video and text formats. This delivery of lecture notes, question banks, assignments etc. is through internet. The CD's of video slides are being sold to students which means delivery if through CD's. Web based E-learning software systems typically involve a dynamic website (web pages whose contents change in accordance with user selections or inputs), a database for storing references to lecture notes (both videos and texts), assignments, and question banks etc., connected through the network to the client computing node. Client computing nodes have a browser that executes the HTML file returned from the server and shows required lectures notes etc. Such a dynamic website is implemented in languages like PHP, active server pages (ASP) etc. Such web page contains the necessary code for accessing (reading, writing etc.) database, transforming user requests into E-learning services etc. With the advancement in web technologies and transition of web from 1.0 to 4.0, most of E-learning software systems are web 2.0 applications, since education delivery through web applications is easier and provides 24×7 accesses.

Web 2.0 applications in educational sector

With the advancement in web technologies, very complex web 2.0 applications had emerged. Such web 2.0 applications are installed on educational organization server and assessed world wise (Internet) or within campus only (Intranet) by using browsers at client side. Web 2.0 applications include all social networking sites like Orkut, Facebook, twitter, yahoo, gmail and tools like Moodle, wiki etc.

Such web 2.0 applications like virtual classroom, Moodle etc. automates various academic activities of educational institutes in following manner:

- Students are allowed to see their daily assignments, sample question papers, model test papers, test marks, grades, announcements etc.
- Students are allowed to submit assignments, take online open book test quiz etc.
- Teachers can upload new questions, assignments, grades, marks, comments, announcements, lecture notes (in various formats), research papers etc.
- Teachers can detect plagiarism among student's assignments and with internet resources.
- Teachers can upload e-books etc.

- It is possible for a renowned expert from distance remote institute to deliver and interact with students using two way audio-visual communication i.e. Video conferencing.
- Students and teachers can post solutions to problems asked by maximum students so that similar problems could be solved reusing solutions of similar problems.
- Students and teachers could interact with each other during non office hours and thus take benefit of virtual classes.

Survey of applicability of E-learning software in education sector: a case study

E-learning software systems could be a boom for both full time and distance mode education. In developing and populated countries like India building strong economy is one of prime interest activity. For sound economy, education is one of main parameter. Education involves both full time and distance mode educations. One of the objectives of any government is to improve the quality of education, and enhance all round development of the country. E-learning software system would be an asset for any educational organization, achieving this objective. This section presents results of the survey conducted using questionnaire among both distance and full time programme students. For full time education, only B. Tech students were employed for this experimentation, while for Distance education, views of students enrolled in both distance and full time programme students were collected.

Applicability of E-learning software in distance education

The applicability E-learning systems in distance education, is analysed by administering questionnaire to 25 students enrolled under distance education and equal number of full time students (total 50 Students). Students were asked two questions:

- Introduction of E-learning system would improve the quality of education.
- The E-learning system would make distance education nearly similar to full time education.

Figures 1 and 2 give the results of the questionnaire send to various students to get answers to the questions being asked.

Figure 1 shows that majority of students think that the introduction of an E-learning system would improve the quality of Distance and full time education. Figure 2 shows that maximum students agreed to the fact that introduction of an E-learning system would make distance education almost similar to full time education. After the analysis of these results, some of the students were asked, why they thinks so? Most of them thought that in distance education, there is less collaboration between students due to less interaction among them and learning revolves around the study material. They were of the opinion that there is little interaction with the counsellor. Students were of the opinion that the E-learning system would make problem solving an interactive collaborative session. Further, such systems would allow them to attend live lectures which would result in matching the full time education.

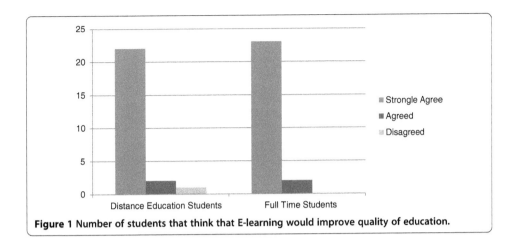

Figure 1 Number of students that think that E-learning would improve quality of education.

Applicability of E-learning software in full time education

To analyze the applicability of such systems, in full time education, the project of "Virtual Classroom" was uploaded on Intranet, for use by B. Tech third year students of the sixth semester. The project aimed at implementing the activities given in Section "Web 2.0 Applications in Educational Sector" (except fewer ones like Video Conferencing etc.). The software tool was implemented in Hyper Text Preprocessor (PHP), Hyper Text Markup language (HTML), Javascript and MySQL technologies. Students were taught "Software Engineering (SE)" without any virtual classroom tool in previous fifth semester. At the end of the sixth semester, total 35 students studying "Multimedia Technologies (MT)" were given questionnaire using GoogleDocs. The scale of 1 to 5 was used, where 5 means higher value and 1 means lower value to question asked. Following were questions asked in the questionnaire:

- Out of "SE" and "MT", which subject do you find interesting?
- Out of the two subjects, which one you consider best for your future research?
- Out of the two subjects, which one really transformed the hidden ideas of mind into practice?
- Out of the two subjects, which one was the highest scoring for you?

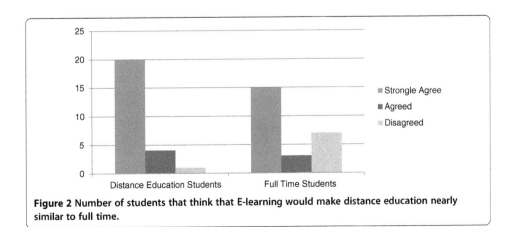

Figure 2 Number of students that think that E-learning would make distance education nearly similar to full time.

- When compared the teaching strategy for the two subjects, how much you rate these components:
  - Easiness.
  - Problem solution oriented.
  - Collaborative.
  - Work Originality due to plagiarism.
  - Practice oriented.
  - Transparency.

The response given by students to the above mentioned questions is given in Figures 3, 4, 5, 6 and 7. The analysis of responses i.e. values allotted for each question by the students highlights the importance of E-learning systems. Such system improves the quality of teaching and not only makes students academically better but also paves the path for future research.

In Figures 3, 4, 5 and 6, only the number of students who rated using values of 5, 4, 3, 2 and 1 are presented graphically. In Figure 7, the ratings of each student for each strategy for two courses are added and presented in the form of graphical representation. Thus, it shows the number of students, categorized in accordance with the value supplied, while Figure 7 presents aggregated allotted values.

Result analysis

Figure 3 show that students found the course of MT very interesting. When asked the reason behind such results, the majority of students reported that due to virtual classroom they got enough time in classrooms, focussing on what is being taught, without any stress of documentation of classroom notes, since they are available of the intranet. Thus, the whole effort is just to listen, comprehend, understand and documentation of important points. Deadline for assignment submission, plagiarism detection, and support for collaboration among students and teachers, due to chat and posting about problems, and solutions, made everyone come forward and perform, required activities within deadline. Since, software does not accept any assignments after the deadline and due to plagiarism detection capability; students were forced to write after a full

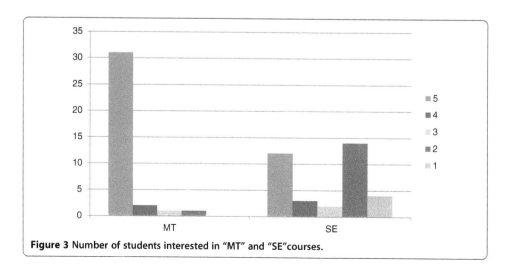

Figure 3 Number of students interested in "MT" and "SE" courses.

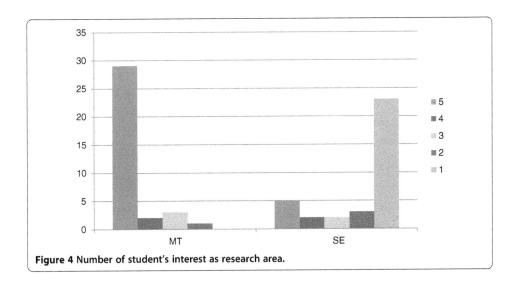

Figure 4 Number of student's interest as research area.

understanding of the application based assignments questions. This allowed them to clear their doubts within a reasonable amount of time, rather than during exam times. Availability of online resources enhanced interest of students, and they were able to work on the problems which required the knowledge and understanding gained during learning processes. Most of the students found problems interesting enough and subsequently expressed their willingness to take up the topics for future research work.

The subject of Multimedia Technologies turned out to be a high scoring subject for students which they passed with very good score. Students found that it is very easy to share problems, find solutions by working collaboratively. Also students were forced to do away the practice of "copy and paste" involved in their daily academic work. Students also reported that use of such tools offers transparency in grades allotment, and overall learning of new subject becomes an easy activity.

In case of the Software Engineering course, since some of the students had applied software engineering knowledge in the implementation of projects, some of these students were also interested in this course. Due to this, few values were also assigned to the various aspects in Figures 3, 4, 5, 6 and 7 but yet these allotted values are far lesser than allotted to "MT" course.

Teaching should be dynamic, means teaching contents must be in consonance with the current research trends. For students, to be able to understand recent research trends, complete basic knowledge and interest in the subject is essential for students.

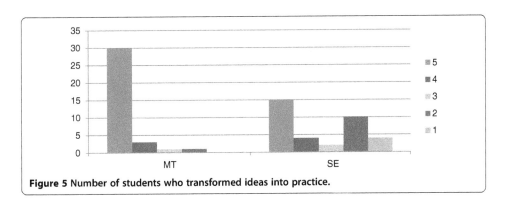

Figure 5 Number of students who transformed ideas into practice.

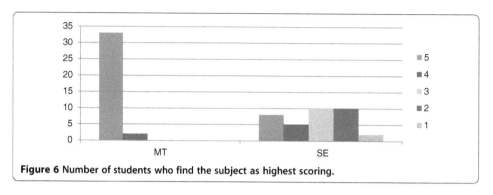

Figure 6 Number of students who find the subject as highest scoring.

Use of E-learning tools, like virtual classroom, made it possible to encourage students to learn while doing the things. Such web 2.0 tools provide 24×7 access worldwide, and hence irrespective of location of tutor or learner, collaboration could be promoted to solve new problems.

From the presented data, it could be easily concluded that effective teaching, and hence a revolution in the area of education sector could be attributable not only to the quality of teachers, quality of notes etc., but also to quality of software employed for the purpose of E-learning. Quality of E-learning software is the main factor in determining the effectiveness of teaching strategy, since quality software can bring revolution in the education sector. This enhances the quality of learning and knowledge among students and teachers, thereby influencing learners and educators of the next generation.

Proposed prioritization model: development of E-learning software system

As discussed in previous sections, for effective teaching, E-learning software system should be employed. E-learning modules could either be uploaded on the Internet or on the Intranet. Such E-learning systems are mostly web 2.0 applications that are read/ write and execute web applications.

The poor quality of such applications would mean complete rejection in the education sector. Effective requirement prioritization should be employed so that the highest priority requirements are implemented in resource constrained environment by satisfying diverse stakeholders and reducing the regression testing efforts during later increments.

In order to support incremental delivery, paper proposes a new requirement prioritization method that selects those requirements for implementation that are required at most, by stakeholders and has a lower regression count, associated with them, thereby reducing regression testing effort. The priority of a requirement is determined by "Customer Satisfaction" and "Regression Count Value", such that the cost of implementation of the selected requirement set is approximately within the allotted budgets.

Figure 8 gives the proposed technique for requirement prioritization. The proposal gives a prioritization method that not only considers the decision aspects like customer satisfaction and cost but also takes into consideration regression testing efforts. The objective is to customers; reduce development cost and also reducing the future regression testing efforts.

The calculation of priority against customer satisfaction and cost is almost similar to cost value approach as proposed in [11].

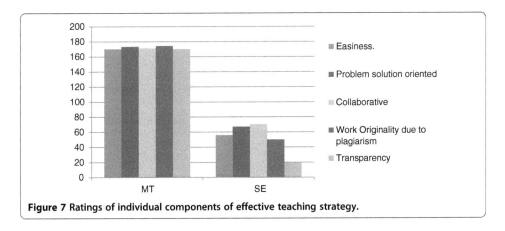

Figure 7 Ratings of individual components of effective teaching strategy.

The working of this proposed prioritization technique is given in form of algorithm in Table 1.

This algorithm generates the set of requirements for implementation. Selected requirements are such that they provide maximum customer satisfaction to its intended users (one of the important criteria for educational sector software success) and lowest cost and highest regression count value. Requirements that provide less value to its customers and have the highest value of regression count are simple ignored since these requirements could never alter project success chances.

The proposed prioritization technique could be named as "CCR" technique where First C stands for Customer satisfaction, second C stands for cost and R stand for Regression count.

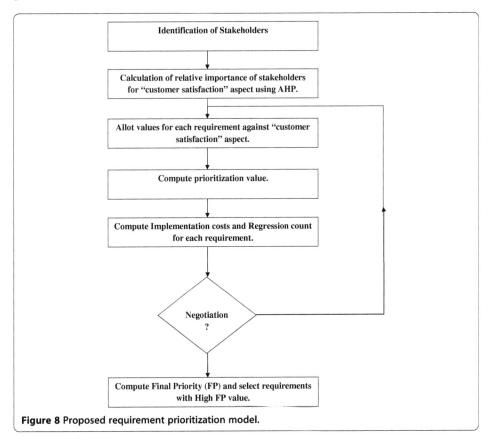

Figure 8 Proposed requirement prioritization model.

Table 1 Algorithm: requirement prioritization of E-Learning software system

Step number	Executable steps
1.	Identify influential stakeholders for prioritizing requirements. As a customers or users, a good combination of experienced teachers, research scholars, students, project staff etc. should be identified. Teachers could better identify those requirements that are very important for them and without which their work will suffer.
2.	Compute the relative importance of each stakeholder against "**customer satisfaction**" aspect using Analytical Hierarchical Process (AHP). AHP is a decision making process that allows stakeholders to fill prioritization matrix using a scale of 1–9. The relative prioritization value is then computed and the results are analyzed for accuracy purpose by calculating a consistency index (CI). A result of execution of this step is computation of the importance of one stakeholder with respect to another. Execution of this step is necessary since experienced teachers should be given higher importance as compared to other stakeholders and voice of students or other project staff with huge development experiences could not be bypassed.
3.	For each requirement against **customer satisfaction** aspect. Each stakeholder allots value using a scale of 1–9 as proposed in [12].
4.	Compute the priority using equation 1: $Priority = (Wa * Va) + (Wb * Vb) + + (Wb * Vb)$ (1) Wi denotes the relative importance of stakeholder "i" and Vi is the value assigned by stakeholder "i". Computation of this step is similar to that in [5].
5.	Compute Implementation costs and Regression count for each requirement. This step requires the involvement of software engineers rather than involving customers and users. The implementation of each requirement would be dependent on the implementation of another requirement. Such dependency implies that changes in particular requirement would create ripple effects in other parts of source code i.e. in source code of dependent requirement. This paper terms number of such dependencies between code parts of one requirement and parts of another one as regression count. To compute regression count, developers use AHP technique, where each requirement is pair wise compared with another. If there is very strong dependency between the two requirements say R_i and R_j, prioritization matrix cell (i, j) is given a value of 9 (scale of 1–9) and for no dependency it is given a value of 1. Finally the relative regression count value is computed. Similar scale is used to represent the implementation cost of each requirement.
6.	Select the highest priority requirement. Such requirements are those that have the highest value of Customers Satisfaction. Denote this set by R'. It varies from organization to organization to have threshold value of the selection. An optimal value could be at least 65%. Requirements with highest regression count and lower development costs are highly desirable. Let R be the set of gathered requirements. Let R" = R – R'. Each requirement of R" is represented by three tuples i.e. (P, C, R) where P represents assigned priority, C is development cost and R is regression count. •Compute cost associated with the set R'. If it exceeds the allotted budget, perform negotiation by holding talks with stakeholders and re allotment of values and thus repeating step 3 and onwards. •Sort the requirements in decreasing order of their priorities. Find the set R''' where, R''' = R" – $R_{(i)}$. The set $R_{(i)}$ denotes the set of those requirements of set R" which are having the highest value of R and lowest value of P. •For remaining requirements belonging to set R''', compute the final value of priority using equation 2: $EP = (p * R)/C$ (2) In this equation, value is "C" is not in monetary terms but in terms of scale of 1–9. Thus the highest cost value 9 represents a high cost requirement.
7.	Implement the set R' and select requirements of set R''' with the highest value of FP until resources permits.

Input: Set of gathered requirements.
Output: Prioritized set of requirements.

Conclusion and future work

The objectives of this paper were twofold i.e. main objective involves accessing the applicability of E-learning software system in the education sector and another is to propose a method to incrementally develop high quality E-learning system such that it could be an asset to education organization. Such a system will be delivered without any delay with almost all preferences of diverse stakeholders implemented in a resource constrained environment.

To achieve the first objective, "Virtual Classroom" E-learning software was employed for teaching a course of "Multimedia Technologies" to the B. Tech students of sixth semester. As compared to courses taught in the fifth semester, students found that they were very comfortable with the course taught using E-learning software system. Such E-learning system provides necessary virtual classroom environment that strengthens classroom face to face in person teaching. Results indicate that students found the use of such E-learning software system as a good database of lecture notes documentation, forces them to collaboratively focus on problems identified by classmates, report unique and original contents, work or findings in assignments. Students also reported that use of such tools provides transparency in grades allotment, and overall learning of new subject becomes an easy activity. E-Learning experience enlightened them with the necessary knowledge of the subject which they were able to transform into practical and thus enabled students to identify topics for future research.

In total 50 students, enrolled under both distance education and full time education (25 in each category) were asked a set of questions and results indicate that E-learning system would bring revolution in the field of education whether study programme is full time, part time or distance education programme.

Educational institutes demands complex E-learning software system. The timely delivery of these systems happens to be a very difficult task. To have timely delivery, paper requirement prioritization technique that prioritizes software requirements are proposed. These requirements provide maximum satisfaction to its customers and lessen regression testing effort. To achieve improved optimizations in regression testing effort, as a heuristic, requirements with highest regression count and lesser customer satisfaction value could be ignored.

The proposed requirement prioritization model needs to be evaluated on live projects and in near future it is expected that the impact of E-learning software system (developed using the proposed model) on educational quality in countries like India, could be evaluated.

Quality of developed E-learning system would influence the quality of teaching in educational sectors, and would useful for educators and learners, both. Country would be benefitted, since economic development depends heavily on education and quality of researchers involved in research projects in the country. E-learning systems overcome the global distances that exist between experts and learners and thereby making the whole world as an education hub.

Thus, it is expected that good quality of E-learning software systems would be developed using the proposed prioritization technique. It is also expected that Mobile compatible E-learning systems would be launched soon so that "any time and any place" access could be provided (M-Learning). Advancement in the area of Software engineering, Mobile Communications and Web Technologies would improve quality of E-learning and hence teaching quality.

Competing interests
The authors declare that they have no competing interests.

Authors' contributions
All the authors of this paper have equally contributed to this paper. All authors read and approved the final manuscript.

Acknowledgements
The work as mentioned in the paper would not have been possible without the active involvement of the students. The efforts on the part of the full time, distance education and B.Tech students are acknowledged with reverential thanks.

Author details
[1]Uttarakhand Technical University, Dehradun, Uttarakhand, India. [2]Department of CSE, National Institute of Technology, Hamirpur, India.

References
1. Sujatha K (2002) Distance Education at Secondary Level in India: The national open school. Report for the UNESCO International Institute for Educational Planning. http://unesdoc.unesco.org/images/0012/001262/126210e.pdf
2. Ramshirish M, Singh P (2006) E-learning: Tools and Technology. DRTC Conference on ICT for Digital Learning Environment, Banglore
3. Sivakumar N, Vivekanandan K, Arthi B, Sandhya S, Katta V (2011) Incorporating agent technology for enhancing the effectiveness of E-learning system. Int J Comput Sci Issues (IJCSI) 8(3):454–460
4. Rajpal S, Singh S, Bhardwaj A, Mittal A (2008) E-Learning Revolution: Status of Educational Programs in India. Vol 1. International Multi Conference of Engineers and Computer Scientists, Hong Kong, pp 846–851
5. Gupta V, Srivastav M (2011a) Web based tool supported requirement prioritization: based on multiple stakeholder preferences. Int J Comput Eng Inf Technol (IJCEIT) 25(1):12–19
6. Gupta V, Srivastav M (2011b) Overcoming global distance in globally distributed developments by Web based framework. CiiT Int J Software Eng Technol, June 2011, DOI: SE062011003
7. Gupta V, Chauhan DS, Dutta K (2012b) Impact analysis of requirement prioritization on regression testing. AWER Procedia Inf Technol Comput Sci 2:379–383
8. Gupta V, Chauhan DS (2011c) Hybrid Regression Testing Technique: A Multi Layered Approach. IEEE annual Conference (INDICON), Hyderabad
9. Gupta V, Chauhan DS, Dutta K (2012) Hybrid Decision Aspect Prioritization Technique for Globally Distributed Developments. Vol 38. Procedia Engineering, Elsevier, pp 3614–3627
10. Clark RC, Mayer RE (2003) E-learning and the science of instruction. Jossey-Bass, San Francisco
11. Jim A, Smith RK, David C (2007) Value-Oriented requirements Prioritization in a Small Development. IEEE software 24(1):32–37
12. Saaty T (1980) The Analytic Hierarchy Process. McGraw-Hill, New York

3

"Intelligent Environments: a manifesto"

Juan C Augusto[1*], Vic Callaghan[2], Diane Cook[3], Achilles Kameas[4] and Ichiro Satoh[5]

* Correspondence:
j.augusto@mdx.ac.uk
[1]Middlesex University, London, UK
Full list of author information is
available at the end of the article

Abstract

We explain basic features of an emerging area called Intelligent Environments. We give a short overview on how it has developed, what is the current state of the art and what are the challenges laying ahead. The aim of the article is to make aware the Computer Science community of this new development, the differences with previous dominant paradigms and the opportunities that this area offers to the scientific community and society.

Basic concepts

Here we explain how the area of *Intelligent Environments* (IE) has developed, what its core values are and how it differs from other areas. By "Environment" we refer here to any space in our surroundings. Although some people may also consider virtual environments here we mostly refer to Physical spaces, in all its diversity, e.g., house, building, street, a field, an area in the sea or space, etc. Our use of the word "Intelligent" applied to Environments mostly refers to Artificial Intelligence, as defined in [1]. An *Intelligent Environment* is one in which the actions of numerous networked controllers (controlling different aspects of an environment) is orchestrated by self-programming pre-emptive processes (e.g., intelligent software agents) in such a way as to create an interactive holistic functionality that enhances occupants experiences.

Historical development of the area

For centuries humans have witnessed scientific and technological leaps that changed the lives of their generation, and those to come, forever. We are no exception. In fact many of those advances are occurring now, in a more or less unperceivable way. Slowly and silently technology is becoming interwoven in our lives in the form of a variety of devices which are starting to be used by people of all ages and as part of their daily routine. As predicted by M. Weiser [2], this technology is gradually disappearing from our cognitive front, as we increasingly take for granted its existence. But this fact alone could not justify a paradigm shift, as we claim in this manifesto.

The emergence of a new paradigm requires the convergence of various domains of human activity, many of which are not technological. It is true that numerous technological advances have taken place during the past two decades worldwide, mainly due to persistent efforts by researchers and systematic funding by governments and markets. Among these advances one could site:

- Miniaturization of hardware components, and at the same time increase in processing power, performance and reliability and better storage management. Figure 1 shows how computers have become progressively available to humans.
- A multitude of different and reliable wireless network protocols, with the deployment of any required infrastructure.
- Large amount of information available, because of the widespread use of information sources (i.e. images from embedded cameras, location data from GPS, indentifers from RFID, user profiles stored in social computing applications, etc), and at the same time efficient knowledge extraction (i.e. for recognition of activity or prediction of intention, etc) and management and proliferation of semantic technologies (i.e. semantic web).
- Development of novel software platforms (i.e. grids, clouds, web 2.0, social computing), the associated middleware for all kinds of heterogeneous devices (from PCs to mobile phones to refrigerators) and the necessary development and end user tools.
- Ubiquitous contextual information, more accurate context representation, and higher order functions (such as adaptation, learning, etc) made possible
- Multi-modal intuitive HCI (i.e. based on natural language, gestures, whole body movements, even emotions) paving the way to direct brain to computer interfaces.

It is also important to note that developments in all of these technological areas not only have reached a level of maturity (i.e. they have been deployed outside labs, some of them

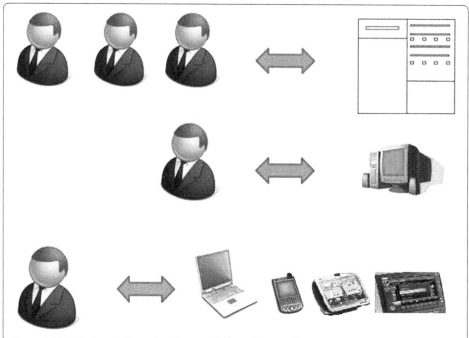

Figure 1 Historical evolution and shift on availability of computing power per person. From top to bottom, initially many users shared a centralized system, then a personal computer became available to a single user, and currently each user (even non-computers specialist) has access to many computing devices, often without realizing.

with commercial success), but they are also converging to define the requirements of IEs. Still, these would not be enough if the society (where ultimately, IEs are deployed) was not ready for a paradigm shift. This is backed by facts such as:

— The widespread user adoption of IE related applications, an indication that people are used in living with this kind of technology, although many concerns are still raised, especially regarding privacy.
— The commercial success that some of IE technological components already enjoy (i.e. mobile phones, ubiquitous cameras and sensors, social computing applications, cloud-based services, etc.) and the continuous investment made in this technology by public and private sector bodies.
— The impact of this technology has on all society sectors (i.e. education, health, employment, administration, entertainment, wellbeing, energy conservation, agriculture, etc) and the emergence of new ones (i.e. new jobs such as AAL expert or technician, smart home engineer, semantic information engineer etc).

This widespread availability of resources forms the technological layer for the realization of a new generation of systems that we refer here under the umbrella term of "Intelligent Environments".

Having the necessary technology is not enough for an area of science to flourish. Previous experiences of people with computers over recent decades have created an interesting context where people's expectations of these systems are growing and their fear of using them has decreased. A significant part of the way our societies work everyday have been adapted to the world's acceptance of existing technology. A new generation of technology consumers are coming and there is increasing appetite and education to make the adoption if IE's feasible.

The emergence of ubiquitous computing is perceived as the third wave in the evolution of computer technology [ref], because it signifies a move from large mainframes to ubiquitous computers in parallel with a move from a many users using one computer to many (embedded) computers being owned or used by one user. But the study of IEs requires a more complex approach, because many different axes of development have that led to their emergence:

— Scale: it is expected that IEs will contain millions of networked computing devices (i.e. hence the need for ZibGee, IEEE 1451 and IPv6 standards) and at the same time call for universal adoption.
— Size: device components become small and invisible at an amazing pace, eventually reaching the molecule level.
— Performance: despite issues of synchronization, heterogeneity and management, individual component and collective system performance are increasing
— Knowledge: the amount of information available for storage, processing and transmission is huge, but what's more important, the amount of knowledge also available for access, processing and transmission is growing fast, leading to a new era for AI.
— Proactiveness: a gradual shift from the reactive device to the proactive, even cognitive one, is witnessed.

– Dependability: this crucial for paradigm adoption factor marks the gradual increase of trust that people show in the new technology, partly as a result of the fault tolerance and autonomic behaviour of the massively distributed systems.

Related concepts and basic principles

There are a number of related areas which have facilitated the development of Intelligent Environments. Many of these areas overlap but they also have significant differences, we will try to clarify how they relate to each other.

Pervasive/ubiquitous computing: studies the provision of distributed computational services which are context-aware and travel with the user seamlessly across different environments [2]. Ubiquitous computing is more broadly associated with Human-Computer Interaction whilst Pervasive computing as a stronger emphasis on devices, their networking and the processing of the data they produce.

Smart environments: an environment enriched with sensing devices, some of them with capability to store and process data locally. See for example [3] for a more comprehensive description [4].

Ambient intelligence: refers to the intelligent software that supports people in their daily lives by assisting them in a sensible way [5]. See [6-8] for a seminal paper and [9] for a more recent survey.

Intelligent environments: builds on all the previous concepts and aims at creating systems which integrate a Smart Environment with Ambient Intelligence and is based in the pervasive/ubiquitous availability of services. See [10] for some up to date picture of work in the area.

In order to help characterizing what we interpret by Intelligent Environments we list below some key principles we believe every Intelligent Environment should aspire to have:

P1) to be intelligent to recognize a situation where it can help.

P2) to be sensible to recognize when it is allowed to offer help.

P3) to deliver help according to the needs and preferences of those which is helping.

P4) to achieve its goals without demanding from the user/s technical knowledge to benefit from its help.

P5) to preserve privacy of the user/s.

P6) to prioritize safety of the user/s at all times.

P7) to have autonomous behaviour.

P8) to be able to operate without forcing changes on the look and feel of the environment or on the normal routines of the environment inhabitants.

P9) to adhere to the principle that the user is in command and the computer obeys, and not viceversa.

These principles summarize the aims of our area. An intelligent Environment has to have a proactive attitude, continuously reasoning on how to help the users of that environment. Identifying correctly when help is needed can be extremely difficult in many situations and heavily depends on the information that is available through the sensors, and the knowledge it has about the user. Knowledge about the related world is also very important to understand what the effects of the system can be on that world and what is realistically feasible to achieve on behalf of the user. The challenge is here to keep a balance between not missing an opportunity when the user expected assistance at the same time the system understands it does not have to assist the user in every action.

Being sensible demands recognizing the user, learning or knowing her/his preferences and the capability to exhibit empathy with the user's mood and current overall situation.

Different users have different preferred modalities of interaction (e.g., auditory, visual, tactile, etc.), this is shaped by education or it could be affected by physical and cognitive capabilities. A system that wants to effectively engage with a user should be prepared to offer assistance in a variety of combinations.

Humans have different attitudes towards privacy, generally this is a sensitive issue for most people and as such it should be approached with care and implemented with the assumption that the user value privacy and is allowed to set up how the system should deal with issues that relate to privacy.

Safety is another important aspect a system will be forced to look after, given this systems primordial role is to assist humans, failing to preserve the safety of humans will render any such system worthless and unusable.

Systems in this area are expected to have a degree of autonomy, the more autonomy the better, provided this does not come at the cost of other principles like safety. The system should be able to inform itself by learning from previous experiences and its intelligence should help adaptation to different circumstances in such a way that it does not require continuous programming.

A fundamental principle to be observed is that users should be always in control and should be able to decline advice from the system, impose their preferences, undo previous decisions and actions from the system and even disconnect the system altogether if it is perceived inconvenient.

Systems of this type should be unobtrusively immersed in the environments we occupy on a daily basis. That is, their introduction should not come at the price of environment and humans which were part of that space having to adapt to or change their fundamental interactions and behaviours.

A delicate balance of the combination of those principles listed above is fundamental for this technology to thrive and to gain widespread acceptance. If a system overwhelms the user offering help, or delivers the wrong assistance or at a time or mode the user does not want it then users will soon get tired and switch the system off. Human assistants are capable to balance all these aspects, some more successfully than others and on that basis they are appreciated or not. Artificial systems should aim to master the subtle skills that distinguish successful human assistants and make them acceptable companions [11].

Fundamental areas

The area of Intelligent Environments supports its developments on the relative maturity and degree of success achieved in several well-known areas of Computer Science (see Figure 2). We explain below how these areas contribute to the realization of Intelligent Environments.

Sensors and Actuators: There is a wide range of sensors with varying capabilities, allowing the measurement of [12,13], for example:

- strain and pressure,

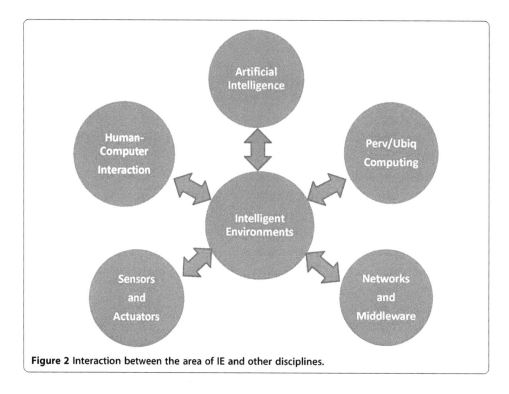

Figure 2 Interaction between the area of IE and other disciplines.

- position, direction, distance and motion,
- light, radiation and temperature,
- solids, liquids and gases,
- identification information, including biometric data,
- sound, and
- images

They provide a variety of different inputs, that can range from a simple on/off value, to values in numerical ranges (e.g., temperature, and weight of a person), to richer data like fingerprints, sound, pictures and video. There is no single formula to combine sensors in an environment for a specific problem and current developments arrange them in an ad hoc manner to suit a specific application.

Networks and Middleware: each intelligent environment has usually a variety of distributed sensors which helps to understand the current status of the environment. This flow of data is channelled to the main system through a wired or wireless network. This process presents the first set of major challenges to the system designers: how to merge in real-time all the influx of information, how to cope with incomplete or corrupt information coming from malfunctioning sensors, how to present the information in a way that can be useful to other higher decision-making modules of the system, and how to manage a huge number of devices and sensors? These and other problems are usually dealt with by a layer of software commonly referred as *middleware* which 'digest' the data coming from sensors to make it more useful to other software layers on top of them. One important task typically assigned to the middleware layer of a system is to facilitate inter-operability, that is, help parts of the system (devices, network, etc.) created by different providers to understand each other and converge into a representation that is understood by software at upper levels of the system architecture [14]. There is still much work to do in this area as there is no standard middleware, i.e., massively adopted by the community worldwide and there is still substantial work to be done to make middleware more useful, for example, being able to describe capabilities, rather than just functionality.

Pervasive/Ubiquitous Computing: is a technological paradigm centred on the dispersion of a variety of devices with, sometimes modest, computing capabilities. This paradigm explores the development of systems which departs from the desktop PC centred paradigm and supports a shift towards a model that follows the user where it goes, transparently across different physical locations. This paradigm is related to user-centred computing and highlights the value of concepts like *Context-awareness* [15], the capability of a system to understand the current situation in the environment, to keep tracks of its evolution and to relate this knowledge to modules within the system that produces proactive reactions.

Artificial Intelligence: Autonomous decision-making is one of the implicit expectations about any intelligent environment, they are precisely deployed to provide services in a similar way other humans will decide to provide in the same circumstances. To achieve this autonomous decision-making capability, systems will usually apply AI techniques which allow them to perform:

- *Learning and Activity Recognition:* the system is capable to detect within the vast amount of data produced by sensor triggering specific patterns of human behaviour which are meaningful to the services that has to provide [16].
- *Reasoning:* cognitive inference is essential for the system to infer whether it has to act or not and what action(s) should be taken. A variety of methods exist here, ranging from systems which are more rule-based to those based in biologically inspired models [17].
- *Autonomy and autonomicity:* provides the system with fundamental independence which is essential to decide when the system should or can act. This independence is needed at all levels, from assisting the users, to energy preservation and other internal decision which are more related to ensuring delivery of service, for example, self-reconfiguration and self-healing [18,19].
- *Embedded and distributed:* data processing and reasoning are tasks which do not necessarily have to be centralized and given an intelligent environment is supported by a number of interconnected devices part of this responsibility can be passed to the increasingly computationally capable devices physically distributed in the environment. [20] describes the benefits that practical experience suggests can be obtained with this approach and the current limitations and challenges developers will face at deployment time.

Relevant to these intelligent systems is the use of *(a) Multiagent systems* provides a flexible paradigm to model the different levels of autonomy and dependency that each component can have in a Smart Environment [21-23], and (b) *Robots:* providing a valuable tool both as an interface and as an actuator within a smart environment. Robots can provide an element of socialization [24]. They can also be disguised in the way of a tool that users can benefit from like an intelligent wheelchair which can help navigate a house to users with mobility challenges [25].

Human-Computer Interaction: Weiser's initial vision was very emphatic on the requirement that technology only will be successful if it becomes adopted to the extent of not being noticed [2], very much the way we use a fridge or a washing machine nowadays. Humans should be able to use devices in a way that does not demand vast amounts of training and specialization, needless to say, most of what it is on offer today in the areas of AmI and SmE fall short of this expectation. It is also fair to say that there is a significant part of the community which is doing interesting progress and is working extremely hard to overcome limitations in this area. Gesture recognition [26], gaze tracking [27], facial expression recognition [28], emotion recognition [29], and spoken dialogue [30], either isolated or combined to form multi-modal interfaces [31], are some of a range of options becoming available to facilitate communication between humans and the system in a natural way.

Challenging Aspects of IEs

There is a variety of problems that makes Intelligent Environments interesting and at the same time difficult to implement. We try to explain some of them in this section.

Users

Users are at the center of Intelligent Environments, in that respect this area overlap with the efforts of the scientific community focused on Person-Centric Computing [32,33]. The system should be able to help people of all ages and educational backgrounds, crucially those who do not have IT knowledge. Figure 3 shows a caricature that is often used in our area to represent the dangers of pushing technology in an insensitive way.

This represent the opposite of the predominant philosophy in our area, a mere accumulation of technology will overwhelm users. The introduction of technology has to be sensitive to the user and abide to the principle that the human is the master and the computer the slave and not the other way round [34]. This principles have been emphasized from the very beginning [2] highlighting the importance that unobtrusiveness and transparency of these services have for its success. Relevant here is also the differentiation made in [35] between System-Oriented, (Importunate Smartness) Systems takes/imposes

Figure 3 Technology as an inadequate tool. (Source of figure: praxis.cs.usyd.edu.au/~peterris).

decisions (e.g., "smart" fridge orders food, sometimes non sensibly) and People-Oriented (Empowering Smartness) Systems which make suggestions (e.g., fridge advises on feasible meals according to fridge content).

Intelligent Environments should also be aware of and be sensitive to multiple users in the same environment. These multiple users may coexist, may be interacting, may be cooperating, or may even be conflicting interests. Systems also have to be resilient enough to cope with users which will try to use the system in unexpected ways and with the richness and variability of human's behaviour on a daily basis.

Environments

The spaces where these systems can be deployed are very diverse. There are closed spaces with relatively well defined boundaries and others which do not have well defined boundaries which we can call open spaces. All of them can be roughly defined by the area (physical space) that the sensors can sense. Examples of closed spaces are: houses, offices, hospitals, classrooms, and cars. Examples of open spaces are: streets, bridges and car parks (for example for surveillance), fields (for agriculture), air (for airplanes) and sea (for underwater pollution measurement and tsunami early warning system). These environments are usually rich, complex, unpredictable, possibly generating substantial 'noisy' data, unstructured and sometimes highly dynamic (i.e., they change continuously or at least often).

Perception of the system

All intelligent environments are embedded in a world they have to act upon. The understanding the system has of the environment where is operating is directly proportional to the quantity and quality of its perceptive capability. In current systems that amounts to the sensing network that is connected to. This sensing network informs but at the same time oversimplifies reality.

The impact of the sensing network in an intelligent environment is huge. The intelligent system at the core of an Intelligent Environment base most of its decision-making on the perceived current situation which is composed out of the information perceived in real-time through the sensors. Sensors allow the system to perceive what happens in a place without a human being necessarily being there. But how accurate and useful this perception is? As a metaphor to understand how distorted the sensed perception of the world is we can think of driving on a foggy day (Figure 4). We are able to see part of the landscape around us, but we do not see all objects, we see some objects partially occluded and we see others in their entirety but fuzzy.

To illustrate the practical implications of this impoverished depiction of reality that sensors bring to the system let us compare them with the richest sensing machine we know: humans. A pressure sensor can sense whether there is certain weight over it, so we can put it on a chair or a sofa and use it to sense whether someone is sitting but that information alone will not tell us univocally whether there is a person or a dog on the sofa and if we know a person is there we do not know whether the person is awake or has fainted. So often several sensors have to be combined in order to support the accurate understanding of a simple aspect of reality. Part of the problem is that underlying these systems there are requirements of achieving aims whilst keeping costs and computational complexity low (Figure 5). On the other hand there are richer means to

Figure 4 A metaphor for how sensors perceive an environment.

gather input data, for example an array of video cameras distributed in various places of a building or a team of robots equipped with cameras and other advanced sensing devices can move around an area and provide 'in situ' understanding of a dynamic environment quite close to what humans in the place may be able to perceive. This however will still have a cost and require such computational skills to process the

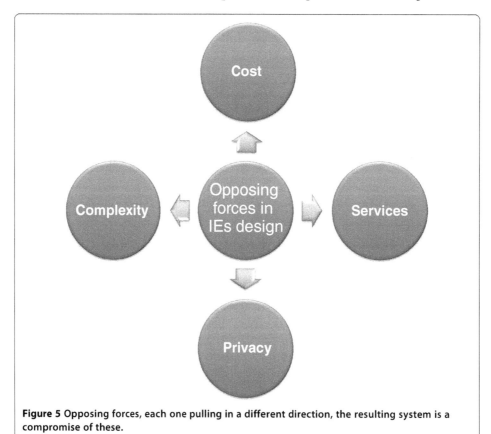

Figure 5 Opposing forces, each one pulling in a different direction, the resulting system is a compromise of these.

rich input which very few can afford and which, despite constant progress in the area, is far from being accessible to the masses. At the same time, the richer the more information a device can extract per time unit, the more invasive and resisted on privacy grounds.

The next section explains how people working in this area applies all the knowledge gained through decades of advances in different fields of Computer Science to allow a system to understand as best as possible an environment and provide valuable decision-making to benefit people that interacts with that environment.

Applications

The range of possible applications for Ambient Intelligence and Smart Environments is vast and we can look at the future of the area with expectation and hope that it will bring to everyday life a range of available solutions. Here we list some emerging applications driven by the demand of users, companies and governmental organizations:

- *Health-related applications.* Hospitals can increase the efficiency of their services by monitoring patients' health and progress by performing automatic analysis of activities in their rooms. They can also increase safety by, for example, only allowing authorized personnel and patients to have access to specific areas and devices. Health can be decentralized and made accessible at home through telecare and telehealth services in what it is commonly termed Ambient Assisted Living [36-38].
- *Transportation.* Transport is already benefiting from technology including satellite services, GPS-based spatial location, vehicle identification, image processing and other technologies to make transport more fluent and hence more efficient and safe. This progress is starting to emerge in the form of Smart Cars and Smart Road Network infrastructure [39,40].
- *Education.* Education-related institutions may use technology to create smart classrooms where the modes of learning are enhanced by technology that support students and lecturers inside and outside the classroom [41].
- *Production-oriented places.* Companies can use RFID sensors to tag different products and track them along the production and commercialization processes. This allows identifying the product path from production to consumer and helps improving the process by providing valuable information for the company on how to react to favourable demand and unusual events like products that become unsuitable for sale [42].
- *Smart offices.* They have been also the centre of attention and some interesting proposals aim at equipping offices with ways to assist their employees to perform their tasks more efficiently [43,44].
- *Intelligent supermarkets:* work has been conducted recently to develop the supermarkets of the future, where objects can interchange with customers auditory and visual information on its characteristics and interpret how customers move objects in what is a simplified version of a sign language between the customer and the shelf containing the objects [45].
- *Energy Conservation:* smart homes were the most prominent early examples of products advertised as intelligent environments which can primarily help house occupants to manage lighting and temperature automatically on behalf of the user.

Part of the marketing implied they will provide a more efficient managing of those resources. People worldwide is taking those issues much more seriously today and Intelligent Environments can be one important instrument to achieve those goals [46].

- *Entertainment:* fun is perceived as an important part of human lives. Many houses contain now a wide range of devices to provide entertainment and fun for a diversity of ages. The sophistication of these games can be highly enhanced by technology which provides more immersive experiences, an important feature in modern gaming [47].

Limitations in current systems

During the last decade or so, this area has increasingly attracted interest, effort and resources. Still the complexities associated with the limitations of the technological infrastructure and its relation to the variety of humans they are supposed to serve is considerable. Below we try to explain the dimension of this gap through some features which can make a substantial difference on technology adoption.

Accurate context-awareness

An intelligent environment needs to made decisions that benefit the environment inhabitants. Naturally, the decision needs to take into account the context of the current situation. Computationally, context may refer to network connectivity, communication costs, and resource availability. The user context may include the user's profile (demographic, gender, preferences, habits) as well as current location, task, and social situation. The environment context may capture internal features such as lighting and temperature levels as well as the current state outside the environment. Also important, time context includes the hour of the day, day of the week, season, and year [48]. By combining heterogeneous sources of information including the user location, automatically-recognized activity, and online information (e.g., Facebook), an intelligent environment can build and use a contextual picture of the situation to reason about and act to improve the current situation.

While context-awareness is crucial for intelligent environments to provide effective decisions and actions, a danger is focusing on a too narrow understanding of the context recognition problem. Sensor data fusion techniques can combine disparate sources of information into a concise, usable contextual description [49]. An intelligent environment should seamlessly adapt to changing context or behaviors at an individual, social group, or community level. Intelligent environments deal with massive amounts of data and highly complex situations. As a result, they also need to make decisions based on insufficient, incomplete and noisy data samples.

Balancing preferences and needs

Preferences (e.g., on meals, entertainment, house environmental conditions) and needs (e.g., medicine and schedules) distinguish us from one another and we even change some of those often due to unforeseen circumstances (e.g., weather) or to our own decision (e.g., we want to see ourselves slimmer). On one side it will be unpractical to design each system from scratch in an ad hoc manner for each person, on the other hand, a "one size fits all" approach to Intelligent Environment development will clearly not address all specific preferences and needs of each user. One option ahead is to create a generic system and then to personalize it, ideally the system should have a learning system which can learn how to serve the user better. However, the capability of the system to recognize, learn and update preferences and needs dynamically is a crucial problem still to be tackled.

"Mindreading"

Related to the problem described above is the problem of how the system can obtain an updated understanding of the preferences and needs of a user at any given moment. Some users may not be willing to speak to the system or to use any keyboard or device to explicitly indicate that the current situation (e.g., bad mood or in the presence of visits) advises against interruptions or that on the contrary a suggestion from the system may be welcomed (e.g., on a new film that has been released). Is there any way a system can understand whether the user is in more of a receptive or introverted mood? Can for example, the activities performed in the last hour and the way they were performed (e.g., slamming doors), biometric data (e.g., perspiration and pulse captured by a watch or ECG measured by a wearable t-shirt), and body language observed (e.g., through video cameras that focus on face gestures) be used to understand the emotional status of the user? So far all these research is reporting some moderated success on achieving specific technical goals [50-53] but they have not yet been used in a holistic and comprehensive manner that is meaningful to the field and to a real practical (e.g., commercial) application.

Coping with multiple occupancy

Working with one user has proved difficult enough to produce reliable affordable systems capable to serve a person. Some advances have been made and some prototypes have been deployed and are currently being tested but it is clear there is still a long way to go. Things get more difficult when the system is supposed to deliver differentiated services to more than one user in the same environment. The first problem is identifying each one of the users at all times. Current technology is such that univocally identifying a person is proportional to the cost and complexity of the identification mechanisms. Let us assume the user wears an ID tag which can be read by a device approaching meaningful points like doors or objects of daily use. This imply the replication of reading devices all along the house to know where the user is and to deliver meaningful services according to the context (e.g., location, time, etc.). This still leave us with the problem that each user may confuse the tags and the system will deliver services to the wrong person. Other technologies can be used, e.g., face recognition through cameras, but they also have negative side effects, e.g., privacy.

An intelligent environment can rely on these biometric approaches to identifying individuals in a space. An alternative approach is to draw from behaviometrics. In this case the environment performs identification by recognizing the movement or behavioral patterns that are typically associated with a specific individual. Using behavior to classify individuals into groups (e.g., friends, threats, salesmen) is a skill all humans possess. Designing intelligent environments to make the same kind of prediction is a natural extension of sensor-based systems [54]. Another typical problem arising when more than one user co-exist in an environment is described in the next section.

Humans have lot in common but it is very difficult to find two human beings with exactly the same preferences and needs. Whether it is on T.V. channels or meals, diversions will arise. How the system should react to those situations? can an artificial system become an effective mediator amongst humans? What happens when all alternatives to reach an agreement fail, will the system give priority to one human, based, for example, on a social hierarchy? [55] This is again an important issue because if some user or group of users find often their needs and preferences are not favored against those of other co-habitants then they will probably feel unsatisfied and consider the system useless.

Deploying reliable systems

Intelligent Environments are designed to assist and support people, in some cases are intended to take care of people in vulnerable situations, the potential for disaster when a system fails is high. Assuming systems should be developed to perfection is naive, companies are decided to exploit this market and the best we can do is to create and make available methodologies and tools that can be easily incorporated to the development process facilitating adoption by industry. There are reports which eloquently explain how the complexity of the software needed to govern these systems can easily develop hidden complex interactions which create instability within the behaviour of the system [56]. Doing nothing and passing the responsibility to the user (which usually is not technically prepared to thoroughly assess what is being installed in an environment) is unethical. This is an aspect our community should take very seriously given the potential to harm other humans.

Software Engineering has been working on these areas for long but the systems we consider here have a mix of sensors, networks, intelligent software, human-computer interfaces and users which makes thorough testing and verification to exceed the complexity traditional techniques and tools can cope with. It is difficult to test context-aware software in comparison with other software, because the former needs to be tested in its target contexts to develop reliable systems. A solution is to run such software with contexts e.g., locations and local-area networks, by emulating context or migrating software to the target locations [57]. Also, we often need formal methodologies to simulate or verify intelligent environments to confirm whether they can satisfy the specifications.

Ethical dimension

Systems which are designed to serve humans have to do so in a sensitive way. This area which aspires to be so intimately connected with our daily lives has to take this dimension very seriously.

Privacy

The more a system knows about us the more is able to serve us as we would like. The system may know we like chocolate ice cream because we have told the system explicitly or because we allowed the system to infer that from the last two months purchases from the supermarket. If we have not told the system we hate pistachio flavoured ice cream then the system may one day incur in what we consider a wrong decision.

We have discussed above the limitations of simple sensors and how they feed the decision-making modules with a simplified perception of reality. From all the data gathering devices we have available, video cameras are the most successful ones in the sense they provide us with fuller and crisper information about the fragment of the environment they are observing. Cameras provide more information that is useful but also have the potential to absorve information the user may not like to be captured by a camera. To illustrate the point think about extreme situations like having a camera in your own bathroom or bedroom at home. Sure there are many other situations where cameras can be used and indeed are being used. What is acceptable or not acceptable to share changes enormously with cultural values and the situation being observed. Some users are happy to give up some degree of privacy in return for increased safety; some humans will never accept a camera recording their daily life activities.

Researchers and developers have to work out systems which adapt to the different degrees of sensitivity users may have when blending technology with daily life affairs.

Multiple stakeholders

Sensors available in an intelligent environment may be owned and managed by different organizations or people. When such sensors in a space acquire information on targets, e.g., people, the information may be held by the targets or the administrators of the space, rather than the owners or operators of the sensors. That is, intelligent environment s tend to have multiple stakeholders. Before using information from intelligent environment s, we must adjust interests among all potential stakeholders. This problem becomes serious when IEs are supported in public spaces, e.g., office buildings and streets.

Furthermore, we need to limit free riders in intelligent environment s, where a free rider is someone who consumes a resource without paying for it, or pays less than the full cost. This is an economic problem in the sense that it leads to the excessive use of a common property resource. However, if too many people do this, users cannot be provided with services from intelligent environments. Intelligent environments need mechanisms to limit free riders. On the other hand, when an emergent situation, e.g., fire and disaster, intelligent environment s should assign much resources and services for some specified users, e.g., rescue teams. Since intelligent environments become social infrastructures in future, researchers and developers have to solve multiple stakeholder problems, including free rider problems.

Safety

Sensors record information about our daily activities and there is technology that can mine the recorded data to extract patterns of behaviour. The idea being that negative behaviours can be indentified and discouraged and positive ones encouraged and reinforced. But what happens if all that private information fall in the wrong hands?

There have been many incidents where sensitive digital information from governments and military forces around the world has been forgotten in a pen drive, CD or laptop at an airport or a train. We can get many unwanted calls per week because a company (e.g., bank or electronics shop where we bought something in installments) stored our personal details in a PC and the company that do back-ups sells the information (most probably without the bank's or shop's knowledge) to SPAM making companies?

It is not unlikely then that the same can happen to sensitive private data and our habits and illnesses can be accessible to groups of people who are eager to take profit of that knowledge. Both economic and personal safety can be compromised as a result of personal data falling in the wrong hands. As a result, users will become more and more aware of this and extra measures have to be provided to bring peace of mind to the early adopters of this technology. If the market is labeled as unsafe by the users then all those involved will lose a fantastic opportunity to benefit society.

Given the inherent intrinsic complexity of systems of this anture and given the extrinsic complexity of humans expectations from technology, these systems will unavoidably fail from time to time in some way or another. [58] alerts of this situation and advocates for all the different stakeholders to emphasize the need to give safety a higher status in the agenda. Four first steps are proposed: a) A more formal software engineering approach to systems design, b) enhanced understanding of human–computer interaction, c) a partnership between the technical level and human, d) a higher ethical dimension. It is also recognized they are not a solution but only a first step in the right direction.

Conclusions

We have provided an account of a new emerging area, one that can have an important role in a transition towards computing devices supporting our daily life to an extent not experimented before.

There are still considerable challenges, which we highlighted above. There are technological limitations both in hardware, which is currently based on limited and unreliable sensors and networks, as well as in software, forced to make good decisions out of a limited perception of reality, and to deal with a number of users with different needs and preferences.

Privacy and safety concerns also have to be carefully considered for these systems to be adopted. At the core of these systems there is a paradox where for us to be served best, the system needs to know more about our daily life, which in turn makes us more vulnerable to system failure.

On the other hand there are important benefits for humanity if this technological enterprise succeeds. Also, a scientific point of view it is an interesting catalyst for blending efforts from different areas of Computer Science which have achieved relative success and maturity (AI, HCI, communications, etc.). An intelligent environment necessarily needs a multi-disciplinary approach, this includes as well the professional expertise incumbent to the application area, hence a Smart Home to support independent living may require the involvement of social workers, nurses and architects.

This is a very interesting source of applications that has an impact on society yet has well defined physical boundaries (e.g., a Smart Home or a Smart Car) where to deploy specific services (e.g., order shopping for me, wake me up if I show signs of falling asleep when driving).

The area is well suited for incremental development, i.e., adding services gradually as the system and user needs unfold. Whilst previous AI research was predominantly inspired by challenges that benefited either a few in very specific places (e.g., expert systems) or all humanity in a very indirect way (e.g., space exploration), this technology can potentially allow us to achieve a variety of benefits for many humans as the services address comfort, economy, safety and other concerns of humans daily living experience in the environments where they live and work.

Still these applications present reasonable challenges (solutions are feasible for the state of the art in a relatively short term) and are a new inspiration for CS professionals to produce something tangible for society which still demands ingenuity and responsible development. This is hopefully the era when computing is finally blended in our lives not to benefit the few but the masses, not in rare occasions but continuously.

Competing interests

The authors declare that they have no competing interests.

Authors' contributions

All authors contributed to the content of all sections.

Author details

[1]Middlesex University, London, UK. [2]University of Essex, Colchester, UK. [3]Washington State University, Pullman, USA. [4]Hellenic Open University, Patras, Greece. [5]National Institute of Informatics, Tokyo, Japan.

References

1. Russell S, Norvig P (2003) Artificial Intelligence: A Modern Approach (Second Edition). Prentice Hall, New York
2. Weiser M (1991) The computer for the 21st century. Sci Am 265(3):94–104
3. Cook D, Das S (2005) Smart Environments: Technology, Protocols and Applications. Wiley-Interscience, USA
4. Nakashima H, Aghajan H, Augusto JC (2012) Handbook on Ambient Intelligence and Smart Environments. Springer Verlag, Berlin
5. Augusto JC (2007) Ambient Intelligence: The Confluence of Pervasive Computing and Artificial Intelligence. In: Schuster A (ed) Intelligent Computing Everywhere. Published by Springer Verlag, Berlin, pp 213–234
6. Aarts E, Harwig R, Schuurmans M (2001) Chapter 'Ambient Intelligence'. In: Denning P (ed) The Invisible Future: The Seamless Integration Of Technology Into Everyday Life. McGraw-Hill Companies, USA
7. Aarts E, Marzano S (2003) The New Everyday: Visions of Ambient Intelligence. 010 Publishers, Rotterdam
8. Ducatel K, Bogdanowicz M, Scapolo F, Leijten J, Burgelman J (2001) Scenarios for Ambient Intelligence in 2010. ISTAG 2001
9. Cook D, Augusto J, Jakkula V (2009) Ambient Intelligence: applications in society and opportunities for AI. Pervasive Mobile Comput 5:277–298, Elsevier
10. Augusto JC, Callaghan V, Zamudio V, Egerton S (eds) (2012) Proceedings of the 8th International Conference on Intelligent Environments (IE 12), Guanajuato. IEEE Press, Mexico
11. Augusto JC, Bohlen M, Cook D, Flentge F, Marreiros G, Ramos C, Qin W, Suo Y (2009) The Darmstadt Challenge (the Turing Test Revisited). In: Proceedings of the International Conference on Agents and Artificial Intelligence (ICAART). INSTICC, Porto, Portugal
12. (2009) Ambient Intelligence and Wearable Computing: Sensors on the Body, in the Home, and Beyond. In: Cook D, Song W (eds) , vol 1, 2nd edn, Journal of Ambient Intelligence and Smart Environments, pp 83–86
13. Delsing J, Lindgren P (2005) Sensor communication technology towards ambient intelligence. Measurment Sci Technol 16:37–46
14. Schiele G, Handte M, Becker C (2009) Pervasive Computing Middleware. In: Nakashima H, Aghajan H, Augusto JC (eds) Handbook of Ambient Intelligence and Smart Environments. Springer, New York
15. Dey A, Salber D, Abowd G (2001) A conceptual framework and a toolkit for supporting the rapid prototyping of context-aware applications. Hum Comput Interact 16(2–4):97–166
16. Aztiria A, Izaguirre A, Augusto JC (2010) Learning patterns in Ambient Intelligence environments: A Survey. Artif Intell Rev 34(1):35–51
17. Doctor F, Hagras H, Roberts D, Callaghan V (2009) A Fuzzy Based Agent for Group Decision Support of Applicants Ranking within Recruitment Systems. IEEE IA:8–15
18. Huebscher M, McCann J (2008) A survey of autonomic computing - degrees, models, and applications. ACM Comput Surv 40(3)
19. Satoh I (2011) Building and Operating Context-aware Services for Groups of Users. Procedia CS 5:304–311
20. Callaghan V, Clarke G, Colley M, Hagras H (2011) Embedding Intelligence: Research Issues in Ubiquitous Computing, Proceedings of 1st Equator IRC Workshop on Ubiquitous Computing. 13-14th of September
21. Cook D, Youngblood M, Das S (2006) A multi-agent approach to controlling a smart environment. In: Augusto J, Nugent C (eds) Designing Smart Homes, The Role of Artificial Intelligence. Springer-Verlag, Berlin, pp 165–182
22. Cook D (2009) Multi-agent smart environments. Diane J. Cook. JAISE 1(1):51–55, IOS Press
23. Satoh I (2008) Context-aware Agents to Guide Visitors in Museums. Proc 8th Int Confer Intell Virt Agents (IVA'08), Lect Notes Artific Intell (LNAI) 5208:441–455
24. de Ruyter B, Aarts A (2006) Social interactions in ambient intelligent environments. In: Augusto JC, Shapiro D (eds) Proceedings of the 1st Workshop on Artificial Intelligence Techniques for Ambient Intelligence (AITAmI2006). Riva del Garda, Italy
25. Matsumoto O, Komoriya K, Toda K, Goto S, Hatase T, Nishimura N (2006) Autonomous travelling control of the "tao aicle" intelligent wheelchair. In: IEEE/RSJ International Conference on Intelligent Robots and Systems (IROS06)., pp 4322–4327
26. Pentland A (2005) Perceptual environments. In: Cook DJ, Das SK (eds) Smart Environments: Technology, Protocols and Applications. Wiley-Interscience, USA
27. Majaranta P, R̈aiḧa K-J (2007) Text entry by gaze: Utilizing eye-tracking. In: MacKenzie I, Tanaka-Ishii K (eds) Text entry systems: Mobility, accessibility, universality. Morgan Kaufmann, Berlin, pp 175–187
28. Partala T, Surakka V, Vanhala T (2006) Real-time estimation of emotional experiences from facial expressions. Interact Comput 18(2):208–226
29. Zhou J, Yu C, Riekki J, Kärkkäinen E (2009) AmE Framework: a Model for Emotion aware Ambient Intelligence. In: Ubiquitous, Autonomic and Trusted Computing (Proceedings of UIC-ATC '09)., pp 428–433
30. McTear M, Raman T (2004) Spoken Dialogue Technology: Towards the Conversational User Interface. Springer, Berlin

31. Aghajan H, Lopez-Cozar Delgado R, Augusto JC (2009) Human-Centric Interfaces for Ambient Intelligence. Academic Press Elsevier, USA

32. Campos P, Nicholas Graham T, Jorge J, Nunes N, Palanque P, Winckler M (2011) Human-Computer Interaction - INTERACT 2011 - 13th IFIP TC 13 International Conference. Lecture Notes in Computer Science 6949. Springer, Lisbon, Portugal

33. Costagliola G, Ko A, Cypher A, Nichols J, Scaffidi C, Kelleher C, Myers B (2011) IEEE Symposium on Visual Languages and Human-Centric Computing (VL/HCC 2011). IEEE Press, Pittsburgh, PA, USA

34. Dertouzos M (2001) Human-centered Systems. In: Denning (ed) The Invisible Future. ACM Press, USA, pp 181–192

35. (2007) The Disappearing Computer, Interaction Design, System Infrastructures and Applications for Smart Environments. In: Streitz N, Kameas A, Mavrommati I (eds) The Disappearing Computer, Interaction Design, System Infrastructures and Applications for Smart Environments. Springer, Berlin

36. Augusto JC, Huch M, Kameas A, Maitland J, McCullagh P, Roberts J, Sixsmith A, Wichert R (2012) Handbook on Ambient Assisted Living – Technology for Healthcare, Rehabilitation and Well-being, vol 11. AISE Book Series, IOS Press, Amsterdam

37. van den Broek G, Cavallo F, Wehrmann C (2010) AALIANCE Ambient Assisted Living Roadmap. Ambient Intelligence and Smart Environments Series, vol 6. IOS Press, Amsterdam

38. Helal S, Mokhtari M, Abdulrazak B (2009) The Engineering Handbook on Smart Technology for Aging, Disability and Independence. In: , Computer Engineering Series John Wiley & Sons, USA, ISBN 978-0-471-71155-1

39. Abdel-Rahim A (2012) Intelligent Transportation Systems. Publisher: InTech. ISBN 978-953-51-0347-9

40. Krumm J, Horvitz E (2006) Predestination: Inferring destinations from partial trajectories. In: Eighth International Conference on Ubiquitous Computing., pp 243–260

41. Augusto JC (2009) Ambient Intelligence: Opportunities and Consequences of its Use in Smart Classrooms. Italics, 8(2), published by the HEA-ICS subject centre, UK, pp 53–63

42. Want R (2004) RFID–a key to automating everything. Sci Am 290:46–55

43. Danninger M, Stiefelhagen R (2008) A context-aware virtual secretary in a smart office environment. In: Proceedings of the 16th ACM international conference on Multimedia, Vancouver, British Columbia, Canada., pp 529–538

44. Ramos C, Marreiros G, Santos R, Filipe Freitas C (2010) Smart Offices and Intelligent Decision Rooms. Handbook Ambient Intelligence Smart Environ VII:851–880, Springer

45. Wahlster W, Feld M, Gebhard P, Heckmann D, Jung R, Kruppa M, Schmitz M, Spassova L, Wasinger R (2010) The Shopping Experience of Tomorrow: Human-Centered and Resource-Adaptive. In: Crocker MW, Siekmann J (eds) Resource-Adaptive Cognitive Processes. Berlin, Springer, Heidelberg, pp 205–237

46. Tomic S, Fensel A, Schwanzer M, Veljovic M, Stefanovic M (2011) Semantics for Energy Efficiency in Smart Home Environments. Applied Semantic Technologies: Using Semantics. In: Sugumaran V, Gulla JA (eds) Intelligent Information Processing. Taylor and Francis, USA

47. Block F, Schmidt A, Villar N, Gellersen H-W (2004) Towards a Playful User Interface for Home Entertainment Systems. In: Proceedings of the European Symposium on Ambient Intelligence. Springer, Berlin, pp 207–217

48. Chen G, Kotz D (2000) A survey of context-aware mobile computing research. Technical Report TR2000-381, Dartmouth College, USA

49. Siegel M, Wu H (2004) Confidence fusion. Proceedings of the IEEE Workshop on Robotic Sensing

50. Kotsia I, Buciua I, and Pitas I (2008) An analysis of facial expression recognition under partial facial image occlusion, Image and Vision Computing, Volume 26, Issue 7. Pages 1052–1067. Elsevier.

51. Mäkinen E (2007) Face Analysis Techniques for Human-Computer Interaction. Ph.D. Thesis. Tampere University, Finland, Available from http://acta.uta.fi/pdf/978-951-44-7184-1.pdf

52. Leon E, Clarke G, Callaghan V, Doctor F (2010) Affect-aware behaviour modelling and control inside an intelligent environment. Pervasive Mobile Comput 6(4):559–574, Elsevier

53. Westerink J, Ouwerkerk M, Overbeek T, Pasveer W, de Ruyter B (2008) Probing Experience: From Assessment of User Emotions and Behaviour to Development of Products, vol 8. Philips Research Book Series

54. Crandall A (2011) Behaviometrics for multiple residents in a smart environment. PhD Dissertation, Washington State University, USA

55. Muñoz A, Botía J, Augusto J (2010) Intelligent Decision-Making for a Smart Home Environment with Multiple Occupants. In: Computational Intelligence in Complex Decision Systems". Atlantic Press, Amsterdam, pp 325–369, ISBN: 978-90-78677-27-7

56. Zamudio V, Callaghan V (2009) Understanding and Avoiding Interaction Based Instability in Pervasive Computing Environments. V. Zamudio, and V. Callaghan. Int J Pervasive Comput Commun 5(2):163–186

57. Satoh I (2003) A Testing Framework for Mobile Computing Software. IEEE Trans Softw Eng 29(12):1112–1121

58. Augusto JC, McCullagh P, Walkden J-A (2011) Living Without a Safety Net in an Intelligent Environment, ICST Transactions on Ambient Systems 1(1). ICST and EAI., http://eudl.eu/doi/10.4108/trans.amsys.2011.e6

4

Shared virtual presentation board for e-Meeting in higher education on the WebELS platform

Arjulie John Berena[1*], Sila Chunwijitra[2], Hitoshi Okada[1] and Haruki Ueno[1]

* Correspondence: berena@nii.ac.jp
[1]National Institute of Informatics, Tokyo, Japan
Full list of author information is available at the end of the article

Abstract

In this paper, the development of a shared virtual presentation board (VPB) for real-time e-Meeting on the Web-based e-Learning System (WebELS) platform is introduced. WebELS is a general-purpose e-Learning system to support flexibility and globalization of higher education in science and technology. In WebELS, the Meeting module consists of online presentation and video conference system, and the combination of both allows the creation of a so-called virtual room for e-Meeting applications where participants convene via the Internet. Online presentation features synchronized slide control between the presenter and the listeners for slide changing, scrolling, zooming, cursor positioning, and playback control for video embedded on the slide. It also features online annotation that allows the presenter to write using a pen function on the slide display panel. The system has video conferencing function that provides an audio-video communication among the meeting participants. This paper discusses briefly the video conference system, and focuses on online presentation based on slide-based synchronization and the development of VPB. VPB is a shared object that resides on the server that is updated every time the presenter client makes mouse events and is periodically accessed by client system in order that listener's presentation viewer synchronized with that of the presenter.

Keywords: e-Learning, e-Meeting, Online presentation, Online annotation, Shared presentation board, WebELS

Introduction

Advancements of technology and the informatization of society are factors that paved the way for shifting the teaching methodologies in higher educational system from the traditional classroom-based method to the use of information and communications technology. In recent years, Internet-based teaching and learning technologies have been widely available enabling e-Learning to become a major form of educational methodology addressing time-limitation and location-limitation between teacher and students [1]. e-Learning infrastructure can be easily carried out because of the advancement in internetworking technologies, multimedia information processing technologies, and software technologies at lower cost and higher quality in a global scale [2].

Unlike e-Learning in middle school and undergraduate programs where course management and automated student assessment are typical features, in higher education, particularly in the graduate school, the system should support self-learning, group meetings, and research presentations [3-6]. The characteristics of an e-Learning system for higher education based on information technology perspective can be best deduced from the three areas as follows:

- *Activities:* A system must support online activities, such as group distance meetings, multi-point distribution of oral presentation in conferences, online collaboration with professors and other researchers in academe and industries, and other similar scenarios.
- *Tools and Materials:* A system must have powerful authoring tool so that professors and students alike can create and edit their own presentation materials on their personal computers. Users should be able to utilize various contents in the form of PDF, PPT and other office documents on various operating systems, such as Windows, Mac OS and Linux.
- *Behavior:* A system must support slide-based presentation and multimedia content, such as audio and video. Users should be able to make comment and annotation to the presentation material and must also be available during online meeting and discussion.

In carrying out the demands of higher education in view of information technology, an e-Meeting system is strongly requested rather than a typical learning management system (LMS) [7,8]. An effective e-Meeting system requires primary features like online slide presentation, online annotation, chat messaging and video conferencing system. Although there are a lot of similar systems, but it is very rare to find an all-in-one system that really answer the need to support e-Meeting for higher education.

In this paper, we discuss the development of a shared virtual presentation board (VPB) for e-Meeting system on the Web-based e-Learning System (WebELS) platform. VPB is a master copy of the presenter's presentation panel environment, stored onto the server and used to achieve slide presentation synchronization between the presenter and the listeners. Synchronization in our context refers to real-time mirroring of slide presentation events that include slide controls for slide changing, vertical and horizontal scrolling, panning, zooming, cursor positioning, annotation, and playback control for video embedded on the slide. The system has a video conferencing function that provides an audio-video communication among the meeting participants. An effective e-Meeting is made possible by combining the online slide presentation and video conference system to create a so-called virtual room, where meeting participants convene via the Internet.

Review of online presentation technologies

With the fast-paced development of Internet application technologies, various online presentation tools have become widely available. We describe some popular related technologies according to their core design, such as screen sharing, document sharing and slide synchronization. We also discuss the benefits and drawbacks for each in view of e-Meeting application for higher education.

Screen sharing technology

Screen sharing technology allows one to transmit the desktop static image of his computer to one or more remotely connected users in the network. Some screen sharing systems allow remote control which shares the ability to control the keyboard and mouse to other users. Some systems that use screen sharing are VNC [9], Skype [10], GoToMeeting [11], WebEx [12], TeamViewer [13], join.me [14], to name a few.

The advantage of screen sharing technique is that presenter can show various applications on his desktop and be seen by other participants. In view of e-Meeting however, presenter have to be careful that sensitive information is not displayed as it can be visible to other meeting participants. Another drawback of screen-sharing technology is the reduced graphic quality that small text cannot be easily read or small objects cannot be easily recognized. Screen sharing technique works well in broadband, but may not operate well in narrowband as it utilizes greater bandwidth for transmitting of encoded pixel data of screen image. Bandwidth demand gets very high if there is a lot of pixel change at a short time, such as when scrolling a window or showing animated presentation may take several seconds to completely display the image at remote site. Another major drawback of screen sharing is that it requires advanced network address translation (NAT), firewall and router configuration such as port forwarding in order for the connection to go through. Other systems are also limited to peer-to-peer connection, and does not support multi-user. Since it is not a web-based system, it is necessary to download and install the software before screen sharing can start up. Some screen sharing systems have an integrated support to Voice over Internet Protocol (VoIP) or teleconferencing (telephone) to realize an e-Meeting. But others do not have and users have to use other VoIP system.

Document sharing technology

Document sharing tools are sometimes referred to as online presentation tool because it is possible to share presentation files online. Some document sharing tools allow one to create a PowerPoint presentation online or upload an existing PowerPoint file onto the server. Other users can then view and edit the shared presentation, such as Google Docs [15] and SlideRocket [16], while others allow anyone to view only but does not allow editing, such as authorSTREAM [17] and SlideShare [18]. Some systems support various file formats [15], but others only support PowerPoint [16-18]. Users sharing a document is not required to be online at a time, thus there is no real time interaction among the users. Document sharing does not employ integrated support for VoIP as the main purpose is to share documents.

Slide-based synchronization technology

Slide-based synchronization technology refers to mirroring of the presentation panel among the meeting participants, i.e., what the presenter see on his display panel will also be replicated on the listeners' display panel. Some popular systems that use slide synchronization are V-Cube [19], Adobe Connect [20], BigBlueButton [21], among others. During online presentation, MS PowerPoint or PDF file is uploaded on-the-fly by the client presenter to the server. At the server, the uploaded file is converted to an image format before it can be viewed by the users. For instance, however, the file document to be uploaded is considerably large, conversion process may take a lot of time, and this may cause delay on the meeting proceedings. It is even more time consuming if the there are several file documents to be used in the meeting. Furthermore, these systems use streaming mechanism to deliver the slide presentation to each connected user. However, images loaded as slides becomes blurred, distorted, and have poor quality as compared to the original. This has been widely reported problem on Flash-based images, and hopefully solution will be on its way. On the brighter side, most web-based conferencing technologies today have built-in audio-video communication support.

WebELS platform overview
System design concepts
WebELS is designed to provide an advanced e-Learning platform for globalizing higher education in science and technology focusing on authoring and dissemination of multimedia contents, aiming to assist instructors to archive their learning materials on the web for on-demand learning and to support online meeting [22].

The design concepts of WebELS can be summarized in the following:

- Supports asynchronous and synchronous e-Learning, i.e., on-demand self-learning and multi-location Internet-based meeting,
- Powerful and easy-to-use content authoring function that supports various documents,
- User-friendly interface for novice and non-IT users,
- Supports multi-operating systems and multi-browser,
- Must be available "anywhere and anytime" and must work even in strict firewall and proxy settings,
- Should be available not only in advanced countries where broadband Internet is widely used but also in developing countries such as in Asia and Africa where narrowband Internet is normally used [23].

System components
WebELS is a Java-based client–server system built with applets and JSP/servlets technology for client and server side programs, respectively. Java applets are used for content authoring and online slide presentation viewing, which requires the users' browser to have Java Runtime Environment (JRE) plug-in. For audio-video conference system, Red5 streaming server is used, and requires the users to have Adobe Flash Player plug-in installed on their computer. The main components required for the WebELS server system are the following: Linux Operating System, Apache HTTP Server, Apache Tomcat, Open JDK, MySQL, Red5 Media Server, FFmpeg, and Apache OpenOffice.

WebELS meeting module
The overview of the WebELS Meeting system is shown in Figure 1. As shown, there are three servers in the server side system - database server, content server and streaming server. Database and content server are used for content and user data management, while streaming server is used for real-time audio-video communication.

Also in Figure 1, content authoring is done using the Java-based content Editor downloaded from the server. Content authoring using the Editor can achieve three operations, such as creating new content, editing content, and importing content from other servers. Existing file in various formats can be used, such as portable document format file (*.pdf), slide presentation file (*.ppt, *.pptx, *.odp), spreadsheet file (*.xls, *.xlsx, *.ods) and word processing file (*.doc, *.docx, *.odt). Files are converted to slide images either at the client or at the server. To create high-quality slides images, MS Office files are converted locally if there exists an MS Office application on the client system,

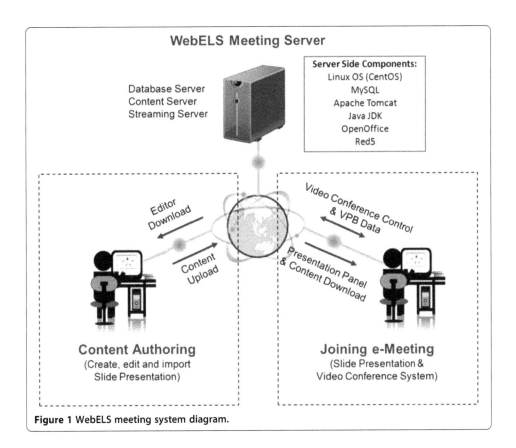

Figure 1 WebELS meeting system diagram.

then it is uploaded to the server. When there is none, files are uploaded to the server and are automatically converted into images by using OpenOffice and GhostScript. PDF and OpenOffice files are converted at the server by default. Video files (*.mpg, *. mov, *.avi) can also be embedded onto a special slide template which is possible to playback when viewing the content.

A virtual room is assigned to each created content and stored on the server. Each user accessing the same content will be able to join a meeting. In Figure 1, joining an e-Meeting requires the user to download the content and the presentation panel. The system stores the downloaded content onto the temporary folder, unzip the content package, and then load the slide images onto the presentation panel. The system prompts the user for username, and when done, displays the online presentation panel.

Online presentation has two user modes, namely (1) Presenter Mode, and (2) Listener Mode. In presenter mode, the user has over-all control of slide change, cursor position, zooming function and annotation function. Users in listener mode can only monitor who have joined the presentation, but does not have the rights to control the slides. The listener's presentation panel serves as a passive listener where it displays what is on the presenter's presentation panel.

The online presentation system implements the concept of a shared virtual presentation board. In this concept, a master copy of the presenter's presentation panel environment is stored onto the server, and used to achieve slide presentation synchronization between the presenter and the listeners. VPB data is updated by the presenter by sending the information in its presentation panel every time there is a user slide event, such as mouse click, mouse drag or button press. Listener of the same content retrieves the VPB data by polling the server, and thus be able to replicate in their presentation panel similar to what is in the presenter's presentation panel.

On the other hand, video conference system provides audio-video communication among the meeting participants who are in the same virtual room. Video conference and slide presentation panels are designed to be independent with each other, because one video conference panel can be used with multiple presentation content. Figure 2 shows the example of video conference and slide presentation.

Synchronized online presentation

Online presentation panel

WebELS Online Presentation Panel shown in Figure 3 is divided into four panels, namely (1) Presentation Display Panel, (2) Content Information Panel, (3) Control Panel, and (4) Collapsible Annotation Toolbar. Presentation display panel serves as the graphical screen of the slide presentation. Content information panel shows the content title and the slide navigator for quick slide changing. Control panel contains the slide control, zoom function, and presentation mode selection buttons. Annotation toolbar is hidden by default, but is displayed when annotation function is activated. It contains pen, pen color palette, pen size palette, eraser, and move tools.

Online presentation features

WebELS Online Presentation features the following important characteristics in implementing an effective e-Meeting system for higher-education:

- *Slide Synchronization*. A technique for real-time mirroring of slide presentation between the presenter and listener. The presentation control panel is equipped with slide control buttons (first slide, next slide, previous slide, and last slide) that

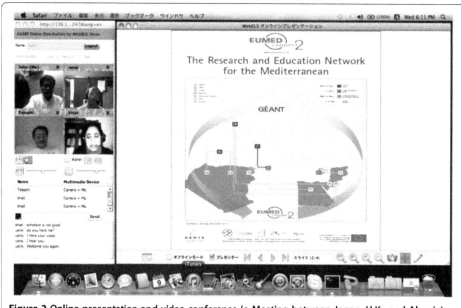

Figure 2 Online presentation and video conference (e-Meeting between Japan, U.K., and Algeria).

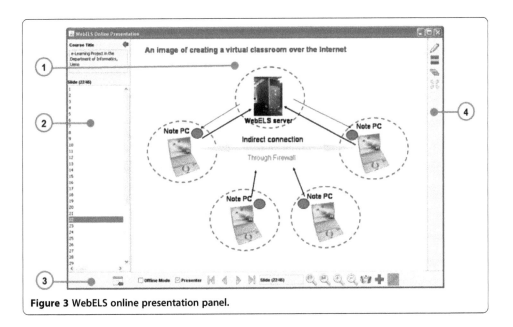

Figure 3 WebELS online presentation panel.

enables slide changing by the presenter, which is synchronized on the listeners'
presentation display panel.

- *Cursor-based Presentation.* A heavy red crosshair cursor displayed as a pointer
  which guides the listener on which part of the slide is being presented. When the
  presenter moves the default cursor and clicks at a certain position on the
  presentation display panel, a heavy red crosshair cursor appears, and will also be
  displayed on the listeners' presentation display panel. See Figure 4a.
- *Pen-based Presentation.* A pen-like function during the presentation for writing
  annotation. Annotation on the presentation display panel is simply done like a
  freehand drawing. By pressing the left-hand mouse and holding it steadily, drag the
  thin crosshair cursor which in turn writes your desired object. Pen color and size
  can be selected. See Figure 4b.
- *Slide Zoom Function.* Slide zooming function is necessary when text or object on
  the slide are not readable or visible during online presentation as in Figure 4c. It is
  also worth mentioning that cursor and annotation function is also possible even in
  zoomed-in presentation display panel. The annotated object after zooming out is
  scaled down equally the same as the slide.
- *Video Playback Function.* Various video content formats (*.mov, *.avi, *.mpg) can be
  embedded onto the slides. Video playback functions such as start, stop and pause
  are also made to synchronize between the presenter and the listener.

Virtual presentation board concept

The concept of a shared virtual presentation board is illustrated in Figure 5. The basic
concept is to make a master copy of the presentation display panel of the presenter at
the server, and it will be made available for the listeners to retrieve this data. The server
keeps the online presentation panel applet, the presentation content, and the VPB data
where it is created only when the content is used for the first time. Using a web
browser, a client joins in a meeting by requesting to download the presentation panel
and content in one compressed package. After downloading the package at the client

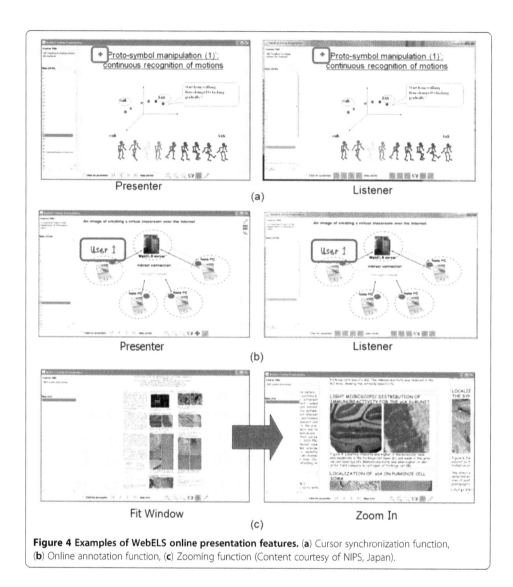

Figure 4 Examples of WebELS online presentation features. (**a**) Cursor synchronization function, (**b**) Online annotation function, (**c**) Zooming function (Content courtesy of NIPS, Japan).

computer, it is uncompressed at the temporary folder, and the presentation panel loads the content accordingly. By default, the client is a listener which polls the server for VPB data. The retrieved data will be used to set the presentation display panel. When there is no existing presenter, the listener can become a presenter by selecting the option. To keep the meeting in order, only one client is allowed to become a presenter at a time, where switching of presenter's right is allowed. The presenter, having the right to control the presentation display panel, is the source of VPB data, wherein every slide event in its presentation display panel, a new VPB data is sent to the server. Slide events include slide changing, cursor positioning, slide zooming, scrollbar positioning, video playback, and annotation functions. At the server, a VPB data file is updated by a write method. For the listeners to mirror the presenter's display panel in a synchronized manner, the client system polls the server, reads and retrieves the VPB data if it exists, and refreshes the presentation display panel. Polling takes place every one second.

VPB data structure

Figure 6 shows the VPB data structure that consists of static and dynamic data. Static data structure is used for slide presentation objects that include presenter status,

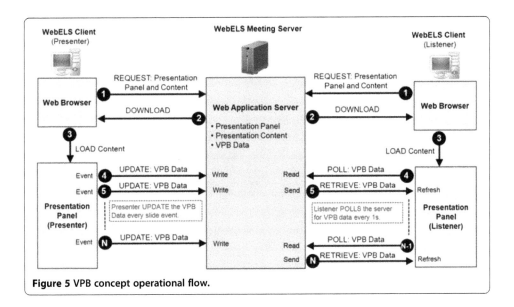

Figure 5 VPB concept operational flow.

presentation mode, slide number, cursor position, zoom data, scrollbar data and video function. These objects are used in cursor-based presentation. The part of the VPB data structure that has dynamic memory is used for the annotation data in a pen-based presentation. It uses a vector type memory that is appropriate for growing array of objects.

The fields of the VPB static data structure are detailed in the following:

- *presenter_status* – an integer data type that tells whether there is a presenter in the online presentation or not. This flag is used to implement one-presenter policy.
- *presentation_mode* – an integer data type that tells the mode of presentation whether cursor-based or annotation-based.
- *slide_number* – an integer data type that tells the current slide being used by the presenter.

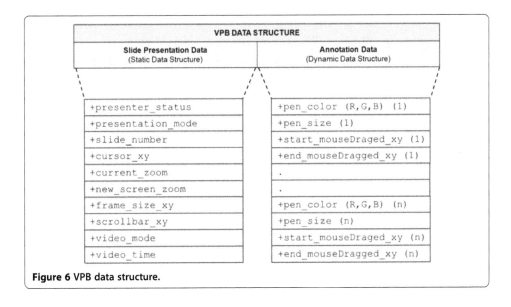

Figure 6 VPB data structure.

- *cursor_xy* – both an integer data type for the x value and y value of the cursor position relative to the display panel.
- *current_zoom* – both a double data type for current zoom-in scale and current zoom-out scale of the display panel.
- *new_screen_zoom* – both an integer data type that tells whether the display panel needs to be fixed or not after a zoom function.
- *frame_size_xy* – both an integer data type that tells the frame size of the presenter panel, which is used in calculating the listener's slide image to avoid mismatched display area.
- *scrollbar_xy* – both an integer data type for x and y scrollbar value that control horizontal and vertical view positions, respectively.
- *video_mode* – an integer data type that represents the mode for video functions whether start, pause, restart and stop.
- *video_time* – an integer data type that specifies the time in milliseconds when video mode is either stop or set time.

The VPB dynamic data are stored onto the vector memory that implements a growing array of objects. The dynamic data structure fields are detailed in the following:

- *pen_color* – three integer data types for RGB components of a color object.
- *pen_size* – float data type used for defining line width with default cap and joint styles rendered with Java Graphics2D object.
- *start_mouseDragged_xy* – both an integer data type for x and y values of cursor position relative to the display panel after the mouse is clicked, kept holding the left-button and dragged.
- *end_mouseDragged_xy* – both an integer data type for x and y values of cursor position relative to the display panel after the mouse is released from mouse dragged event.

Audio-video communication support

WebELS Meeting is equipped with a video conferencing system that provides audio-video communication among the users in a shared virtual room. With this system, effective e-Meeting can take place because users can discuss in a face-to-face like environment alongside with the online synchronized slide presentation.

The video conference system adopted by WebELS uses Real Time Messaging Protocol (RTMP). RTMP is a protocol used for streaming audio, video and data over the Internet between Flash player on client side and streaming server. The Red5 streaming server uses port 443 (the default for HTTPS) as RTMP port, however it switches automatically to RTMP Tunneled (RTMPT) when the network communication cannot transverse through firewall due to security issues of certain network location. In RTMPT, RTMP data is encapsulated and exchanged via HTTP, and messages from the client, i.e., the Flash media player, are addressed to port 80 (the default for HTTP) on the server. The reason that we don't use RTMPT from the beginning of the network connection is because the speed of communication via RTMPT is slower than RTMP, where we want to keep the quality of audio-video communication as high as possible.

Parameters for audio-video quality have been optimized in order for the system to adapt the users' network environment without suffering from bad audio-video quality. These parameters include video resolution, video frame rate, video encoding quality, and audio sampling rate are used to provide three video quality settings such as low, medium and high, which can be selected in manual or automatic mode.

The system has administrator functions for keeping an orderly flow of the e-Meeting. Several administrator functions are mute user, mute all, set presenter, and block user. The system also has an automatic reconnection function that monitors the network connection status. When the network connection is lost, it waits for the new connection to establish, and login process automatically starts again by using the latest user environment and conference information [24].

Performance evaluation and discussion

Presentation image quality

In WebELS Meeting online presentation implemented in Java, slide presentation files are converted into series of slide images, archived on a compressed package and stored on the server. Before starting a meeting, content must be downloaded from the server onto the client system, uncompressed to the temporary folder, and loaded onto the presentation panel. During the meeting, slide control is implemented using shared VPB. Since slide images are now in client system, high-quality images can be displayed on the presentation panel as shown in Figure 7b and look exactly the same as the original image shown in Figure 7a. Inset in Figure 7b shows the zoom-in image bearing smaller text information, but still readable.

As for the Flash-based online presentation systems, slide presentation file is also converted into series of slide images. During the meeting, when the presenter share the slide image, the URL link for that image is shared unto the server via a message stream, which in turn is shared to the connected clients. Clients get the image from the server using the URL link. Image quality in Flash is blurry that small text cannot be recognized anymore as shown in the inset in Figure 7c. The image sharing process is handled by a shared object class which offer real-time data and object sharing between multiple Flash application clients or remote server [25].

In presentation using screen sharing technology, image quality becomes degraded because it requires compression algorithms in order to transmit huge data in real-time. Sophisticated compression algorithms produce encoded image size around 100 kbytes for 800 × 600 true color screen image (i.e., 1.44 Mbytes in size) [26]. With this data size and moderate frame rate, however, it is still required to use broadband Internet for better quality. Image rendering at the client side experience flickering resulting to distorted image when the presenter changes the slide or scrolls the window that takes several seconds to completely display the image as shown in Figure 7d.

Comparing all three technologies for image quality in online presentation, WebELS Meeting based on Java has the best image quality than in Flash-based online presentation and screen sharing technology. Flash-based images are blurry that small texts are difficult to recognized, while presentation based on the screen sharing have flickering effect resulting to distorted image when changing slide or scrolling window.

Online presentation data size

Online presentation is achieved by sharing data between the remote user and the server. Shown in Table 1, the data size and the transmit frequency between the client and the server for various online presentation technology. For WebELS cursor-based presentation

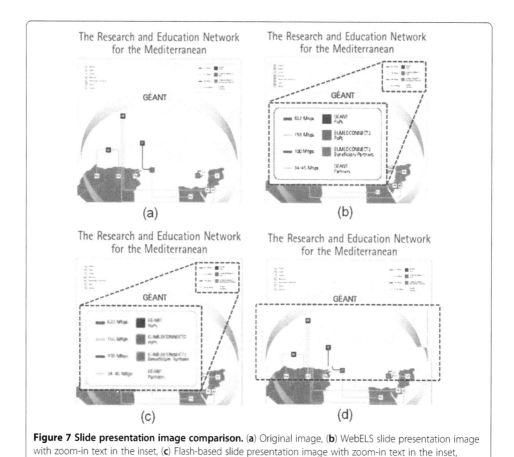

Figure 7 Slide presentation image comparison. (a) Original image, (b) WebELS slide presentation image with zoom-in text in the inset, (c) Flash-based slide presentation image with zoom-in text in the inset, (d) Screen sharing image with flickering.

mode, the VPB data contains slide control which range from 34 to 54 bytes, which is transmitted to the server for update every slide control events. For pen-based presentation mode, data size depends on how many the annotation is. In normal online meeting, annotation data range from 100 bytes to 10 kbytes, which is transmitted to the server for update every mouse drag release event. In Flash-based online presentation, sharing of image to other remote users is handled by a shared object class that sends the URL link of that image for other users to fetch. The typical image size of about 1 Mbytes is transmitted every slide change, while the annotation data also range from 100 bytes to 10 kbytes. For screen sharing technology, an 800 × 600 true color screen image after compression is about 100 kbytes. Screen image must be transmitted at a higher frame rate for better quality between the sender and receiver. In Table 1, the data size shared between the remote user and the server to achieve online presentation synchronization is comparatively minimal for WebELS than with the Flash-based online presentation and screen sharing technology.

Client network bandwidth requirement

Bandwidth utilization depends on the data size transmitted over a period of time between the client and the server. Based on the data in Table 1, WebELS VPB data for cursor-based presentation mode does not pose high bandwidth utilization since the data size is very small and slide control events are not that frequent. For VPB data in pen-based presentation mode, the more annotation is done, the larger the data sent

Table 1 Online presentation data size and transmit frequency

Data types	Data size (bytes)	Transmit frequency
WebELS VPB Data for cursor-based presentation mode	34 ~ 54	Every slide control events
WebELS VPB Data for pen-based presentation mode	100 ~ 10,000	Every mouse drag release
Flash-based Slide Synchronization (using SharedObject class for fetching the image)	≈ 1,000,000	Every slide change
Flash-based Slide Synchronization (using SharedObject class for fetching annotation)	100 ~ 10,000	Every mouse drag release
Compressed Screen Share Image Size	≈ 100,000	Pre-set frame per second (fps)

every mouse release. As for the Flash-based online presentation, slide image is transferred from the server to the client every slide change. Though high quality images are typically around 1 Mbytes, slide change is not that frequent that would cause high bandwidth utilization. But in screen sharing technology, there is a requirement for broadband network to achieve better quality. Among the different online presentation technologies, VPB concept works well even in narrowband Internet environment, say a 56 kbps line. On the other hand, slide synchronization delay between the presenter and listener using VPB is minimal because of its optimized data size, and delay would depend mainly on the network distance, i.e., round-trip propagation and transmission delay. Slide synchronization delay of 1 or 2 seconds is negligible in online distance presentation.

Server requirements

Synchronized online slide presentation consumes server resources for every connected user, but not as much as the video conferencing system do. For each video user connected to Red5 streaming server, CPU, memory, and I/O resources are utilized. However, with the current development in computer hardware technology, these are not very critical. The performance bottleneck that limits the number of users the server would accommodate with higher quality of service (QoS) depends on the network channel capacity.

The server uplink/downlink data rate with the number of users in a face-to-face meeting mode in an actual measurement is shown in Figure 8. Face-to-face meeting mode refers to a video conferencing scenario where all users use web-camera and microphone. Video qualities were optimized by setting the video parameters that results to average video stream bandwidth for low-quality, medium-quality and high-quality as 72, 120, 240 kbps, respectively. Due to video-codec algorithm, video stream bandwidth fluctuates, i.e., gets higher when the image is in motion and gets lower when it is almost steady. The receive data rate at the server increases linearly with respect to the number of users, where each user uses the same video quality. As for the send data rate, it can be estimated by using the equation:

$$BW_{send} = n * (n-1) * bw \qquad (1)$$

where: BW_{send} - total send data rate at the server

bw – bandwidth for one video stream

n – number of users

In order to increase the number of concurrent users in face-to-face meeting mode, a conservative video quality should be used, i.e., low-quality having a video stream bandwidth of around 72 kbps.

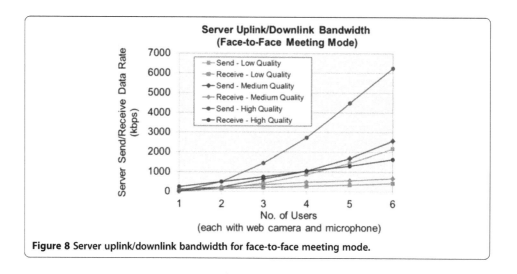

Figure 8 Server uplink/downlink bandwidth for face-to-face meeting mode.

The server downlink data rate with the number of users in broadcast mode is shown in Figure 9. Broadcast mode is a usage scenario where the presenter use web camera to distribute video and share the slide presentation, but listeners do not use web camera. One example is distributing a presentation in a conference with remote viewers. The data in Figure 9 shows a linear increase in send data rate with the number of users. By selecting a conservative video quality for distribution, number of concurrent users can be increased largely in broadcast mode.

Content-based meeting system

WebELS Meeting is a content-based meeting system, i.e., content to be presented during the meeting must be pre-uploaded to the server before starting a meeting, although it is possible to upload another content when the meeting has already started. Since online presentation and video conference panels are separated, video conference connection can be kept while the meeting participants change their presentation panel to load another content. This scenario is efficient for a meeting with several participants where each has slide presentation to show, i.e., no wasted time for uploading new content

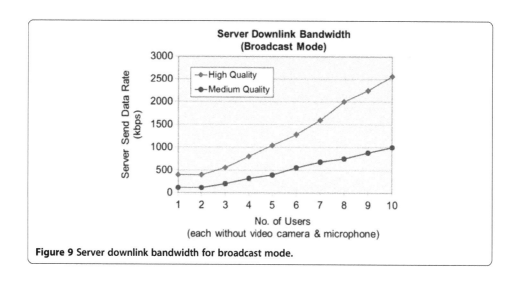

Figure 9 Server downlink bandwidth for broadcast mode.

when changing the presenter. Unlike in Flash-based web-conferencing system that uploading of content is done on-the-fly. Uploading of content takes several seconds to few minutes for a large file since this process involves the conversion of uploaded file into series of slide images. Thus, content-based meeting system is also suitable for distributing live presentation of the conference proceedings to remote viewers because contents are already uploaded unto the server and changing of presentation does not consume much time. As an example, Figure 10 shows the list of presentation contents during the Asia-Arab Sustainable Energy Forum (AASEF) held at Nagoya, Japan last August 23–26, 2011.

Summary

This paper presented the online presentation based on a shared virtual presentation board (VPB) for e-Meeting on the WebELS platform. VPB is a data structure that defines several objects that represents the presentation panel of the presenter. In an e-Meeting, the presenter is the source of VPB data that is sent to the server, the server updates the master copy, the listener polls the server for the data periodically, and the retrieved data is used to set the presentation panel to achieve slide synchronization. Online presentation combined with video conference system creates a so-called virtual room for e-Meeting where participants convene via the Internet.

With VPB concept implemented on a content-based meeting system such as the WebELS Meeting, high-quality e-Meeting performance can be achieved. Meetings proceedings would not be interrupted by necessary on-the-fly uploading of content for presentation, since content must be pre-uploaded before a virtual meeting room is created. Because of this, the system is also suitable for distributing live presentation of the conference proceedings to remote viewers. Moreover, slide images are pre-downloaded on the users' local computer, thus there is no blurry and distorted slide presentation

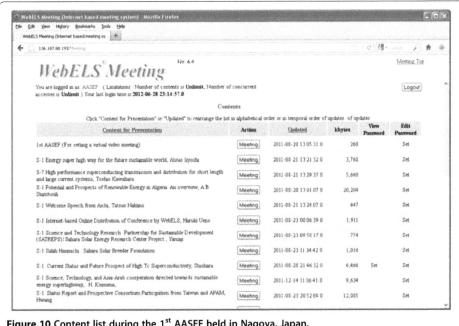

Figure 10 Content list during the 1st AASEF held in Nagoya, Japan.

images. Online presentation can be attained smoothly because slide synchronization delay is minimized due to minimal VPB data that is shared between users and the server. More online presentation features are showcased, such as slide synchronization, cursor synchronization, freehand annotation function, zooming function, and embedded video playback. Moreover, the system works well in narrowband Internet as well as in a cloud environment.

Competing interests
The authors declare that they have no competing interests.

Authors' contributions
HU conceptualized the core functions of the Web-based E-Learning System (WebELS). AB carried out the design and implementation of shared virtual presentation board. All authors participated in the testing and evaluation of the system. AB drafted the manuscript and did the final revision. All authors read and approved the final manuscript.

Acknowledgment
The authors would like to express sincere thanks to all persons who supported the WebELS project of NII, Japan, especially to Dr. Vuthichai Ampornarambeth, Dr. Zheng He and Dr. Pao Sriprasertsuk for contributions in designing and implementing the WebELS system. The project is funded by Science Research Foundation of Japan, The Telecommunications Advancement Foundation, Amada Foundation for Metal Work Technology, Japan Science and Technology Agency (JST) and The Graduate University of Advanced Study (SOKENDAI). We express sincere thanks to Genetec Co. for a collaborative development, and to the e-Learning Project of UNESCO Jakarta Office and the Sahara Solar Breeder (SSB) Project for collaborations using WebELS.

Author details
[1]National Institute of Informatics, Tokyo, Japan. [2]The Graduate University for Advanced Studies, Tokyo, Japan.

References
1. Ueno H (2002) Internet-Based Distance Learning for Lifelong Engineering Education - A Personal View and Issues. J Inf Syst Educ 1(1):45–52
2. Blinco K, Mason J, McLean N, Wilson S (2004) Trends and Issues in E-Learning Infrastructure Development. A Whitepaper for alt-i-lab 2004. Prepared on behalf of DEST (Australia) and JISC-CETIS (UK). http://www.jisc.ac.uk/uploaded_documents/Altilab04-infrastructureV2.pdf
3. Ampornarambeth V, Zhang T, Hadiana A, Shimamoto N, Ueno H (2006) A Web-Based e-Learning Platform for Postgraduate Education. Proceedings of the 5th IASTED International Conference on Web-based Education (WBE'06). ACTA Press, Anaheim, CA, USA, pp 388–393
4. Sriprasertsuk P, Berena AJ, Chunwijitra S, Ueno H (2009) A Study on an Open Source for Distance Real-Time Learning Environment. IEICE Technical Report, KBSE 2009–57:53–58
5. Ueno H, He Z, Yue J (2009) WebELS: A Content-Centered E-Learning Platform for Postgraduate Education in Engineering. Proceedings of the 13th International Conference on Human-Computer Interaction, Part IV: Interacting in Various Application Domains. Springer-Verlag Berlin Heidelberg, CA, USA, pp 246–255
6. Berena AJ, Sriprasertsuk P, He Z, Ueno H (2009) An Open Source Integrated e-Learning/e-Communication Platform for Postgraduate Education and Corporate Cyber Meeting. IEICE Technical Report, ET 109(193):33–37
7. (2011) Moodle. http://moodle.org
8. (2011) Joomla LMS. http://www.joomlalms.com
9. (2011) RealVNC. http://www.realvnc.com
10. (2011) Skype. http://skype.org
11. (2011) GoToMeeting. http://www.gotomeeting.com
12. (2011) WebEx. http://webex.com
13. (2012) TeamViewer. http://www.teamviewer.com
14. (2012) join.me. https://join.me
15. (2011) Google Docs. http://docs.google.com
16. (2011) SlideRocket. http://sliderocket.com
17. (2011) AuthorStream. http://www.authorstream.com
18. (2012) SlideShare. http://slideshare.com
19. (2012) V-Cube. http://vcube.com
20. (2012) Adobe Connect. http://adobe.com/products/adobeconnect.html
21. (2012) BigBlueButton. http://www.bigbluebutton.org
22. (2012) WebELS. http://webels.ex.nii.ac.jp
23. He Z, Yue J, Ueno H, WebELS (2009) A Multimedia E-Learning Platform for Non-broadband Users. Proceedings of the International Conference on Computer Engineering and Technology, pp 177–181

24. Chunwijitra S, Berena AJ, Okada H, Ueno H (2011) Design of Suitable Meeting Management Model for WebELS Meeting to Meet the Business Situations. Proceedings of the First International Conference on Advanced Collaborative Networks, Systems and Applications, Luxembourg, pp 62–67

25. (2012) ActionScript Documentation Reference for Adobe Flash Platform. http://help.adobe.com/en_US/FlashPlatform/beta/reference/actionscript/3/flash/net/SharedObject.html

26. Lin T, Hao P (2005) Compound Image Compression for Real-Time Computer Screen Image Transmission. IEEE Trans Image Process 14:993–1005

5

Detecting misinformation in online social networks using cognitive psychology

KP Krishna Kumar[*†] and G Geethakumari[†]

*Correspondence:
kpkrishnakumar@gmail.com
[†]Equal contributors
Department of Computer Science
and Information Systems,
BITS-Pilani, Hyderabad Campus,
Jawahar Nagar, Hyderabad, India

Abstract

The paper explores the use of concepts in cognitive psychology to evaluate the spread of misinformation, disinformation and propaganda in online social networks. Analysing online social networks to identify metrics to infer cues of deception will enable us to measure diffusion of misinformation. The cognitive process involved in the decision to spread information involves answering four main questions viz *consistency of message, coherency of message, credibility of source* and *general acceptability of message*. We have used the cues of deception to analyse these questions to obtain solutions for preventing the spread of misinformation. We have proposed an algorithm to effectively detect deliberate spread of false information which would enable users to make informed decisions while spreading information in social networks. The computationally efficient algorithm uses the collaborative filtering property of social networks to measure the credibility of sources of information as well as quality of news items. The validation of the proposed methodology has been done on the online social network 'Twitter'.

Keywords: Online social network; Misinformation; Disinformation; Cognitive psychology

Introduction

Internet is a great source of information. It is also called the Web of deception. The use of communication channels of the Internet to propagate false information has become quite common. The advent of social networks has made every user a self-publisher with no editing, checking for factual accuracy and clearly with no accountability. The facts are presented with no authority and for millions of users seeing them on their computer screen is itself a certificate of truthfulness of information being presented to them. In [1], the dangers in the use of Internet like deliberate deception, deliberate misinformation, and half-truths that can be used to divert a user from the real information being sought have been discussed. The use of technologies by people to support lies, deception, misdirection, fraud, spin control, propaganda as discussed in the book have come true with online social networks like Facebook and Twitter being used for purposes for which they were not intended for. Validating the data on the Internet is a challenging proposition and pitfalls by new users and experienced ones are far too often.

Online Social Networks (OSN) have become an important source of information for a large number of people in the recent years. As the usage of social networks increased, the abuse of the media to spread disinformation and misinformation also increased many fold. The spread of information or misinformation in online social networks is context specific and studies have revealed topics such as health, politics, finances and technology trends are prime sources of misinformation and disinformation in different contexts to include business, government and everyday life [2]. The number of information diffusion models do not take into consideration the type of information while modeling their diffusion process. The information diffusion in social networks due to misinformation or disinformation could follow different patterns of propagation and could be as a result of an orchestrated campaign to mimic widespread information diffusion behaviour. The lack of accountability and verifiability afford the users an excellent opportunity to spread specific ideas through the network.

The detection of misinformation in large volumes of data is a challenging task. Methods using machine learning and Natural Language Processing (NLP) techniques exist to automate the process to some extent. However, because of the semantic nature of the contents, the accuracy of automated methods is limited and quite often require manual intervention. The amount of data generated in online social networks is so huge as to make the task computationally expensive to be done in real time. In this paper, we propose a methodology to detect misinformation content using concepts based in cognitive psychology. We analysed the literature on cognitive psychology to understand the process of decision making of an individual. An individual is seen to make decisions based on cues of deception or misinformation he obtains from the social network. Analysing the social network data using suitable metrics to detect the same cues of deception would enable us to identify patterns of spread of misinformation. This could be used by an online user to take correct decisions about authenticity of information while spreading them. A framework which would enable prevention of spread of inaccurate information would be more effective than one which proposes counter measures after the information diffusion process. We have implemented our proposed framework in Twitter.

Twitter has emerged as one of the more popular micro-blogging sites. Twitter enables propagation of news in real time. Information propagates in Twitter in the form of short messages of maximum 140 characters called 'tweets'. The system enables one to subscribe to another's tweets by following them. It allows quick information dissemination by retweeting the tweets one has received. The ability to post tweets from mobile devices like smart phones, tablets and even by SMS have resulted in Twitter becoming the source of information for many users. These capabilities also make Twitter a platform for spreading misinformation easily.

Background and literature review
Concepts of information, misinformation and disinformation
How they differ?
It is essential to understand the related concepts of information, misinformation, disinformation and propaganda. The definition of information is clear by its very nature to the users. But what needs to be defined is the different forms it can take. We are more interested in the usage of social networks to spread specific kind of information to alter the behaviour or attitude of people. In the cyber space, manipulation of information so as to affect the semantic nature of information and the way in which it is interpreted by users is often called semantic attacks. Semantic attacks in social networks could be a result of

propagation of information in various forms. This could take the shape of misinformation, disinformation or propaganda. The distinction between information, misinformation and disinformation is difficult to be made [3]. The three concepts are related to truth, and to arrive at a universal acceptance of a single truth is almost impossible.

The term information is defined by the Oxford dictionary as 'facts provided or learned about something or someone'. The other forms of information are defined by Oxford dictionary as under:

- *Misinformation* is false or inaccurate information, especially that which is deliberately intended to deceive.
- *Disinformation* is false information that is intended to mislead, especially propaganda issued by a government organization to a rival power or the media.
- *Propaganda* is defined as information, especially of a biased or misleading nature, used to promote a political cause or point of view.

The three definitions have small differences and the most important fact is they involve the propagation of false information with the intention and capability to mislead at least some of the recipients. The advent of social networks has made the speed of propagation of information faster, created large number of sources of information, produced huge amounts of information in short duration of time and with almost no accountability about the accuracy of data. The term 'Big Data' is often associated with the data in social networks. Finding credible information after sifting out the different forms of false information in online social networks has become a very challenging computational task. In this paper, we intend to use the basic tenets of cognitive psychology to devise efficient methods by which the task can be done. Our methodology involves detecting cues of deception in online social networks to segregate false or misleading information with the intention of developing an effective tool for evaluating the credibility of information received by a user based on the source of the message as well its general acceptability in the network.

Conceptual explanation of the distinguishing features

The concept of information, misinformation and disinformation have been differentiated with respect to five important features by Karlova et al. [2]. They are truth, accuracy, completeness, currency and deceptiveness. While all the three are informative in nature, only disinformation is deliberatively deceptive information. The authors have also given a social diffusion model of information, misinformation and disinformation as products of social processes illustrating the way they are formed and disseminated in social networks. The model suggests that people use cues to credibility and cues to deception to make judgements while participating in the information diffusion process.

Accuracy of the information is one of the important measures of quality of information. Honest mistake in the spread of inaccurate information is misinformation, whereas when the intention is to deceive the recipient, it is disinformation. In [4], authors have outlined the main features of disinformation.

- Disinformation is often the product of a carefully planned and technically sophisticated deceit process.
- Disinformation may not come directly from the source that intends to deceive.

- Disinformation is often written or verbal communication to include doctored photographs, fake videos etc.
- Disinformation could be distributed very widely or targeted at specific people or organizations.
- The intended targets are often a person or a group of people.

In order to classify as disinformation, it is not necessary that the disinformation has to come directly from the source of disinformation [4]. In the chain of dissemination of information, most of the people could actually be transmitting misleading information (hence misinformation), though only one of the intermediaries may believe that the information is actually misleading (hence disinformation). This is especially true for social networks where the chain of propagation could be long and quite a few people involved in the process.

Social networks with its freedom of expression, lack of filtering mechanisms like reviewing and editing available in traditional publishing business coupled with high degree of lack of accountability have become an important media for spread of misinformation. Summarily, the propagation of different versions of information, viz misinformation, disinformation and propaganda involves the spread of false or inaccurate information through information diffusion process involving users of social networks where all the users may not be aware of the falsehood in the information. We have used the term misinformation to denote any type of false information spreading in social networks.

Misinformation

The acceptance of misinformation or misleading information by the people depends on their prior beliefs and opinions [5]. People believe things which support their prior thoughts without questioning them. The same is also supported by research in cognitive psychology [6]. The authors have brought out that preexisting political, religious or social views make people accept information without verification if it conforms to their beliefs. Countering such ideological and personal beliefs is indeed very difficult. Another important finding was that countering the misinformation may lead to amplifying the beliefs and reenforcing them.

Political astroturfing in the form of propagation of memes in Twitter was studied by the Truthy team [7,8]. Investigating political election campaigns in US in the year 2010, the research group uncovered a number of accounts sending out duplicate messages and also retweeting messages from the same few accounts in a closely connected network. In another case, 10 different accounts were used to send out thousands of posts, many of them duplicates slightly altered to avoid detection as spam. With URL shorteners available, messages containing links could be altered to give different shortened links to the same source and hence escaping the spam filters.

Decision making out of ignorance is often based on heuristics and the level of confidence on the decision is also low, making correction easier. Such decisions are often correct and are generally not catastrophic. False beliefs based on misinformation are held strongly and often result in greater support for a cause. Such beliefs are also very contagious and the person makes efforts to spread them to others. The persistence of misinformation in the society is dangerous and require analysis for their prevention and early detection [6,9].

Misinformation during an event as it unfolds like casuality figures in a natural calamity, are seldom accurate initially and the figures get updated or changed over a period of time. Such spread of misinformation is often considered benign though media is considered as one of the most important sources of misinformation. The other important sources of misinformation are governments and politicians, vested interests and rumours and works of fiction. Information asymmetry due to new media like social networks play a big role in the spread of misinformation. Social networks spread information without traditional filters like editing. The advent of Web 2.0 has resulted in greater citizen journalism resulting in increase in the speed of dissemination of information using multiple online social media like social networks, blogs, emails, photo and video sharing platforms, bulletin boards etc. The creation of cyber–ghettos has been discussed where the cyber space has become echo chambers and blogs and other social media primarily link to like minded sites propagating similar views than providing contrarian views. This leads to fractionation of the information landscape and consequent persistence of misinformation in large sections of the society for a long period of time. This often result in people holding on to their views on matters of pubic, political and even religious importance due to their misinformed world views and ideology.

In [10], authors have enumerated a number of possible instances of misinformation in the Internet. They include incomplete, out-of-date and biased information, pranks, contradictions, improperly translated data, software incompatibilities, unauthorized revisions, factual errors and scholarly misconduct. However, with the advent of Web 2.0 the list has grown many times and social media is described as one of the biggest sources of information including misinformation. Internet acts as a post modern Pandora's box-releasing many different arguments for information which are not easily dismissible [11].

Countering the spread of misinformation

Misinformation is easily another version of information. Countering spread of misinformation is not an easy task. The simple technique of labelling the other side as wrong is ineffectual. Education of people against misinformation is necessary but not sufficient for combating misinformation. An analysis of the counter measures proposed and modeled in the literature against the spread of misinformation in OSNs are at times not in consonance with the effectiveness of the measures as suggested in studies of cognitive psychology. Theoretical framework for limiting the viral propagation of misinformation has been proposed in [12,13]. The authors have proposed a model for identifying the most influential nodes whose decontamination with good information would prevent the spread of misinformation. The solution to the problem of limiting the spread of misinformation by starting a counter campaign using k influential nodes, called the *eventual influence limitation* problem has been proposed in [14]. The influence limitation problem has also been studied in the presence of missing information. In both the papers, the basic assumption is that when an infected node is presented with correct information, it would become decontaminated. Studies in psychology have proved that removing misinformation from infected persons is not easy [6]. The best solution to the spread of misinformation is early detection of misinformation and launch of directed and effective counter campaigns. In [15], the authors have proposed ranking based and optimization-based algorithms for identifying the top k most suspected sources of misinformation in a time bound manner.

The strategies proposed in [6] for effective counter measures include:

- Providing credible alternative explanation to the misinformation.
- Repeated retractions to reduce the effect of misinformation without repeating the misinformation.
- Explicit warnings before mentioning the misinformation so as to prevent the misinformation from getting reinforced.
- Counter measures be suitably biased towards affirmation of the world view of the receiver.
- Simple and brief retractions which are cognitively more attractive than the corresponding misinformation.

Analysis of work done so far

We have analysed the cognitive process of adoption of information from studies in psychology. The difficulties associated with distinguishing between misinformation, disinformation and true information have been highlighted by most of them [2,3,6]. The cognitive factors which decide the credibility of messages and their consequent acceptance by users can be effectively modulated in OSNs as seen during US elections [7,8]. The inherent beliefs of a user play a very important part in accepting news items and fractionation of cyber space is a consequence of this aspect of human mind. We explore different factors contributing towards deciding the credibility of news items in the next section.

Misinformation has been widely accepted in the society, it becomes extremely difficult to remove. This has been suitably demonstrated during July 2012, when mass exodus of thousands of people took place in India due to a sustained misinformation campaign by vested interests using social media and other telecommunication networks [16]. Preventing the spread of misinformation is a more effective method of combating misinformation, than its subsequent retraction after it has affected the population. Significant contributions towards successful debiasing of misinformation have been made in [6].

While studies in cognitive psychology are sufficient to understand the process of adoption of information by users, we would like to explore the process of diffusion of information. Process of diffusion is a group phenomenon, where we study the process of adoption by different users over a period of time. Patterns arising out of diffusion of information are better studied using algorithms from computer science. We study the process in detail using 'Twitter' in Section "Credibility analysis of Twitter".

A generic framework for detection of spread of misinformation

While formulating a generic framework for detecting spread of misinformation, it is important to understand the cognitive decision making processes of individuals. A study of individual decision making process from a cognitive psychology point of view followed by a generic framework for detection of misinformation using the cues of deception is given in the following subsections.

Identifying cues to deception using cognitive psychology

The presence of misinformation in the society and real world social networks have been studied from psychological point of view extensively. An excellent review of the mechanisms by which misinformation is propagated and how effective corrective measures can be implemented based on cognitive psychology can be found in [6]. As per the authors, the spread of misinformation is a result of a cognitive process by the receivers based on their assessment of the truth value of information. Acceptance of information is more the norm than otherwise for most of the people. When people evaluate the truth value of any information they take into account four factors. The factors are characterised by asking four relevant questions. These questions are given below and illustrated in Figure 1, where we have summarised all relevant issues of misinformation.

1.   **Consistency of message.** Is the information compatible and consistent with the other things that you believe?
2.   **Coherency of message.** Is the information internally coherent without contradictions to form a plausible story?
3.   **Credibility of source.** Is the information from a credible source?
4.   **General Acceptability.** Do others believe this information?

Information is more likely to be accepted by people when it is **consistent** with other things that they believe is true. If the logical compatibility of a news item has been evaluated to be consistent with their inherent beliefs, the likelihood of acceptance of misinformation by the receiver increases and the probability of correcting the misinformation goes down. Preexisting beliefs play an important part in the acceptance of messages. Stories are easily accepted when the individual elements which make them up are **coherent** and without internal contradictions. Such stories are easier to process and easily processed stories are more readily believed. The familiarity with the sender of a message, and the sender's perceived **credibility** and expertise ensure greater acceptance of the message. The acceptability of a news item increases if the persons are subjected to repeated exposure of the same item. Information is readily believed to be true if there is a perceived social consensus and hence **general acceptability** of the same. Corrections to the misinformation need not work all the time once misinformation is accepted by a receiver.

The rest of the paper is organised as follows. In Section "Research design and methodology" we give our research design and methodology where we explain the generic framework for the detection of misinformation in online social networks. As part of its implementation in 'Twitter', we carried out an analysis of the work done in estimating the credibility

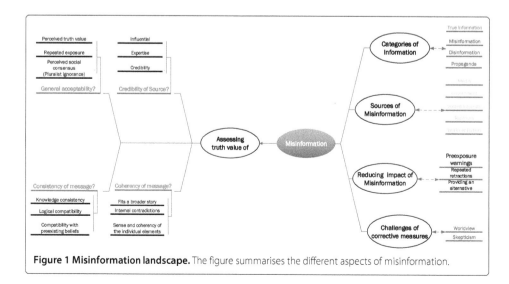

Figure 1 Misinformation landscape. The figure summarises the different aspects of misinformation.

of information propagation in 'Twitter'. In Section "Methods" we explain our method-ology and algorithm for speedy detection of spread of misinformation in Twitter to aid a user to recognise misinformation and consequently prevent him from spreading it. In Section "Results and discussion" we show the results obtained using two different Twitter data sets. We outline our future work and conclude in Section "Conclusions".

Research design and methodology

Generic framework for detection of spread of misinformation

Based on the analysis of cognitive process, it becomes clear that the receiver obtains cues of deception or misinformation from the online social network to decide on the accu-racy of information. The same cues could be used by a social media monitoring system to detect spread of misinformation, disinformation or propaganda. The proposed frame-work for such a system is given in Figure 2. The evaluation process of truth value of information begins with identification of suitable credibility metrics of the social network being studied. The metrics would reflect the cues by which a user would have made his decision of estimating the accuracy of information. The subsequent stages of evaluation of truth value of information would involve using the identified metrics to establish the credibility of the source and estimate the general acceptability of the message. A user should be able to make informed decisions regarding the truthfulness of messages with this help from the system and applying his own coherency and consistency values.

We have implemented the proposed framework for Twitter. The details of implemen-tation is given in the subsequent sections. The first step involves the identification of suitable metrics for evaluating the credibility of information propagated in Twitter. For this, we have carried out a detailed analysis of the work done to study the credibility of information propagated in Twitter with a view to identify the most appropriate parame-ters which would enable detection of misinformation. We classified the parameters using concepts of cognitive psychology and selected the most appropriate metrics.

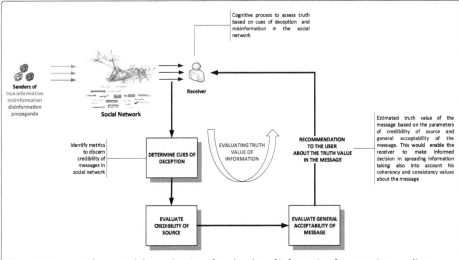

Figure 2 A generic framework for evaluation of truth value of information for a user in an online social network. The figure gives a broad framework for detecting misinformation using cues of deception to help a user to make informed decisions.

Credibility analysis of Twitter

An analysis of the literature to categorize tweets based on the four aspects of *consistency of message, coherency of message, credibility of source* and *general acceptability* as given in the previous section was done. A number of automated techniques using machine learning algorithms have been proposed in the literature to classify tweets based on their characteristic features.

Twitter as a social filter

The credibility of tweets propagated through Twitter has been analyzed in [17]. The authors have used automated methods to assess the credibility of tweets related to trending topics. The features used by the authors include the re-tweeting behaviour, texts of the posts and links to external sources. The authors used supervised learning techniques to build a classifier to estimate the credibility of tweets. The types of features used to characterize each tweet were of four types: message based features, user based features, topic based features and propagation based features. Use of message features included length of the message, positive or negative sentiments, presence of question marks or exclamation marks, and also the use of hashtags and retweets. User based features included number of followers and followees, number of past tweets etc. Topic based features were derived from user based and message based features to include fraction of tweets that contained hashtags, URLs and positive and negative sentiments. The propagation based features included the depth of the retweet tree and number of initial tweets of a topic. Best results of automatic classification of tweets were achieved using J48 learning algorithm. Sentiment features were found to be very relevant for predicting the credibility of tweets. The fraction of tweets with negative tweets was found to be more credible as well as tweets with greater number of retweets. The ability of the Twitter community to act as social filter of credible information has been clearly brought out in the paper. Credible users with large number of followers and followees along with large tweet activity have better reputation score and tend to propagate credible news. While validating the best features to be used for automatic determination of credibility of tweets, the propagation based features were ranked the best. The text and author based features alone are not sufficient to determine the credibility of tweets. The credibility of tweets increases when propagated through authors who have a higher reputation score, having written a large number of tweets before, originate at a single or few users in the network and have many retweets.

Twitter during critical events

Reliability of Twitter under extreme circumstances was also investigated in [18]. The analysis of tweets related to earthquake in Chile in 2010 has revealed that the propagation of rumours in Twitter is different from spread of credible news as rumours tend to be questioned more. The authors selected confirmed news and rumours manually from the set of tweets after the earthquake to analyse patterns of diffusion of information in the form of re-tweets in the network. The use of Twitter as a collaborative-filter mechanism has been proved with the help of this study. Further, the authors have verified the validity of the use of aggregate analysis of tweets to detect rumours.

Credibility of tweets during high impact events was studied in [19]. The authors used source based and content based features to indirectly measure the credibility of tweets and their sources. Content based features in the tweets like number of words, special symbols, hashtags, pronouns, URLs and meta data like retweets were used. Source based features like number of followers, number of followees, age etc were used to measure the credibility of a user. The features were analysed for credibility using RankSVM and Relevance feedback algorithms. The limitation of their work is the requirement to establish ground truth using human annotation.

Spread of rumours and influence in Twitter

The spread of rumours in micro blogs was investigated in [20]. In particular, the authors investigated the spread of rumours in Twitter to detect misinformation and disinformation in them. The authors have proposed a framework using statistical modeling to identify tweets which are likely to be rumours from a given set of general tweets. They used content based, network based and microblog-specific memes for correctly identifying rumours. NLP techniques in sentiment analysis of the tweets was used for automatic detection of rumours. Content based features like lexical patterns, part-of-speech patterns, features corresponding to unigrams and digrams for each representation were used for classification of tweets. The authors used these techniques for rumour retrieval i.e., identifying tweets spreading misinformation. The belief classification of users to identify users who believe in the misinformation was done using the re-tweet network topology. The importance of re-tweet network topology has been clearly brought out in the paper. The authors have also used Twitter specific features like hashtags and URLs.

The measure of influence as given by the retweet mechanism offers an ideal mechanism to study large scale information diffusion in Twitter [21]. The degree of influence of nodes measured by calculating the number of followers and number of retweets showed different results with little correlation between the two. The relationship between indegree, retweets and mentions as measures of influence have been further analysed in [22]. The authors have supported the claim that the users having large number of followers are not necessarily influential in terms of retweets and mentions. Influential users have significant influence across a number of topics. Influence in terms of retweets is gained only after concerted efforts. Surveys have also shown that the users are poor judge of truthfulness based on contents alone and are influenced by the user name, user image and message topic when making credibility assessments [23].

Orchestrated semantic attacks in Twitter

Detection of suspicious memes in microblog platforms like Twitter using supervised learning techniques has been done in [7,8]. The authors have used supervised learning techniques based on the network topology, sentiment analysis and crowd-sourced annotations. The authors have discussed the role of Twitter in *political astroturf* campaigns. These are campaigns disguised as popular large scale grassroots behaviour, but actually carried out by a single person or organization. As per the authors, orchestrating a distributed attack by spreading a particular meme to a large population beyond the social network can be done by a motivated user. The paper discusses methods to automatically identify and track such orchestrated and deceptive efforts in Twitter to mimic the organic spread of information. The authors have described *Truthy*, a Web service to track political memes in Twitter to detect astroturfing and other misinformation campaigns. The importance of the use of retweets to study information diffusion in Twitter has been highlighted by the authors. Network analysis of the diffusion of memes followed by sentiment analysis was used by the system to detect coordinated efforts to spread memes. The importance of detection of the spread of memes at an early stage itself before they spread and become indistinguishable from the real ones was also highlighted in the paper.

Being in the first page of the search results of any search engine is often regarded as an indicator of popularity and reputation. Search engines have introduced real time search results from social networking sites like Twitter, blogs and news web sites to appear in their first pages. A concentrated effort to spread misinformation as in political astro-turf campaigns could have far reaching consequences if such search results are displayed prominently by search engines like Google. While studying the role of Twitter in spread of misinformation in political campaigns, Mustafaraj et al. have concluded that one is likely to retweet a message coming from an original sender with whom one agrees [24]. Similarly repeating the same message multiple times indicates an effort to motivate others in the community to accept the message. The authors described an attack named *Twitter-bomb* where the attackers targeted users interested in a spam topic and send messages to them, relying on them to spread the messages further. The authors have highlighted the ability of automated scripts to exploit the open architecture of social networks such as Twitter and reach a very wide audience. Measuring hourly rate of generation of tweets seems to be a meaningful way of identifying the spam accounts.

Analysis of measuring credibility of tweets

A summary of the analysis of the literature on measuring the credibility of information propagation in Twitter along with the pointers towards detection of misinformation is given in Table 1. The present efforts to detect the spread of misinformation in online social networks can be broadly classified with relation to the questions of *consistency of message, coherency of message, credibility of source* and *general acceptability* as given in Section "A generic framework for detection of spread of misinformation".

The analysis has brought out the following aspects:

- Automated means of detecting tweets are accurate, but computationally intensive and manual inputs are required.

Table 1 Comparison of metrics for measuring credibility of tweets

Criteria	Metrics	Authors	Accuracy	Complexity	Usefulness for fast detection	Remarks
Consistency of message	Retweets, mentions	[7,8,17,19, 22,24]	Retweets are better than mentions	No	Yes	
Coherency of message	Questions, affirms, denial, no of words, pronouns, hashtags, URLs, exclamation marks, negative and positive sentiments, NLP techniques	[7,8,17-20]	Decision tree algorithms with a combination of various factors are accurate	Yes	Computationally intensive, requires ground truth	Content analysis required. Metrics are an indirect measure
Credibility of Source	Tweets, retweets, mentions, indegree, user name, image, followers, followees, age	[7,8,17,19, 21,24]	Retweets are more accurate	No	Yes	
General acceptability	Retweets	[7,8]	Good	No	Yes	

- Retweets form a unique mechanism available in Twitter for studying information propagation and segregating misinformation.
- Analysing the information propagation using models in Computer Science and concepts of Cognitive Psychology would provide efficient solutions for detecting and countering the spread of misinformation.

Methods

We want to examine the information propagation pattern in Twitter to detect the spread of misinformation. The cognitive psychology analysis revealed that source of information is an important factor to be considered while evaluating the credibility. Moreover, the difference between misinformation and disinformation is in the intention of the source in spreading false information. The retweet feature of Twitter would enable us to understand the information propagation and grouping tweets based on their sources would reveal patterns which would enable us to estimate the credibility of the information being propagated.

Out of the four parameters stated above, *consistency of message* and *coherency of message* are internal to the user. These would be the first tools the user would employ to confirm the authenticity of the received information. A user who is convinced of the authenticity of the message or lack of it by these two parameters would not be bothered about using the other parameters to come to a decision. The external parameters of *credibility of source* and *general acceptability* would be used when the user has greater suspicion of the news item. We would assume that most of the news items spreading misinformation would fall in this category and a user accepts and forward them after evaluating the source of the message as well as the perceived general acceptance of the message.

Data sets

We carried out experimental evaluation on data sets obtained from the online social network 'Twitter'. We collected data using Twitter API for two different topics. The spreadsheet tool TAGS v5 used for collection of tweets using the Search API was provided by Martin Hawskey [25]. The topics enabled us to define the context for the study of spread of information. We had carried out our studies on a number of data sets obtained from Twitter using different keywords. Tweets were obtained for events like natural calamities, acts of terrorism, political events etc. Here we describe two of those to bring out our results. The keywords refer to different types of news items as explained below and the statistical details are given at Table 2:

- **Egypt.** Heavy political unrest and massive protests spread in Egypt during the months of Aug-Sep 2013. The news related to the these events were captured using the keyword 'egypt' for the period from 13 Aug 2013 to 23 Sep 2013.
- **Syria.** The use of chemical weapons in Syria in the month of Aug 2013 attracted worldwide criticism. The reflection in Twitter of the events was tracked using the keyword 'syria' for the period from 25 Aug 2013 to 21 Sep 2013.

Table 2 Details of the data set

Data set	#Tweets	#Retweets	#Senders	#Re-tweeters	Period
Egypt	141682	51723	10850	27532	13 Aug 2013 to 23 Sep 2013
Syria	104867	44708	11452	25415	25 Aug 2013 to 21 Sep 2013

Methodology

We now describe the methodology we adopted to analyse the data sets to detect misinformation in them. We aim to detect non credible information which have the potential to spread and possible collusion between users in spreading them. We outline the steps and then give the complete algorithm in the form of a flow chart.

Step 1: Consider only the retweets

We use the Twitter user as the first stage of social filter by not considering any tweets which are not retweets. The effectiveness of retweets to determine the credibility of information in Twitter has been verified already by our review of work done in the field. Retweets are the easiest means by which tweets are propagated and any person retweeting a tweet personally has validated the information content in the tweet. Further, this would also remove personal chats, opinions and initial misinformation not considered credible. The fact that a tweet has not been retweeted also indicates that the probability of it spreading to a sizeable proportion of the population is minimal.

Step 2: Evaluate the source of retweets

The credibility of the source is the next important factor to be considered. For this we identified and segregated the retweets as per the source. This step would enable us to estimate the unique tweets of the source which are being retweeted and the unique number of users who are retweeting the same. The pattern of retweeting was analysed. Human annotation was done to determine the credibility of the information. We found greater unevenness amongst the users retweeting tweets of a source, when the credibility of the source was poor. The sources spreading misinformation were being retweeted heavily by a limited proportion of users who have at least retweeted the source once. This points towards collusion between the users and deliberate attempts being made to spread misinformation. Favouritism in the retweeting behaviour is most often due to questions of credibility as has been validated in all the data sets studied.

The disparity in the retweeting behaviour was measured using Gini coefficient. Gini coefficient is a measure of inequality of a distribution. The metric is more often used to measure the disparity in income of a population. In the retweet graph, we wanted to measure the pattern of distribution of retweets of the tweets of a particular source. A value of Gini Coefficient nearer to zero would indicate a more even retweet behaviour and a value above 0.5 and nearer 1 would indicate greater disparity in that a few users are involved in retweeting a large number of tweets from the source and hence the possibility of misinformation in the contents and reduced credibility of the source.

We calculate the Gini coefficient, G using the approximation of the Lorenz curve, where it is approximated on each interval as a line between consecutive points. Let X_k be the cumulative proportion of the 'users' variable, for k = 0, ... n and $X_0 = 0$ and $X_n = 1$ and let Y_k be the cumulative proportion of the retweeets, for k = 0, ··, n and $Y_0 = 0$ and $Y_n = 1$. If X_k and Y_k are indexed such that $X_{k-1} < X_k$ and $Y_{k-1} < Y_k$, the Gini coefficient, G is given by

$$G = 1 - \sum_{k=1}^{n} \left(X_k - X_{k-1}\right)\left(Y_k + Y_{k-1}\right) \tag{1}$$

The patterns of retweet behaviour of sample users from the two data sets are shown in Figures 3 and 4. The graphs in Figures 3 and 4 depict the distribution of retweets

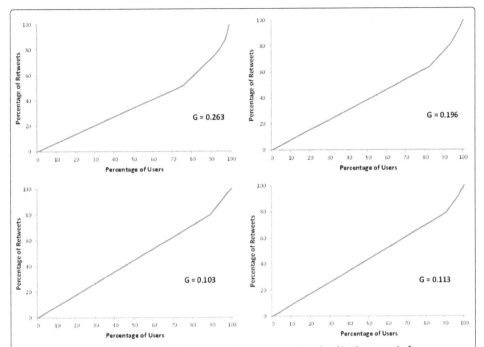

Figure 3 Distribution of retweets from four sample sources not involved in the spread of misinformation. The figure shows the retweeting pattern of tweets of non misinforming sources of information. The Gini coefficient is nearer to zero for all such source nodes.

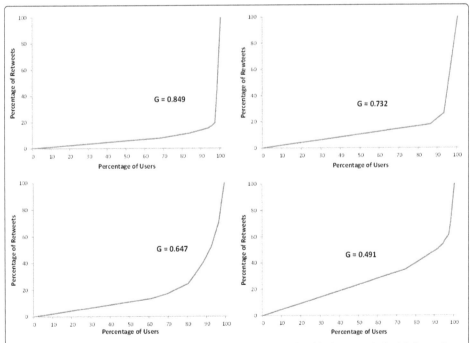

Figure 4 Distribution of retweets from four sample sources involved in the spread of misinformation. The figure shows the retweeting pattern of tweets of misinforming sources of information. The Gini coefficient is normally high and always above a minimum value of 0.4.

amongst the users for four different sources. The differences in patterns of distribution of retweets of the sources are quite obvious in the graphs. The graphs in Figure 3 are for sources who are not spreading misinformation. The equitable distribution of retweets is indicated by the low value of Gini coefficient G. A value of G equals zero would indicate perfectly even distribution. A value of unity for G would indicate just the opposite with one user completely taking all the share. The graphs in Figure 4 depict the distribution for sources involved in the spread of misinformation. We measured a threshold of G as 0.5, above which the sources were classified as spreading misinformation. The high values of G and the consequent different shapes of the graph are easily identifiable. All the sources involved in deliberate spread of misinformation had a high G value. But all the sources having a high G value were not found to spread misinformation. We conclude that the user would forward only tweets which he feels as possible misinformation and hence the high G value would indicate sources of misinformation for all the messages which had to be classified by automated techniques.

Step 3: Construct a retweet graph

We construct a retweet graph as in Figure 5. In the figure, the source 'S' has made three tweets RT1, RT2 and RT3, which have been subsequently retweeted by user nodes U1, U2, U3 and U4. Hence there are directed edges from the tweets to the source 'S' and from the 'retweeters' to the tweets. While U1, U3 and U4 have retweeted only one tweet of source 'S', U2 has retweeted all the three tweets.

Step 3: Evaluate the general acceptability of the tweet

We constructed a retweet graph similar to Figure 5 but involving all the sources and the tweets which have been retweeted. The graph is a bipartite graph with two types of nodes - user nodes and retweet nodes. This graph would clearly depict who tweeted what and the nodes responsible for their propagation in the network. The general acceptability of the tweet was measured using PageRank algorithm in this retweet graph [26]. The PageRank

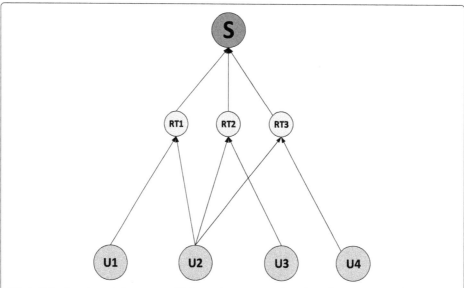

Figure 5 A retweet graph for a source 'S'. A sample retweet graph to show the construction of the retweet graph for a source 'S'.

of the source node is dependent on the PageRanks of its retweet nodes and then PageRank of the retweet nodes are in turn dependent on the number and type of user nodes retweeting them. A higher PageRank would indicate greater acceptability of the tweet - due to more number of retweets and being retweeted by more credible user nodes. A tweet can be considered generally acceptable if it has a higher PageRank. The threshold value is taken as the value at which the tailed distribution begins. As seen in the data sets most of the tweets have very low PageRank indicating that only a small proportion of the tweets are getting retweeted more number of times. The PageRank of a node n_i - retweet node or a user node, $PR(n_i)$ was calculated based on the equation:

$$PR(n_i) = \frac{1-d}{N} + d \sum_{n_j \varepsilon S(n_i)} \frac{PR(n_j)}{L(n_j)} \tag{2}$$

Here, $n_1, n_2, \cdots, n_N$ are the nodes in the retweet graph. $S(n_i)$ is the set of nodes that have a link to node n_i. $L(n_j)$ is the number of outgoing links from the node n_j. N is the total number of nodes in the bipartite retweet graph. We used the standard value of damping factor d as 0.85. Like all social computing strategies, PageRank is also susceptible to manipulation. This would happen when there is collusion between the users where each of them retweet the others' tweets. Such collusion would invariably result in greater communication edges between the nodes involved. The resulting favoritism in retweet behavior can be detected to a large extent using the Gini coefficient explained earlier.

Step 4: Content analysis of the finally filtered items

The output of the previous steps is given to the user. Based on his evaluation of the consistency and coherency of the message, and the additional quantified inputs of the credibility of the source and the general acceptability of the tweet, the user would be able to make an informed decision on the authenticity of the tweet. This would prevent more number of people from retweeting misinformation. Preventive measures such as these are bound to be more effective than any counter measures launched after the misinformation has spread to a large section of the population.

Proposed framework for speedy detection of misinformation in Twitter

The proposed framework would evaluate the credibility of the source and the general acceptability of the news items using collaborative filtering techniques to enable the user to make informed decisions and thus possibly avoid spreading misinformation. We have already outlined the steps for detection of sources involved in the spread of misinformation. The decision tree we constructed to implement the proposed sequence of actions is given at Figure 6.

Summary of the steps involved

The algorithm would do the following:

- Identify the original source of information (tweets) in the network.
- Evolve a methodology to rate the credibility of the source based on the acceptance of the tweets by the receivers.
- Construct a retweet graph to evaluate and measure the 'misinformation content' of a tweet and determine its credibility by the level of its acceptance by all the affected users using Gini coefficient.

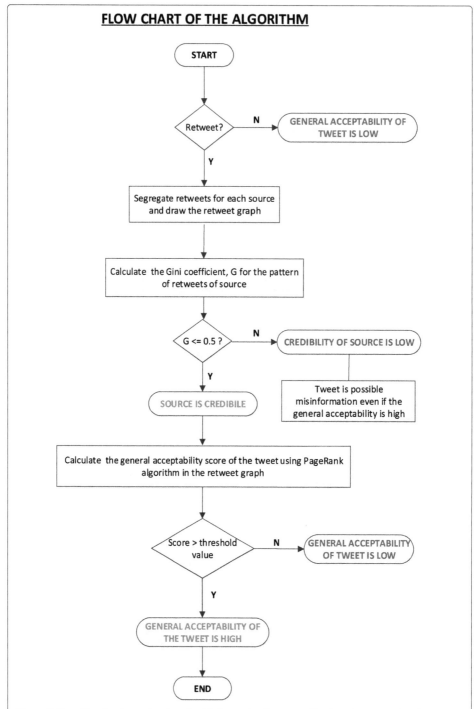

Figure 6 Algorithm for determination of misinformation in tweets. The flowchart giving the algorithm to detect misinformation using a retweet graph to estimate the general acceptability of tweets and credibility of sources.

- Segregate the possible sources of misinformation as non credible users and the corresponding tweets.
- Evaluate the general acceptance of tweets from credible users using PageRank algorithm in the retweet graph.

- Present the credibility of the source and the general acceptance of the tweet to the user to help him evaluate the information contents of the tweet.

Results and discussion

We evaluated the proposed algorithm in all the data sets. The retweet graphs of the data sets were visualised using the software Gephi [27]. In Figures 7 and 8 we show the retweets graphs of the Egypt data set. While Figure 7 gives the broader view of the retweet graph, an exploded view of a section of the retweet graph showing the internal details like name, PageRank and modularity class of the nodes is shown in Figure 8. The nodes with names starting with 'RT' are the retweets and the others are the user nodes in the bipartite graph. Similar results were observed for the Syria data set also.

Measuring credibility of tweets

A plot of the Gini coefficients obtained for the Egypt and Syria data sets are given at Figures 9 and 10 respectively. They show a heavy tailed distribution where the Gini coefficients of most of the user nodes are 0. The figure corroborates the fact that most of the communication are not misinformation. The user nodes with higher Gini coefficients are fewer in number and hence they can be monitored effectively. A threshold value of 0.5 is

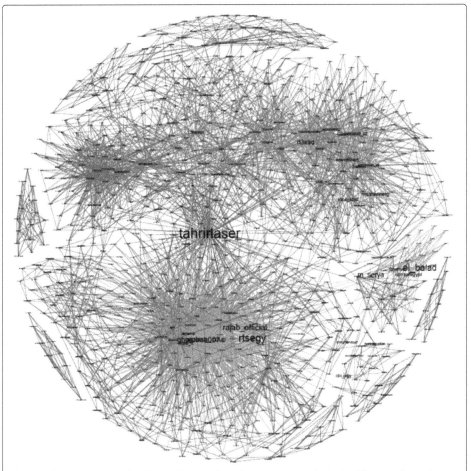

Figure 7 The Retweet graph of Egypt data set. Part of the retweet graph obtained from the Egypt data set showing the retweet nodes and user nodes. The graph has been made using the software 'Gephi'.

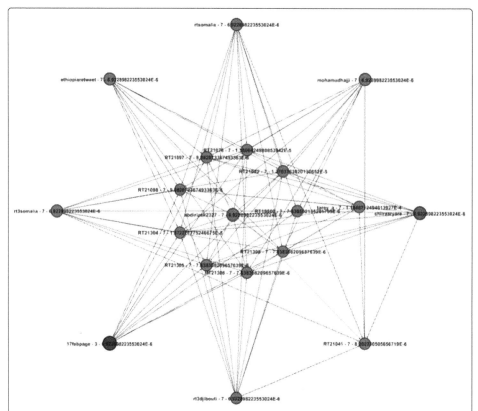

Figure 8 The magnified view of a section of the retweet graph of the Eqypt dataset. A section of the retweet graph has been magnified to show the two types of nodes and the modularity number and PageRank of the nodes.

meaningful to separate out the misinforming users, which has been validated by verifying them. A plot of the PageRank scores obtained for the Egypt and Syria data sets are given at Figures 9 and 10 respectively. As expected, they also show a heavy tailed distribution, with few retweets and user nodes having higher PageRank values. This again supports the fact that a few tweets would be retweeted more heavily than others.

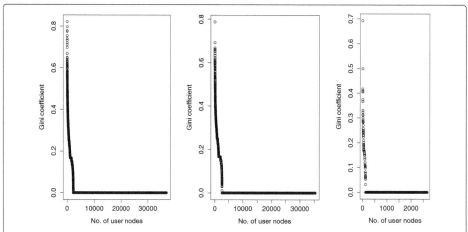

Figure 9 Distribution of Gini coefficients in the Egypt data set. The figure shows the tailed distribution of Gini coefficients of all the user nodes in the retweet graph in the Egypt data set. Majority of the user nodes have Gini coefficients nearer to zero, indicating that spreading misinformation is limited to a very small set of nodes.

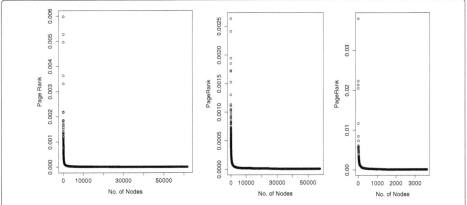

Figure 10 Distribution of Gini coeffcients in the Syria data set. The figure shows the tailed distribution of Gini coefficients of all the user nodes in the retweet graph in the Syria data set. The results are similar to the Egypt data set and majority of the user nodes have Gini coefficients nearer to zero, indicating that spreading misinformation is limited to a very small set of nodes.

Analysis

Using Gini coefficient, the True positive rate to correctly identify all sources of misinformation was over 90%. The False positive rate, where users were wrongly identified as sources of misinformation, was less than 10%. The False negative rate, where the algorithm failed to identify sources of misinformation was less than 10%. The tailed distribution of the spread of Gini coefficients in the data sets revealed that the sources involved in the spread of deliberate misinformation were few as expected.

The Process of diffusion of information is more effectively understood using metrics like Gini coefficient. If we consider retweets as a measure of adoption of information, differences in adoption behaviour would indicate differences in perceived credibility of information. Misinformation or disinformation are context specific and hence responses of users assume great significance. If information from a certain source is accepted as credible uniformly by a large number of users, quite possibly that source is credible. On the other hand, if there are variations in the acceptance levels, the simple explanation is apparent non credibility of messages of the source. Similarly if most of the users receiving users do not repropagate information from a source also, his credibility is low. However, gini coefficient value would be low as the the variations in acceptance are not pronounced. This result is also acceptable, as we are unable to detect misinforming tweets which have been decided by the collective intelligence of the network users to be non credible. Our algorithm would segregate messages which are repropagated differently by a significant section of users, which has the potential to create a certain perceived level of social consensus. By deploying our proposed framework at the client end, we give better inputs regarding social consensus and credibility of sources.

The PageRank algorithm could correctly identify the tweets which were being retweeted in greater numbers. The threshold value would decide the level of classification of a news item as generally acceptable or not. We had taken a threshold value of the PageRank score before it starts to even out to near zero levels. In all cases, the acceptability of the tweets were correctly evaluated.

The algorithm is proposed to be used by an user to detect the credibility of sources and general acceptability of the tweets. It would also use the cognitive powers of the user to carry out the initial screening of messages. With that, the false positives of the algorithm would be minimum and the algorithm would provide valid inputs to the user in an accurate manner. The users who have a high degree of communication with the segregated sources could also be now identified along with the tweets involved in the spread of false information.

Conclusions

The paper has explored the application of principles of cognitive psychology in evaluating the spread of misinformation in online social networks. We have proposed an effective algorithm for speedy detection of spread of misinformation in online social networks taking Twitter as an example. Analysing the entire content of a social network using linguistic techniques would be computationally expensive and time consuming. The aim was to propose an algorithm which would use the social media as a filter to separate misinformation from accurate information. We were also interested only in misinformation which were likely to spread to a large section of the social network. Analysing the problem from a cognitive psychology point of view enabled us to understand the process by which a human mind determines the credibility of information. The literature review of the work done in detection of misinformation in Twitter brought out the critical features of Twitter which would help us identify the cues to deception in tweets. Our proposed algorithm is simple and effective in limiting the computation required to identify the users involved in spread of misinformation and estimate the level of acceptance of the tweets.

Prevention is better than cure. The spread of misinformation can be prevented if users are enabled to make correct decisions while retweeting the messages they receive. The algorithm would enable the user to make informed decisions while spreading information in OSNs. The implementation of the algorithm at the client end can be done in the form of a browser plug-in or a Twitter app. The proposed plug-in or the app would help the user to make correct decisions while forwarding messages and thus prevent large scale misinformation cascades. The important feature of the algorithm is that it does not make use of any specific features of Twitter. The proposed methodology would be applicable for other online social networks also which support easy re-propagation like Facebook, with its 'share' feature, Diggs with its 'voting' mechanism or even e-mail networks with their 'forwarding' features.

Competing interests
The authors declare that they have no competing interests.

Authors' contributions
The work was carried out as part of research on online social networks and is a result of equal contribution by each of the authors. Both authors read and approved the final manuscript.

Acknowledgements
The authors want to acknowledge BITS-Pilani, Hyderabad campus for the facilities provided. We also want to thank Agrima Srivastava, our co-researcher for her excellent inputs during various brainstorming sessions.

References
1. Mintz AP (2002) Web of deception: Misinformation on the Internet. Information Today, Inc., New Jersey, USA
2. Karlova NA, Fisher KE (2013) "Plz RT": A social diffusion model of misinformation and disinformation for understanding human information behaviour. Inform Res 18(1):1–17
3. Stahl BC (2006) On the difference or equality of information, misinformation, and disinformation: A critical research perspective. Inform Sci: Int J Emerg Transdiscipline 9:83–96

4. Fallis D (2009) A conceptual analysis of disinformation. iConference, Chapel Hill, NC, California, USA
5. Libicki MC (2007) Conquest in cyberspace: National security and information warfare. Cambridge University Press, New York, USA
6. Lewandowsky S, Ecker UK, Seifert CM, Schwarz N, Cook J (2012) Misinformation and its correction continued influence and successful debiasing. Psychol Sci Public Interest 13(3):106–131
7. Ratkiewicz J, Conover M, Meiss M, Goncalves B, Patil S, Flamini A, Menczer F (2010) Detecting and tracking the spread of astroturf memes in microblog streams. arXiv preprint arXiv:1011.3768
8. Ratkiewicz J, Conover M, Meiss M, Goncalves B, Patil S, Flammini A, Menczer F (2011) Truthy: mapping the spread of astroturf in microblog streams. In: Proceedings of the 20th International Conference Companion on World wide Web. ACM, Hyderabad, India, pp 249–252
9. De Neys W, Cromheeke S, Osman M (2011) Biased but in doubt: Conflict and decision condence. PLoSONE 6(1):e15954
10. Fitzgerald MA (1997) Misinformation on the internet: Applying evaluation skills to online information. Emerg Libr 24(3):9–14
11. Kata A (2010) A postmodern pandora's box: Anti-vaccination misinformation on the internet. Vaccine 28(7):1709–1716
12. Nguyen NP, Yan G, Thai MT, Eidenbenz S (2012) Containment of misinformation spread in online social networks. In: Proceedings of the 3rd Annual ACM Web Science Conference. ACM, Illinois, USA, pp 213–222
13. Nguyen NP, Yan G, Thai MT (2013) Analysis of misinformation spread containment in online social networks. Comput Netw 57(10):2133–2146
14. Budak C, Agrawal D, El Abbadi A (2011) Limiting the spread of misinformation in social networks. In: Proceedings of the 20th International Conference on World Wide Web. ACM, Hyderabad, India, pp 665–674
15. Nguyen DT, Nguyen NP, Thai MT (2012) Sources of misinformation in online social networks: Who to suspect?" In: Military Communications Conference, MILCOM 2012. IEEE, Orlando, USA, pp 1–6
16. Reuters IANS (2013) Ethnic riots sweep assam, at least 30 killed. [Online]. Available: http://in.reuters.com/article/2012/07/24/india-assam-riots-floods-idINDEE86N04520120724. Last accessed 21 August 2014
17. Castillo C, Mendoza M, Poblete B (2011) Information credibility on twitter. In: Proceedings of the 20th International Conference on World Wide Web. ACM, Hyderabad, USA, pp 675–684
18. Mendoza M, Poblete B, Castillo C (2010) Twitter under crisis: Can we trust what we RT? In: Proceedings of the First Workshop on Social Media Analytics. ACM, 2010: Washington DC, USA, pp 71–79
19. Gupta A, Kumaraguru P (2012) Credibility ranking of tweets during high impact events. In: Proceedings of the 1st Workshop on Privacy and Security in Online Social Media. ACM, Lyon, France, p 2
20. Qazvinian V, Rosengren E, Radev DR, Mei Q (2011) Rumor has it: Identifying misinformation in microblogs. In: Proceedings of the Conference on Empirical Methods in Natural Language Processing. Association for Computational Linguistics, Edinburg, UK, pp 1589–1599
21. Kwak H, Lee C, Park H, Moon S (2010) What is twitter, a social network or a news media? In: Proceedings of the 19th International Conference on World Wide Web. ACM, Raleigh, USA, pp 591–600
22. Cha M, Haddadi H, Benevenuto F, Gummadi KP (2010) Measuring user in uence in twitter: The million follower fallacy. In: Proceedings of the 4th International Conference on Weblogs and Social Media (ICWSM) 14. AAAI, Washington DC, USA, pp 10–17
23. Morris MR, Counts S, Roseway A, Hoff A, Schwarz J (2012) Tweeting is believing?: understanding microblog credibility perceptions. In: Proceedings of the ACM 2012 Conference on Computer Supported Cooperative Work. ACM, Raleigh, USA, pp 441–450
24. Mustafaraj E, Metaxas PT (2010) From obscurity to prominence in minutes: Political speech and real-time search. In: WebSci10: Extending the Frontiers of Society On-Line. The Web Science Trust, Raleigh, USA p 317
25. Hawksey M (2013) Twitter Archiving Google Spreadsheet TAGS v5. JISC CETIS MASHe: The Musing of Martin Hawksey (EdTech Explorer). http://mashe.hawksey.info/2013/02/twitter-archive-tagsv5/, [Online: Last accessed: 21 August 2014]
26. Page L, Brin S, Motwani R, Winograd T (1999) The pagerank citation ranking: bringing order to the web. Stanford InfoLab, California, USA
27. Bastian M, Heymann S, Jacomy M (2011) Gephi: an open source software for exploring and manipulating networks. 2009. In: International AAAI Conference on Weblogs and Social Media, Barcelona, Spain, pp 361–362

6

Illumination invariant head pose estimation using random forests classifier and binary pattern run length matrix

Hyunduk Kim[*], Sang-Heon Lee, Myoung-Kyu Sohn and Dong-Ju Kim

* Correspondence: hyunduk00@ dgist.ac.kr
Department of Convergence, Daegu Gyeongbuk Institute of Science & Technology (DGIST), 50-1 Sang-Ri, Hyeongpung-Myeon, Dalseong-Gun, 711-873 Daegu, South Korea

Abstract

In this paper, a novel approach for head pose estimation in gray-level images is presented. In the proposed algorithm, two techniques were employed. In order to deal with the large set of training data, the method of Random Forests was employed; this is a state-of-the-art classification algorithm in the field of computer vision. In order to make this system robust in terms of illumination, a Binary Pattern Run Length matrix was employed; this matrix is combination of Binary Pattern and a Run Length matrix. The binary pattern was calculated by randomly selected operator. In order to extract feature of training patch, we calculate statistical texture features from the Binary Pattern Run Length matrix. Moreover we perform some techniques to real-time operation, such as control the number of binary test. Experimental results show that our algorithm is efficient and robust against illumination change.

Keywords: Head pose estimation; Random forests; Binary pattern; Run Length matrix; Illumination-invariant

Introduction

Determining head pose is one of the most important topics in the field of computer vision. There are many applications with accurate and robust head pose estimation algorithms, such as human-computing interfaces (HCI), driver surveillance systems, entertainment systems, and so on. For this reason, many applications would benefit from automatic and robust head pose estimation systems. Accurately localizing the head and its orientation is either the explicit goal of systems like human computer interfaces or a necessary preprocessing step for further analysis, such as identification or facial expression recognition. Due to its relevance and to the challenges posed by the problem, there has been considerable effort in the computer vision community to develop fast and reliable algorithms for head pose estimation [1]. The several approaches to head pose estimation can be briefly divided into two categories: appearance-based and model-based approaches, depending on whether they analyze the face as a whole or instead rely on the localization of some specific facial features.

The model-based approaches combine the location of facial features (e.g. eyes, mouth, and nose tip) and a geometrical face model to calculate precise angles of head orientation [2]. In general, these approaches can provide accurate estimation results for a limited range of poses. However, these approaches have difficulty dealing with low-resolution images due to invisible or undetectable facial points. Moreover, these approaches depend on the accurate detection of facial points. Hence, these approaches are typically more sensitive to occlusion than appearance-based methods, which use information from the entire facial region [3].

The appearance-based approaches discretize the head poses and learn a separate detector for each pose using machine learning techniques that determine the head poses from entire face images [3]. These approaches include multi-detector methods, manifold embedding methods, and non-linear regression methods. Generally, multi-detector methods train a series of head detectors each attuned to a specific pose and assign a discrete pose to the detector with the greatest support [1,4]. Manifold embedding based methods seek low-dimensional manifolds that model the continuous variation in head pose. These methods are either linear or nonlinear approaches. The linear techniques have an advantage in that embedding can be performed by matrix multiplication; however, these techniques lack the representational ability of the nonlinear techniques [1,5]. Nonlinear regression methods use nonlinear regression tools (e.g. Support Vector Regression, neural networks) to develop a functional mapping from the image or feature data to a head pose measurement. These approaches are very fast, work well in the near-field, and give some of the most accurate head pose estimates in practice. However, they are prone to error from poor head localization [1,6].

Recently, random forests have become a popular method in computer vision given their capability to handle large training datasets, their high generalization power and speed, and the relative ease of implementation. Decision trees can map complex input spaces into simpler, discrete or continuous output spaces, depending on whether they are used for classification of regression purposes. A tree splits the original problem into smaller ones, solvable with simple predictors, thus achieving complex, highly non-linear mappings in a very simple manner. A non-leaf node in the tree contains a binary test, guiding a data sample towards the left or right child node. The tests are chosen in a supervised-learning framework, and training a tree boils down to selecting the tests which cluster the training such as to allow good predictions using simpler models. Random forests are collections of decision trees, each trained on a randomly sampled subset of the available data; this reduces over-fitting in comparison to trees trained on the whole dataset, as shown by Breiman. Randomness is introduced by the subset of training examples provided to each tree, but also by a random subset of tests available for optimization at each node [7,8].

The proposed approach can be summarized as follows.

1. Random Forests is employed for classifier. Due to this classifier, system can be operated in real time and deal with the large set of training data.
2. The binary pattern run length matrix is proposed for binary test. This method is a combination of a binary pattern and a run length matrix. The binary pattern was calculated by randomly selected operator, such as Local Binary Pattern, Centralized Binary Pattern and Local Directional Pattern. The statistical texture features, such as Short Run Emphasis and Long Run Emphasis, is employed. Due to this strategy, system can be robust to illumination variance and classification performance is improved.
3. The key parameters of the binary test of each node are optimized using information gain. The resulting optimum binary test improves the discriminative power of individual trees in the forest.

4. In order to achieve a more efficient data split, we increase the number of iteration for parameter generation. By this strategy, the patches are split roughly at the beginning depths, and are divided more finely at deeper depths.

The remainder of this paper is organized as follows. We describe several binary patterns and gray-level run length matrix in Section Related work. In section Proposed head pose estimation algorithm, the proposed method is introduced in detailed. Experiments results and a discussion of those results are reported in Section Experiments. Finally, we offer our conclusions in Section Future works.

Related work

Head pose estimation

The model-based approach

In the feature-based methods, the head pose is inferred from the extracted features, which include the common feature visible in all poses, the pose-dependent feature, and the discriminant feature together with the appearance information.

Vatahska et al. [9] use a face detector to roughly classify the pose as frontal, left, or right profile. After his, they detect the eyes and nose tip using AdaBoost classifiers, and the detections are fed into a neural network which estimates the head orientation. Whitehill et al. [10] present a discriminative approach to frame-by-frame head pose estimation. Their algorithm relies on the detection of the nose tip and both eyes, thereby limiting the recognizable poses to the ones where both eyes are visible. Yao and Cham [11] propose an efficient method that estimates the motion parameters of a human head from a video sequence by using a three-layer linear iterative process. Morency et al. [12] propose a probabilistic framework called Generalized Adaptive View-based Appearance Model integrating frame-by-frame head pose estimation, differential registration, and keyframe tracking.

The appearance-based approach

In the appearance-based methods, the entire face region is analyzed. The repre-sentative methods of this type include the manifold embedding method, the flexible-model-based method, and the machine-learning-based method. The performance of both kinds of methods may deteriorate as a consequence of feature occlusion and the variation of illumination, owing to the intrinsic shortcoming of 2D data. Generally, the appearance-based methods outperform the feature-based methods, because the latter rely on the error-prone facial feature extraction.

Balasubramanian et al. [13] propose the Biased Manifold Embedding (BME) framework, which uses the pose angle information of the face images to compute a biased neighborhood of each point in the feature space, before determining the low-dimensional embedding. Huang et al. [14] present Supervised Local Subspace Learning (SL2), a method that learns a local linear model from a sparse and non-uniformly sampled training set. SL2 learns a mixture of local tangent spaces that is robust to under-sampled regions, and due to its regularization properties it is also robust to over-fitting. Osadchy et al. [15] describe a method for simultaneously detecting faces and estimating their pose in real time. The method employs a convolutional network to map images of faces to points on a low-dimensional manifold parameterized by pose, and images of non-faces to points far away from that manifold.

Random forests

Random Forests have become a popular method in computer vision because of their capability to handle large training datasets, their high generalization power and speed, and the relative ease of implementation. In the context of real time pose estimation, multi-class random forests have been proposed for the real time determination of head pose from 2D video data.

Li et al. [3] propose person-independent head pose estimation method. The half-face and tree structured classifiers with cascaded-Adaboost algorithm to detect face with various head poses. After localization, the random forest regression is trained and applied to estimate head orientation. Huang et al. [16] propose Gabor feature based multi-class random forest method for head pose estimation. In order to enhance the discriminative power, they employed LDA technique for nodetests.

Binary pattern

The local binary pattern

Recently, the Local Binary Pattern (LBP) has been extensively exploited for facial image analysis, including face detection, face recognition, facial expression analysis, gender/age classification, and so on [17]. The Original LBP operator labels the pixels of an image by thresholding a 3×3 neighborhood of each pixel with the center value and considering the results as a binary number, of which the corresponding decimal number is used for labeling. Formally, given a pixel at (x_c, y_c), the resulting LBP can be derived by:

$$LBP(x_c, y_c) = \sum_{n=0}^{7} s(i_n - i_c) 2^n,$$ (1)

where n runs over the 8 neighbors of the central pixel, i_c and i_n are gray-level values of the central pixel and the surrounding pixels, respectively, and the sign function $s(x)$ is defined as:

$$s(x) = \begin{cases} 1 & if \quad x \geq 0 \\ 0 & otherwise \end{cases},$$ (2)

According to the definition above, the LBP operator is invariant to the monotonic gray-scale transformations that preserve the pixel intensity order in local neighborhoods. The histogram of LBP labels calculated over a region can be exploited as a texture descriptor.

The centralized binary pattern

Fu and Wei [18] introduced the Centralized Binary Pattern (CBP) for facial expression recognition. CBP compares pairs of neighbors which are in the same diameter of the circle, and also compares the central pixel with the mean of all the pixels (including the central pixel and the neighboring pixels), given the largest weight to strengthen the effect of the central pixel. Compared to the original LBP, CBP produces less binary units, and thus reducing the feature vector length. Formally, given a pixel at (x_c, y_c), the resulting CBP can be derived by:

$$CBP(x_c, y_c) = \sum_{n=0}^{3} s(i_n - i_{n+4}) 2^n + s(i_c - i_T) 2^4,$$ (3)

where i_c and i_n are gray-level values of the central pixel and the surrounding pixels, respectively, i_T is the mean gray-level value of all the pixel and the sign function $s(x)$ is just as Equation (2).

From Equation (3) we can see CBP operator considers the center pixel and gives it the largest weight. This strengthens the effect of center pixel and is beneficial for discrimination of CBP. Moreover, CBP captures better gradient information through comparing pairs of neighbors.

The local directional pattern

More recently, a Local Directional Pattern (LDP) method was introduced for a more robust facial representation [19]. While the binary patterns such as LBP and CBP use the information of intensity changes around pixels, the LDP uses the edge response values and encodes the image texture. Given a central pixel in the image, the eight-directional edge response values are computed by Kirsch masks, and are converted to absolute values. Then, the most prominent directions of the number with high response values are selected to generate the LDP code. In other words, bit responses of are only set to 1, and the remaining bits are set to 0. Formally, given a pixel at (x_c, y_c), the resulting LDP can be derived by:

$$LDP(x_c, y_c) = \sum_{n=0}^{7} s(i_n - i_k) 2^n,$$ (4)

where i_n and i_k are gray-level values of the surrounding pixels and k-th most significant directional response, respectively and the sign function $s(x)$ is just as Equation (2). Figure 1 shows the example of binary pattern containing LBP, CBP and LDP.

Gray level run length matrices

The Gary Level Run Length (GLRL) method is a way of extracting higher order statistical texture features [20]. This technique has been described and applied by Galloway and by Chu et al. A set of consecutive pixels with the same gray level, collinear in a given direction, constitutes a gray level run. The run length is the number of pixels in the run, and the run length value is the number of times such a run occurs in an image.

A Gray Level Run Length Matrix (GLRLM) is a two-dimensional matrix in which each element $p(i, j|\theta)$ gives the total number of occurrences of runs of length j at gray level i, in a given direction θ. Figure 2 shows a 4×4 picture having four gray levels (0–3) and the resulting gray level run length matrices for the four principal directions.

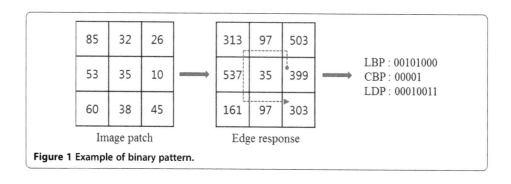

Figure 1 Example of binary pattern.

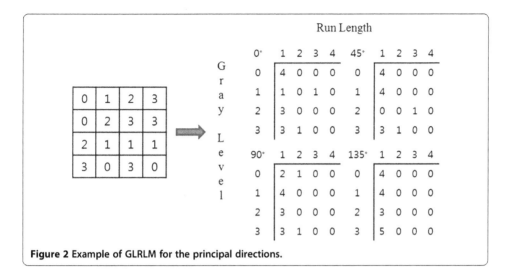

Figure 2 Example of GLRLM for the principal directions.

Let G be the number of gray levels in the image, R be the longest run and n be the number of pixels in the image. In order to obtain numerical texture measures from the matrices, statistical texture features can be extracted from the GLRLM as follows:

1. Short Run Emphasis

$$SRE(p) = \sum_{i=1}^{G}\sum_{j=1}^{R}\frac{p(i,j|\theta)}{j} \Big/ \sum_{i=1}^{G}\sum_{j=1}^{R}p(i,j|\theta) \tag{5}$$

Short Runs Emphasis (SRE) divides each run length value by the length of the run squared. This tends to emphasize short runs. The denominator is the total number of runs in the image and serves as a normalizing factor.

2. Long Runs Emphasis

$$LRE(p) = \sum_{i=1}^{G}\sum_{j=1}^{R}j^2 p(i,j|\theta) \Big/ \sum_{i=1}^{G}\sum_{j=1}^{R}p(i,j|\theta) \tag{6}$$

Long Runs Emphasis (LRE) multiplies each run length value by the length of the run squared. This should emphasize long runs. The denominator is a normalizing factor, as above.

Proposed head pose estimation algorithm
Random forests framework
A tree T in a forest $F = \{T_i\}$ is built from the set of annotated patches $P = \{P_i = (I_i, c_i)\}$ randomly extracted from the training images, where I_i and c_i are the intensity of patches and the annotated head pose class labels, respectively. Starting from the root, each tree is built recursively by assigning a binary Test $\phi(I) \rightarrow \{0, 1\}$ to each non-leaf node. Such test sends each patch either to the left or right child, in this way the training patches P arriving at the node are split into two sets, $PL(\phi)$ and $PR(\phi)$.

The best test ϕ^* is chosen from a pool of randomly generated ones ($\{\phi\}$): all patches arriving at the node are evaluated by all tests in the pool and a predefined information gain of the split $IG(\phi)$ is maximized:

$$\phi^* = Arg\,\max_\phi IG(\phi) \qquad (7)$$

The process continues with the left and the right child using the corresponding training sets PL(ϕ^*) and PR(ϕ^*) until a leaf is created when either the maximum tree depth is reached, or less than a minimum number of training samples are left [21].

Training

All the trees are trained on different training sets. These sets are generated from the original training set using the bootstrap procedure. For each training set, we randomly select N data in the original set. The data are chosen with replacement. That is, some data will occur more than once and some will be absent. Then, we randomly extract M patches with fixed size.

Our binary tests $\phi_{f, r, s, \tau, type}(I)$ are defined as:

$$f(BPRLM(r)) - f(BPRLM(s)) > \tau, \qquad (8)$$

where f is the statistical texture feature, r and s are pixel coordinate, τ is a threshold, θ is the direction, $type$ is the type of Binary Pattern, and $BPRLM(r)$ is the Binary Pattern Run Length Matrix (BPRLM) at gray level $I(r)$. During training, we use the different statistical texture feature, such as Short Run Emphasis and Long Run Emphasis, which is introduced in Section Random Forests. Short Run Emphasis tends to emphasize short runs, i.e., this feature represents the global texture measure. On the other hand, Long Run Emphasis tends to emphasize long runs, i.e., this feature represents the local texture measure. Therefore, we use Long Run Emphasis up to middle depth and then we use Short Run Emphasis.

The Binary Pattern Run Length Matrix is the combination between the Binary Pattern and Run Length matrix, which can be calculated by the following steps. First, the binary patterns at $I(r)$ and $I(s)$ using predetermined binary pattern operator, such as LBP, CBP or LDP operator. Second, construct the Run Length matrices from the binary patterns in a direction $0°$. Figure 3 shows an example of a Binary Pattern Run Length matrix using LBP operator.

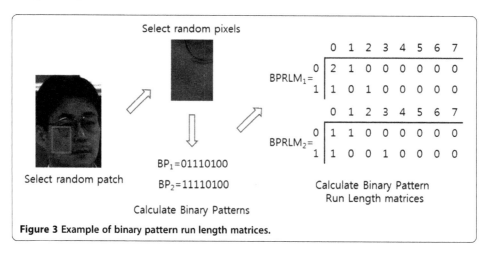

Figure 3 Example of binary pattern run length matrices.

During training, for each non-leaf node starting from the root, we generate a large pool of binary tests $\{\phi^k\}$ by randomly choosing f, r, s, τ, *type*. For efficiency reason, the number of binary tests is determined depend on the depth of the tree. That is, the number of the binary test increases with increasing the depth of the tree. The test which maximizes a specific optimization function is picked. Our information gain IG (ϕ) is defined as follows:

$$IG(\phi) = \sum_{i \in \{L,R\}} (\mu_i - \mu)^2 - \sum_{i \in \{L,R\}} \frac{n_i}{n_i + n_j} \left[\sum_{j=1}^{n_i} (c_{ij} - \mu_i)^2 \right],$$ (9)

where n_i and μ_i are the number of samples and the mean of class at the child node i, respectively, c_{ij} is the head pose class label of the *j-th* patch contained in child node i, and μ is the mean of class at the parent node. The information gain $IG(\phi)$ indicates the difference between the within variance and weighted between variance.

For each leaf, the class distribution $p(c_i|T)$ is stored. The distributions are estimated from the training patches that arrive at the leaf and are used for estimation the head pose.

Algorithm 1 Training the random forest

Input: T_{max}: the maximum number of trees to grow
$\quad\quad\ D_{max}$: the maximum depth of trees to extend
$\quad\quad\ B_{max}$: the maximum number of binary tests to split
$\quad\quad\ S$: training sets
$\quad\quad\ $Initialize: $i = 0$, $j = 0$

Loop: $T_i < T_{max}$
$\quad\quad\ i = i + 1$
$\quad\quad\ $Select n new boostrap samples from training set S.
$\quad\quad\ $Extract m sample patches from each sample.

$\quad\quad\ $Loop: $D_j < D_{max}$
$\quad\quad\quad\quad\ j = j + 1$
$\quad\quad\quad\quad\ $1.　Grow an unpruned tree using the *nm* sample patches.
$\quad\quad\quad\quad\ $2.　Each internal node, randomly generate $B_{max}D_j/D_{max}$ binary tests and
$\quad\quad\quad\quad\quad\quad\ $determines the best binary test. The binary test $\phi(I)$ iteratively splits
$\quad\quad\quad\quad\quad\quad\ $the training data into left node P_L and right node P_R using equation
$\quad\quad\quad\quad\quad\quad\ $(10).

$$P_L = \{I_i \in P \mid \phi(I_i) < \tau\},$$
$$P_R = P \setminus P_L$$ (10)

$\quad\quad\quad\quad\ $The threshold τ is randomly chosen by the binary test $\phi(I)$ in
$\quad\quad\quad\quad\ $the range $\tau \in (\min \phi(I), \max \phi(I))$
$\quad\quad\ $Loop end

$\quad\quad\ $Add the *i*-th decision tree to the random forests.
$\quad\ $Loop end

Output: random rorest F

Testing

Given a new gray image of a head, patches that have the same size as the ones used for training are densely sampled from whole image and passed through all trees in the forest. Each patch is guided by the binary tests stored at the nodes. A stride parameter controls how densely patches are extracted, thus easily steering speed and accuracy of the classification. At each node of a tree, the stored binary test evaluates a patch, sending it either to the right of left child, all the way down until a leaf. Arriving at a leaf, a tree outputs the class distribution and the class label c that received the majority of votes. Because leaves with a low probability are not very informative and mainly add noise to the estimate, we discard all votes if $p(c|T)$ less than an empiric threshold P_{max}. The final class distribution is generated by arithmetic averaging of each remained distribution of all trees as follows:

$$p(c_i|F) = \frac{1}{|F|}\sum_{t=1}^{|F|} p(c_i|T_t) \quad (11)$$

We choose c_i as the final class of an input image if $p(c_i|F)$ has the maximum value.

Experiments

We evaluate the performance of our algorithm based on the CMU Multi-PIE database, which contains more than 750,000 images of 337 people recorded in up to four sessions over the span of five months. Subject were imaged under 15 view points and 18 illumination conditions while displaying a range of facial expressions [22]. In our paper, first session, 249 person, neutral expression, 18 illuminations and 7 view points, which consist of 0°, ±15°, ±30°, and ±45°, were employed. All of these face images were cropped to 32×32. Among these images, 50% were used for training and the rest for testing. Figure 4 shows an example of the CMU multi-PIE databases.

Training a forest involves the choice of several parameters. A set of values of parameters used for all experiments are given as follows. The patch dimension is 16×16 pixels; the minimum patch number for split is 20 (m); the number of trees in the forest is 100 (T_{max}); the maximum tree depth is 10 (D_{max}); the number of training images for each tree is 3,000 (n); the number of patch of each training image is 10; the maximum threshold is 0.5 (P_{max}); the maximum number of binary test is 4000 tests, i.e., 200 different combinations of f, r, s, $type$ in Equation (8), each with 20 different thresholds τ.

In order to evaluate the performance of the proposed head pose estimation, we employed a combination of several methods. First, the Local Binary Pattern, Centralized

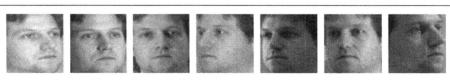

Figure 4 Example of CMU Multi-PIE databases.

Table 1 Comparison of classification accuracies (CA) of different algorithms

Algorithm	Raw image	LBP image	CBP image	LDP image
PCA + SVM	64.6%	69.0%	70.3%	75.9%
LDA + SVM	73.9%	76.4%	78.7%	80.0%
Proposed	93.1%	-	-	-

Binary Patterns, and Local Directional Pattern were employed for preprocessing. Second, Principal Component Analysis (PCA) and Linear Discriminant Analysis (LDA) were employed for feature extraction. Finally, a Support Vector Machine (SVM) was employed for the classifiers. In this experiment, 100 principal components are employed for PCA, Radial basis function (RBF) kernel is used for SVM.

Table 1 shows the comparison results of the classification accuracies (CA) of the different algorithms. Because of the illumination change, the results of the LBP, CBP and LDP image were better than those of the raw images. Also, classification accuracy using LDP image showed better performance compared to other images transformed by binary pattern operators such as LBP and CBP. Furthermore, the proposed method has performance better than that of other methods, about 17% higher than that of LDP + PCA + SVM, and 13% higher than that of LDP + LDA + SVM. Figure 5 shows the comparison results of the classification accuracies of the different class. Furthermore, we summarized the classification accuracies in Table 2. As a result, maximum classification accuracies are 90.5%, 92.1%, and 97.2% when PCA + LDP + SVM, LDA + LDP + SVM, and proposed algorithm, respectively. Here, we can observe that proposed algorithm shows the less variance of classification accuracy than that of other algorithm. To further disclose the relationship between the recognition rate and the number of the trees, we showed the recognition results along with number of trees in Figure 6.

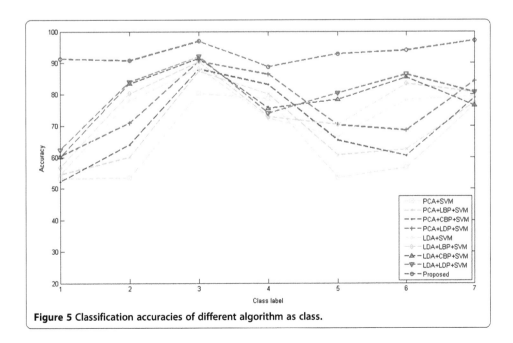

Figure 5 Classification accuracies of different algorithm as class.

Table 2 Comparison of classification accuracies (CA) of different class

Algorithm	Class1	Class2	Class3	Class4	Class5	Class6	Class7
PCA + LDP + SVM	60.4%	70.9%	90.5%	86.4%	70.2%	68.5%	84.3%
LDA + LDP + SVM	62.4%	84.0%	92.1%	74.5%	80.4%	86.7%	80.6%
Proposed	91.3%	90.6%	96.8%	88.7%	92.7	93.9%	97.2%

Future works

Recently, 3D sensing devices have become available and computer vision researchers have started to leverage the additional depth information for solving some of the inherent limitations of image-based methods. Even though depth sensors can solve much of the ambiguities inherent of standard video and even if their prices recently dropped, resolution of depth image is still low. Hence, the future work on head pose estimation could use color images in addition to depth data, as an RGB camera is available in the most common depth sensors.

Conclusion

In this paper we proposed to use a Binary Pattern Run Length matrix based on the random forests method for head pose estimation. In order to make this method robust in terms of illumination, the Binary Pattern Run Length matrix was employed; this matrix is the combination of a Binary Pattern and a Run Length matrix. Binary pattern is calculated using various operators, such as Local Binary Pattern, Centralized Binary Patterns, and Local Directional. In order to evaluate the discriminative power of the random tree method, a novel information gain was employed. Experiments on public databases show the advantages of this method over other algorithm in terms of accuracy and illumination invariance.

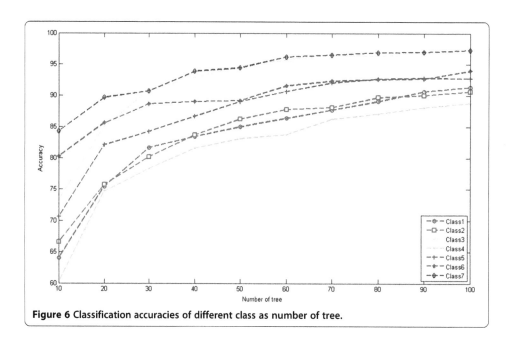

Figure 6 Classification accuracies of different class as number of tree.

Competing interests
The authors declare that they have no competing interest.

Authors' contributions
HDK and SHL conceptualized the core functions of head pose estimation algorithm and drafted the manuscript. MKS and DJK conducts the implementation including algorithm design, experiments and acquisition of evaluation data. All authors read and approved the final manuscript.

Acknowledgement
This work was supported by the DGIST R&D Program of the Ministry of Education, Science and Technology of Korea (14-IT-03). It was also supported by Ministry of Culture, Sports and Tourism (MCST) and Korea Creative Content Agency (KOCCA) in the Culture Technology (CT) Research & Development Program (Immersive Game Contents CT Co-Research Center).

References
1. Murphy-Chutorian E, Trivedi MM (2009) Head pose estimation in computer vision: a survey. IEEE Trans Pattern Anal Mach Intell 607:626
2. Gee A, Cipolla R (1994) Determining the gaze of faces in images. Image and Vision Computting 639:647
3. Li Y, Wang S, Ding X (2010) Person-independent head pose estimation based on random forest regression. IEEE Int Conf Image Processing 1521:1524
4. Huang C, Ai H, Li Y, Lao S (2007) High-performance rotation invariant multiview face detection. IEEE Trans Pattern Anal Mach Intell 671:686
5. Raytchev B, Toda I, Sakaue K (2004) Head pose estimation by nonlinear manifold learning. IEEE Int Conf Pattern Recognition 462:466 (204)
6. Li Y, Gong S, Liddell H (2000) Support vector regression and classification based mult-view face detection and recognition. IEEE Int Conf Automatic Face and Gesture Recognition 300:305
7. Fanelli G, Gall J, Van Gool L (2011) Real time head pose estimation with random regression forests. IEEE Int Conf Computer Vision and Pattern Recognition 617:624
8. Breiman L (2001) Random Forests. Machine learning. 5:32
9. Vatahska T, Bennewitz M, Behnke S (2007) Feature-based head pose estimation from images. IEEE-RAS Int Conf Humanoid Robots 330:335
10. Whitehill J, Movellan JR (2008) A discriminative approach to frame-by-frame head pose tracking. IEEE Int Conf Automatic Face and Gesture Recognition 1:7
11. Yao J, Cham WK (2004) Efficient model-based linear head motion recovery from movies. IEEE Int Conf Computer Vision and Pattern Recognition 414:421
12. Morency LP, Whitehill J, Movellan JR (2008) Generalized adaptive view-based appearance model: integrated framework for monocular head pose estimation. IEEE Int Conf Automatic Face and Gesture Recognition 1:8
13. Balasubramanian VN, Ye JP, Panchanathan S (2008) Biased manifold embedding: a framework for person-independent head pose estimation. IEEE Int Conf Computer Vision and Pattern Recognition 1:7
14. Huang D, Storer M, De la Torre F, Bischof H (2011) Supervised local subspace learning for continuous head pose estimation. IEEE Int Conf Computer Vision and Pattern Recognition 2921:2928
15. Osadchy M, Miller ML, LeCun Y (2007) Synergistic face detection and pose estimation with energy-based models. Mach Learning Research 1197:1215
16. Huang C, Ding XQ, Fang C (2010) Head pose estimation based on random forests for multiclass classification. IEEE Int Conf Computer Vision and Pattern Recognition 934:937
17. Ojala T, Pietkainen M, Maenpaa T (2002) Multiresolution gray-scale and rotation invariant texture classification with local binary patterns. IEEE Trans Pattern Anal Mach Intell 971:987
18. Fu X, Wei W (2008) Centralized binary patterns embedded with image Euclidean distance for facial expression recognition. IEEE Int Conf Natural Computation 115:119
19. Jabid T, Kabir MH, Chae O (2010) Robust facial expression recognition based on local directional pattern. J ETRI 784:794
20. Galloway MM (1975) Texture analysis using gray level run lengths. Computer Graphics and Image Processing 172:179
21. Fanelli G, Danotone M, Gall J, Fossati A, Van Fool L (2013) Random forests for real time 3D face analysis. International J of Computer Vision 437:458
22. Gross R, Matthews I, Cohn JF, Kanade T, Baker S (2010) Multi-PIE. Image Vis Comput 807:813

7

Discriminative histogram taxonomy features for snake species identification

Alex Pappachen James[1,2]*, Bincy Mathews[2], Sherin Sugathan[2] and Dileep Kumar Raveendran[3]

* Correspondence: apj@ieee.org
[1]School of Engineering, Nazarbayev University, Astana, Kazakhstan
[2]Enview R&D Labs, Thiruvananthapuram, India
Full list of author information is available at the end of the article

Abstract

Background: Incorrect snake identification from the observable visual traits is a major reason for death resulting from snake bites in tropics. So far no automatic classification method has been proposed to distinguish snakes by deciphering the taxonomy features of snake for the two major species of snakes i.e. Elapidae and Viperidae. We identify 38 different taxonomically relevant features to develop the Snake database from 490 sample images of Naja Naja (Spectacled cobra), 193 sample images of Ophiophagus Hannah (King cobra), 88 images of Bungarus caeruleus (Common krait), 304 sample images of Daboia russelii (Russell's viper), 116 images of Echis carinatus (Saw scaled viper) and 108 images of Hypnale hypnale (Hump Nosed Pit Viper).

Results: Snake identification performances with 13 different types of classifiers and 12 attribute elevator demonstrate that 15 out of 38 taxonomically relevant features are enough for snake identification. Interestingly, these features were almost equally distributed from the logical grouping of top, side and body views of snake images, and the features from the bottom view of snakes had the least role in the snake identification.

Conclusion: We find that only few of the taxonomically relevant snake features are useful in the process of snake identification. These discriminant features are essential to improve the accuracy of snake identification and classification. The presented study indicate that automated snake identification is useful for practical applications such as in medical diagnosis, conservation studies and surveys by interdisciplinary practitioners with little expertise in snake taxonomy.

Keywords: Snake classification; Snake database; Taxonomy; Classifiers; Feature analysis

Background

Snake is a cold blooded reptile that is in majority perceived to be deadly to humans [1-5]. Since the ancient times, Snakes have been worshipped, feared and disliked by people across the world. Snake remain a painful reality in the daily life of millions of affected people and is largely one of the most misunderstood species [6,7]. At the same time, they are more perilous than the wild animals due to their close existence near human habitation [2]. World Health organization reports around five million snake bites every year resulting in millions of envenomation, hundreds of thousands of amputations and deaths. In cities like Thiruvananthapuram in Kerala, that has high humidity environment, where we started our study, on daily approximately 25–30 Snakes sightings are reported. Majority of these sighted snakes were identified to equip with enough venom to kill a human in the course of few hours.

In tropical regions of the world, most of the snake bite cases are caused by four venomous snakes often referred to as "Big Four" snakes [8]. They include Spectacled Cobra (Naja naja), Common Krait (Bungarus caeruleus), Russell's Viper (Daboia russelii) and Saw Scaled Viper (Echis carinatus) [7]. Another snakes which causes major snake bite cases and is very commonly found are King cobra (Ophiophagus Hannah) and Hump nosed Pit Viper (Hypnale hypnale). Due to this reason we restrict our study in this paper to these six deadly snakes [9,10].

Although anti-venom is produced in sufficient quantities by several public and private manufacturers, most snake bite victims don't have access to good quality care, and in populated countries like India, both morbidity and mortality due to snake bite is high. Because of serious misreporting, the true burden of snake bite is not known. Doctors mostly inject polyvalent anti-venom to the snake bite victim. This is injected without considering which snake has bitten the person, even under the situation when the patient has knowledge about some observational features of the snake under consideration. The taxonomy of the snake is not well understood by majority of the medical practitioners making the correct identification of the snake from the remarks of the victims or eye witness. The polyvalent anti-venom injected by the medical practitioner contains antibodies raised against two or more species of snake, which may neutralize the venom injected by a single snake bite. Since there is only one type of venom injected by a snake bite, the remaining non-neutralized part of the polyvalent anti-venom used for treating the patient creates further risk to the human health. So proper identification of the snake is very important for the proper medical treatment to save the life of the snake bite victims [9-11].

To our knowledge, there has been no research reported yet on computer based approach to automatically distinguish snake classes. This may be largely due the lack of database for this purpose and less awareness of snake taxonomy research. The lack of database of venomous snakes in India makes this research very challenging, as the collection of images often involve well trained snake catchers, photographers and expert biologists. Through this paper we provide an early set of snake images that are collected in a view to identify relevant features based on snake taxonomy. In addition, the images contain a wide range of features from different snakes that can help with gaining newer understanding on snake taxonomy. The Indian snake taxonomy is a topic that is not investigated with rigor and there is lack of expert taxonomists. This makes the first line snake identification difficult in life threatening situations that are essential for recommending accurate treatment to the snake bite victims.

Materials and methods

Snake database

The snake images for the experiment were collected from forest across different parts of Kerala, India with the help of snake catchers from Pujappura Panchakarma Serpentarium, Trivandrum, India, through the close and 1 year long interaction with the subjects under study. The total number of images used for this experiment is 1299 that are obtained from 10–15 wild snakes of each species taken at different occasions and time.

Table 1 shows the taxonomically relevant features and their logical grouping based on the top, bottom, side or body view of the snake in the captured image, and Figure 1 shows the visual description of taxonomy features for each of snake class. The descriptions of the snakes are included as a supplementary file (Additional file 1). In total, 38 taxonomy based features are identified for creation of the feature database from 1299 snake images collected. There are a total of 490 images of spectacled cobra, 304 images of Russell's viper, 193 images of king cobra, 88 images of common krait, 116 images of saw scaled viper and 108 images of hump nosed pit viper. For creating the feature database, the 1299 snake images are manually converted by taxonomist to form feature vectors representing 38 taxonomically relevant features. This database file is included as a supplementary material to this article (Additional file 2).

Feature ranking and selection

Out of 38 taxonomically relevant features, top features that have highest impact on classification are determined. In order to find the top features from the complete database following 12 Attribute Elevators are used: ChiSquared AttributeEval [12], CfsSubsetEval [13], ConsistencySubsetEval [14], FilteredAttributeEval [15], FilteredSubsetEval [16], GainRatioAttributeEval [17], InfoGainAttributeEval [18], OneRAttributeEval [19], PrincipalComponents [20], ReliefFAttributeEval [21], SVMAttributeEval [19], SymmetricalUncertAttributeEva [19], along with combination of certain search methods [21,22] like Genetic Search, Greedy Stepwise, Linear Forward Selection, Rank Search, Scatter Search, Subset Size Forward Selection and Ranker. The histogram of the feature counts from these attribute elevators is then plotted to get the ranking of the taxonomically relevant features that are most useful for the classification as shown in Figure 2. The concept of ranking and histograms used in this method is useful for identifying the relevance of the features [23-25]. The rank table is made with the help of this histogram based on the total number of repetitions of each features in the experiment. The repetitions of the feature results from the repeated ranking of features using different feature ranking method. The features that share same number of repetitions are then ranked on the basis of their average classification score taken independently for that feature i.e. features with highest average classification score among the features with same repetition is ranked first. Table 2 shows the ranking of all the 38 features using the attribute elevators with search method and classification score. The rank list of features is used to prepare 38 feature subsets with different numbers of features from 1 to 38 starting from the top feature to the last feature of Table 2. The numbers of features in the feature subsets are referred to as feature size.

Classifier selection and training

In order to perform automated snake classification following 13 classifiers are used: Bayes Net [26], Naïve Bayes [27], Multilayer perception [26], Ada BoostM1 [28], Multi BoostAB [29], RBF network [30], IB1 [30], IBk [31], LWL [32], NB Tree [33], J48 [34], Random Sub Space [35], and Bagging [36]. In the setting up the classification experiment, the database is split into training and test set. The training set is the one that will train the classifier parameter, while the test set is used to assess the performance of the classifier in terms of classification accuracy, F-score value, the area under the receiver operator characteristic curve, precision and recall rates. The selection of less number of samples per snake class in the training set makes the problem challenging and performance

Table 1 The table shows the grouping of the taxonomy features and its idealistic feature values for the creation of the database for automatic classification purpose

Feature group	Features	Feature name	Spectacled cobra	King cobra	Common krait	Russel's viper	Saw scaled viper	Hump nosed pit viper
Top	F_1	Rostral	1	1	1	1	1	1
	F_2	Internasal	2	2	2	1	1	2
	F_3	Prefrontal	2	2	2	1	1	2
	F_4	Supraocular	2	2	2	1	1	2
	F_5	Frontal	2	2	2	1	1	2
	F_6	Parietals	2	2	2	1	1	2
	F_7	V mark on head	0	0	0	1	0	0
	F_8	Triangular head	0	0	0	1	0	1
	F_9	Two dark patch on head	0	0	0	1	0	0
	F_{10}	Number of scales between Supraoculars	1	1	1	6-9	6-9	1
	F_{11}	Big occipital	0	1	0	0	0	0
	F_{12}	Plus sign in the head	0	0	0	0	1	0
Side	F_{13}	Small nostril	1	1	1	0	1	1
	F_{14}	Round pupil	1	1	1	0	0	0
	F_{15}	Big nostril	0	0	0	1	0	0
	F_{16}	Elliptical pupil	0	0	0	1	1	1
	F_{17}	Loreal	0	0	0	1	1	1
	F_{18}	Nasorostral	0	0	0	1	0	0
	F_{19}	Supranasal	0	0	0	1	0	0
	F_{20}	Triangular brown streaks below/behind eyes	0	0	0	1	0	0
	F_{21}	Subocular	0	0	0	1	1	1
	F_{22}	Nasal	2	2	2	1	3	1
	F_{23}	Preoculars	1	1	1	4	4	4
	F_{24}	Postoculars	3	3	2	4	4	4
	F_{25}	Supralabial scale	6-7	6-7	6-7	9-11	9-11	9-11
	F_{38}	Pit between eyes and nose	0	0	0	0	0	1
Bottom	F_{26}	Mental	1	1	1	1	1	1
	F_{27}	Asterior sublingual	1	1	1	1	1	1
	F_{28}	Posterior sublingual	1	1	1	1	1	1
Body	F_{29}	Round/smooth scale	1	1	1	0	0	0
	F_{30}	Hood	1	0	0	0	0	0
	F_{31}	Spectacled mark on hood	1	0	0	0	0	0
	F_{32}	Keeled scale	0	0	0	1	1	1
	F_{33}	Spots on dorsal scale	0	0	0	1	1	1
	F_{34}	White/yellow stripes on dorsal scale	0	1	1	0	0	0
	F_{35}	Black stripes on ventral scale	0	1	0	0	0	0

Table 1 The table shows the grouping of the taxonomy features and its idealistic feature values for the creation of the database for automatic classification purpose *(Continued)*

F_{36}	Enlarged and Hexagonal vertebral scale	0	0	1	0	0	0
F_{37}	Ventral scale	1	1	1	1	1	1

If certain features are visible in the image, corresponding values are assigned else for every invisible or missing feature '0' is assigned.

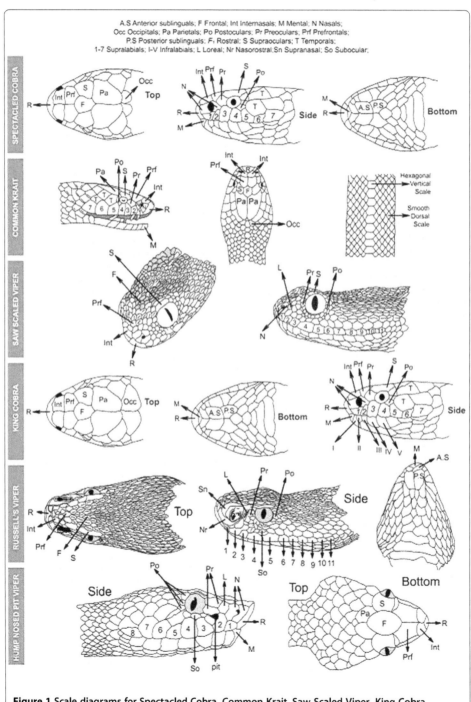

Figure 1 Scale diagrams for Spectacled Cobra, Common Krait, Saw Scaled Viper, King Cobra, Russell's viper and Hump Nosed Pit Viper observed at different natural view angles.

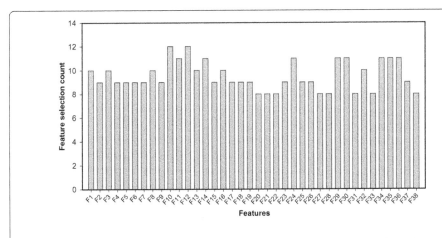

Figure 2 The histogram of the results from 12 Attribute Elevators in combination with certain search methods showing the top relevant features for classification.

measures in such situations indicates classifiers applicability in practice. In our study, we use 5% of the samples from each snake class for the training set, while remaining 95% is selected as test set. The classifier that performs the best in terms of performance measures can be selected as a possible candidate for implementation.

The research and work submitted do conform to the guidelines for care and use of animals in scientific research. We've followed the guidelines published by Indian National Science Academy. The Ethics committee of Enview R&D Labs gave approval for the research work.

Results and discussion

The feature database of the snakes is as explained in Table 1 and Figure 1 is used for analysing the classification performance of this six class classification problem. The feature database contains 38 features of each sample. Now using Table 2, we perform our further experiments for databases with different feature size. The samples in the databases are randomly split into 5% samples in training set and 95% in test set and performance evaluated on individual classifiers. The selection of features is performed on the training set. To ensure statistical correctness, the selection and testing is repeated 100 times, and the resulted reported in Table 3. The testing is done such that test and training set are non-overlapping in samples. Table 3 shows the comparisons of average performance measures of 38 feature size databases. The performances indicated are percentage accuracy of correct classification, F-score value, the area under the receiver operator characteristic curve, precision and recall rates. Table 3 shows the variation of performance measures with the increase in feature size i.e. the number of features in the feature-subset. As shown in Table 3, the correct classification accuracy increases considerably till feature size 15 which contain top 15 features of rank list in the database and tend to drop from feature size 31. This proves that these top 15 features are alone enough for the automated snake identification instead of 38 taxonomically relevant features.

Tables 4 and 5 shows the performance of the automatic snake classification using Bayes Net [37], Naive Bayes [27], Multilayer perception [26], Ada BoostM1 [28], Multi BoostAB [29], RBF network [30], IB1 [31], IBk [31], LWL [32], NB Tree [33], J48 [34],

Table 2 Ranking of all the 38 features based on the results from 12 attribute elevators with certain search method and the average classification score taken individually for all the features

Feature number	Number of times repeated	Classification - score
F_{12}	30	43.66 ± 1.51
F_{29}	28	57.02 ± 1.27
F_{35}	28	47.95 ± 1.11
F_{34}	28	47.59 ± 1.23
F_{10}	27	51.16 ± 2.59
F_{24}	27	46.46 ± 3.70
F_{30}	25	47.51 ± 1.47
F_{36}	25	39.92 ± 1.89
F_{32}	23	54.79 ± 1.28
F_{11}	22	36.80 ± 1.13
F_{16}	20	50.60 ± 1.50
F_{13}	20	44.73 ± 2.23
F_{14}	17	50.23 ± 1.46
F_{1}	16	36.82 ± 1.84
F_{8}	15	45.80 ± 2.05
F_{25}	15	45.77 ± 3.11
F_{37}	15	36.24 ± 1.96
F_{23}	14	45.56 ± 2.88
F_{26}	14	43.14 ± 1.92
F_{3}	14	36.47 ± 1.42
F_{15}	12	50.23 ± 1.61
F_{33}	12	41.16 ± 2.01
F_{38}	12	37.50 ± 1.46
F_{17}	11	48.50 ± 1.78
F_{9}	11	41.22 ± 1.61
F_{27}	11	39.67 ± 2.48
F_{22}	11	37.81 ± 3.47
F_{6}	11	36.42 ± 1.40
F_{19}	10	49.05 ± 1.67
F_{18}	10	48.46 ± 1.91
F_{20}	10	48.02 ± 1.86
F_{7}	10	44.97 ± 2.06
F_{31}	10	36.83 ± 0.98
F_{4}	10	36.30 ± 1.48
F_{2}	10	36.26 ± 2.14
F_{5}	10	36.21 ± 1.58
F_{21}	9	48.60 ± 1.63
F_{28}	9	41.26 ± 2.48

Random Sub Space [35], and Bagging [36] classification methods for top 15 selected snake feature database and 38 snake feature database respectively. The performances indicated are percentage accuracy of correct classification, F-score value, the Area under the receiver operator characteristic curve, precision and recall rates. The RBF

Table 3 Comparison of average classification result from 13 classifier in different feature size snake database with 5% train and 95% test of the total samples

Feature size	% Correct	F-score	AUC	Precision (%)	Recall (%)
1	43.69 ± 1.51	0.55 ± 0.00	0.55 ± 0.02	39 ± 0.02	95 ± 0.03
2	63.16 ± 1.83	0.81 ± 0.01	0.75 ± 0.02	64 ± 0.02	91 ± 0.03
3	72.41 ± 2.38	0.89 ± 0.01	0.84 ± 0.03	79 ± 0.03	92 ± 0.02
4	73.73 ± 3.01	0.93 ± 0.01	0.88 ± 0.03	86 ± 0.05	93 ± 0.01
5	75.23 ± 2.65	0.93 ± 0.01	0.88 ± 0.03	85 ± 0.05	93 ± 0.02
6	76.81 ± 2.83	0.94 ± 0.01	0.89 ± 0.03	85 ± 0.04	95 ± 0.02
7	77.21 ± 2.82	0.94 ± 0.01	0.89 ± 0.02	85 ± 0.03	94 ± 0.01
8	77.86 ± 2.84	0.94 ± 0.01	0.90 ± 0.03	86 ± 0.04	94 ± 0.01
9	77.89 ± 2.95	0.94 ± 0.02	0.89 ± 0.03	84 ± 0.05	96 ± 0.03
10	77.82 ± 2.96	0.94 ± 0.02	0.89 ± 0.03	84 ± 0.05	95 ± 0.03
11	77.65 ± 2.92	0.94 ± 0.02	0.89 ± 0.03	84 ± 0.05	91 ± 0.03
12	77.76 ± 3.03	0.94 ± 0.02	0.88 ± 0.03	84 ± 0.05	92 ± 0.03
13	78.05 ± 2.97	0.94 ± 0.02	0.88 ± 0.03	83 ± 0.05	93 ± 0.03
14	77.66 ± 2.95	0.94 ± 0.02	0.88 ± 0.03	83 ± 0.05	93 ± 0.03
15	78.80 ± 3.05	0.94 ± 0.02	0.89 ± 0.03	83 ± 0.05	95 ± 0.03
16	78.19 ± 3.14	0.94 ± 0.02	0.88 ± 0.03	83 ± 0.05	94 ± 0.04
17	78.31 ± 3.03	0.94 ± 0.02	0.88 ± 0.03	83 ± 0.05	94 ± 0.04
18	78.29 ± 3.06	0.94 ± 0.02	0.88 ± 0.03	83 ± 0.05	96 ± 0.04
19	78.05 ± 2.93	0.94 ± 0.02	0.88 ± 0.03	83 ± 0.05	96 ± 0.04
20	78.00 ± 2.94	0.94 ± 0.02	0.88 ± 0.03	83 ± 0.05	96 ± 0.04
21	78.44 ± 2.55	0.94 ± 0.02	0.88 ± 0.03	83 ± 0.05	96 ± 0.04
22	78.52 ± 2.74	0.94 ± 0.02	0.88 ± 0.03	83 ± 0.05	96 ± 0.04
23	78.61 ± 2.80	0.94 ± 0.02	0.88 ± 0.03	83 ± 0.05	96 ± 0.04
24	78.47 ± 2.79	0.94 ± 0.02	0.88 ± 0.03	82 ± 0.05	96 ± 0.04
25	78.41 ± 2.84	0.94 ± 0.02	0.88 ± 0.03	82 ± 0.05	95 ± 0.04
26	78.24 ± 2.85	0.94 ± 0.02	0.87 ± 0.03	82 ± 0.05	95 ± 0.04
27	78.10 ± 2.87	0.94 ± 0.02	0.87 ± 0.03	82 ± 0.05	95 ± 0.04
28	78.09 ± 2.89	0.94 ± 0.02	0.87 ± 0.03	82 ± 0.05	95 ± 0.04
29	78.03 ± 2.90	0.94 ± 0.02	0.87 ± 0.03	82 ± 0.05	95 ± 0.04
30	78.05 ± 2.89	0.94 ± 0.02	0.87 ± 0.03	82 ± 0.05	95 ± 0.04
31	77.99 ± 2.92	0.94 ± 0.02	0.87 ± 0.03	82 ± 0.05	95 ± 0.04
32	77.97 ± 2.92	0.94 ± 0.02	0.87 ± 0.03	82 ± 0.05	95 ± 0.04
33	77.96 ± 2.94	0.94 ± 0.02	0.87 ± 0.03	82 ± 0.05	95 ± 0.04
34	77.90 ± 2.91	0.94 ± 0.02	0.87 ± 0.03	82 ± 0.05	95 ± 0.04
35	77.83 ± 2.95	0.94 ± 0.02	0.87 ± 0.03	82 ± 0.05	95 ± 0.04
36	77.74 ± 2.99	0.93 ± 0.02	0.87 ± 0.03	82 ± 0.05	95 ± 0.04
37	77.67 ± 2.98	0.93 ± 0.02	0.87 ± 0.03	82 ± 0.05	94 ± 0.04
38	77.55 ± 2.96	0.93 ± 0.02	0.87 ± 0.03	82 ± 0.05	94 ± 0.04

network, IBk and IB1 classifiers showed higher classification performance as opposed other classifiers. The classification accuracy of above 85% in-dicates robustness of the taxonomically relevant features in the automatic classification process. Multilayer perception [26], RBF Network [30], IB1 [31], IBk [31], and J48 [34] shows good recognition

Table 4 Comparison of different classifiers when 5% of the class samples are used as gallery and remaining 95% of sample are used as test on top 15 selected snake feature database

Method	% Correct	F-score	AUC	Precision (%)	Recall (%)
Bayes net [37]	81.26 ± 4.00	0.98 ± 0.01	0.92 ± 0.03	88 ± 0.05	96 ± 0.04
Naïve Bayes [27]	81.64 ± 3.05	0.98 ± 0.01	0.93 ± 0.03	91 ± 0.04	96 ± 0.04
Multilayer perceptron [26]	86.64 ± 2.71	0.97 ± 0.01	0.92 ± 0.02	90 ± 0.04	95 ± 0.03
Ada BoostM1 [28]	57.52 ± 1.27	0.80 ± 0.03	0.75 ± 0.02	63 ± 0.04	95 ± 0.04
Multi BoostAB [29]	57.52 ± 1.27	0.80 ± 0.03	0.75 ± 0.02	63 ± 0.04	95 ± 0.04
RBF network [30]	88.75 ± 2.69	0.97 ± 0.02	0.94 ± 0.02	93 ± 0.04	96 ± 0.03
IB1 [31]	86.05 ± 3.35	0.93 ± 0.03	0.91 ± 0.04	89 ± 0.04	94 ± 0.07
IBk [31]	87.50 ± 2.35	0.95 ± 0.01	0.92 ± 0.02	88 ± 0.04	96 ± 0.03
LWL [32]	69.57 ± 4.17	0.97 ± 0.01	0.86 ± 0.04	77 ± 0.06	96 ± 0.03
J48 [33]	84.71 ± 2.90	0.95 ± 0.02	0.91 ± 0.03	87 ± 0.06	96 ± 0.03
Random sub space [34]	79.77 ± 4.01	0.98 ± 0.01	0.89 ± 0.03	82 ± 0.06	98 ± 0.02
Bagging [35]	81.34 ± 3.93	0.97 ± 0.02	0.90 ± 0.03	85 ± 0.06	96 ± 0.03
NB Tree [36]	82.10 ± 4.02	0.96 ± 0.02	0.91 ± 0.03	87 ± 0.05	96 ± 0.03

performance among the tested classifiers at 5% training data. While increasing the training dataset size to 30% the multilayer perception [26] classifier results in 94.31 ± 1.00% classification accuracy. The results indicate the difficulty of automatic classification of snakes, nonetheless, is indicative of the practical use in as a first line prediction of the snake classification. These early results opens up two major directions of research: (1) as to identify the taxonomy features of unknown snakes using feature automatic feature analysis and (2) to develop accurate feature classification and recognition methods for automatic snake. To use of real-time applications such as in diagnosis an ambitious 100% accuracy is preferred, which is by far a challenging problem posed through these results. In addition, the results on 5% training data, is likely to be more useful in real-time systems as in real applications the size of the test data keeps on

Table 5 Comparison of different classifiers when 5% of the class samples are used as gallery and remaining 95% of sample are used as test on 38 snake feature database

Method	% Correct	F-score	AUC	Precision (%)	Recall (%)
Bayes net [37]	78.81 ± 2.27	0.98 ± 0.01	0.89 ± 0.03	83 ± 0.07	97 ± 0.03
Naïve Bayes [27]	77.69 ± 2.11	0.97 ± 0.01	0.89 ± 0.02	90 ± 0.05	89 ± 0.03
Multilayer perceptron [26]	86.85 ± 2.59	0.98 ± 0.01	0.92 ± 0.02	90 ± 0.04	94 ± 0.04
Ada BoostM1 [28]	57.39 ± 1.44	0.80 ± 0.03	0.75 ± 0.02	62 ± 0.04	95 ± 0.05
Multi BoostAB [29]	57.39 ± 1.44	0.80 ± 0.03	0.75 ± 0.02	62 ± 0.04	95 ± 0.05
RBF network [30]	85.00 ± 3.05	0.95 ± 0.02	0.91 ± 0.03	92 ± 0.05	89 ± 0.04
IB1 [31]	85.82 ± 2.45	0.93 ± 0.02	0.91 ± 0.02	88 ± 0.04	93 ± 0.04
IBk [31]	86.38 ± 2.47	0.94 ± 0.01	0.91 ± 0.02	88 ± 0.04	94 ± 0.03
LWL [32]	68.37 ± 6.26	0.97 ± 0.01	0.82 ± 0.05	72 ± 0.07	96 ± 0.03
NB Tree [36]	83.79 ± 2.87	0.95 ± 0.02	0.91 ± 0.03	88 ± 0.05	95 ± 0.04
J48 [33]	78.92 ± 4.37	0.98 ± 0.01	0.87 ± 0.04	80 ± 0.06	97 ± 0.03
Random sub space [34]	80.50 ± 3.29	0.97 ± 0.02	0.90 ± 0.03	85 ± 0.06	96 ± 0.04
Bagging [35]	80.91 ± 4.48	0.94 ± 0.03	0.88 ± 0.04	83 ± 0.06	93 ± 0.04

growing at a rate higher than the training data, mainly because of the labor intensive processes involved in the preparation and validation of the training data.

Conclusion

In this paper, we presented an automatic snake identification problem by developing a taxonomy based feature targeted for use by the computer scientist and herpetologist. The feature-subset analysis indicated that only 15 features are sufficient for snake identification. In a real-life situation, the snake feature database reflects a situation when the bite victim has seen the snake, and based on the observed features it is required to identify the class of the snake. In addition to the venom detection research required for treating the bite victims, the proposed automatic snake recognition method could provide valuable information to administer correct medication and treatment in life threatening situation. Survey of snakes in wild is another major activity in the process to ensure the preservation of snake population and diversity. This is however a very challenging task and require prohibitive investments in manpower. The automatic classification using snake image database can be extended to the analysis of snake images captured remotely with minimal human intervention. The progress in snake taxonomy research is in the decline for the last 60 years, and has resulted in lack of expertise for environmental surveys and help required for medical practitioners in emergency situations. With a computerized analysis on the images of snakes using the proposed database and classification approach, we hope that more studies would come out to generate interest on this topic.

Additional files

Additional file 1: Snake Feature Database. http://www.hcis-journal.com/imedia/2229930941022190/supp1.doc.
Additional file 2: Supplementary info. http://www.hcis-journal.com/imedia/1032655649102219/supp2.xls.

Competing interests
We declare that there are no competing interests.

Authors' contributions
AJ carried out the problem formulation, algorithm development and drafted the manuscript. BM organized the dataset and performed the feature analysis. SS helped in the implementation of algorithm. DR collected the original snake images. All authors read and approved the final manuscript.

Acknowledgements
The authors thank the snake catchers in Trivandrum for the assistance with the creation of the database. The assistance of Balaji Balasubramaniam (TRDDC) and Anaswara Krishnan (Department of Zoology, Kerala University) is also acknowledged. Dileep Kumar R would like to acknowledge the support of Prof Ommen V Ommen for the encouragement and support for this research.

Author details
[1]School of Engineering, Nazarbayev University, Astana, Kazakhstan. [2]Enview R&D Labs, Thiruvananthapuram, India. [3]Department of Computational Biology and Bioinformatics, University of Kerala, Trivandrum, India.

References
1. Smith MA (1981) Reptilia and Amphibia, vol 3, Serpentes. Today & Tomorrow's Printers & Publishers, India
2. Whitaker R, Captain A, Ahmed F (2004) Snakes of India: the field guide. Draco Books, Chengalpattu
3. Mattison C (1999) Snake. Dorling Kindersley, New York,USA
4. Firth SMJWJR (2002) Snake. Scholastic, India
5. Weidensaul S (1996) Snakes of the World. Grange Books Ltd, Chartwell House, London
6. Mertens T (1995) Deadly & Dangerous Snakes. Magic Bean. Era Publications, Flinders Park, South Australia
7. Backshall S (2007) Venomous Animals of the World. Johns Hopkins University Press, Maryland, USA

8.   Stevens D (2011) The Big Four Snakes: The Indian Cobra, the Common Krait, the Russell's Viper, and the Saw-Scaled Viper. Webster's Digital Services, USA
9.   Premawardhena A, De Silva C, Fonseka M, Gunatilake S, De Silva H (1999) Low dose subcutaneous adrenaline to prevent acute adverse reactions to antivenom serum in people bitten by snakes: randomised, placebo controlled trial. BMJ: Brit Med J 318(7190):1041
10. Warrell DA (1999) The clinical management of snake bites in the Southeast Asian region. Southeast Asian J Trop Med Public Health 1(Suppl 1):1–89
11. Calvete JJ, Ju'arez P, Sanz L (2007) Snake venomics. Strategy and applications. J Mass Spectrom 42(11):1405–1414
12. Sorower MS, Yeasin M (2007) Robust Classification of Dialog Acts from the Transcription of Utterances. In ICSC 2007. IEEE International Conference on Semantic Computing, 3-10
13. Chanda P, Cho YR, Zhang A, Ramanathan M (2009) Mining of attribute interactions using information theoretic metrics. In: Data mining workshops, ICDMW'09. IEEE International Conference on Data Mining, Florida, USA, pp 350–355
14. Devi MI, Rajaram R, Selvakuberan K (2008) Generating best features for web page classification. Webology 5., http://www.webology.org/2008/v5n1/a52.html
15. Marquez-Vera C, Romero C (2011) Ventura S: Predicting school failure using data mining. In Proceedings of the 4th International Conference on Educational Data Mining 271–276
16. John GH, Kohavi R, Pfleger K (1994) Irrelevant features and the subset selection problem. In Proceedings of the eleventh international conference on machine learning, Volume 129, San Francisco 121–129
17. Jensen R, Shen Q (2007) Fuzzy-rough sets assisted attribute selection. Fuzzy Systems, IEEE Transactions on 15:73–89
18. Meng YX (2011) The practice on using machine learning for network anomaly intrusion detection. In IEEE International Conference on Machine Learning and Cybernetics (ICMLC), 2011, Vol. 2, 576-581
19. Indra Devi M, Rajaram R, Selvakuberan K (2007) Automatic web page classification by combining feature selection techniques and lazy learners. In conference on computational intelligence and multimedia applications, 2007. Int Conference on 2:33–37
20. Koonsanit K, Jaruskulchai C (2011) Band selection for hyperspectral image using principal components anal-ysis and maxima-minima functional. In: Knowledge, Information, and Creativity Support Systems. Thailand, Springer, pp 103–112
21. Frank E, Hall M, Holmes G, Kirkby R, Pfahringer B, Witten IH, Trigg L (2005) Weka. In: Data Mining and Knowledge Discovery Handbook. Springer, USA, pp 1305–1314
22. Hall M, Frank E, Holmes G, Pfahringer B, Reutemann P, Witten IH (2009) The WEKA data mining software: an update. ACM SIGKDD Explorations Newsletter 11:10–18
23. James AP, Dimitrijev S (2012) Ranked selection of nearest discriminating features. Hum-centric Comput Inform Sci 2:12
24. Milacic M, James AP, Dimitrijev S (2013) Biologically inspired features used for robust phoneme recognition. International Journal of Machine Intelligence and Sensory Signal Processing 1(1):46–54
25. James AP, Maan AK (2011) Improving feature selection algorithms using normalised feature histograms. Electron Lett 47(8):490–491
26. Longstaff ID, Cross JF (1987) A pattern recognition approach to understanding the multi-layer perception. Pattern Recogn Lett 5(5):315–319
27. Kim SB, Han KS, Rim HC, Myaeng SH (2006) Some effective techniques for naive bayes text classification. Knowledge and Data Engineering, IEEE Transactions on 18(11):1457–1466
28. Freund Y, Schapire RE (1995) A desicion-theoretic generalization of on-line learning and an application to boosting. In Computational learning theory, Springer 23–37
29. Benbouzid D, Busa-Fekete R, Casagrande N, Collin FD, Kégl B (2012) MultiBoost: a multi-purpose boosting package. J Mach Learn Res 13:549–553
30. Buhmann MD (2003) Radial basis functions: theory and implementations, Volume 12. Cambridge university press
31. Aha DW, Kibler D, Albert MK (1991) Instance-based learning algorithms. Machine learning, Boston,USA, pp 37–66, 6
32. Atkeson CG, Moore AW, Schaal S (1997) Locally weighted learning for control. Artif Intell Rev 11(1–5):75–113
33. Kohavi R (2001) Bayes rule based and decision tree hybrid classifier. [US Patent 6,182,058]
34. Kotsiantis SB, Zaharakis ID, Pintelas PE (2006) Machine learning: a review of classification and combining techniques. Artif Intell Rev 26(3):159–190
35. Ho TK (1998) The random subspace method for constructing decision forests. Pattern Anal Mach Intel, IEEE Transactions on 20(8):832–844
36. Breiman L (1996) Bagging predictors. Mach Learn 24(2):123–140
37. Singhal A, Brown C (1997) Dynamic Bayes net approach to multimodal sensor fusion. In Proceedings of the SPIE-The International Society for Optical Engineering, Volume 3209, 2–10

8

The art of software systems development: Reliability, Availability, Maintainability, Performance (RAMP)

Mohammad Isam Malkawi

Correspondence:
mmalkawi@aimws.com
Jordan University of Science and
Technology, Irbid 21410, Jordan

Abstract

The production of software systems with specific demand on reliability, availability, maintenance, and performance (RAMP) is one of the greatest challenges facing software engineers at all levels of the development cycle. Most requirements specification tools are more suited for functional requirements than for non-functional RAMP requirements. RAMP requirements are left unspecified, specified at a later stage, or at best vaguely specified, which makes requirements specifications more of an art than a science. Furthermore, the cost of testing for RAMP requirements is quite often prohibitive. In many cases, it is difficult to test for some of the RAMP specifications such as maintainability, reliability, and high availability. Even the test for performance is quite often workload dependent and as such the performance numbers provided at test time or at system commissioning time may not be achievable during actual system workload. What makes the subject matter more difficult is the absence of a clear set of rules or practices, which, if followed closely, produce a system with acceptable RAMP specifications. As such, and until the design of RAMP software systems becomes a well understood theme, the development of such systems will be a fine art, where the tools and capabilities of developing such systems will depend on the particular system to be developed, the environment in which it will run, and the level of expertise and knowledge deployed. Just like no two pieces of art produced by the same artist are the same, no two software systems will have the same RAMP characteristics.

This paper will focus on the paradigms involved in the production of RAMP software systems through several case studies. The purpose is to promote the interest of researchers to develop more specific guidelines for the production of SW systems with well defined RAMP qualities.

Introduction

The production of software systems with specific demand on reliability, availability, maintenance, and performance (RAMP) is one of the greatest challenges facing software engineers at all levels of the development cycle. Most requirements specification tools, e.g., Accent, Nu Thena, SES, Rational, are more suited for functional requirements than for non-functional RAMP requirements [1-5]. RAMP requirements are left unspecified, specified at a later stage, or at best vaguely specified, which makes requirements specifications more of an art than a science [6-8]. Furthermore, the cost of testing for RAMP requirements is quite often prohibitive. In many cases, it is difficult to test for some of the RAMP specifications such as maintainability, reliability and high availability. Even the test for performance is quite often workload dependent and as such the performance numbers provided at test time or at system commissioning time may not be achievable during actual system workload. What makes the subject matter more difficult is the absence of a clear set of rules or practices which, if followed closely, produce a system with acceptable RAMP specifications. As such, and until the design of RAMP software systems becomes a well understood theme, the development of such systems will be a fine art, where the tools and capabilities of developing such systems will depend on the particular system to be developed, the environment in which it will run, and the level of expertise and knowledge deployed [8]. Just like no two pieces of art produced by the same artist are the same, no two software systems will have the same RAMP characteristics. Software system design and development is by and large more complex than the programming phase of it, which was perceived as an art by Donald Knuth in his classic book "The Art of Computer Programming" [9].

There has been quite a bit of argument in the literature on what constitutes an art or a science in the software production cycle. This is evident in several arguments carrying a debate whether SW development is an art or engineering [10,11]. In a post on the internet titled "Software Development: Art or Science", Sammy Larbi from the University of Houston writes: "There is a seemingly never-ending debate (or perhaps unconnected conversation and misunderstandings) on whether or not the software profession is science or art, or specifically whether "doing software" is in fact an engineering discipline [12,13]".

In an article titled "The Art, Science, and Engineering of Software Development" [14], Steve McConnell argues that SW development is art, science, craft, and many other things.

Naveen Gunti [15] examines the benefits of using function point analysis in the context of the art of SW engineering. Robert Glass in his book "Software Conflict 2: The Art and Science of SW Development" agrees with earlier findings that SW design is a model that emerges in the human mind [16] similar to how a piece of art emerges in the mind of an artist. Jim Waldo, a distinguished engineer at SUN Microsystems [17] writes "Software engineering is a lot less like other kinds of engineering than most of us would like to think. There is an aspect of art to what we do, that is learned not in school but by finding a master and serving an apprenticeship".

The purpose of this paper is not to argue whether SW development is an art or science, or what is a science or an art in the cycle of SW development. Rather, this paper will focus on the paradigms involved in the production of RAMP software systems through several case studies. The purpose is to promote the interest of researchers to develop more specific guidelines for the production of SW systems with well defined RAMP qualities. The performance paradigm section, we will discuss the performance paradigm as one of the main pieces of software design. The reliability paradigm section will present the reliability and availability paradigms. Maintainability issues will be discussed in section Discussion. Section Conclusion will address the necessity for the development of guidelines and best practices for RAMP software system development, where a general framework for RAM is proposed. Concluding remarks are discussed in Discussion section.

The performance paradigm

My most recent encounter with a performance paradigm was related to the modeling of water flow in cases of flood, tsunami, cyclones, river floods and similar cases. Simulating 72 hours of water flow in some cases requires more than 12 hours of execution on a mid size server. Is there a need to enhance the performance of the software? What should the performance requirements be? And how to achieve the required performance in a cost effective manner? Another case, involved a software tool used to mitigate intermodulation interference problems in telecommunication systems. In some cases, the SW tool would run for several hours, overflow the disk space with data, and cause the system to crash. Should the performance of the tool be improved? What are the performance requirements, how to achieve them in a cost effective manner? A more interesting question would target the limits of performance, which can be achieved on the system! Yet, one more example, involving the modeling and simulation of the evacuation of large facilities in case of natural or human inflected disasters. The simulation time can run for several hours for a given scenario. How much improvement is required, if any?

When performance requirements are analyzed independently from the concept of productivity [18], the above scenarios may not warrant a performance improvement. In the above examples, it is often required to repeat the study with different parameters and scenarios. An optimal solution in most cases is a must due to the safety and security nature of the studies. Repeating the experiments for several hours each time can be a frustrating practice for the engineer, which may lead to the introduction of approximation techniques or compromising optimality. Besides, the longer the process runs on the system, the more likely it will experience faults and errors during the execution process [19-21]. In the case of the interference analysis SW tool, one engineer explains: "If I can run the SW in less than one hour, I can generate more studies per day. I can make more money. Each study costs $2000.00".

Once we get to the point where a performance enhancement is needed, then we have to answer the following questions: "How much improvement are we looking for"? This (requirement) question has to be answered by the end user of the SW system. What is the limit of performance improvement? This (specification) question has to be answered by SW engineers, who should take into consideration the economics of the hardware settings. But the most difficult (architecture) question is: "How do you achieve the performance gains". Figure 1 shows a general framework for performance improvement. Details of the framework will be further discussed through the following study cases.

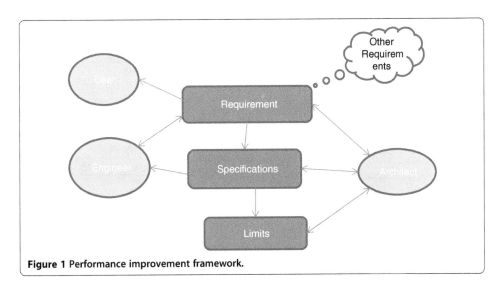

Figure 1 Performance improvement framework.

Case 1: initialization problem

Failure recovery is one of the important factors related to availability. Failure recovery in-volves the recovery mode, the time to recover and the recovery success rate. One of the recovery modes, after a complete system failure, is the restart of the failed system and/or the applications on the same system. In order to achieve a certain level of availability (5 NINES for example) [22-26], the system must be restarted (reboot, initialize, restore checkpoints) within a certain time constraint. The minimum acceptable recovery time is determined using technique such as Markov process analysis [27] or stochastic activity network simulation [28]. This is a case where the **performance requirement** is deter-mined based on another higher level requirement, e.g., availability requirement.

In the course of analysis, the recovery time is further decomposed into subtasks based on the time consumed by each subtask. Performance budgeting is then used to estimate the potential enhancement of each subtask, if possible at all. Performance budget, in this context, defines the limits of performance improvement. Some of the subtasks that con-sume most of the budgeted time, in our example, include the boot image loading time, the kernel initialization time, and the payload components initialization time. It is essential to determine if any of the sub-tasks can be skipped in order to save time and speed up the process of initialization. For example, memory tests can be skipped at initialization time only to be performed later, when the system is not too busy. Also, the initialization of some payload components may be deferred until the system is completely recovered.

In our example, we draw the attention on the loading time of the boot image of the device; assuming that the boot image does not reside on the device, as is the case in wireless infrastructure devices. When evaluating the boot image load time using ftp protocols, it was noticed that the speed of ftp load depends on the file size as well as on the number of concurrent ftp load sessions. We evaluated two versions of the ftp protocol. We measured the load time for different file sizes and different parallel loads. Figure 2 shows that the load time is minimal when using version 2 of the ftp load protocol with 11.6 MB file size. The best results can be achieved when 4 download ses-sions are performed in parallel. We observed that increasing the number of open ftp sessions beyond 4 will increase the overall loading time. This is an example, where per-formance improvement requires careful selection of protocols and parameter setting.

The initialization example reveals several important points.

1. The dependence of performance requirement on other requirements (see Figure 1) such as availability and reliability. In this case, the recovery time (a performance parameter) depends on the recovery time, in the availability model.

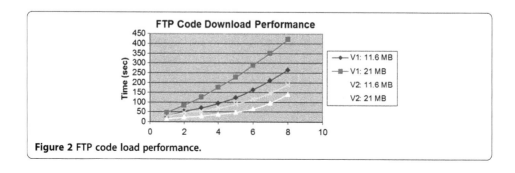

Figure 2 FTP code load performance.

2. The impact of parameter configuration, environment settings, and tuning on performance. The setting and configuration of parameters require expertise in experimentation, data collection, and analysis. The complexity of parameter setting and tuning can be very large; therefore, selection of the proper parameters and setting the proper values remain an act of art unless extensive experiments are used to validate the selected parameters and their values.

3. Setting a parameter may produce counter intuitive results. For example, increasing the number of parallel downloads results in longer download times rather than shorter one. Another example is priority inversion of threads, where a starvation or deadlock may occur when priority inversion is actually used to prevent starvation or deadlock.

Case 2: the interference sort and search problem

This case deals with the problem of intermodulation interference in telecommunications network systems. Intermodulation interference occurs due to the mixture of radio frequency (RF) signals in nonlinear devices. The resulting new RF combinations can be very large. For a total of (n) RF signals, the Kth order intermodulation produces a total of (n^k) combinations. Only a subset of the (n^k) combinations may interfere with other signals at receiving devices. In order to resolve or prevent interference, it is essential to search for those combinations which may cause interference. The complexity of the search grows exponentially with the growth of the number of original signals [29].

This is an example with several facets of art and design. Radio frequency engineers require a SW that can solve the interference problem in relatively short time. The SW should be robust enough not to overload the memory or the disk space. The SW should also be able to adapt easily to new sources of data with different data formats as well as to different technologies (e.g., CDMA, GSM, WiFi, WiMax, LTE).

Note that none of the requirements is defined in a clear quantitative manner. For example, RF engineers will not come clearly and say that we need a system that performs 2nd or 3rd order intermodulation for (N) signals in less than (X) seconds. Ironically, the telecomm industry until today states the requirement for completing an intermodulation interference analysis for a given site in days (typically 48 hours) rather than minutes or seconds. This is due to the complexity of the analysis which includes sorting and searching billions of elements in large files. It is also due to the lack of well defined strategy for defining the performance requirement of such system. Industry, however, acknowledges the need to address interference analysis in a timelier manner [30-32]. To illustrate the complexity of the issue, consider the following example.

Consider 2nd order intermodulation with 5 signals (S_1, S_2, S_3, S_4, S_5). One potential list of intermodulation combinations would be the sum of any two signals (S_1+ S_2, S_1+ S_3, S_1+ S_4, S_1+ S_5, S_2+ S_3, S_2+ S_4, S_2+ S_5, S_3 + S_4, S_3+ S_5, S_4+ S_5). It is required to find all signals (S_i + S_j) that are larger than a given signal (S_g). When the number of combinations (S_i + S_j) is relatively small, we can sort this list (using a quick sort algorithm for example) and use a fast search algorithm, e.g., binary search, and locate the desired signals. This is a typical SW engineering practice well known by any engineer in the field. However, when the number of original signals is relatively large, say 10,000 and the intermodulation order is 3 instead of 2, then we have to deal with 10^{12} permutations. This is too large of a number to deal with, which could easily cause the paging algorithm to thrash, and the time to sort and search to be in the order of hours rather than minutes.

This is a good example to illustrate how the art of SW engineering can help reduce the time complexity of the algorithms. Instead of looking at the combinations above as a linear array, let's view them as a lower half of a matrix as in Table 1 below. Only the original signals (Si) need to be sorted (Sort N signals instead of sorting N^2 signals).

Note that, if $(S2 + S3) > S_g$ in the third column, then all elements following $(S2 + S3)$ in this column and in the following columns will also be larger than S_g. Similarly, if $(S1 + S4) > S_g$, then all the elements in the second column following $S1 + S4$ will be larger than S_g. Note that this representation of the data provides a sorted view of each of the columns. Search within each column can be as fast as a binary search. The solution provided for this problem is more of an art than simply SW engineering. In this case, it is the presentation layout of the data that leads to a productive solution. The complexity of algorithms developed using this representation is 2 orders of magnitude better than those with classical view of the data [30].

The intermodulation complexity problem reveals that the limit of performance improvement depends on the method of data presentation. This is especially true for big data processing. For each problem, the optimal data presentation must be identified by the system architect, who can then determine the limits of achievable performance.

Case 3: data mining and management

This case deals with large data manipulation and maintenance. Consider the following problem in telecomm data management systems. In a typical service provider network several switches control a certain segments of the network. Each switch controls several cell sites. One of the functions of a switch is to collect performance and radio frequency service measurement data related to the network segment (RFSM) as well as per call management data (PCMD) [33]. RFSM and PCMD Data are released by the switch at a certain time, e.g., on top of the hour. The amount of data released per hour can be very large depending on the number of cells in the territory of the switch and activity of the network. The data released per unit time can be in the order of gigabytes per hour. Moreover, the data released by the switch changes in format, type, and structure every time a new switch version is released. This change calls for a change in the code responsible for parsing and loading the data as well as in the schema of the database which hosts the RFSM and PCMD data. The switch experiences major release changes several times a year; in some cases it can be 4 releases per year. During the transition from one release to another and the subsequent code modification, the data management system could become unavailable for an unidentified time (depending on the success and duration of system upgrade). The cost of maintenance is non-

Table 1 Data representation for intermodulation problem

Signal	S1 + Sj (J = 2..5)	S2 + Sj (J = 3..5)	S3 + Sj (J = 4..5)	S4 + Sj (J = 5..5)
S1				
S2	S1 + S2			
S3	S1 + S3	S2 + S3		
S4	S1 + S4	S2 + S4	S3 + S4	
S5	S1 + S5	S2 + S5	S3 + S5	S4 + S5

trivial in terms of money and the period in which the system remains either unstable or unavailable.

Another issue related to performance is the time required to perform queries or to generate reports. Obviously, query and report generation performance depends on the size of the DB, the schema structure, and the organization/distribution of data within and across the tables. The well known rules of DB performance tuning can achieve limited performance improvement. The data is too large and diverse, which makes the process of data analysis difficult and time consuming. Finally, the reliability of the host servers has a direct impact on the reliability of the system at large. Hosting all the data in one DB and on one server is the least reliable and has the highest performance hit. Hosting each switch on its own separate DB and then on its own server is the most reliable, with best performance and highest cost.

What matters to the user at the end is how soon would data be available for him to query and browse, and how fast he can generate reports when they are requested by a manager?

In a complex system like the one described above, there is no single set of rules that can be specified, and if followed closely, the required performance will be achieved. And that is where the art of system architecture plays a great role. The proposed architecture of the system is shown in Figure 3. The figure appears as a piece of art whose components are squares, rectangles, circles, and arrows. Each of these components contributes to the overall system performance, reliability and availability.

The art begins with the selection of data transfer mechanism and application, e.g., ssh (secure shell file transfer), sshfs (secure shell to share files [34], ftp, ODBC (open database connectivity) or others. In the selection process, one needs to consider the tradeoffs of security, performance and reliability.

Another key performance parameter is the speed at which we can parse the raw data, prepare if for the loader, and load the data into DB tables. If this process fails to complete in less than (x) minutes, then the query and report performance will lag behind. Parsing and loading design requires the selection among languages, loading mechanisms, file structures, and inter-communication with the DB servers. For

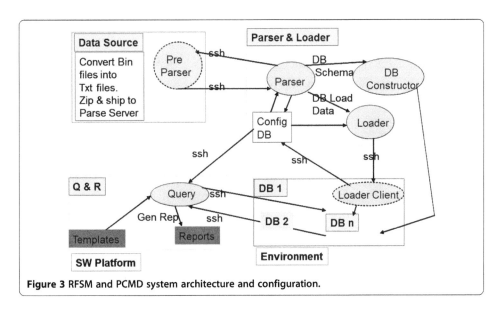

Figure 3 RFSM and PCMD system architecture and configuration.

example, Perl scripting language allows parsing very complicated text structures more efficiently than other languages such as C# or VB. However, loading the parsed and structured files into the DB is faster and more efficient using C#.

At the database level, we have to worry about how fast we load data into the DB and how fast we pull data out. The raw data as it comes from the source lends itself to large tables with millions of records and thousands of fields. Key to high performance is the ability to partition the tables in a meaningful manner. The irony is that there is no clear definition for what would be a meaningful manner. What we can say in general, is that larger number of tables allows for more parallel loads of tables into the DB. Also, smaller table sizes mean faster query and report generation. Too many tables, on the other hand, may slow down the queries and reports if they happen to scan large number of tables. A DB designer would like to store homogenous data (data commonly requested in a given report or query) in the same table; this design improves the data locality structure and leads to faster access of data, although it puts more burden on the parser and loader. In a relatively small DB system, this is easily done by investigating the semantics of the data. In systems like the one described in this example, this task is next to impossible.

Here comes the art part of the DB design. We can watch and monitor the access patterns of the DB, and overtime we learn which data fields are commonly retrieved in a given query or report. Based on access pattern recognition, we build intelligence into the mechanism responsible for partitioning the data. Table partitioning, and data migration between tables can be implemented in a mechanism, we call, the DB Constructor. Using this mechanism, the database is no longer a static repository structure. The DB schema changes over time, and the data migrates between tables. The more we access the DB, the better it performs. This phenomenon is exactly opposite to the well known SW aging phenomenon, where SW performance and reliability falls down with age.

The RFSM and PCMD case reveals the following important factors related to performance

1. Data partitioning has significant impact on performance. In large systems, it is very difficult to find an optimal partition. Adaptive learning algorithms can be used to find an optimal data partition.
2. Tools and languages must be carefully selected, observing that each subtask may require tools different from those used for other tasks.
3. Intercommunication between various modules is a major performance bottleneck. Proper intercommunications solutions allow for better performance optimization.

The reliability paradigm

SW reliability continues to be a major reliability bottleneck in large and complex systems. Compared to HW reliability, SW systems are more difficult to design for reliability, more difficult to test, and could constitute a safety and economic hazardous. A 2002 study commissioned by the National Institute of Standards and Technology found software bugs cost the U.S. economy about $59.5 billion annually [35]. More recently, a study conducted by Cambridge University researchers estimates the total annual cost at $312 worldwide [36]. SW failures have contributed to major system failures in the past few years including the August 14, 2003 Blackout of Northeast Power Grid [37], Mars Climate Orbiter (September 23rd, 1999) [38], USS Yorktown (1998), Ariane 5 rocket explosion (1996) and many others [39]. Although, the SW industry has become more experienced in measuring and testing for reliability, we are still far behind in issues related to the design of highly reliable SW systems.

Problems like memory leak, memory corruption, memory overflow, deadlock and others have been known for quite a long time. Today, most SW systems still contain scores of bugs related to these problems. In a study, recently conducted on a large and complex SW system, where data was tracked for several years, it was observed that the system overall reliability does not improve over time. Figure 4 shows 3 releases of a system observed over 10 years time period. Note that the time it takes to stabilize the system (stability period) increases in the second and third releases. Also, the rate of defects per month goes up. It is true that the system also grows in size and complexity, but the expectation is that with time, the knowledge and expertise will also grow. This phenomenon is generally observed in many complex SW systems.

One of the main challenges in SW reliability is stress and accelerated life testing. For hardware, this is a well known procedure. For SW, there is no unified method on what would constitute a stress or accelerated test [40]. The choice of tools, methods, coverage, confidence levels, and ways of interpreting results remain an art for most of SW engineers.

In many cases, reliability depends on performance. For example, a fault not detected within (x seconds) may propagate and cause the system to be unstable. This was the case in the Arian 5 explosion (1995) [39], where the SW system failed to convert a 64-bit floating number into a 16-bit integer. The fault was detected, but only after the error has propagated and a command to shut down the system was issued; the rocket exploded shortly after.

Measuring SW reliability is by and large harder than that of hardware reliability. When a piece of HW is delivered out of the factory, the expected lifetime of that piece is known with a good degree of certainty. Stress testing and accelerated life testing methods have been used successfully for a long time. When it comes to SW reliability, the problem is much harder. The complexity of the problem stems sequence from the fact that the input data to a given SW is time and conditions variant. Different methods have been used to measure SW reliability. Among these methods are code coverage tools, number of code lines, and number of defects/bugs found in a given number of lines [41].

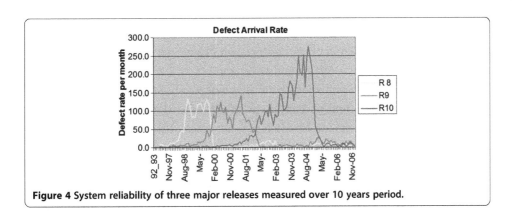

Figure 4 System reliability of three major releases measured over 10 years period.

Commenting on the number of code lines as a measure of reliability, Bill Gates says that "measuring programming progress by lines of code is like measuring aircraft building progress by weight". The number of defects/bugs found in a SW system during testing is a measure of how unreliable the system was before debugging and testing. The remaining bugs/defects in the system can turn to be a major cause of outage or safety hazard (e.g. the failure of patriot missile to track down an incoming scud missile due to arithmetic rounding errors [42]. Code coverage tools produce as good of a reliability measure as the covered code in a given test.

The artistic part of reliability measurement lies in the design of the various tests and procedures to stress the system and find out all possible errors, bugs and defects. For example, when a function erroneously deletes a pointer, resulting in a memory leak, and the function is never called at testing time, the leak will persist in the SW system. The lack of robust testing likely contributed to the radio system outage over the skies of parts of California, Nevada and Arizona. The system failed to failover to a backup server during a data overload failure scenario [43,44]. Testing did not cover this scenario.

Consider the following example which shows the limitation of stress accelerated testing. A truncation error in a 24-bit fixed point arithmetic can be as small as 0.000000000000000000000001 (decimal 0.00000009). If we were to represent 1/10 of a second using this arithmetic, then the truncation error can grow to 0.3 seconds after 100 hours of operation. Obviously, the error will not be detected if the accelerated test was run for less than 100 hours. Depending on what application the SW will be used in, the error can be either detected (after 100 hours of runtime) or remains hidden (if the application terminates in less than 100 hours).

The main problem which reliability engineers have to resolve is the design of the proper tests which reveal the majority of unreliable parts of the system they are designing. There is no set of well defined rules to follow. The variable space, which includes the input space, the failure modes, and applications, can be infinitely large.

In order to reduce the subjectivity of SW reliability testing and measurement, it is highly recommended to make use of well kept dictionaries and databases of failure modes and scenarios. One method, which can be used in this regard is the failure scenario analysis (FSA) [45]. FSA is recommended as a guide for continued reliability improvement. Failure modes are described both qualitatively and quantitatively. For example, for a given failure mode, there should be a description of the methods used to detect, isolate, contain and recover the failure. Also, there should be a specification of the time required to detect, isolate, contain and recover the failure. The times have to be carefully specified for each different application. The dictionary of the failure modes should be maintained during development, testing, and deployment.

Measuring the availability of a SW system is yet another challenge and piece of art. The availability of a system depends mostly on how fast it can be recovered after experiencing a failure mode as well as how frequently it fails. Most of the availability numbers used by various vendors are based on real-time measurement of availability of systems in the field. However, it is very difficult to provide an accurate measure of availability of a system when it is ready to be deployed. Different modeling and analysis techniques exist for availability measurement including analytical methods and simulation methods [27,28]. It is not uncommon to hear the phrase "there is no good availability model; but there is a valid one". In my experience as a SW reliability engineer, I have not seen anything more art oriented than availability modeling.

As an example, consider the models in Figure 5. Figure 5a shows a model where the system failure is represented by one failure rate which will be the sum of the failure rate of all components. Figure 5b shows a more detailed failure and recovery behavior for each failure mode. The system fails at different rates, has different recovery mechanism for each failure mode and different recovery success rate (ρ). Figure 5b can also represent the case, where failure modes can be categorized into categories and each category represents a group of failures with similar failure and recovery behavior. All three models are correct representation of the system. Which is a better model, though, depends on how much details are available about the system and how close the system availability needs to be monitored.

Art of budgeting for availability

Availability is quite often measured in downtime minutes, outage duration and frequency. A FIVE nine availability system allows for 5.24 minutes downtime per year. The distribution of these 5.24 minutes among various system components is not always a straightforward matter. Quite often the distribution of downtime minutes needs to be negotiated among the owners of system components. More interesting even is how the system gets partitioned into components or subsystems. The broadest partitioning is the typical hardware/software partitions. Such partition makes it very difficult to design for the proper recovery when a failure occurs. More detailed partitioning, however, makes it very difficult to achieve the required availability or outage requirement. An

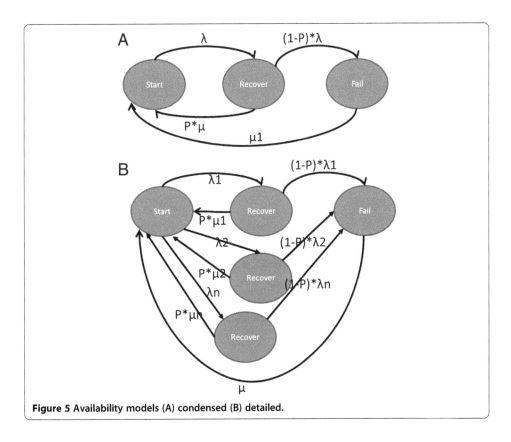

Figure 5 Availability models (A) condensed (B) detailed.

optimal distribution of outage time among the various hardware and software components is a fine art orchestrated by expert system architects.

Take for example, the system depicted in Figure 3. One way of distributing outage time is to evenly distribute it among the four subsystems. This is easy and straightforward. However, this distribution places a great burden on the DB environment where the number of transactions executed per unit time is very high. In this system, we have built N load sharing DB servers with auto failover, where a DB server can failover to the least loaded server. This implementation allowed more downtime to be allocated to the secure shell (ssh) communication, which turns out to be the least reliable in the system.

Art of design for reliability and availability

The greatest question of all remains "how to design and implement a reliable and highly available software system?" Is there a way to develop a system without memory leak, without memory corruption, without address space violation, without buffer overflow, without timing and synchronization errors, without data format translation errors, and the list goes on and on? Can we design a system where an error can be detected before it generates a serious failure and possibly a catastrophe like the explosion of a rocket or air flight control mishaps? Can we eliminate interface errors when two or SW modules are linked to form a more complex system? How much education, training, code inspection, debugging, and testing are needed before a SW can be certified for reliability and availability? The best answer to any of these questions is "we will try our best".

The most reliable SW development continues to be an art which involves several instruments. Such instruments include the selection of personnel skills (both development and management), the selection of development tools (including language, development environment), the selection of code coverage tools and code coverage strategies, the selection of code inspection tools and methods, the setting of the testing environment (including test suites, benchmarks, testing time), as well as the careful selection of third party SW components. The combination of selected instruments at a given SW production house dictates the level of SW reliability and availability.

In essence, reliability and availability is not a single task or product. Rather, it is a set of availability work products [23] as shown in Figure 6. Once implemented, the AWP can deliver a robust, reliable, and highly available system.

Discussion

The study cases discussed in this paper show how difficult it is to satisfy various RAMP requirements. Each and every software system has its own characteristics which are different from others. The process of achieving RAMP requirements remains an art that engineers and architects need to possess. The expertise of several engineers and architects may have to be integrated. In order for this art to be more effective and controllable, a peformability framework, which combines the four non-functional requirements (performance, reliability, availability, and maintainability), is proposed and shown in Table 2.

The reliability requirement, for example, has specific performance requirements such as failure rate (λ), fault detection time, fault isolation time, and fault containment time. These parameters must be defined in order to achieve a certain level of reliability. Similarly, availability can only be achieved if availability parameters meet

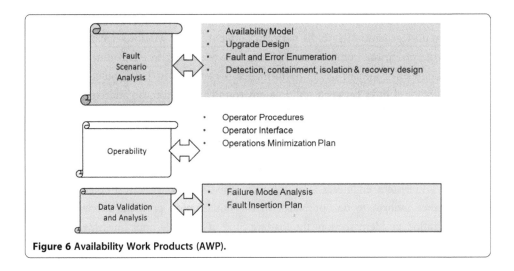

Figure 6 Availability Work Products (AWP).

certain performance requirements, e.g., the time to recover from a failure and the rate of successful recovery from failures (ρ). Also, specific performance requirements (throughput, speed/speedup, and bandwidth) need to be defined in terms of reliability, availability, and maintenance parameters. For example, the throughput of a wireless system can be obtained only under specific packet loss rate. The system speedup, when multiple units are used, can only be defined in terms of the redundancy mode; for example, M out of N load sharing mode sets the maximum speedup to M, although the system has N > M units.

The performability framework also defines the interaction between various stakeholders of the system under consideration. The example of InterMod60 is a clear example where the restructuring of the intermodulation algorithms required the knowledge of RF and software engineers.

Another example is the use of asynchronous versus synchronous processes. In the example used in section case 3: data mining and management (Figure 3), the use of asynchronous processes was the proper solution for achieving the required availability. The use of time-synchronized processes would have been the preferred choice for achieving higher throughput. The skills and expertise of the architects had to be carefully deployed to decide which of the techniques is more useful. Same applies to the selection of the language and the run-time environment. In the example used in this study (Figure 3), it turns

Table 2 Performability framework

	Reliability	Availability	Maintenance
Performance	• Failure rate (λ)	• Recovery time	• Maintenance rate (μ)
	• Fault detection, isolation, containment time	• Recovery success rate (ρ)	• Maintenance success rate
		• Downtime	
Throughput	• Failure rate (λ)	• Downtime	• Maintenance rate (μ)
		• # NINES	• Maintenance method
Speed/speedup	• Redundancy mode	• Recovery mode	• Maintenance mode
Bandwidth	• Failure rate,	• Recovery success rate (ρ)	
	• Redundancy mode		
	• Detection		

out that the Linux environment is more suitable for the parser and loader processes. However, the report generation systems perform better in a MS windows environment. Thus it is worth solving the communication links between multiple environments than settling for a single environment where performance is compromised. Of course, the security and reliability of links between multiple environments need to be addressed. This was an example, where the diversity of tools was the solution for achieving both performance and reliability requirements.

The study also shows that proper performance metrics must be used. Where throughput is the main performance index for one system, response time can be the index for another system. The system engineers and architects must specify without ambiguity the main performance indexes to be optimized. In the initialization problem, discussed in Case 1: initialization problem section, the loading time of multiple boot images was the performance index. However, this index depends on another one, which comes from a higher level system, the availability of the network; in this example, the recovery time (an availability parameter) defined the boot image load time (a performance parameter). Hence, the relation between performability indexes of the various components of the system must be observed.

It should be noted that performance requirements may require modeling and simulation in order to set the proper performance values. Modeling and simulation are generally used to define the limits of performance, for example, the maximum throughout achievable under certain conditions. The limits of achievable performance should be well defined. This allows more realistic performance requirement setting. This in turns requires the selection of workloads and benchmarks. In the initialization problem discussed in section Case 1: initialization problem, the selection of the workload for testing the performance of ftp had to be carefully selected. As another example, the call model used in the evaluation of networking and telecomm systems has a direct impact on the performance requirements and measurements.

Testability is of equal importance. Any performability requirement must be measurable both in the lab (during development) and in the field. Requiring a transaction to be completed in the order of nanoseconds for example, where the lowest granularity of measurement devices is in microseconds is counterproductive.

The selection of the data representation model is of utmost significance as we illustrated in the example given in section case 2: the interference sort and search problem. Trends within large data sets might be better revealed when using one data representation model versus another. Therefore, the system engineers and architects must give enough consideration to the selection of the data representation model. In our example, the performance improvement would not have been possible without the proper selection of the data representation model.

The example of large data mining (discussed in section case 3: data mining and management) shows the challenge of organizing data in various tables. Database update and queries heavily depend on the data distribution among tables. The optimal distribution of data may not be easily attainable due to the complexity of the system measured by large number of tables and large number of attributes; (in our example, the number of tables exceeded 2000 tables, and the number of attributes in some tables exceeded 200). In this case, it is essential to develop adaptive algorithms to shuffle data across tables throughout the lifetime of the system, thus creating a dynamic database schema. In the case presented in section case 3: data mining and management section, performance was dramatically improved after deploying dynamic data migration among the tables of the database.

The selection of tools and languages to be used in the course of the SW system development is shown to directly affect the overall performance of the system. The selection of the tools and languages should be performance oriented rather than dictated by the available skills of the development team.

The performance requirements should not be set in isolation by only one part of the system development, whether the architect, the user, or the system engineers. Rather, this process must be integrated by all parts. The end user, the architect, the test and the system engineers all need to participate in defining the performance requirements of the system. The requirements of the complex system presented in section case 3: data mining and management section were established by all parties involved: the end user, the architects, the software engineers, and the testing engineers.

Reliability and availability requirements face more challenges than performance requirements. For example failure rates are very difficult to quantify for software systems unless accelerated software testing is performed. SW accelerated life testing has not matured enough in the SW industry and remains an open area of research and development.

Also, testing for reliability and availability is a challenge. Reliability and availability models are as good as the parameters used to drive the models, such as failure rates, recovery success rate, and recovery and maintenance time. The state space of SW systems can be very large such that the use of analytical availability models becomes prohibitive. Consequently, simulation models with significant approximations become the only means of measuring availability and reliability.

The use of failure scenario dictionaries and failure mode and effect analysis can be very useful in improving system reliability and availability. Keeping a history of defects, their means of detection, containment, isolation, and recovery will certainly help in mitigating future defects of the same type. We recommend the use of availability work products shown in Figure 6.

Proper budgeting for reliability and availability is essential for building reliable systems. For example, when the total down time of a system is set to a certain number (60 seconds per year for example), it is absolutely necessary to distribute the 60 seconds among the subcomponents of the system. The proper distribution of the budget is key to being able to achieve the requirement. The example given in section Case 1: initialization problem (the initialization problem) was based on availability budget allocation.

In summary, the process of building software systems with well-defined RAMP requirements is an art, where the engineers must choose and select among a very large number of parameters such as tools, languages, models, architectures, design methods, benchmarks and workloads, testing environment, performability indexes and more.

However, this art is not an open ended one. Rather, it is confined to methodologies and practices. The availability work products constitute a methodology by which the art engineer can use to build a robust high availability system. Benchmarking, work load characterization, performance metrics definition, and evaluation constitute a methodology by which the art engineers can build systems with well-defined performance requirements.

Conclusions

This paper presented the challenges of building systems with certain non-functional performability requirements (performance, reliability, availability, and maintainability).

Several case studies are presented to illustrate the performability paradigms, particularly the performance, reliability and availability, maintainability, and budgeting. The paper presents a framework, which shows that the art of software engineering for non-functional requirements can be engineered in a rather systematic manner. The author has used the presented framework to work out several cases, to achieve significant improvements in performance, reliability, availability and maintainability. The performance of intermodulation interference system (Intermode60) achieved an order of magnitude speed improvement. The availability of the data mining system achieved more than four NINES availability through the utilization of diverse languages and environment, and adaptive algorithms for dynamic maintenance of the massive database system. Finally, the paper shows that achieving the required performability parameters is human centric and depends on the integration of diverse skills of engineers, and the sense of art embodied by those engineers.

Competing interests
The authors declare that they have no competing interests.

Authors' contributions
MM investigated the impact of non-functional requirements such as reliability, availability, maintainability and performance (RAMP) on the overall system architecture. The author provided a framework to facilitate the implementation of RAMP requirements in a rather deterministic manner rather than a mere art of software development as is the current state of the art. MM read and approved the final manuscript.

References
1. Eushiuan T (1999) Requirements and Specifications. Carnegie Mellon University, 18-849b Dependable Embedded Systems
2. Ascent® Logic website. http://www.alc.com
3. Nu Thena® Systems website. http://www.lynuxworks.com/
4. Rational® Software website. http://www-01.ibm.com/software/rational/
5. Scientific and Engineering Software® website. https://www.ece.cmu.edu/~koopman/des_s99/requirements_specs/
6. Eushiuan T (1999) Requirements & Specifications. Dependable Embedded Systems. Spring. http://www.ece.cmu.edu/~koopman/des_s99/requirements_specs/
7. Lattemann F, Lehmann E (1997) A methodological Approach to the Requirement Specification of Embedded Systems. In: Proceedings of the First IEEE International Conference on Formal Engineering Methods, ISBN 0-8186-8002-4; Nov. 12–14, 1997. Hiroshima, Japan, pp 183–191
8. Patridge D (1995) Where do Specifications Come From? In: Achievement and Assurance of Safety - Proceedings of the Third Safety-Critical Systems Symposium. , Brighton, United Kingdom, pp 302–310
9. Donald Ervin K (1974) The Art of Computer Programming, Volume I: Fundamental Algorithms, 3rd edition. Addison-Wesley International. ISBN 0201896834
10. John C (2012) Art and Science of Software Engineering. University of Washington Blogs. http://blogs.uw.edu/ajko/2012/08/22/john-carmack-discusses-the-art-and-science-of-software-engineering/
11. Ko AJ, et al. The State of the Art in End-User Software Engineering. ACM Surveys Vol. 43, No. 3, Article 21, April 2011; http://faculty.washington.edu/ajko/papers/Ko2011EndUserSoftwareEngineering.pdf
12. Loka RR (2007) Software Development: What Is the Problem? Computer 40(2):110–112
13. Victoria R (2011) Software Engineering: Art or Science. SD Times, Nov. 8, 2011; http://sdt.bz/content/article.aspx?ArticleID=36088&page=1
14. Steve MC (1998) The Art, Science, and Engineering of Software Development. IEEE Softw 15(1):118–120
15. Naveen G (2006) Art of Software Engineering, Function Point Analysis Examined. Avenue Razorfish. http://people.eecs.ku.edu/~saiedian/Teaching/Sp13/811/Papers/fun-point-analysis-explained.pdf
16. Glass R (2006) Software Conflict 2.0: The Art and Science of Software Development. Books International. ISBN 0977213307
17. Waldo J (2001) DSP Laboratory for Real-Time Systems Design and Implementation: Software Engineering and the Art of Design. Proceedings of the 2001 American Society for Engineering and Education Annual Conference; session 1526. http://www.artima.com/weblogs/viewpost.jsp?thread=7600
18. Votta L, et al. (2004) Measuring High Performance Computing Productivity. Int J High Perform Comput Appl 18 (4):459–473
19. Wilkins D (2002) The Bathtub Curve and Product Failure Behavior. The Reliability HotWire in Weibull.com. issue 21, November 2002; http://www.weibull.com/hotwire/issue21/hottopics21.htm
20. Wood A (2003) Software Reliability from the Customer View. IEEE Comp Soc 36(8):37–42
21. Iyer RK, Rossetti DJ (1985) Effect of System Workload on Operating System Reliability: A Study on IBM 3081. IEEE Trans Software Eng SE-11(12):1438–1448

22. Jun X, Zbigniew K, Ravishankar KI (1999) Networked Windows NT System Field Failure Data Analysis. In: Proceedings of IEEE Pacific Rim Intl' Symp. Dependable Computing (PRDC). , Hong Kong, China

23. Malkawi M, Votta L, Ignatius G, Moore B (2001) Availability Work Products – A Strategic Approach. IEEE Signal Processing Society 5th WSES International Conference, Crete

24. Malkawi M, et al. (2002) Analysis of Failure and Recovery Rates in a Wireless Telecommunications System. In: Proceedings of the International Conference on Dependable Systems and Networks (DSN), pp 687–693

25. Malkawi M, Votta L (2000) Software Systems Availability Modeling and Analysis. Motorola Report and Motorola Symposium on Software Engineering. , Phoenix, AZ

26. Malkawi M (1999) High Availability Models for Common Platform BTS. Motorola Inc. Internal Report #R1999HAM01

27. Sahner RA, Trivedi KS, Antonio P (1996) Performance and Reliability Analysis of Computer Systems: An Example-Based Approach Using the SHARPE Software Package. Kluwer Academic Publishers, Netherlands. ISBN 0-7923-9650-2

28. Courtney T, Daly D, Derisavi S, Lam V, Sanders WH (2003) The Möbius Modeling Environment. In: Tools of the 2003 Illinois International Multiconference on Measurement, Modeling, and Evaluation of Computer-Communication Systems. Universität Dortmund Fachbereich Informatik, Germany, pp 34–37. research report no. 781/2003

29. Malkawi M, Malkawi A (2005) Spectrum Management and Rebanding. Mobile Radio Technology (MRT) J. June 2005

30. Malkawi M, Malkawi A (2002) A Comprehensive Analysis of External Interference. white paper published at http://www.glob-tel.com/index.html

31. Babcock WC (1953) Intermodulation Interference in Radio Systems. Bell Syst Tech J 32(1):63–73

32. Jacobsmeyer JM (2007) Solving Inermodulation Interference in Radio Systems. Mobile Radio Technology. (MRT) J; July 1, 2007

33. Lucent Technologies User manual Document 401-610-133 Issue 28- Flexnet/Autoplex Wirless Networks Executve Cellular Processor (ECP) Release 24.:4-125–4-127

34. Williams S Analysis of the SSH Key Exchange Protocol. Cryptology ePrint Archive, Report 2011/276. http://eprint.iacr.org/2011/276, 2011

35. Patrick T Buggy software costs users, vendors nearly $60B annually. Computerworld. June 25 2002; http://www.computerworld.com/s/article/72245/Study_Buggy_software_costs_users_vendors_nearly_60B_annually

36. Fiorenza B Cambridge University Study States Software Bugs Cost Economy $312 Billion Per Year. PRWeb Online Visibility from Focus, Cambridge Judge Business School. http://www.prweb.com/releases/2013/1/prweb10298185.htm

37. U.S.-Canada Power System Outage Task Force August 14th, 2003 Blackout: Causes and Recommendations. http://energy.gov/sites/prod/files/oeprod/DocumentsandMedia/BlackoutFinal-Web.pdf

38. Stephenson A, et al. (1999) Mars Climate Orbiter Mishap Investigation Board, Phase I Report on Project Management in NASA, pp 16–22. http://science.ksc.nasa.gov/mars/msp98/misc/MCO_MIB_Report.pdf

39. Lions JL Arian 5 flight 501 Failure, Report by the Inquiry Board. http://www.ima.umn.edu/~arnold/disasters/ariane5rep.html

40. Matz S (2001) GoAhead Stress Test Definition; Motorola Internal Report; Rep. ##R2001ALT01

41. Jones TC (1978) Measuring Programming Quality and Productivity. IBM Syst J 17(1):39

42. Information Management and Technology Division, GAO/IMTEC-92-26 Patriot Missile Software Problem, B-247094, February 4, 1992. http://www.fas.org/spp/starwars/gao/im92026.htm

43. Douglas A (1992) Two disasters caused by computer arithmetic errors. Institute of Mathematical Applications, University of Minnesota. http://www.ima.umn.edu/~arnold/455.f96/disasters.html

44. Dominik GC, Pangan Oliver I (2004) Cultural Influences on Disaster Management: ACase Study of the Mt. Pinatubo Eruption. Int J Mass Emergencies Disasters 22(2):31–58

45. Dobrica L, Niemela E (2002) A survey on software architecture analysis methods. IEEE Trans Software Eng 28(7):638–654

9

An optimizing pipeline stall reduction algorithm for power and performance on multi-core CPUs

Vijayalakshmi Saravanan[1][*], Kothari Dwarkadas Pralhaddas[1], Dwarkadas Pralhaddas Kothari[2] and Isaac Woungang[1]

*Correspondence:
vsaravan@rnet.ryerson.ca
[1] WINCORE Lab, Ryerson University, Toronto, Canada
Full list of author information is available at the end of the article

Abstract

The power-performance trade-off is one of the major considerations in micro-architecture design. Pipelined architecture has brought a radical change in the design to capitalize on the parallel operation of various functional blocks involved in the instruction execution process, which is widely used in all modern processors. Pipeline introduces the instruction level parallelism (ILP) because of the potential overlap of instructions, and it does have drawbacks in the form of hazards, which is a result of data dependencies and resource conflicts. To overcome these hazards, stalls were introduced, which are basically delayed execution of instructions to diffuse the problematic situation. Out-of-order (OOO) execution is a ramification of the stall approach since it executes the instruction in an order governed by the availability of the input data rather than by their original order in the program. This paper presents a new algorithm called Left-Right (LR) for reducing stalls in pipelined processors. This algorithm is built by combining the traditional in-order and the out-of-order (OOO) instruction execution, resulting in the best of both approaches. As instruction input, we take the Tomasulo's algorithm for scheduling out-of-order and the in-order instruction execution and we compare the proposed algorithm's efficiency against both in terms of power-performance gain. Experimental simulations are conducted using Sim-Panalyzer, an instruction level simulator, showing that our proposed algorithm optimizes the power-performance with an effective increase of 30% in terms of energy consumption benefits compared to the Tomasulo's algorithm and 3% compared to the in-order algorithm.

Keywords: Instruction pipeline; Stall reduction; Optimizing algorithm

Introduction

Instruction pipeline is extensively used in modern processors in order to achieve instruction level parallelism in pipelined processor architectures [1]. In a conventional pipelined processor, there are 5- pipe stages, namely FETCH (FE), DECODE (DE), EXECUTE (EXE), MEMORY (MEM) and WRITE-BACK (WB). In the first stage, the instruction is read from the memory, loaded into the register, then the decoding of an instruction takes place in the succeeding stage. In the third stage, the execution of an instruction is carried out and in the fourth stage, the desired value is written into the memory; and finally, the computed value is written into a register file. For example, in pipelined processors, if there is any dependency between two consecutive instructions, then the instruction in the decode stage will not be valid. The Tomasulo hardware algorithm is used to overcome this situation. Typically, it is a hardware dynamic scheduling algorithm, in which a separate hardware unit (so-called forwarding) is added to manage the sequential instructions that would normally stall (due to certain dependencies) and execute non-sequentially (This is also referred to as out-of-order execution). Due to data forwarding, there is at least a clock cycle delay and the stall is inserted in a pipeline. These no-operation (NOP) or stalls are used to eliminate the hazards in the pipeline. The NOP instructions contribute to the overall dynamic power consumption of a pipelined processor by generating a number of unnecessary transitions. Our main goal is to minimize such stalls which in turn increases the CPU throughput, thus saves the power consumption.

Generally, the time taken by computing devices is determined by the following factors:

- Processor cycle time.
- Number of instructions required to perform certain task.
- Number of cycles required to complete an instruction.

The system performance can be enhanced by reducing one or more of these factors. Pipelining does just that by dividing the workload into various sub units and by assigning a processing time to each unit, thereby reducing the waiting time period which occurs if the sequential execution was adopted. Various approaches can be to increase the pipeline stages, and various strategies can be used to reduce the stalls caused by the pipeline hazards. To solve this hazard, one can use a large and faster buffer to fetch the instructions and perform an out of order execution. Though, this method increases the hardware complexity cost. It also reduces the branch penalty by re-arranging the instructions to fill the stalls due to branching instruction. But, this requires the use of a suitable scheduling algorithm for the instruction [2]. There is an ongoing research on variable pipeline stages, where it is advocated that processor's pipeline stages can be varied within a certain range. In this type of processors, one can vary the workload and power consumption as per our requirement.

Our proposed work on the analysis of stall reduction of pipelined processors is motivated by the following facts: (1) How to identify the power consumption of the instruction execution in a pipelined processor, i.e. does the power consumption of a instruction execution caused by the number of instructions or the type of executions (such as in-order or out-of-order execution) and why? (2) How to balance both the power and performance in instruction execution.

Recently, a new trend has been established by multi-threaded and multi-core processors. The demand for these processors are due to the inability of the conventional processor to meet higher performance memory-intensive workloads, which in turn may lead to high cache miss rates. In addition, a conventional processor cannot utilize the pipeline effectively, in the sense that a high percentage of the processor resources are wasted. The state-of-the-art architectural methods and algorithms such as pre-fetching and out-of-order execution are not suitable enough for these types of pipelined processors.

In this paper, an alternative strategic algorithm is proposed, in which the instructions are divided into a number of stages, then sorted and executed simultaneously, thereby increasing the throughput. In other words, our algorithm performs a combination of in-order and out-of-order execution for sequential instructions. Our algorithm is then compared against two traditional benchmark algorithms, namely the in-order algorithm and the Tomasulo algorithm. We have also pointed out that just increasing pipeline stages will not always be beneficial to us.

The paper is organized as follows: Section 'Related work' presentssome related work. In Section 'Proposed algorithm', our proposed algorithm for effective stall reduction in pipeline design on multiprocessors is presented. In Section 'Comparison of LR vs. Tomasulo algorithm', the simulation results are presented. Finally, Section 'Conclusions' concludes our work.

Related work

The length of the pipeline has an impact on the performance of a microprocessor. Two architectural parameters that can affect the optimal pipeline length are the degree of instruction level parallelism and the pipeline stalls [3]. During pipeline stalls, the NOP instructions are executed, which are similar to test instructions. The TIS tests different parts of the processor and detects stuck-at faults [4,5].

Wide Single Instruction, Multiple Thread architectures often require static allocation of thread groups, executed in lockstep. Applications requiring complex control flow often result in low processor efficiency due to the length and quantity of the control paths. Theglobal rendering algorithms are an example. To improve the processor's utilization, a SIMT architecture is introduced, which allows for threads to be created dynamically at runtime [6].

Branch divergence has a significant impact on the performance of GPU programs. Current GPUs feature multiprocessors with SIMT architecture, which create, schedule, and execute the threads in groups (so-called wraps). The threads in a wrap execute the same code path in lockstep, which can potentially lead to a large amount of wasted cycles for a divergent control ow. Techniques to eliminate wasted cycles caused by branch and termination divergence have been proposed in [7]. Two novel software-based optimizations, called iterative delaying and branch distribution were proposed in [8], aiming at reducing the branch divergence.

In order to ensure consistency and performance in scalable multiprocessors, cache coherence is an important factor. It is advocated that hardware protocols are currently better than software protocols but are more costly to implement. Due to improvements on compiler technologies, the focus is now placed more on developing efficient software protocols [9]. For this reason, an algorithm for buffer cache management with pre-fetching was proposed in [10]. The buffer cache contains two units, namely, the main cache unit and the prefetch unit; and blocks are fetched according to the one block lookahead prefetch principle. The processor cycle times are currently much faster than the memory cycle times, and the trend has been for this gap to increase over time. In [11,12], new types of prediction cache were introduced, which combine the features of pre-fetching and victim caching. In [13], an evaluation of the full system performance using several different power/performance sensitive cache configurations was proposed.

In [14,15], a pre-fetch based disk buffer management algorithm (so-called W2R) was proposed. In [16], the instruction buffering as a power saving technique for signal and multimedia processing applications was introduced. In [17], another buffer management technique called dynamic voltage scaling was introduced as one of the most efficient ways to reduce the power consumption because of its quadratic effect. Essentially, the micro-architectural-driven dynamic voltage scaling identifies program regions where the CPU can be slowed down with negligible performance loss. In [18], the run-time behaviour exhibited by common applications with active periods alternated with stall periods due to cache misses, was exploited to reduce the dynamic component of the power consumption using a selective voltage scaling technique.

In [19], a branch prediction technique was proposed for increasing the instructions per cycle. Indeed, a large amount of unnecessary work is usually due to the selection of wrong-path instructions entering the pipeline because of branch mis-prediction. A hardware mechanism called pipeline gating is employed to control the rampant speculation in the pipeline. Based on the Shannon expansion, one can partition a given circuit into two sub-circuits in a way that the number of different outputs of both sub-circuits are reduced, and then encode the output of both sub-circuits to minimize the Hamming distance for transitions with a high switching probability [20].

In [21], file Pre-fetching has been used as an efficient technique for improving the file access performance. In [22], a comprehensive framework that simultaneously evaluates the tradeoffs of energy dissipations of software and hardware such as caches and main memory was presented. As a follow up, in [23], an architecture and a prototype implementation of a single chip, fully programmable Ray Processing Unit (RPU), was presented.

In this paper, our aim is to further reduce the power dissipation by reducing the execution of the stall instruction passes through the pipe stages using our proposed algorithm. Therefore, our algorithm aims at reducing the unnecessary waiting time of the instruction execution and clock cycles, which in turn will maximize the CPU performance and save some amount of energy consumption.

Proposed algorithm

Performance improvement and power reduction are two major issues that are faced by computer architects, and various methods and algorithms have been proposed to optimize the performance and power. To add on these, other methodsrely on reducing the pipeline hazards and increasing the efficiency of a processor. Processors have evolved into two main categories, namely, in-order execution and out-of-order execution.

In-order execution: In this method, instructions are fetched, executed and completed in a compiler generated order. Instructions are scheduled statically, and if one stall occurs, the rest all are stalled. The Alpha and Intel Atom processors in-order models have been implemented with peak performance. However, complex designs are required for the integration of peak capacity and increase in clock frequency.

```
example of in-order instruction execution:
lw $3, 100($4) in execution, cache miss
add $2, $3, $4 waits until the miss is satisfied
sub $5, $6, $7 waits for the add
```

Out-of-order execution: In the previous method, data dependencies and latencies in functional units can cause reduction in the performance of the processor. In order to overcome this issue, we have uses an out-of-order (OOO) method which is the traditional way to increase the efficiency of pipelined processors by maximizing the instruction issued by every cycle [24]. But, this technique is very costly in terms of its implementation. Most of the high level processors (such as DEC and HP) execute the instructions in out-of-order. In this method, the instructions are fetched in a compiler generated order and the execution of the instruction takes place in pipeline as one which is not dependent on the current instruction, i.e. independent instructions are executed in some other order. The instructions are dynamically scheduled and the completion of instruction may be in in-order or out-of-order.

```
Example of out-of-order instruction execution:
lw $3, 100($4) in execution, cache miss
sub $5, $6, $7 can execute during the cache miss
add $2, $3, $4 waits until the miss is satisfied
```

Tomasulo's algorithm: As a dynamic scheduling algorithm, it uses a hardware-based mechanism to remove the stalls at the runtime. It allows sequential instructions that would normally be stalled due to certain dependencies to execute non-sequentially (out-of-order execution). It also utilizes the concept of register renaming, and resolves Write-after-Write (WAW), Read-after-Write (RAW) and Write-after-Read (WAR) computer architecture hazards by register renaming, which allows the continual issuing of instructions. This algorithm also uses a common data bus (CDB) on which the computed values are broadcasted to all the reservation stations that may need it. This allows for improved parallel execution of instructions, which may otherwise stall. The Tomasulo algorithm was chosen because its order of instruction execution is nearly equivalent to that of our proposed algorithm. Both algorithms are scheduled statically at the micro-architecture level.

Proposed algorithm (LR(Left-Right)): The above mentioned methods and algorithms have their own merits and demerits while executing an instruction in a pipelined processors. Instead of using some other methods to reduce the power consumption, we have

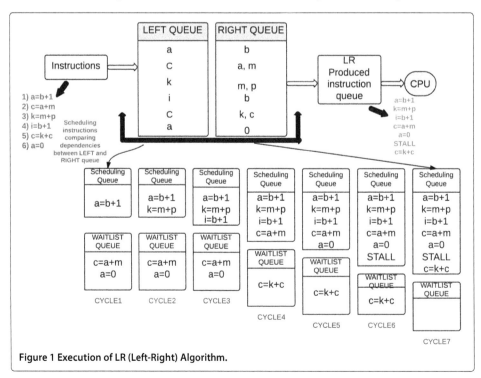

Figure 1 Execution of LR (Left-Right) Algorithm.

proposed an algorithm which performs the stall reduction in a Left-Right (LR) manner, in sequential instruction execution as shown in Figure 1. Our algorithm introduces a hybrid order of instruction execution in order to reduce the power dissipationl. More precisely, it executes the instructions serially as in-order execution until a stall condition is encountered, and thereafter, it uses of concept of out-of-order execution to replace the stall with an independent instruction. Thus, LR increases the throughput by executing independent instructions while the lengthy instructions are still executed in other functional units or the registers are involved in an ongoing process. LR also prevents the hazards that might occur during the instruction execution. The instructions are scheduled statically at compile time as shown in Figure 2. In our proposed approach, if a buffer in presence can hold a certain number of sequential instructions, our algorithm will generate a sequence in which the instructions should be executed to reduce the number of stalls while maximizing the throughput of a processor. It is assumed that all the instructions are in the form of op-code source destination format.

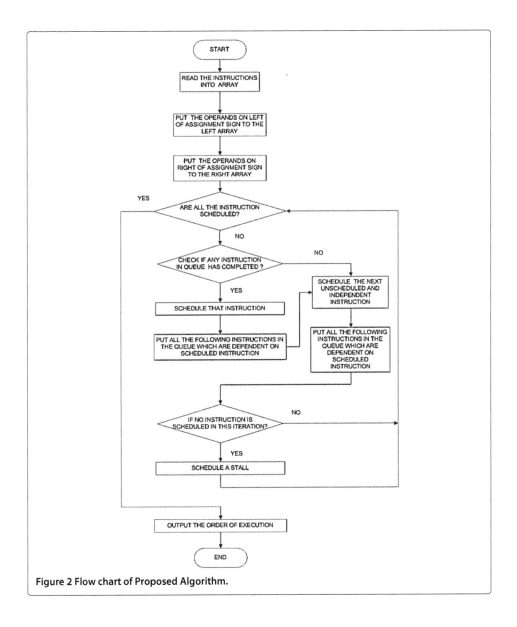

Figure 2 Flow chart of Proposed Algorithm.

Comparison of LR vs. Tomasulo algorithm

In this section, the performance and power gain of the LR and the Tomasulo algorithms are compared.

Simulation and power-performance evaluation

As our baseline configuration, we use an Intel core i5 dual core processor with 2.40GHZ clock frequency, and 64-bit operating system. We also use the Sim-Panalyzer simulator [25]. The LR, in-order, and Tomasulo algorithms are developed as C programs. These C programs were compiled using arm-linux-gcc in order to obtain the object files for each of them, on an ARM microprocessor model.

At the early stage of the processor design, various levels of simulators can be used to estimate the power and performance such as transistor level, system level, instruction level, and micro-architecture level simulators. In transistor level simulators, one can estimate the voltage and current behaviour over time. This type of simulators are used for integrated circuit design, and not suitable for large programs. On the other hand, micro-architecture level simulators provide the power estimation across cycles and these are used in modern processors. Our work is similar to this kind of simulator because our objective is to evaluate the power-performance behaviour of a micro-architecture level design abstraction. Though, a literature survey suggests several power estimation tools such as CACTI, WATTCH [26], and we have choose the Sim-Panalyzer [25] since it provides an accurate power modelling by taking into account both the leakage and dynamic power dissipation.

The actual instruction execution of our proposed algorithm against existing ones is shown in Algorithms 1 and 2. In the LR algorithm, an instruction is executed serially in-order until a stall occurs, and thereafter the out-of-order execution technique comes to play to replace the stall with an independent instruction stage. Therefore, in most cases, our proposed algorithm takes less cycle of operation and less cycle time compared to existing algorithms as shwon in algorithm [2]. The comparison of our proposed algorithm against the Tomasulo algorithm and the in-orderalgorithm is shown in Table 1. The next section focusses on the power-performance efficiency of our proposed algorithm.

Algorithm 1 Pseudo code of the proposed Left-Right (LR) algorithm.

1: **Read** the instruction into an array;
2: Separate the **left operands** and **right operands** of assignment sign into left array and right array respectively;
3: Check if all the instructions have been **scheduled**. If **yes** goto step 7 **else** go to *4a*.
4: *4a*: Check if the instruction in the **queue** has completed **two stalls**. If **yes** go to step *4b* **else** go to step *5a*; *4b*: Schedule that instruction and send all the **dependent instruction** into the **queue**. Go to step *5a*.
5: *5a*: **Schedule** the next independent and **unscheduled instruction**; *5b*: Send all the **dependent instruction** into the **queue**. Go to step 6.
6: If **no instruction** was scheduled in the last iteration then schedule a **stall** and go to step 3.
7: **Output** the order of execution.

Algorithm 2 Actual Instruction execution of proposed algorithm LR(Left-Right) vs. In-order, Tomasulo

---

1: Instructions: 1) a=b + 1; 2) c=a + m; 3) k=m + p; 4) i=b + 1; 5) c=k + c; 6) a=0;

2: LEFT Operand: a, c, k, i, c, a

3: RIGHT Operand: [b,1] [a,m] [m,p] [b,1] [k,c] [0,0]

4: Cycle Operation: 1 2 3 4 5 6

5: First Step: Schedule 1st instruction. And put 2nd and 6th instruction in queue. Then, schedule a 3rd instruction and 4th instruction.

6: Then, 2nd instruction from queue, schedule 6th instruction, **WAIT** for a cycle then schedule 5th instruction.

7: This will give rise to the following sequence for **proposed algorithm (LR):** 1 3 4 2 6 Stall 5

8: **In-order:** 1 Stall 2 3 4 Stall 5 6

9: **Tomasulo:** 1 3 4 2 6 Stall 5. Though, tomasulo takes same cycle time as LR, due to hardware unit high power dissipation to perform the same operation than LR.

Performance evaluation

In general, computer architects use simulation as a primary tool to evaluate the computer's performance. In this setting, instructions per cycle (IPC) represents a performance metric that can be considered, and it is well-known [27] that an increase in IPC generally yields a good performance of the system. The use of instructions per cycle (IPC) to analyze the performance of a system is challenged at least for the multi-threaded workloads running on multiprocessors. In [27], it was reported that work-related metrics (e.g. time per transaction) are the most accurate and reliable way to estimate the multiprocessor workload performance. We have also proved that our algorithm produces less IPC compared to that generated by the Tomasulo algorithm (see Figure 3(b)). According to this result, work-related metrics such as *time per program* and *time per workloads* are the most accurate and reliable methods to calculate the performance of the system. The time

Table 1 Comparison of algorithms

In-order execution	Tomasulo's algorithm	Proposed algorithm (LR)
Static-scheduling	Hardware dynamic-scheduling	Static-scheduling
Compiler tries to reorder the instructions during the compilation time in order to reduce the pipeline stalls	The dynamic scheduling of the hardware tries to rearrange the instructions during run-time to reduce the pipeline stalls	Compilation time instruction execution
Uses less hardware	More hardware unit added	Use more powerful algorithmic techniques (sorting)
Sequential-order	Register-renaming is used to reduce the stall	Sorting takes place first, then execution of an instruction
Bottom-up approach	Re-ordering of CPU instructions	Hybrid order of an in-order and OOO
For ex: char x; //read x, starts on cycle 1 & completes on cycle 2; int a= 10 + 20; // assignment to a, starts on cycle 3 & completes on cycle 4; print char x; // starts on cycle 5 & completes on cycle 6;	char x; // read x, starts on cycle 1 & completes on cycle 2; int a= 10 + 20; // assignment to a, starts on cycle 2 & completes on cycle 3; print char x; // starts on cycle 3 & completes on cycle 4;	char x; // read x, starts on cycle 1 & completes on cycle 2; int a= 10 + 20; // assignment to a, starts on cycle 2 & completes on cycle 3; print char x; // starts on cycle 3 & completes on cycle 4; Due to hardware unit, more power dissipation

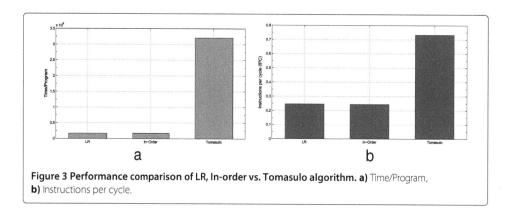

Figure 3 Performance comparison of LR, In-order vs. Tomasulo algorithm. a) Time/Program,
b) Instructions per cycle.

per program is calculated as shown in Eq. (1) and Eq. (2). We use time per program and
IPC as performance metrics.

$$Time/Program = Instructions/Program \times Cycles/Instruction \times Time/Cycle, \qquad (1)$$

$$Time/Program = CP \times CPI \times IPP$$

where TP- time per program, CP- clock period, CPI- Cycles per instruction and IPP-
instructions executed per program. We have executed our program on the same machine,
therefore the clock period will be the same. Hence, Eq. (1) becomes,

$$Throughput(\%) = 100 - \left[(CPI \times IPP)_{LR}/(CPI \times IPP)_{In-order}\right] \times 100 = 98 \qquad (2)$$

$$Throughput(\%) = 100 - \left[(CPI \times IPP)_{LR}/(CPI \times IPP)_{Tomasulo}\right] \times 100 = 95 \qquad (3)$$

By using Eq. 1, we calculated the time per program for the proposed LR algorithm,
and its efficiency iscompared against the traditional in-order and Tomasulo's algorithm
as shown in Table 2.

Power consumption evaluation

In simulation-based power evaluation methods, the system is integrated with various
components such ALU, level-1 I-cache, D-cache, irf (register files), and clock. The energy
consumption of a program is estimated as the sum of all these components as shown
in Table 3 and the mean power dissipation results from Sim-Panalyzer for the same
experiment are shown in Table 4.

Result analysis and discussions

To analyse the efficiency of our proposed algorithm, we have simulated both algorithms
on the Sim-Panalyzer and obtained the average power dissipation of the ALU, level-1
instruction (il1) and data (dl1) caches as well as the internal register file (irf) and the clock

Table 2 Performance estimation of LR vs. in-order

Metrics	LR	In-order	Tomasulo
Instructions per cycle (IPC)	0.2462	0.2442	0.7327
Clocks per instruction (CPI)	4.061	4.09	1.3648
Simulation speed (inst/sec)	785	606	98021.9
Total number of instructions executed	40516	41004	2350639
Time/Program	164535.476	167706.36	3207982.549

Table 3 Average power dissipation for LR, in-order vs. Tomasulo's algorithm

Component	Simulation parameters	LR	In-order	Tomasulo
ALU	alu avg power # Avg power for alu	0.0001	0.0001	0.0003
dl1	dl1.avgswitching #dl1 avg in switching power dissipation	0.0060	0.0079	0.0172
	dl1.avginternal #dl1 avg internal power dissipation	0.0192	0.0199	0.0431
	dl1.avgleakage #dl1 avg leakage power dissipation	0.0029	0.0029	0.0029
	dl1.avgpdissipation #dl1 avg power dissipation	0.223	0.2208	0.2459
il1	il1.avgswitching #il1 avg in switching power dissipation	0.0343	0.0338	0.0950
	il1.avginternal #il1 avg internal power dissipation	0.0861	0.0849	0.2384
	il1.avgleakage #il1 avg leakage power dissipation	0.0029	0.0029	0.0029
	il1.avgpdissipation #il1 avg power dissipation	0.4274	0.4292	0.4525
irf	irf.avgswitching # irf avg in switching power dissipation	0.0063	0.0066	0.0162
	irf.avginternal #irf avg internal power dissipation	0.0085	0.0089	0.0218
	irf.avgleakage #irf avg leakage power dissipation	0.0001	0.0001	0.0001
	irf.avgpdissipation #irf avg power dissipation	0.041	0.0414	0.0407
Clock	clock.avgleakage #clock avg leakage power dissipation	191.13	191.13	191.13

power dissipation. We have plot the energy consumptions of the different components of both algorithms as shown in Figure 4.

It can be observed that with Tomasulo's algorithm, the absolute power dissipation differs significantly between LR and in-order. In terms of ALU power dissipation, it can be observed there is not much improvement in power-performance. But on comparing the results for dl1 and il1, it can be noticed that there is a significant difference in power dissipation in the level-1 data and instruction caches. In both dl1 and il1, the average switching power dissipation (resp. the average internal power dissipation) show up to 60% less power dissipation in LR than in the Tomasulo algorithm. Also, the power dissipation generated by LR is 2.5% less compared to that generated by the Tomasulo algorithm.

From Eq. 2 and Table 2, it can be concluded that LR performs 95% better than Tomasulo. Figure 3a and 3b, Table 3 depict the IPC & time per program of both algorithms. The instruction execution efficiency of the Tomasulo algorithm is 1% and the data efficiency is

Table 4 Total power dissipation of LR, In-order vs. Tomasulo algorithm

Component	LR algorithm	In-order algorithm	Tomasulo	(%) Improvement (Tomasulo)
ALU	0.0001	0.0001	0.0003	33.3
il1	0.5507	0.5508	0.3091	21.1
dl1	0.2527	0.2515	0.7888	33.5
irf	0.0559	0.057	0.0788	33.5

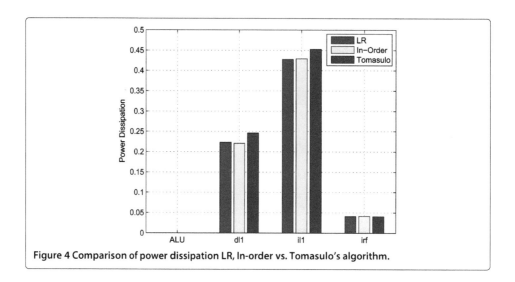

Figure 4 Comparison of power dissipation LR, In-order vs. Tomasulo's algorithm.

2% higher than that of the LR algorithm. In terms of overall power-performance benefits, our proposed LR algorithm outperforms the Tomasulo algorithm. In our experiment, it was also observed that the fraction of clock power dissipation is almost the same for both algorithms. This significant increase of clock power in Sim-Panalyzer is mostly due to the fact that it is dependent on the dynamic power consumption.

Discussions

With this simulator, we are able to obtain power-performance of various below mentioned components , and compared our results.

1. **ALU:** As shown in Table 1, the average power dissipation in ALU indicates the usage of ALU during the simulation of both algorithms. The maximum power dissipation is noticed to be equal for both the algorithm but the average power dissipation in LR shows a 66% improvement against Tomasulo. This simply states that for the processing LR requires less computation as compared to Tomasulo to order the instructions.

2. **DL1:** dl1 represents the level -1 data caches and in the experiment, LR shows an overall improvement of 21% as compared to Tomasulo in the average power dissipation in dl1. This exemplifies that the usage of cache and the cache hit ratio is improved in LR then in the Tomasulo.

3. **IL1:** il1 represents the level -1 instruction caches and in the experiment LR shows an overall improvement of 33% as compared to Tomasulo in the average power dissipation in il1. Hence, we can deduce that the cache used for holding instructions performs better while processing for LR as compared to Tomasulo.

4. **IRF:** IRF indicates the usage of the internal register file. The average power dissipation in LR is 33% less than Tomasulo's. IRF indicates that the register's usage is less in LR and hence the power consumption is less than the Tomasulo.

Overal, thel improvement in average power dissipation of LR comes out to be 30% better than that of the Tomasulo algorithm. Also, a slight performance-power improvement of LR against in-order is also achieved. Hence, it can be concluded that our algorithm increases the throughput of the pipelined processor by reducing the stalls, and the power-performance of our algorithm is better than that of the Tomasulo's algorithm.

Conclusions

We have presented a stall reduction algorithm for optimizing the power-performance in pipelined processors. Our algorithmic technique is based on the hybrid order of instruction execution and it operates at a higher level of abstraction than more commonly used hardware level algorithms in instruction level power-performance estimation do. Simulation results have been conducted to validate the effectiveness of our proposed algorithm, revealing the following findings: (1) Our proposed algorithm is able to optimize the stall reductions during instruction scheduling in the pipelined processor; (2) It can also help preventing the data hazards that might occur; (3) Compared to the Tomasulo algorithm chosen as benchmark, it can achieve up to 30% of power and 95% of performance improvement on simulation in a pipelined processor; (4) the performance-power exhibited by in-order execution are relatively low compared to that performed by our algorithm; and (5) Our algorithm is statically scheduled, and it performs better in terms of power and performance than the existing stall reduction algorithm. As futre work, the proposed algorithm can further be enhanced by using more advanced sorting techniques, for instance, techniques that can help overlapping the instructions, making them more data dependable.

Competing interests
The authors declare that they have no competing interests.

Authors' contributions
All authors read and approved the final manuscript.

Author details
[1]WINCORE Lab, Ryerson University, Toronto, Canada. [2]I.I.T. Delhi, India.

References
1. Kogge PM (1981) The Architecture of pipelined computers. McGraw-Hill advanced computer science series, Hemisphere, Washington, New York, Paris, Includes index
2. Johnson WM (1989) Super-scalar processor design. Technical report
3. Hartstein A, Puzak TR (2002) The optimum pipeline depth for a microprocessor. SIGARCH Comput Archit News 30(2):7–13
4. Shamshiri S, Esmaeilzadeh H, Navabi Z (2005) Instruction-level test methodology for cpu core self-testing. ACM Trans Des Autom Electron Syst 10(4):673–689
5. Patterson DA, Hennessy JL (2006) In praise of computer architecture: a quantitative approach. Number 704. Morgan Kaufmann
6. Steffen M, Zambreno J (2010) Improving simt efficiency of global rendering algorithms with architectural support for dynamic micro-kernels. In: Proceedings of the 2010 43rd Annual IEEE/ACM International Symposium on Microarchitecture. MICRO '43, IEEE Computer Society, Washington, DC, USA. pp 237–248
7. Frey S, Reina G, Ertl T (2012) Simt microscheduling: Reducing thread stalling in divergent iterative algorithms. In: Proceedings of the 2012 20th Euromicro International Conference on Parallel, Distributed and Network-based Processing PDP '12. IEEE Computer Society, Washington, DC, USA. pp 399–406
8. Han TD, Abdelrahman TS (2011) Reducing branch divergence in gpu programs. In: Proceedings of the Fourth Workshop on General Purpose Processing on Graphics Processing Units, GPGPU-4, ACM, New York, NY, USA. pp 3:1–3:8
9. Lawrence R (1998) A survey of cache coherence mechanisms in shared memory multiprocessors
10. Chaudhary MK, Kumar M, Rai M, Dwivedi RK (2011) Article: A Modified Algorithm for Buffer Cache Management. Int J Comput Appl 12(12):47–49
11. Bennett JE, Flynn MJ (1996) Reducing Cache Miss Rates Using Prediction Caches. Technical report
12. Schnberg S, Mehnert F, Hamann C-J, Hamann Clj, Reuther L, Hrtig H (1998) Performance and Bus Transfer Influences. In: In First Workshop on PC-Based Syatem Performance and Analysis

13. Bahar RI, Albera G, Manne S (1998) Power and performance tradeoffs using various caching strategies. In: Proceedings of the 1998 international symposium on Low power electronics and design, ISLPED '98, ACM, New York, NY, USA. pp 64–69

14. Jeon HS, Noh SH (1998) A database disk buffer management algorithm based on prefetching. In: Proceedings of the seventh international conference on Information and knowledge management, CIKM '98, ACM, New York, NY, USA. pp 167–174

15. Johnson T, Shasha D (1994) 2Q: A Low Overhead High Performance Buffer Management Replacement Algorithm. In: Proceedings of the 20th International Conference on Very Large Data Bases. VLDB '94, Morgan Kaufmann Publishers Inc., San Francisco, CA, USA. pp 439–450

16. Bajwa RS, Hiraki M, Kojima H, Gorny DJ, Nitta K, Shridhar A, Seki K, Sasaki K (1997) Instruction buffering to reduce power in processors for signal processing. IEEE Trans. Very Large Scale Integr Syst 5(4):417–424

17. Hsu C-H, Kremer U (2003) The design, implementation, and evaluation of a compiler algorithm for cpu energy reduction. SIGPLAN Not 38(5):38–48

18. Marculescu D (2000) On the Use of Microarchitecture-Driven Dynamic Voltage Scaling

19. Manne S, Klauser A, Grunwald D (1998) Pipeline gating: speculation control for energy reduction. In: Proceedings of the 25th annual international symposium on Computer architecture. ISCA '98, IEEE Computer Society, Washington, DC, USA. pp 132–141

20. Ruan S-J, Tsai K-L, Naroska E, Lai F (2005) Bipartitioning and encoding in low-power pipelined circuits. ACM Trans Des Autom Electron Syst 10(1):24–32

21. Lei H, Duchamp D (1997) An Analytical Approach to File Prefetching. In: In Proceedings of the USENIX 1997 Annual Technical Conference. pp 275–288

22. Li Y, Henkel Jrg, Jrghenkel Y (1998) A Framework for Estimating and Minimizing Energy Dissipation of Embedded HW/SW Systems

23. Woop S, Schmittler J, Slusallek P (2005) Rpu: a programmable ray processing unit for realtime ray tracing. In: ACM SIGGRAPH 2005 Papers. SIGGRAPH '05. ACM, New York, NY, USA. pp 434–444

24. Johnson M, William M (1989) Super-Scalar Processor Design. Technical report

25. Whitham J (2013) Simple scalar/ARM VirtualBox Appliance. Website. http://www.jwhitham.org/simplescalar

26. Brooks D, Tiwari V, Martonosi M (2000) Wattch: a framework for architectural-level power analysis and optimizations. SIGARCH Comput Archit News 28(2):83–94

27. Alameldeen AR, Wood DA (2006) Ipc considered harmful for multiprocessor workloads. IEEE Micro 26(4):8–17

10

A dynamic attention assessment and enhancement tool using computer graphics

Geeta U Navalyal* and Rahul D Gavas*

* Correspondence: kle.geeta@gmail.
com; rahulgavas@gmail.com
Department of Computer Science &
Engg, KLE Dr. M.S.S CET, Udyambag,
Belgaum, India

Abstract

Training Programs to enhance Math Solving Skills, Memory, Visualization, etc in children are gaining popularity worldwide. Any skill is better acquired, when attention, the basic cognitive ability of the trainee is improved. This study makes an attempt to devise a technique in the form of a Brain Computer Interface (BCI) Game, to assist the trainers in monitoring and evaluating the attention levels of the trainees, at regular intervals during the training period.

The gaming environment is designed using Open Source Graphics Library (OpenGL) package and the game control is through the player's brain waves using the BCI technology. The players control the movement of an object from a source to a destination location on the screen by focussing their thought processes. The time taken to complete one game can be recorded. More the time taken, lesser would be the attention sustaining capacity of the player.

Thirteen subjects under different levels of the ABACUS Math Solving training program controlled the ball movement while solving math problems mentally, the time taken reduced for most of the subjects as they reached higher levels of their training course, indicating the benefit of such training programmes. The game was also played by eight non-abacus literates. The evaluation procedure was found to be very easy and fast.

Index terms: ADHD; BCI; EEG

Introduction

Concentration or sustained attention is the basic cognitive ability of a person to perform any task or develop a skill. The timely monitoring of this ability is important when his/her performance enhancement is concerned. Though the existing methodologies to assess ones cognitive abilities in the form of mathematical, linguistic-aptitude questionnaires, face to face interaction are well established, practicing these techniques in the present day scenario seems to be time consuming and less appealing, especially in case on online training programmes. Also, many current assessment techniques stress on task completion rather than the overall process responsible for it. To improve the quality of the output, be it a task performance or a skill attainment, the entire process of it has to be monitored and evaluated [1].

Today computer games are being developed not only for entertainment of the players but in the field of health and education to improve one or more cognitive abilities of the users. Brain Computer Interface is one technology, which has facilitated the assessment of user behaviour through games [2]. These games can enhance problem solving abilities in children. Many "Serious" games for health and education for children are also popular [3].

The states of the brain can be recorded in a non-invasive and a flexible way through Electroencephalogram (EEG) [4]. Research has shown that EEG based applications were first developed to help disabled people to communicate with machines [5,6], then they were used in video games as game controllers [7] and then in Neurofeedback Games [8]. Children with Attention Deficit Hyperactivity Disorder (ADHD) syndrome are treated primarily with behavioural therapy than pharmacologically, as medications are bound to cause side effects [9-11].

Also training programs to help children, to focus and improve mental skills are increasingly becoming popular. Abacus is one such training program designed to develop math solving skills in children in the age groups of five to fourteen. This program is divided into many levels with increased complexity in solving skills at each level. The skills acquired at each of the levels are manually tested by specifying time limits to complete a calculation. This can be a burden on the trainer to make observations of a trainee's performance before he/she is allowed to take up the next level.

These existing techniques test the trainees solving skills, which also reflect their attention and concentration levels. So as an alternative measure, the trainees can be tested for their improvement in concentration at different stages and their progress tracked. It can also aid self evaluation to the user. This paper shows a game implementation to test the progress of the trainees with a more flexible and interesting approach. It is a simple gaming application using visualization techniques to increase enthusiasm without being aware of being tested. As the system makes use of a subject's direct attention to control a game, it works on a feed-forward mechanism [12].

As inexpensive, wireless, portable and easy-to-use EEG headsets are available in the market from vendors like Neurosky and Emotiv [13,14], BCI game implementations have become very easy and assessing attention and meditation values of the users are found to be reliable [15].

Section 3 deals with the proposed game design philosophy. Game implementation details are discussed in section 4 and 5. Results of the implementation are discussed in section 6. In section 7 and 8, the conclusion and future work are discussed.

Game design

Any gaming application uses a graphics tool for the design of the gaming environment and user interface along with devices like keyboard, mouse or a joystick type of controllers to control the game. An EEG based game uses "thoughts" to control game. Our implementation uses OpenGL software for designing the gaming environment and an EEG device and its driver software from Neurosky.

The game design schema was done by taking into consideration the following points: The hardware used should be inexpensive and easy to maintain. It should use simple GUI so as to make a novice get accustomed to it in a short span. It was also necessary for it to use neurofeedback to give a visual representation of his attention levels and thus aid him to enhance it in a rather playful manner.

Game implementation

The hardware includes a Lenovo Intel i5 processor based laptop and EEG device "Mindwave Mobile" from Neurosky. The implementation platform is Windows 7 and the game is developed using Visual C++ with OpenGL graphics library.

Details of NeuroSky Mindwave mobile EEG

Software

Thinkgear software provided with the EEG device is used to connect the EEG device to the computer. It allows special applications and games to be run according to the states of mind as detected by EEG headset with NeuroSky's ThinkGear sensor. It runs as a background process continuously by keeping an open socket on the computer system, thereby allowing applications to connect to it. The applications receive information from the connected ThinkGear devices. It is provided as an executable for Mac OS X and Windows platforms.

Hardware

The device is a single lobe, dry sensor electrode based, non-invasive EEG device.

ThinkGear is the technology which is embedded in every NeuroSky product. It enables connectivity with brainwaves of the wearer. It comprises of a sensor that touches the forehead to collect brain wave data centered at the frontal cortex, the contact and the reference points located on the ear pad. The data is processed using the onboard chip included on it. Both the eSense Meters (Meditation and Attention) and raw brainwaves are calculated on the ThinkGear Chip.

Signal acquisition

The MindWave Mobile Headset includes the sensor that touches the forehead, the contact and reference points located on the ear pad, and the onboard chip that processes all of the data and provides this data to software and applications in digital form through Bluetooth connectivity. Figure 1 shows the setup for the game.

The EEG electrode is placed on the user's forehead (on the frontal cortex) during the play. The headset safely measures and outputs the EEG power spectrums (alpha waves, beta waves, etc), attention, meditation and eye blink values. Attention and Meditation are indicated and reported on a meter with a relative eSense scale of 1 to 100.

This scale has a set of grouping schemata for the ranges of values and a particular state of mind is attributed to it. Values between 20-40 are reduced levels and from 1-20 they are considered strongly lowered eSense. A value lying in the range of 40-60 is considered to be neutral. Values above 60 are considered to be values higher than the normal or "slightly elevated". Values in the range of 80-100 are considered to be high levels of eSense.

Attention as an unsigned one-byte value indicates the intensity of a user's level of mental "focus" or "attention", such as that which occurs during intense concentration and directed (but stable) mental activity. Its value ranges from 0 to 100. Distractions, wandering thoughts, lack of focus or anxiety lower the Attention meter levels.

Gaming strategy

The input to this gaming application is through the attention values. The 3D ball moves from a source location to a destination location when the users focus on the task been assigned to them. Our implementation uses the eSense value 50 as a threshold value for a

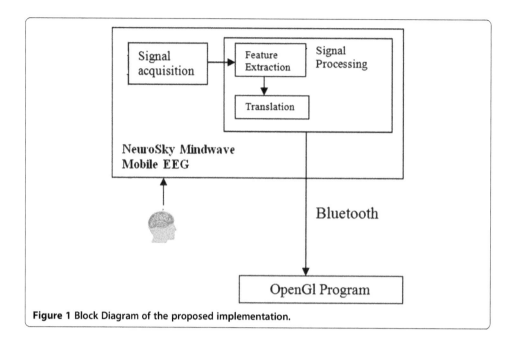

Figure 1 Block Diagram of the proposed implementation.

fair attention value, since it is the middlemost value lying on the eSense scale and is considered to be average balanced state of mind. When this value is crossed, the players ball moves forward towards the destination else it descends. On reaching the destination, a golden pot appears on the screen as a reward of the achievement.

Methodology

The subjects were devoid of any mental or physical disabilities and normal environmental conditions prevailed during the experimentation.

EEG data was gathered from subjects from 4 different areas and age groups.

Areas included 13 Abacus students (8-Males, 5-Females) in the age groups of 6 -15 years, 3 under graduate students (2-males, 1-Female) in the age group of 20 – 22, 3 professionals (2-Males, 1-Female) in the age groups of 40 – 50 and 2 senior citizens (1-Male, 1-Female) above 60 years. All of them hailed from Karnataka, India. Out of the four groups, for two groups the data was collected when they were involved in mental activities performing a task, than using the gaming tool. The subjects involved in the experimentation were either playing a game or involved in a mental activity and each of these activities induce a perceptible concentration level in the participants which the application records. The recorded data are further evaluated.

Algorithm

The following algorithm defines work flow of the proposed BCI game. The second step in the algorithm comprises of setting up proper connectivity with the EEG device and the system, initializing OpenGL features like lighting, shading and material properties and drawing the required graphics objects on the OpenGL window.

Input: *Attention eSense values.*
Output: *Attention assessment using computer graphics.*

1. Start.
2. Set up the environment for the game.
3. Read the input and start the timer.
4. If (input value > threshold).

Move the graphics object forward.
Else.
Move it backward.

5. When the graphics object reaches the destination, stop timer.
6. Stop.

Figure 2 shows the snapshot of the BCI game developed using OpenGL.

Results

Figure 3 shows the graph of abacus training levels on the X-axis and the time taken in seconds to accomplish the BCI task assigned to them on the Y-axis.

The experimentation was carried out on students from various levels of abacus training. The students in the lower abacus training levels deal with simple addition and subtraction problems. Hence they performed better.

The students in the higher abacus training levels had to perform floating point calculations and were given multiple operations, so switching between multiple tasks hindered their attention. But the students, who had practised for more time in every level, did not panic and could perform calculations at higher attention levels.

Nervousness curbs attention values whereas confidence, self-esteem enhances it.

Figure 4 shows the graph of the age of non-abacus practitioners in years on the X-axis and the time taken in seconds to play the game on the Y-axis.

Attention can be divided into classes of ages. Too young (below 10 years) and too old ones (above 70 years) lack attention whereas teenagers are consistent in this regard.

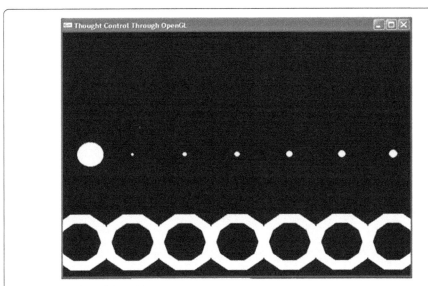

Figure 2 Snapshot of the BCI game.

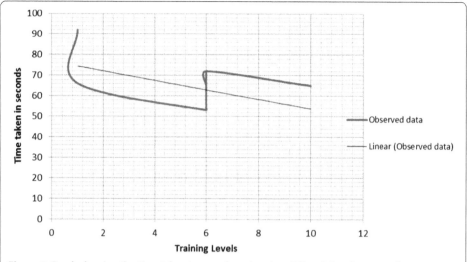

Figure 3 Graph showing the time taken to complete the given BCI task by abacus students at different levels of training.

Further it considerably reduces with age. The subjects selected were not trained with special mental skills.

The linear trendline is a best-fit straight line for the data sets obtained which follows the equation given below to calculate the least squares fit for a line:

y = mx + c, where m is the slope and c is the intercept.

The application was tested on an assortment of subjects from mind training institutes like abacus institute. Surprisingly, these subjects could navigate the sphere with greater ease in contrast with the normal subjects.

Conclusion

As a summary, the paper draws sharp inferences of the mental activities with conjunction to the factors like age, mental training, etc. The visual game aids as a tool in this regard. The graphical analysis reveals the correlation that exists between the attention values and their enhancement for subjects undergoing mental training skills like abacus and non-abacus subjects. It also reveals the

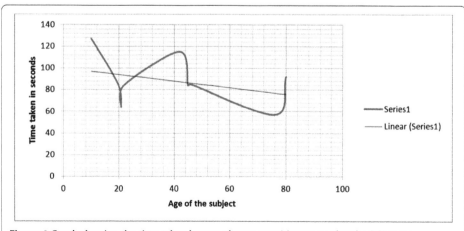

Figure 4 Graph showing the time taken by non-abacus practitioners to play the BCI game.

benefits of such training programmes. The application has the ability of providing feedback to children on their performance and monitoring their progress over time.

Future work

Visual modelling features of OpenGL can be added to distract a user during the game, which through control of thoughts could be overcome and could aid children with ADHD disorder to improve concentration. Playing such games on regular basis could enhance one's attention and focussing capabilities considerably.

Authors' contributions

Both the authors, GU and RG, have equally contributed in implementation of the proposed system, data acquisition and analysis, and documentation. All authors read and approved the final manuscript.

Author's information

Prof Geeta N. has graduated in Electronics and Communication Engineering from GIT, Belgaum and completed Post-graduation in Computer Networking from VTU Belgaum. Currently she is working as Assoc. Prof in Computer Science and Engineering at KLE Dr. M.S.S College of Engineering and Technology, Belgaum, Karnataka. Her areas of interest include cognitive computing, brain-computer interface, computer networks and parallel processing.
Mr. Rahul Dasharath Gavas is pursuing his Bachelor of Engineering in Computer Science and Engineering from KLE Dr. M.S.S College of Engineering and Technology, Belgaum, India. His areas of interest include cognitive computing, brain-computer interface and unpredictability theory.

Acknowledgements

The authors are immensely grateful to the valuable guidance provided by Dr. Nandini Sidnal, HOD, Department of Computer Science & Engg, KLE Dr. M.S.S CET, Udyambag, Belgaum.

References

1. Ferris GR, Munyon TP, Basik K, Buckley MR (2008) The Performance Evaluation Context: Social, Emotional, Cognitive, Political, and Relationship Components, Human Resource Management Review 18. Elsevier, pp 146–163, doi:10.1016/j.hrmr.2008.07.006
2. Payam Aghaei P, Tauseef G, Omar AZ, Gaetano G, Calvo RA (2008) Brain-Computer Interface: Next Generation Thought Controlled Distributed Video Game Development Platform. IEEE Symposium on Computational Intelligence and Games (CIG'08). doi:10.1109/CIG.2008.5035647
3. Wang Q, Sourina O, Nguyen MK (2010) EEG-based "Serious" Games Design for Medical Applications. Cyberworlds, International Conference, Singapore, IEEE Computer Society. doi:10.1109/CW.2010.56
4. Nunez PL, Srinivasan R (2006) Electric fields of the brain: the neurophysics of EEG. Oxford University Press, Inc, New York
5. Rebsamen B, Burdet E, Guan C, Zhang H, Teo CL, Zeng Q, Ang M, Laugier C (2006) A brain-controlled wheelchair based on P300 and path guidance. Biomedical Robotics and Biomechatronics. The First IEEE/RAS-EMBS International Conference. pp 1101–1106, doi:10.1109/BIOROB.2006.1639239
6. Rebsamen B, Teo CL, Zeng Q, Ang VMH, Burdet E, Guan C, Zhang H, Laugier C (2006) Controlling a wheelchair indoors using thought. IEEE Intelligent Systems 22:18–24, 2007. doi:10.1109/MIS.2007.26
7. Lécuyer A, Lotte F, Reilly RB, Leeb R, Hirose M, Slater M (2008) Brain-computer interfaces, virtual reality, and videogames. Computer 41:66–72
8. Hammond DC (2006) What is neurofeedback? Journal of Neurotherapy 10:25–36, 2006. doi:10.1300/J184v10n04_04
9. Lim CG, Lee TS, Guan C, Sheng Fung DS, Cheung YB, Teng SS, Zhang H, Krishnan KR (2010) Effectiveness of a brain-computer interface based programme for the treatment of ADHD: a pilot study. Pscyopharmacological Bulletin 43(1):73–82
10. Gevensleben H, Birgit H, Björn A, Schlamp D, Kratz O, Studer P, Wangler S, Rothenberger A, Moll GH, Heinrich H (2009) Distinct EEG effects related to neurofeedback training in children with ADHD: A randomized controlled trial. International Journal of Psychophysiology 74:149–157, doi:10.1016/j.ijpsycho.2009.08.005
11. Cowan JD, Markham L (1994) EEG biofeedback for the attention problems of Autism - A case study. Biofeedback and Self-Regulation 19:287–287
12. Lopetegui E, Zapirain BG, Mendez A (2011) Tennis Computer Game With Brain Control Using EEG Signals. Computer Games (CGAMES), 2011 16th International Conference. doi:10.1109/CGAMES.2011.6000344
13. Neurosky Mindwave Mobile. Available at: http://www.Neurosky.com
14. Emotive EEG System. Available at: http://www.emotiv.com
15. Crowley K, Aidan S, Pitt I, Murphy D (2010) Evaluating a brain-computer interface to categorise human emotional response. ICALT doi:10.1109/ICALT.2010.81

11

Collective intelligence within web video

Konstantinos Chorianopoulos

Correspondence: choko@ionio.gr
Department of Informatics, Ionian
University, 7 Tsirigoti square, Corfu
49100, Greece

Abstract

We present a user-based approach for detecting interesting video segments through simple signal processing of users' collective interactions with the video player (e.g., seek/scrub, play, pause). Previous research has focused on content-based systems that have the benefit of analyzing a video without user interactions, but they are monolithic, because the resulting key-frames are the same regardless of the user preferences. We developed the open-source SocialSkip system on a modular cloud-based architecture and analyzed hundreds of user interactions within difficult video genres (lecture, how-to, documentary) by modeling them as user interest time series. We found that the replaying activity is better than the skipping forward one in matching the semantics of a video, and that all interesting video segments can be found within a factor of two times the average user skipping step from the local maximums of the replay time series. The concept of simple signal processing of implicit user interactions within video could be applied to any type of Web video system (e.g., TV, desktop, tablet), in order to improve the user navigation experience with dynamic and personalized key-frames.

Keywords: Video; Web; User-based; Key-frame; Collective intelligence; Signal processing; Analytics

Introduction

In this research, we examine the benefits of Web video platforms for the simplest type of user interaction, such as pause/play, skip/scrub. The convergence of diverse video and TV systems toward Web-based technologies has transformed the static conceptualization of the viewer, from consumer of content, to active participant. For example, IP-based video has become a popular medium for creating, sharing, and active interaction with video [1-3]. At the same time, IP-based video streaming has become available through alternative channels (e.g., TV, desktop, mobile, tablet). In the above diverse, but technologically converged scenarios of use, the common denominator is the increased interactivity and control that the user has on the playback of the video. For example, the users are able to pause and, most notably, to seek forward and backward within a video, regardless of the transport channel (e.g., mobile, web, broadcast, IPTV). In this work, we suggest that user-based video thumbnails that dynamically summarize and visualize the structure of a video are beneficial for all Web-based TV systems.

Before the emergence of Web video and TV systems, content-based research has established the need for video thumbnails [4], video summaries [5], and the usefulness of automatic detection of key-frames for user navigation [6,7], but has not regarded the benefits of user-based approaches. In this work, we explore the modeling of user interest based on simple user interactions that are common to any Web video platform, such as play/pause, seek/scrub. User-based research on web video has focused on the meaning of the comments, tags, re-mixes, and micro-blogs, but has not examined simple user interactions with the web-based video player [8]. Although there are various methods that collect and manipulate user-based data, the majority of them are considered burdensome for the users, because they require an extra effort. Moreover, the percentage of users leaving a comment is rather small when compared to the real number of viewers [3]. In this research, we have implemented and empirically evaluated a system that leverages seamless user interactions for extracting useful information about a video. In particular, we let the viewer browse the video, we store all the interactions with the player (e.g. play, pause, seek), and we model them as a continuous signal, which we analyze with simple signal processing techniques, in order to automatically generate key-frames of interesting video segments.

In the remaining of the paper, we examine the properties of the open source SocialSkip system, and we present the results of user-based key-frame extraction.

Related work

Previous research has explored several techniques in order to improve users' navigation experience. One of the major goals in multimedia information retrieval is to provide abstracts of videos. Abstraction techniques are a way for efficient and effective navigation in video clips [9]. Indeed, stationary images have proven an effective user interface in video editing, [10], as well as in video browsing [11]. According to Truong and Venkatesh [7] those techniques are classified in: 1) video skims, which provide moving images that stand for the important parts of the original video, and 2) key-frames, which provide stationary pictures of key moments from the original the video. According to Money and Agius [6], there is another interesting classification for video summarization techniques: 1) internal summarization techniques that analyse information sourced directly from the video stream, and 2) external ones that analyse information not sourced directly from the video stream. Notably, Money and Agius [6] suggest that the latter techniques hold the greatest potential for improving video summarization/abstraction, but there are rare examples of contextual and user-based works.

There are several research works on content-based key-frame extraction from videos, because a collection of still images is easier to deliver and comprehend when compared to a long video stream. Girgensohn et al. [12] found that clustering of similar colors between video scenes is an effective way to filter through a large number of key-frames. SmartSkip [13] is an interface that generates key-frames by analyzing the histogram of images every 10 seconds of the video and looking at rapid overall changes in the color and brightness. Li et al. [14] developed an interface that generates shot boundaries using a detection algorithm that identifies transitions between shots. Nevertheless, the techniques that extract thumbnails from each shot are not always efficient for a quick browse of video content, because there might be too many shots in a video (Figure 1, left).

In practical systems, web video players (e.g., Google Video, YouTube) provide thumbnails to facilitate user's navigation within a video and between related videos (Figure 1, left). Nevertheless, most of the existing content-based techniques that extract thumbnails at

Figure 1 Video-frames are an important part of user navigation within and between videos (left), but the research issue is that content-based techniques produce too many video thumbnails, which might not be representative, because they are selected by the video uploader (right).

regular time intervals, or from each shot are inefficient, because there might be too many shots in a video (e.g., how-to), or few (e.g., lecture). In the case of Google Video, there are so many thumbnails that a separate scroll bar has been employed for navigating through them. At the same time, search results and suggested links in popular video sites (e.g., YouTube) are represented with a thumbnail that the video authors have manually selected out of the three fixed ones (Figure 1, right). Moreover, by analogy to the early web-text search engines that were based on author definition of important keywords, the current video search engine approach puts too much trust on the frames selected by the video author. Besides the threat of authors tricking the system, the author-based approach does not consider the variability of users' knowledge and preferences, as well as the comparative ranking to the rest of the video frames within a video. Thus, there is a need for ranking video-frames according to the collective action of video users (i.e., viewers), in order to reveal important video segments.

Previous research has already identified the benefits of user-based analysis of content (e.g., tags, comments, micro-blogs), but there is limited work on implicit indicators, such as seek/scrub within video. Social video interactions on web sites are very suitable for applying community intelligence techniques [15]. Levy [16] outlined the motivation and the social benefits of collective intelligence, but he did not provide particular technical solutions to his vision. In the seminal user-based approach to web video, Shaw and Davis [17] proposed that video representation might be better modeled after the actual use made by the users. In this way, they have employed analysis of the annotations [17], as well as of the re-use of video segments in community re-mixes and mash-ups [18] to understand media semantics. Nevertheless, the above approaches are not complete, because they are content-based, or they require increased user effort. Shamma et al. [19] has explored whether micro-blogs (e.g., Twitter) could structure a TV broadcast, but the timing of a micro-blog might not match the semantics of the respective cue point in a video, since there is common time duration for writing a short comment. Notably, Yew et al. [20] have recognized the importance of scrubs (fast forward and rewind), but they have only included counts in their classifier and not the actual timing of the scrub events. Thus, we propose to leverage implicit user activity (e.g., pause/play, seek/scrub), in order to dynamically identify video segments of interest.

In summary, content-based techniques, such as pattern recognition algorithms that focus on the contents of a video (e.g., detection of changes in shots, and scenes) are static. In contrast, the community (or crowd-sourced) intelligence of implicit user activity within web video is dynamic, because it continuously adapts to evolving users' preferences. In the following section, we describe the design and the implementation of a system that collects and analyses the collective intelligence of implicit user interactions within web video.

Design

SocialSkip is an open-source platform we developed to gather and analyze interactions of users while they browse a video. Based on these interactions, representative thumbnails of the video are dynamically generated, according to simple signal processing (Figure 2).

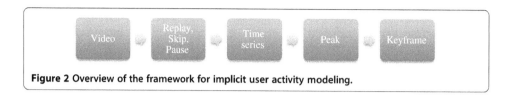

Figure 2 Overview of the framework for implicit user activity modeling.

Broadcast-, PC-, and web-based experimental systems

Researchers have developed various applications, in order to evaluate novel abstraction methods. Kim et al. [21] built a special-purpose system for their experimental environment. They wanted the subjects to believe that the content was being broadcast live. They used an interactive TV monitor, a TV encoder, a simulation server and an infrared remote control. Macromedia Director, a multimedia application platform, was used to develop SmartSkip [13]. The system was running on a desktop computer, it was connected to a television monitor, and a TV remote control was used by the participants for browsing. Crockford and Agius [22] designed a system as a wrapper around an ActiveX control of Windows Media Player. In summary, the majority of previous systems runs locally, needs special modification on software, and at the same time on video clips. Besides (broadcast and PC) stand-alone applications, there are few web-based systems. Fischlar [14] is a web-based system for capturing, storing, indexing and browsing broadcast TV material, but it only features content-based techniques. In the next sub-sections, we present a cloud-based system for user-based key-frame detection.

Cloud-based and open-source software architecture

In contrast to previous broadcast-, PC-, and Web-based systems, we used the Google App Engine (GAE) cloud platform (Platform-as-a-Service) and the YouTube Player API (YT API). At the time of writing, it is the first time that cloud-based technologies are used to build a system for key-frame extraction. SocialSkip (Figure 3) is a web application and has several advantages in contrast to stand-alone applications. Firstly, users do not have to go through an installation process, they just have to visit the link and if there is an updated version they just have to refresh the page. Secondly, the system architecture is modular and it allows re-use of the components. For example, a developer might decide to deploy a custom tablet video player and connect it to the cloud-based application logic, which tracks user activity and dynamically identifies interesting key-frames. Although we employed a simple Web-based video player, any player could connect to the application logic of the SocialSkip system.

There are several benefits of the selected tools (GAE, YouTube, Google accounts). GAE enables the development of web-based applications, as well as maintenance and administration of the traffic and the data storage. YT API allows developers to use the

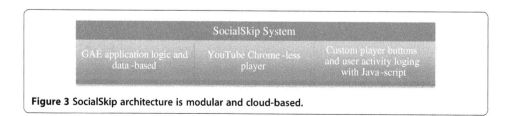

Figure 3 SocialSkip architecture is modular and cloud-based.

infrastructure of YouTube and therefore YouTube videos. In particular, the YT API provides a chrome-less user interface, which is a YouTube video player without any controls. This facilitates customization within Flash or HTML 5. In this way, we used JavaScript to create custom buttons and to implement their functions. Additionally, users of SocialSkip should have a Google account in order to sign in and watch the uploaded videos. In this way, we accomplish user authentication and we avoid the effort of implementing a user account system just for the application. Thus, users' interactions are recorded and stored in Google's database alongside with their Gmail addresses (Figure 4).

The Google App Engine database (Datastore) is used to store users' interactions. Each time a user signs in the web video player application, a new record is created. Whenever a button is pressed, an abbreviation of the button's name and the time it occurred are stored. This record includes four fields: a unique id, the username of the user's Google account, the date and a Text variable including all the interactions with the buttons of the web video player (Figure 5).

The SocialSkip video player (Figure 6) employs custom buttons, in order to be simple to associate user actions with video semantics. We have modified the classic forward and backward buttons to "GoBackward" and "GoForward." The first one jumps backwards 30 seconds and its main purpose is to replay the last 30 seconds of the video, while the GoForward button jumps forward 30 seconds and its main purpose is to skip insignificant video segments. Therefore, the player provides a subset of the main functionality of a typical VCR device [22]. We decided to use buttons that are similar to the main controls of VCR remote controls because they are familiar to users. Although we employed a fixed-step skip, we suggest that natural user interactions from any real system could be mapped to an average user skip-step. Thus, the assumption of the fixed-step skip should have external validity to field data, as well.

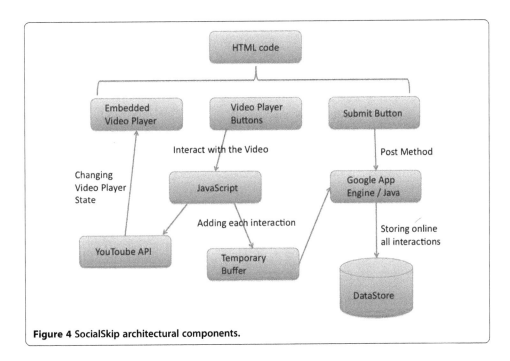

Figure 4 SocialSkip architectural components.

☐ ID/Name	author	content		date
☐ id=22001	videoskipuser3	p:0.1 gf:1.10 gb:32.044 a:3.337 gf:3.33		2010-11-06 00:04:03.066000
☐ id=27001	videoSkipuser1	p:0 gf:0 gb:0.186 gb:16.55 gf:0.567000 gf:0.26 gf:31.832 gf:63.697 gf:93.697		2010-11-15 15:27:30.744000

Figure 5 A screenshot of the records' table showing the id, the username (author), the content of the interactions and the date.

User interest modeling

The transition from the implicit user activity log data to a time series requires some form of user interest modeling. Previous research in user interest modeling has explored several functions that map user behavior to levels of interest. In a content-based approach, Ma et al. [5] made the assumption that video viewers are visually attracted by faces and sudden camera motion, as well as by sudden sounds. Olsen and Moon [23] have proposed that the interest function might be related to user interactions. Most notably, Peng et al. [24] have developed a system that connects the interest function to actual user attention, as measured through eye tracking and face recognition. In summary (Table 1), the main drawback of previous related works has been: 1) the inherent difficulty of modeling either user interest according to video cue time, and/or 2) the lack of any common infrastructure available to all users across Web-based video systems. As a remedy, we propose user interest modeling based on implicit user interaction with the video player buttons, which is common along any of the Web-based video systems (TV, mobile, desktop, tablet).

In this work, we consider that every video is associated with an array of k cells, where k is the duration of the video in seconds. Initially, the array has zero values. Each time the user presses the GoBackward/GoForward button the cells' values matching the last/next thirty seconds of the video, are incremented/decreased by one (Figure 7). We make the assumption that the user replays a video segment either because there is something interesting, or because there is something difficult to understand, while the user skips forward a video segment because there is nothing of interest. In this way, an experimental time series is constructed for each button and for each video—a depiction of collective users' activity over time.

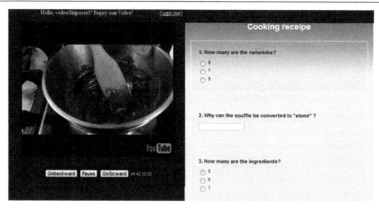

Figure 6 The SocialSkip video player has familiar buttons, as well as a questionnaire functionality, in order to experimentally simulate the collective interest to particular video segments.

Table 1 Previous user interest modeling research has established the significance of mapping user actions to video semantics, but there are drawbacks in all approaches

User interest modeling	Advantages	Disadvantages
Ma et al. [5]	Assumes that viewers are interested in particular well defined and easy to retrieve content features (e.g., faces)	Content-based and thus static vocabulary of what is interesting
Shaw and Davis [17]	User comments and tags	Do not have time information
Shaw and Davis [17]	Remix of popular video segments	Only a portion of users perform re-mixes of video
Shamma et al. [19]	Micro-blogs are associated to TV broadcast	The timing information might not correspond to video cue time
Carlier et al. [25]	Zoom denotes areas of interest within a video frame	Zoom is not a common feature
Olsen and Moon [23]	Interest function	Explicit ratings
Peng et al. [24]	Eye tracking and face recognition	Web camera

In order to extract pattern characteristics from each time series a key-frame detection scheme is developed based on the proposed user interest model. Figure 7 shows a flow-chart of the proposed scheme. In this scheme, the component user interest models are first computed; then, a composite user interest time series is generated by linear combination. The user interest is composed of a time series of the interest values associated with each second in a video sequence. After smoothing, we can identify a number of local maximums. According to the definition of user interest model, the video segments with peaks are most likely to attract the viewers' interest. Therefore, it is reasonable to assume that key-frames should be extracted from the area that is close to those local maximums. A similar approach (i.e., activity graph, smoothing window, local maximum) to the construction of time series from micro-blogs (e.g., Twitter) has been followed by a growing number of researchers (e.g., see citations to [19]). Next, we have to compute the exact location of the proposed key-frame in comparison to an established ground truth. Notably, the interest value of a key-frame can be used as the importance measure of the key-frame. Based on such a measure the most highly ranked key-frames can be used as representative frames of a video in search results and lists of related videos, instead of the fixed ones (Figures 1,2).

Evaluation

The evaluation of a key-frame extraction and video summarization systems has been considered a very difficult problem, as long as user-based systems are concerned. Notably, Ma et al. [5] have argued that: "Although the issues of key-frame extraction and

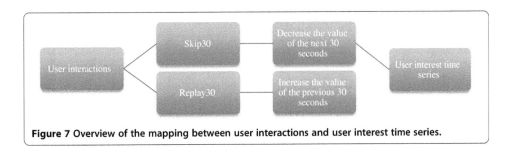

Figure 7 Overview of the mapping between user interactions and user interest time series.

video summary have been intensively addressed, there is no standard method to evaluate algorithm performance. The assessment of the quality of a video summary is a strong subjective task. It is very difficult to do any programmatic or simulated comparison to obtain accurate evaluations, because such methods are not consistent with human perception." In content-based research (e.g., TRECVID), researchers have defined a set of ground-truths that are used as benchmarks during the evaluation of novel algorithms. In this work, we propose that the evaluation of user-based key-frame extraction systems could be transformed into an objective task as long as there is a set of ground truths about the content. In particular, we select videos that are relevant to the users and we ask the users to retrieve information from the video, in order to answer a set of questions in an experimental setting. In the following sub-sections, we are describing the selection of the videos, of the users, and of the questions.

Materials

We selected videos that are as much visually unstructured as possible, because content-based algorithms have already been successful with those videos that have visually structured scene changes. In particular, the lecture video included typical camera pans and zooms from speaker to projected slides, the documentary included a basic narrative and quick scene changes, and the how-to (cooking) video consisted of rapid changes of shots between the people and the cooking activity. In order to experimentally replicate user activity we developed a questionnaire that corresponds to several segments of each video. According to Yu et al. [26] there are segments of a video clip that are commonly interesting to most users, and users might browse the respective parts of the video clip in searching for answers to some interesting questions. In this way, we can assume that during the experimental process the questions that the users are asked to answer stand for interesting topics and that the respective video segments are semantically interesting. In the field (e.g., YouTube), when enough user data is available, user behavior might exhibit similar patterns even if they are not explicitly asked to answer questions, at least for those videos that users browse for utilitarian purposes (e.g., lecture, how-to).

Our main interest is with lecture videos for two reasons: 1) they lack any meaningful visual structure that might have been helpful in the case of a content-based system, and 2) they contain lots of audio-visual (verbal and non-verbal) information that a user might actively seek to retrieve. In addition to video lecture, we employed a how-to (cooking) video because it has a rather complicated and has an active visual structure, which might have created too many false positives for a content-based approach. Finally, we employed a documentary video, which provides a baseline for evaluation with narrative-based videos. The questionnaire employed very simple questions that could not be answered by previous knowledge of the users Table 2.

Procedure

The goal of the user experiment is to collect activity data from the users, as well as to establish a flexible experimental procedure that can be replicated and validated by other researchers. There are several suggested approaches to the evaluation of interactive information retrieval systems [27]. Instead of mining real usage data, we have designed a controlled experiment, because it provides a clean set of data that might be easier to

Table 2 Example questions from each video

Video	Indicative questions
Lecture A	Which are the main research topics?
	What the students did not like?
	What time does the first part of the talk end?
Documentary B	What time do you see the message "coming next"?
	What is the purpose of hackers?
	What is the name of the girl in the video?
Cooking C	How many are the ramekins?
	How many are the ingredients?
	Which is the right order for mixing the ingredients?

analyze. The experiment took place in a lab with Internet connection, general-purpose computers and headphones. Twenty-three university students (18–35 years old, 13 women and 10 men) spent approximately ten minutes to watch each video (buttons were muted). All students had been attending the Human-Computer Interaction courses at the Department of Informatics at a post- or under-graduate level and received course credit in the respective courses. Next, there was a time restriction of five minutes, in order to motivate the users to actively browse through the video and answer the respective questions. We informed the users that the purpose of the study was to measure their performance in finding the answers to the questions within time constraints. After a basic understanding between the user behavior data and the key-frame detection is established, further research could progress to larger scale studies, or even to field studies and data mining of large data-sets.

Results

According to the proposed implicit user-based key-frame detection scheme (Figure 8), we created graphs that facilitated the visual comparison between the original user interest, the ground truth (interesting video segments), and smooth versions of the user interest time series (Figure 9). We explored alternative smoothing windows for each one of the three types of time series (Replay30, Skip30, Composite). We observed that in all cases the smoothing window should be at least 30 seconds (equal to the fixed skip-step), in order to provide a smooth signal with clear peaks. Moreover, we found that the ideal moving window ranges between 30, 45, and 60 seconds for each one of the three videos respectively (Documentary, Cooking, Lecture). Since we have a controlled experiment (equal number of users, time, total interactions), we suggest that the variability of the smoothing window might depend on the number and duration of the interesting video segments. We do not have conclusive results on this issue, because this was an unexpected finding that should be considered for elaboration in further research.

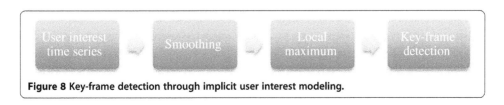

Figure 8 Key-frame detection through implicit user interest modeling.

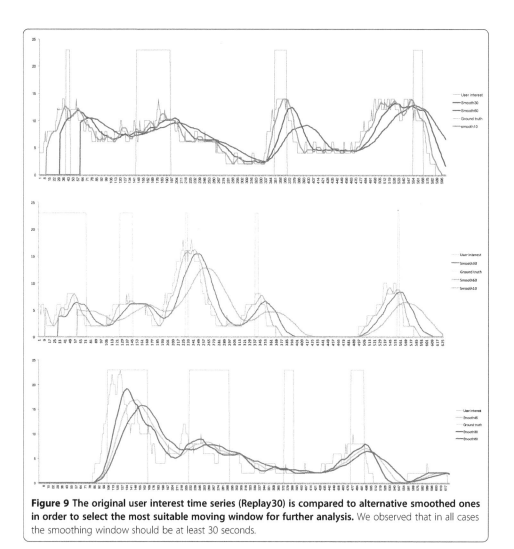

Figure 9 The original user interest time series (Replay30) is compared to alternative smoothed ones in order to select the most suitable moving window for further analysis. We observed that in all cases the smoothing window should be at least 30 seconds.

Next, we visually compared the smooth versions of the component and composite times series to the ground truth (Figure 10). We observed that in most cases the Replay30 time series closely matched the ground truth. Neither the Skip30, nor the composite time series seem to match the ground truth (Figure 10). Therefore, we computed the local maximums of the Replay30 time series for each one of the three videos.

Finally, we found that a simple heuristic could provide key-frames that are positioned at the start of each interesting video segment. In order to calculate this heuristic we observed that in all cases the distance of the local maximum of the Replay30 time series from the start of the respective ground truth is less than 60 seconds. This simple heuristic detects 100% of the interesting video segments (n = 13). Moreover, we observed that approximately 70% (9 out of 13) of the interesting video segments are within 30 seconds and before the local maximum. There is only one case that the local maximum is before the start of the interesting video segment (Cooking video, S3). It is notable that the observed 60 seconds distance is twice the duration of the fixed skip-step. Therefore, we suggest that the position of interesting key-frames can be automatically approximated for any video with informational content by locating the local maximums of the Replay30 time series and then moving back twice the size of the (average) replay step (Table 3).

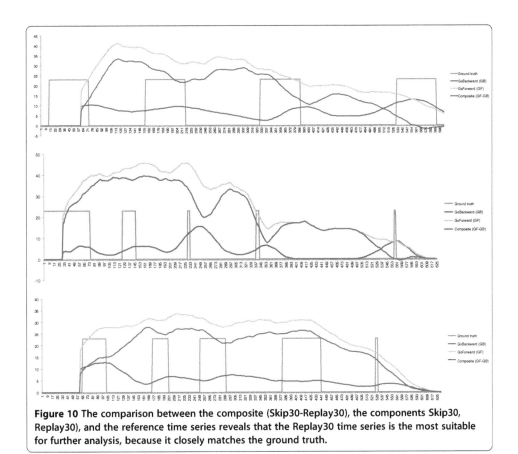

Figure 10 The comparison between the composite (Skip30-Replay30), the components Skip30, Replay30), and the reference time series reveals that the Replay30 time series is the most suitable for further analysis, because it closely matches the ground truth.

The experimental system also kept a log of the answers to the questions alongside the video interaction log, which was used to model the areas of interest. We considered separating the analysis of the user activity logs with correct answers of those with incorrect answers, but we realized that in many cases with incorrect answers the users did search for the answer at the right time of the video. Therefore, we decided that there is no reason to distinguish between correct and incorrect answers, because most users actively searched for interesting video segments.

Discussion

Key-frame detection system for research and practice

The open-source implementation of SocialSkip[a] is based on simple, modular, and well-established software components. SocialSkip is a cloud-based application, which uses cloud-based resources (bandwidth, processing, storage), open user-terminal software (any video streaming player), and videos provided by open video databases (e.g., YouTube). The SocialSkip architecture does not require any extra equipment beyond a computer and an internet connection. Previous efforts have introduced several applications in order to evaluate methods for understanding video content. The majority of related studies developed stand alone applications in order to avoid the elaborate installation, processing and streaming problems of broadcast systems. In terms of the user-based data, the most relevant work is the Hot-spots tool, which is part of the YouTube Insight video account. The Hot-spots tool is employing the same set of data as suggested here, but there is no open

Table 3 The distance of the local maximum of the replay30 time series from the start of the respective pulse (inside parentheses) in the ground truth time series

Distance of local replay30 maximum (from ground truth start)	Lecture A	Documentary	Cooking
S1	33 (40)	58 (1)	45 (105)
S2	13 (145)	19 (126)	21 (230)
S3	48 (350)	16 (229)	−13 (374)
S4	1 (554)	15 (338)	21 (475)
S5		1 (557)	

documentation on the technique employed to map user interactions to a graph. Moreover, Hot-spots has been designed as a tool for video authors, but SocialSkip is proposed as a back-end tool that might improve navigation for all video viewers. Most notably, researchers and practitioners have been cooperating for more than a decade on a large-scale video library and tools for analyzing the content of video. The TRECVID workshop series provides a standard-set of videos, tools, and benchmarks, which facilitate the incremental improvement of sense making for videos [28]. In similar way, we provide open access to both source code and the growing data-set of user interactions, which might facilitate further implementations, as well as alternative user-centric key-frame extraction algorithms.

Key-frame detection process through Implicit user-interest modeling

Although many corporations and academic institutions are making lecture videos and seminars available online, there have been few and scattered research efforts to understand and leverage actual user browsing behavior. He et al. [29] derive user activity (e.g., play, pause, random seek), but did not take advantage of them. Yu et al. [26] made the assumption that there is a shortest path in each video and evaluated user navigation among key-frames with link analysis. Syeda-Mahmood and Ponceleon [30] modeled implicit user activity according to the user's sentiment (e.g., user is bored, or interested). In context of video editing in a studio environment [31], collective user behavior has been proven an effective way to understand and collaborate on video. The benefits of collective intelligence for web video have been noted by Carlier et al. [25], in the case of zoom-able video user interface. Yew et al. [20] have recognized the importance of scrubs (fast forward and rewind), but they have only included counts in their classifier and not the actual timing of the scrub events. Moreover, Martin and Holtzman [32] highlight the value of implicit interactions (views) on news items, but they did not explore this concept within a web video, in order to identify particular segments. Olsen and Moon [9] have devised a degree of interest (DOI) function for American football, which depends on the availability of different camera angles, on "plays", and user ratings, but these features are not generic to all videos. Finally, Peng et al. [24] have examined the physiological behavior (eye and head movement) of video users, in order to identify interesting key-frames, but this approach is not practical because it assumes that a video camera should be available and turned-on in the home environment. In summary, SocialSkip proposes a very simple and generic approach that applies to any viewer and any video on Web-based TV systems.

Further research

In this work, we have focused on the design, development, and experimental evaluation of the system. Future work should consider the optimization of the key-frame-extraction algorithm and its adaptation to different users groups and video contents. For example, SocialSkip could also connect to other growing (lecture and how-to) video libraries, such as Vimeo, and khan academy.

Video key-frames provide an important navigation mechanism and a summary of the video, either with thumbnails, or with video-skims. There are significant open research issues with video-skims: 1) the number and relative importance of segments that are needed to describe a video, and 2) the duration of video-skims. The number of segments depends on several parameters, such as the type and length of the video. Therefore, it is unlikely that there are a fixed number of segments (or a fixed video skim duration) that describes a particular category of videos (e.g., lectures). If the required number of segments is different for each video, then, besides the segment extraction technique, we need a ranking to select the most important of them. Moreover, the duration of each video skim should not be fixed, but should depend on the actual duration of user interest for a particular video segment.

Although the replay user activity seems suitable for modeling user interest, further research should consider the rest of the implicit user activities. We decided to ignore the "pause" interaction because, during the pilot tests, we noticed that the users paused the player to write down the answer to a question. Thus, the pause frequency distribution perfectly matched the ground truths, but this pattern might not have external validity. Nevertheless, in field data, a "pause" might signify an important moment, but a pause that is too long might mean that the user is away.

Another direction for further research would be to perform data mining on a large-scale web-video database. Nevertheless, we suggest that the experimental approach might be more flexible than data mining for the development phase of the system. In particular, the incremental and experimental approach is very suitable for user-centric information retrieval, because it is feasible to connect user behavior with the respective data-logs. In contrast to data mining in large data-sets, a controlled experiment has the benefit of keeping a clean set of data that does not need several steps of frequency domain filtering, before it becomes usable for any kind of simple time-based signal processing.

Finally, we suggest that user-based content analysis has the benefits of continuously adapting to evolving users' preferences, as well as providing additional opportunities for the personalization of content. For example, researchers might be able to apply several personalization techniques, such as collaborative filtering, to the user activity data. In this way, video pragmatics is emerging as a new playing field for improving user experience.

Conclusion

We have developed an implicit user-based key-frame detection system and we have demonstrated that the collective intelligence of users' interactions with a familiar video player could be analyzed in order to generate user-based key-frames. Although we designed the SocialSkip system as a web-based one, the concept of mapping implicit user interactions to a time-series for further analysis has a much broader application. Every second millions of users enjoy video streaming on a diverse number of terminals

(TV, desktop, smart phone, tablets) and create billions of simple interactions. This amount of data might be converted into useful information for the benefit of all video users. As long as the community of users watching videos on Web-based video systems is growing, more and more interactions are going to be gathered and therefore, dynamic thumbnails would represent in a timely fashion the most important scenes of a video according to evolving user interests. We also expect that the combination of richer user profiles and content metadata provide opportunities for additional personalization of the thumbnails. Overall, our findings support the concept that we can learn a lot about an unstructured video just by analyzing how it is being used, instead of looking at the content item itself. In the end, we expect that a balanced mix of hybrid algorithms (content-based and user-based) might provide an optimal solution for navigating inside video content.

Endnotes
[a]Open-source project: http://code.google.com/p/socialskip/

Ethical approval
This research has been approved by Ionian University (Corfu, Greece) and it is in compliance with the Helsinki Declaration.

Competing interests
The authors declare that they have no competing interests.

Acknowledgements
We are thankful to the participants of the user study, and to Markos Avlonitis, David Ayman Shamma, Ioannis Leftheriotis, and Chryssoula Gkonela for assisting in the implementation and evaluation of the system, as well as for providing feedback on early drafts of this paper. The work reported in this paper has been partly supported by project CULT (http://cult.di.ionio.gr). CULT (MC-ERG-2008-230894) is a Marie Curie project of the European Commission (EC) under the 7th Framework Program (FP7).

References
1. Cha M, Kwak H, Rodriguez P, Ahn Y, Moon S (2007) I tube, you tube, everybody tubes: analyzing the world's largest user generated content video system. In: Proceedings of the 7th ACM SIGCOMM Conference on internet Measurement (San Diego, California, USA, October 24–26, 2007). IMC '07. ACM, New York, NY, pp 1–14
2. Cheng X, Dale C, Liu J (2008) Statistics and social network of YouTube videos. In: Quality of service. IWQoS 2008. 16th International Workshop on, IEEE, pp 229–238
3. Mitra S, Mayank A, Amit Y, Niklas C, Derek E, Anirban M (2011) Characterizing Web-based video sharing workloads. ACM Trans Web 5(2):Article 8, May 2011
4. Davis M (1995) Media streams: an iconic visual language for video representation. In: Baecker RM, Jonathan G, Buxton WAS, Saul G (eds) Human-computer interaction. Morgan Kaufmann Publishers Inc, San Francisco, CA, USA, pp 854–866
5. Ma Y-F, Lu L, Zhang H-J, Li M (2002) A user attention model for video summarization. In: Proceedings of the tenth ACM international conference on multimedia (MULTIMEDIA '02). ACM, New York, NY, USA, pp 533–542
6. Money AG, Agius H (2008) Video summarisation: a conceptual framework and survey of the state of the art. J Vis Comun Image Represent 19(2):121–143
7. Truong BT, Venkatesh S (2007) Video abstraction: A systematic review and classification. ACM Trans Multimedia Comput Commun Appl 3:1, Article 3 (February 2007)
8. Chorianopoulos K, Leftheriotis I, Gkonela C (2011) SocialSkip: pragmatic understanding within web video. In: Procecdings of the 9th international interactive conference on Interactive television (EuroITV '11). ACM, New York, NY, USA, pp 25–28
9. Lienhart R, Pfeiffer S, Effelsberg W (1997) Video abstracting. Commun ACM 40(12):54–62
10. Baecker R, Rosenthal AJ, Friedlander N, Smith E, Cohen A (1997) A multimedia system for authoring motion pictures. In: Proceedings of the fourth ACM international conference on Multimedia (MULTIMEDIA '96). ACM, New York, NY, USA, pp 31–42
11. Boreczky J, Girgensohn A, Golovchinsky G, Uchihashi S (2000) An interactive comic book presentation for exploring video. In: Proceedings of the SIGCHI conference on human factors in computing systems (CHI '00). ACM, New York, NY, USA, pp 185–192
12. Girgensohn A, Boreczky J, Wilcox L (2001) Keyframe-based user interfaces for digital video. Computer 34(9):61–67

13. Drucker SM, Glatzer A, De Mar S, Wong C (2002) SmartSkip: consumer level browsing and skipping of digital video content. In: Proceedings of the SIGCHI conference on human factors in computing systems: changing Our world, changing ourselves (Minneapolis, Minnesota, USA, April 20–25, 2002). CHI '02. ACM, New York, NY, pp 219–226

14. Li FC, Gupta A, Sanocki E, He L, Rui Y, Rui Y (2000) Proceedings of the SIGCHI conference on human factors in computing systems (the Hague, the Netherlands, April 01–06, 2000). CHI '00. In: Proceedings of the SIGCHI conference on human factors in computing systems (the Hague, the Netherlands, April 01–06, 2000). ACM, New York, NY, pp 169–176

15. Zhang D, Guo B, Yu Z (2011) The emergence of social and community intelligence. Computer 44(7):21–28

16. Levy P (1997) Collective intelligence: Mankind's emerging world in cyberspace. Perseus Publishing

17. Shaw R, Davis M (2005) Toward emergent representations for video. In: Proceedings of the 13th annual ACM international conference on multimedia (MULTIMEDIA '05). ACM, New York, NY, USA, pp 431–434

18. Shaw R, Schmitz P (2006) Community annotation and remix: a research platform and pilot deployment. In: Proceedings of the 1st ACM international workshop on human-centered multimedia (HCM '06). ACM, New York, NY, USA, pp 89–98

19. Shamma DA, Lyndon K, Elizabeth F (2009) Tweet the debates: understanding community annotation of uncollected sources, Proceedings of the first SIGMM workshop on Social media (WSM '09). ACM, New York, NY, USA, Churchill, pp 3–10. doi:10.1145/1631144.1631148

20. Yew J, Shamma DA, Churchill EF (2011) Knowing funny: genre perception and categorization in social video sharing. In: Proceedings of the 2011 annual conference on Human factors in computing systems (CHI '11). ACM, New York, NY, USA, pp 297–306

21. Kim J, Kim H, Park K (2006) Towards optimal navigation through video content on interactive TV. Interact Comput 18(4):723–746

22. Crockford C, Agius H (2006) An empirical investigation into user navigation of digital video using the VCR-like control set. Int J Hum-Comput Stud 64(4):340–355

23. Olsen DR, Moon B (2011) Video summarization based on user interaction. In: Procceddings of the 9th international interactive conference on interactive television (EuroITV '11). ACM, New York, NY, USA, pp 115–122

24. Peng W-T, Chu W-T, Chang C-H, Chou C-N, Huang W-J, Chang W-Y, Hung Y-P (2011) Editing by viewing: automatic home video summarization by viewing behavior analysis. Multimedia, IEEE Transactions on 13(3):539–550

25. Carlier A, Charvillat V, Ooi WT, Grigoras R, Morin G (2010) Crowdsourced automatic zoom and scroll for video retargeting. In: Proceedings of the international conference on multimedia (MM '10). ACM, New York, NY, USA, pp 201–210

26. Yu B, Ma W-Y, Nahrstedt K, Zhang H-J (2003) "Video summarization based on user log enhanced link analysis", Proceedings of the eleventh ACM international conference on Multimedia - MULTIMEDIA'03. ACM Press, New York, New York, USA, p 382

27. Kelly D (2009) Methods for evaluating interactive information retrieval systems with users. Foundations and Trends in Information Retrieval: 3(1–2):1–224

28. Snoek CGM, Worring M (2009) Concept-based video retrieval. Foundations and Trends in Information Retrieval 2 (4):215–322

29. He L, Sanocki E, Gupta A, Grudin J (1999) "Auto-summarization of audio-video presentations", Proceedings of the seventh ACM international conference on Multimedia (Part 1) - MULTIMEDIA'99. ACM Press, New York, New York, USA, pp 489–498

30. Syeda-Mahmood T, Ponceleon D (2001) "Learning video browsing behavior and its application in the generation of video previews", Proceedings of the ninth ACM international conference on Multimedia - MULTIMEDIA'01. ACM Press, New York, New York, USA, p 119

31. Cohen J, Withgott M, Piernot P (1999) Logjam: a tangible multi-person interface for video logging. In: Proceedings of the SIGCHI conference on human factors in computing systems: the CHI is the limit (CHI '99). ACM, New York, NY, USA, pp 128–135

32. Martin R, Holtzman H (2010) Newstream: a multi-device, cross-medium, and socially aware approach to news content. In: Proceedings of the 8th international interactive conference on interactive TV\&\#38; video (EuroITV '10). ACM, New York, NY, USA, pp 83–90

12

Assessment of combined textural and morphological features for diagnosis of breast masses in ultrasound

Kadayanallur Mahadevan Prabusankarlal[1,2*], Palanisamy Thirumoorthy[3] and Radhakrishnan Manavalan[4]

* Correspondence:
kmsankar@gmail.com
[1]Research & Development Centre, Bharathiar University, Coimbatore 641046, India
[2]Department of Electronics & Communication, K.S.R College of Arts & Science, Tiruchengode 637215, India
Full list of author information is available at the end of the article

Abstract

The objective of this study is to assess the combined performance of textural and morphological features for the detection and diagnosis of breast masses in ultrasound images. We have extracted a total of forty four features using textural and morphological techniques. Support vector machine (SVM) classifier is used to discriminate the tumors into benign or malignant. The performance of individual as well as combined features are assessed using accuracy(Ac), sensitivity(Se), specificity(Sp), Matthews correlation coefficient(MCC) and area A_Z under receiver operating characteristics curve. The individual features produced classification accuracy in the range of 61.66% and 90.83% and when features from each category are combined, the accuracy is improved in the range of 79.16% and 95.83%. Moreover, the combination of gray level co-occurrence matrix (GLCM) and ratio of perimeters (P_{ratio}) presented highest performance among all feature combinations (Ac 95.85%, Se 96%, Sp 91.46%, MCC 0.9146 and A_Z 0.9444).The results indicated that the discrimination performance of a computer aided breast cancer diagnosis system increases when textural and morphological features are combined.

Keywords: Breast ultrasound; Feature extraction; Textural features; Morphological features; Machine learning; SVM classifier

Introduction

The most frequently diagnosed cancer all over the world is the Breast cancer, accounting for 23% (1.38 million) of total cancer cases. It is responsible for about 14% (458,400) of the total cancer deaths in 2008, as leading cause of mortality in females. Almost half of the breast cancer cases and 60% of the mortality present in economically developing countries such as India. The availability of early detection facilities in developed countries contribute to the variation in incidence rates [1].

Mammography has been the primary investigating tool for breast cancer screening. Besides the ionizing radiation of mammography increases the health risk of patients and radiologists, depending on the age and breast density of the patient, mammography screening is associated with a false-negative rate of 10–20% [2]. Also, mammography can hardly detect breast cancer in adolescent women with dense breasts. Ultrasound (US) imaging shows increasing interest in breast cancer detection and diagnosis as an effective alternative to mammography. Ultrasound can be used to characterize a breast lesion as solid or cystic. It is efficient in staging breast cancer more precisely and assists physician in guided biopsy [3]. Ultrasound is an effective, convenient, inexpensive, real-time and ionizing radiation-free imaging tool for the diagnosis of breast tumors in clinics [4].

Employing computer algorithms in ultrasound images improves radiologists' accuracy in distinguishing malignant from benign breast masses [5]. The computer-aided diagnosis (CAD) systems have been introduced to improve the capability of radiologist in interpretation and recognition of breast masses [6,7]. The CAD system increases the efficiency of radiologists and their interpretation can also be improved in terms of accuracy, sensitivity and consistency in discrimination of masses. The overall productivity has been increased by reducing the time required for reading the ultrasonagrams manually by radiologists [8].

It is essential to quantify the characteristics of breast tumors for the detection as well as discrimination, which are quite often difficult to grasp due to intrinsic limitations of the ultrasound imaging process, such as low contrast, speckle noise, heterogeneity or artifacts. It is significant to explore the feature, or set of features, which provide better quantifications of the characteristics of tumors [9]. Some general guidelines [10] for identifying significant features which leads to accurate diagnosis are discrimination, reliability, independence and optimality. However, simply combining the number of best performed features does not make the system effective, but the objective is to identify a set of effective features to classification stage by reducing the redundancy [11].

Textural features, extracted from ultrasound images are efficient features for classifiying breast tumors [12]. Gomes et al. [13] extracted twenty two textural features through gray level co-occurrence matrix (GLCM) using 436 breast ultrasound images and obtained a good classification rate with an area A_Z of 0.87. The histogram, GLCM, gray level run length matrix (GLRLN) were used to extract textural features from 5500 prostate cancer images [14]. An accuracy of 92.83% was achieved in differentiating tumors by combining all the three features [14]. However, the textural features are effective with a specific ultrasound system and its precision reduces with images acquired from different US systems or with different US settings. The use of morphological features of the tumor which are almost independent of sonographic gain setting or different US machines is an alternative solution [15]. Huang et al. [15] extracted nineteen morphological features from 118 breast ultrasound images and using support vector machine(SVM) classifier, they achieved an A_Z of 0.909. Seven morphological parameters for distinguishing malignant from benign breast tumors in ultrasound images were investigated by Alveranga et al. [16]. The morphological features were derived through convex polygon technique and normalized radial length (nrl) to achieve an A_Z of 0.865.

Very few works in the literature have concentrated about combining textural and morphological features in the diagnosis of breast tumors in ultrasound. Wu et al. [17] combined auto-covariance texture features and morphological features extracted from 210 breast ultrasound images to discriminate breast tumors in ultrasound images. An accuracy of 92.86% was achieved using SVM classification. In a later work [18] using the same database, they achieved an accuracy of 96.14% using SVM-genetic algorithm based classifier. Alvaranga et al. [19] evaluated the combined performance of twenty textural and seven morphological features in distinguishing breast tumors. An accuracy of 85.37% was achieved on a database of 246 ultrasound images using fisher linear discriminant analysis(FLDA) classification.

In this work, our objective is to assess the individual and combined performance of textural and morphological features for discriminating breast masses in ultrasound images. Figure 1 shows the four stages of an automated computer aided diagnosis system. We have extracted the thirty nine textural and five morphological features from each region of interest (ROI) of breast ultrasound images in the entire database using an automated segmentation method. Support Vector Machine Classifier along with a 10 fold cross-validation scheme has been used for the assessment of individual and combined features using statistical parameters and ROC analysis.

Methods

Image database

The Breast ultrasound database consists of 120 images including 70 benign and 50 malignant images. The images used in this study are collected through [20], which complies with the HONcode (Health On the Net Foundation) standard for trustworthy health information. The Study protocols are approved by institution's ethics committee of Gelderse Vallei Hospital, Ede, the Netherlands with the consent of the patients.

Pre processing and segmentation

The speckle noise, a characteristic artifact in ultrasound images, significantly degrades the image quality and hinders finer details, which are essential for discrimination.

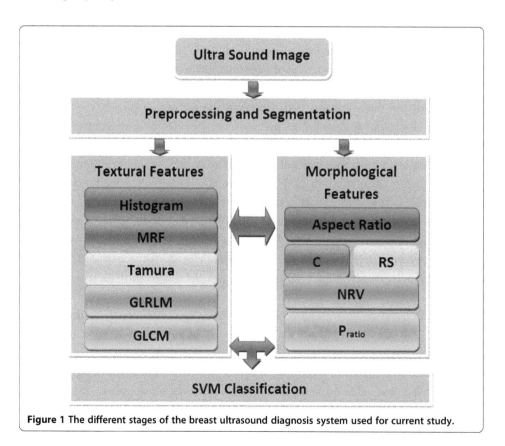

Figure 1 The different stages of the breast ultrasound diagnosis system used for current study.

Image segmentation divides an image into nonoverlapping regions and it is essential to detect breast lesions and to make correct diagnoses in CAD systems [21]. Accurate segmentation requires removal of speckle noise [22], and enhancement of lesion edges [23]. The Non-Local Means (NLM) filter proposed by Buades et al. [24] is based on self similarity or photometric closeness between two pixels. It measures the similarity between two pixels by evaluating the distance between small patches, centered on these two pixels [24,25]. The NLM has been proved to be an effective and suitable filter for removing speckle noise without affecting fine details present at the tumor region in medical ultrasound images [26]. In block-wise NLM [24], for each overlapping block B_{ik} centered around pixels ik, the NLM restoration takes place as,

$$NL(u)(B_{ik}) = \sum_{j \in I} \omega(B_{ik}, B_j) u(B_j) \tag{1}$$

where, $u(B_j)$ is the intensity of block B_j and $\omega(B_{ik}, B_j)$ is the weight assigned to $u(B_j)$ in the restoration of block B_{ik}. For a pixel i included in several blocks B_{ik}, several estimations of the restored intensity $NL(v)(i)$ are obtained in different $NL(v)(B_{ik})$. The weights [24] are defined as

$$\omega(B_{ik}, B_j) = \frac{1}{Z_{ik}} e - \frac{\|uB_{ik} - uB_j\|_2^2}{h^2} \tag{2}$$

where Z_{ik} is the normalization constant which also ensures $\sum_{B_j} \omega(B_{ik}, B_j) = 1$. The

similarity term $\|uB_{ik} - uB_j\|_2^2$ is measured as a diminishing function of the weighted Euclidean distance. The h is the filtering parameter. We used a smaller search window size of 13 X 13, patch size of 5 X 5 and filtering parameter h = 15 as suggested in [27]. The Figure 2 shows a benign and Figure 3 shows a malignant breast ultrasound images. The original images are shown in (A), the speckle removed images using NLM method [24] are shown in (B).

An automatic clustering based segmentation method [28] is employed in order to obtain the contour of the lesion. The Fuzzy C Means (FCM) clustering [28,29], a complex non linear model is employed for segmentation. The objective function of FCM is given by

$$J = \sum_{i=1}^{c} \sum_{j=1}^{n} \mu_{ij}^m \|s_j - a_i\|^2 \tag{3}$$

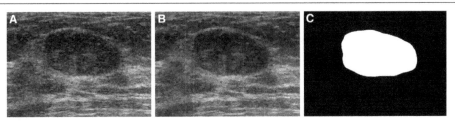

Figure 2 An image of a benign cyst. (A) Original image **(B)** Preprocessed image using NLM filter **(C)** Segmented image.

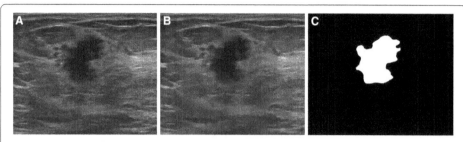

Figure 3 An image of a malignant tumor (A) Original image (B) Preprocessed image using NLM filter (C) Segmented image.

where, $a_1, a_2, ..., a_c$ are the c cluster centres. The μ_{ij} represents the membership of pixel s_j in the i th cluster and a_i is the cluster centre. The constant m controls the fuzzyness and the membership functions and cluster centres are updated as follows:

$$\mu_{ij} = \frac{1}{\sum_{k=1}^{c} \left(\frac{\|s_j - a_i\|}{\|s_j - a_k\|}\right)^{2/(m-1)}} \tag{4}$$

$$a_i = \frac{\sum_{j=1}^{n} \mu_{ij}^m s_j}{\sum_{j=1}^{n} \mu_{ij}^m}, i = 1, 2, ..., c \tag{5}$$

By iterating Eqs. (4) and (5), a_i and μ_{ij} will vary towards the direction that minimize the objective function gradually and when the change of a_i or μ_{ij} is within the given tolerance, the iteration is stopped. However, the algorithm initializes c cluster centers randomly and the solution is sought by iterating cluster centers and partition matrix through local search strategy based on gradient method. Thus the FCM is sensitive to initial values, and the different initial cluster centers lead to different clustering results. Also it often get stuck at local minima and the result is largely dependent on the choice of the initial cluster centers [29], the particle swarm optimization (PSO) algorithm is employed to exploit the searching capability of FCM.

The PSO, a population-based heuristic method based on the inspirations of group behavior of flocks of birds to find optimal solution to the non-linear numeric problems. In PSO, a particle is individual, and a number of particles are grouped as a swarm [29]. The velocity and position of the particle at next iteration are calculated using the following equations:

$$V_i(t+1) = w \cdot V_i(t) + c_1 \cdot r_1 \cdot (P_i - X_i) + c_2 \cdot r_2 \cdot (P_g - X_i) \tag{6}$$

$$X_i(t+1) = X_i(t) + V_i(t+1) \tag{7}$$

where, $V_i = [v_{i,1}, v_{i,2}, ..., v_{i,n}]$ and $X_i = [x_{i,1}, x_{i,2}, ..., x_{i,n}]$ represent the velocity and position of the particle i. The P_i and P_g represent the local and global best positions of the particle. The w is the inertia weight that controls the impact of previous velocity of particle on its current one; c_1 and c_2 are acceleration coefficients; r_1 and r_2 are two independent as well as uniformly distributed random variables with a range between 0 and 1. The PSO, with its efficient and adaptive search process provide near optimal solutions of an evaluation (fitness) function in an optimization problem and averts the FCM from trapping into local minima. A set of morphological operations [28] are performed as post processing in order to obtain the exact contour of the tumor. The parameters used for PSOFCM clustering are, number of particles n = 50, maximum inertia weight w_{max} = 0.9, minimum inertia weight w_{min} = 0.4, c_1 = 2 and c_2 = 2 [28,29]. The segmented images after morphological operations are shown in Figure 2(C) and Figure 3(C).

Feature extraction

The features in the breast ultrasound images can be divided into four categories; Texture, Morphology, Model based and Descriptor [30]. Relevant features from a specific category or set of features from two or more categories need to be extracted and selected for discriminating tumors in the classification stage [11].

Textural features

An important characteristic for identifying an object or regions of interest in an image is the texture. Though the texture and tone bear an inextricable relationship to one another in an image patch, the dominant property is the texture, when the patch has wide variation of features of discrete gray tone [31]. The textural features used in this work include six Histogram features, Markov Random Fields (MRF) based feature, three Tamura features, seven features of Grey Level Run-Length Matrix (GLRLM) and twenty two features of Gray Level Co-occurrence Matrix (GLCM).

Histogram features

The intensity histogram of an image is closely related to the characteristic of image such as brightness and contrast [14]. These features are computed from the histogram distribution of the image. The Six histogram features namely Mean, Variance, Skewness, Kurtosis, Entropy and Energy (F01 –F06) are listed in Additional file 1 along with their equations.

MRF features

Markov Random Fields (MRF) represents the distribution of conditional probabilities over elements in a lattice. Whereas, the probability assumed by an element depends only on the values of its neighbors [32]. In this context, each pixel in the image is considered as a random variable X_r which assume $x_r \in \{0, 1, 2, ... G - 1\}$, where G is the gray level. If η_r is the neighbor set of X_r, the conditional probability is given as $P(X_r = x_r | \eta_r)$.

The auto-logistic probability distribution model of MRF (F07) is presented as [32]

$$P(X_r = x_r | \eta_r) = \frac{e^{x_r T}}{1 + e^T} \tag{8}$$

where, T depends on the neighborhood and the features used by the classifier are the free parameters contained in T and the number of parameters depends on the neighborhood order[32].

Tamura features

Six textural features were defined by Tamura et al. [33] (coarseness, contrast, directionality, line-likeness, regularity and roughness). Coarseness is a fundamental texture feature related to scale and repetition rates in an image. Coarseness identifies the largest size at which a texture exists. Contrast represents the dynamic range of grey levels in an image. Directionality, a global property, describes total degree of directionality over a region. The values for these features are calculated for each pixel to form a Tamura CND image [34]. The descriptions of the three features (F08-F10) are given in Additional file 1.

GLRLM

The texture, a pattern of grey intensity pixel in a particular direction from the reference pixels; the grey level run-length matrix (GLRLM) is a matrix, from which features can be extracted [35]. The number of adjacent pixels with the same grey intensity in a specific direction is known as the run length. Such set of consecutive and collinear pixel points with same gray level is gray level run. GLRLM is a two-dimensional matrix in which each element represents the number of elements j with the intensity i, in the direction θ. The GLRLM [35] is computed as

$$R(\theta) = \left(g(i,j)\big|\theta\right), 0 \leq i \leq N_g, 0 \leq j \leq R_{max} \tag{9}$$

where N_g is the maximum gray level and R_{max} is the maximum length. Additional file 1 is the list of name and descriptions of seven GLRLM features (F11-F17).

GLCM

The gray level co-occurrence matrix (GLCM) is a second-order method to generate texture features. The GLCM comprises the joint frequencies of all pairwise gray level combinations (i, j) with a separation of d along direction θ. By using a distance of one pixel and angles quantized to 45° intervals, four matrices of horizontal, first diagonal, vertical, and second diagonal are used [31,36]. For the four principle directions the unnormalized frequency is defined as follows:

$$P(i,j,d,\theta) = \# \begin{cases} ((k,l),(m,n)) \epsilon \left(L_x \times L_y\right) \times \left(L_x \times L_y\right)| \\ (k-m = 0, |l-n| = d) \text{ or } (k-m = d, l-n = -d) \text{ or } (k-m = -d, l-n = d) \\ \text{or}(|k-m| = d, l-n = 0) \text{ or } (k-m = d, l-n = d) \text{ or } (k-m = -d, l-n = -d), \\ I(k,l) = i, I(m,n) = j \end{cases} \tag{10}$$

Where # is the number of elements in the set, (k, l) and (m, n) the coordinates with gray levels i and j, L_x and L_y the horizontal and vertical spatial domains and $(L_x \times L_y)$ are the set of resolution cells [36]. Totally twenty two features (F18-F39) are extracted through GLCM. The features along with their descriptions are given in Additional file 1.

Morphological features

The morphologic features are obtained from some local characteristics such as shape and margin of the breast lesion. It is an established fact that the borders of benign tumors are smoother than the borders of malignant ones; breast tumors can be evaluated based on their morphological information [16]. Five morphological features (F40-F44) are derived using convex polygon technique, based on the determination of the convex hull [15-19,36,37].

The overlap ratio (RS) is the ratio between actual area and the convex hull (F40) which is given as [16]

$$RS = \frac{A(S)}{A(S_0)} \qquad (11)$$

where, the convex hull (S_0) is established for region S. It is the ratio of number of pixels in area S and S_0.

The aspect ratio (F41) is the ratio of a tumor's depth and width. If the depth exceeds its width (or the ratio is greater than 1) the tumor has the higher probability of being malignant [15].

$$Aspect\ ratio = \frac{D_{depth}}{D_{width}} \qquad (12)$$

The circularity (C) is an important parameter in breast tumor classification [16]. The circularity is the ratio of square of the perimeter to the tumor area (F42). It is given as

$$C = \frac{P^2}{A(S)} \qquad (13)$$

The normalized residual value (NRV) [16] is given as (F43)

$$NRV = \frac{A(S_0) - A(S)}{P_0} \qquad (14)$$

where, P_0 is the perimeter of convex hull S_0. The NRV is the ratio between the residual area and perimeter.

The length of the tumor perimeter is an important indicator of malignancy, as malignant tumors usually have irregular shapes with a large tumor perimeter [15]. The ratio between the perimeter of the convex hull (P_0) and the perimeter of the tumor (P_{ratio}) (F44) is given as [18]

$$P_{ratio} = \frac{P}{P_0} \qquad (15)$$

It is important to note that unlike textural features; the morphological features have the advantage of being independent of settings of US systems or different US machines in the diagnosis of breast tumors [18].

Classification

Support vector machine (SVM) is an effective learning technique which constructs an optimal separating hyper plane in the high dimensional feature space. The SVM map the input vectors into a high-dimensional feature space through non-linear mapping and then an optimal separating hyperplane is chosen. The classification process involves training and testing of data which consist of some instances [38,39]. To create the optimal separating hyperplane between the classes, the SVM use training data.

For a given set of points $\{(x_i, y_i)_{1 \leq i \leq N}\}$, where $x_i \in R^n$ is the ith input vector and $y_i \in \{-1, 1\}$ is the desired output (class label), the SVM finds a hyperplane to separate the training data with a maximal margin. This optimal separating hyperplane (OSH) w: $wx + b = 0$ maximizes the margin of the closest data points. The data points on the margin border are called support vectors. The classification solution [38] is given by the function:

$$f(x) = sign\left(\sum_{i=1}^{N} \alpha_i y_i\, K(x_i, x) + b\right) \tag{16}$$

where α_i is the positive Lagrange multiplier, x_i is the support vector (a total of N) and $K(x_i, x)$ is the kernel decision function. Among the several kernel functions used in SVM such as linear, polynomial, and radial basis kernel functions (RBF), the RBF is most often used since it is suitable for classifying multidimensional data. The RBF [39] is given as

$$K(x, y) = \exp\left(\gamma\|x{-}y\|^2\right) \tag{17}$$

Moreover, the RBF has fewer parameters such as C and γ which should take appropriate values.

Results

The ROIs are generated for the all 120 US images in the database through image segmentation. For each ROI, totally forty four features, including six histogram, MRF, three Tamura, seven GLRLN and twenty two GLCM features are extracted separately along with five morphological features. We have used 10 fold cross-validation [39] for classification ($k = 10$), where the total 120 images are divided into 10 partitions. A total of k runs are required to complete the overall classification task with a set of features. In our method, among the k parts of data, (k-1) parts are used to train the classifier while one part is kept under testing. This process is repeated for 10 times to ensure all parts of data are tested. The experiments have been run using MATLAB 7.0 (Mathworks Inc, USA), on a computer which has Intel Core i3 processer (Intel Corp, USA), 8 GB RAM and Windows 7 operating system (Microsoft Corp, USA).

Statistical parameters

The effectiveness of the features is evaluated in terms of statistical parameters; accuracy, sensitivity, specificity and Matthews correlation coefficient (MCC) [30] as shown in contingency table (Figure 4). The MCC is a powerful accuracy evaluation criterion for machine learning methods, with unbalanced number of positive and negative samples in specific [30].

Evaluation of individual features

The individual feature vectors derived from textural and morphological methods are made as inputs of SVM classifier along with 10 fold validation scheme. The individual features, derived from the entire images of database are arranged as separate datasets. The diagnosed outcome is compared with pathologically proven facts. The values of all input features are normalized into the range of [−1,1], The output class of SVM is corresponded to either 0 or 1 depends on the discriminated tumor is benign or malignant. If the calculated value from the suspicious tumor region is nearer to 1, the image is classified as malignant. If the value is low enough to be considered as 0 and the image region is diagnosed as benign. The performance of individual features is shown in

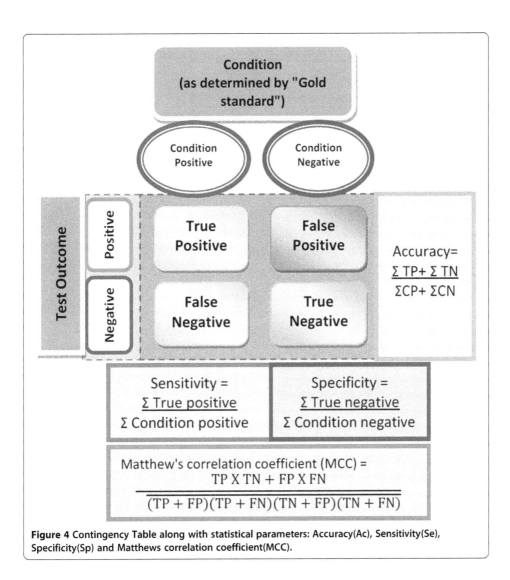

Figure 4 Contingency Table along with statistical parameters: Accuracy(Ac), Sensitivity(Se), Specificity(Sp) and Matthews correlation coefficient(MCC).

Table 1. Highest classification rates are achieved through GLCM features (Ac 90.83%, Se 90%, Sp 91.42% and MCC 0.8120), whereas with morphological features, the P_{ratio} yielded highest classification values(Ac 85.83%, Se 90%, Sp 82.85% and MCC 0.7193).

Evaluating combined features

In order to evaluate the performance of combined textural and morphological features, we combined top performing features from three textural categories (F08-F10, F11-F17 and F18-F39) and three morphological categories (F42, F43 and F44). The nine combinations of selected features (Table 2) are then used for the second set of experiments and the improvement has been observed in terms of statistical parameters is also shown in Table 2. The results suggest that the highest values in all parameters are achieved using the combination of GLCM and P_{ratio} (Ac 95.83%, Se 96%, Sp 95.71% and MCC 0.9146).

ROC analysis

The evaluation of overall value of a diagnosis test can be made through the use of a receiver operating characteristic (ROC) curve [40]. The curve is a plot between true

Table 1 Individual performance of the textural features (thirty nine features in five categories) and five morphological features sorted by accuracy value

Features	Accuracy %	Sensitivity %	Specificity %	MCC
Textural features				
Histogram features(F01-F06)	66.66	60.00	71.42	0.3143
MRF (F07)	76.66	74.00	78.57	0.5230
Tamura features(F08-F10)	77.50	78.00	77.14	0.5456
GLRLN features(F11-F17)	85.00	84.00	85.71	0.6936
GLCM features(F18-F39)	90.83	90.00	91.42	0.8120
Morphological features				
RS(F40)	61.66	66.00	58.57	0.2424
Aspect ratio(F41)	69.16	70.00	68.57	0.3808
C (F42)	74.16	76.00	72.86	0.4823
NRV (F43)	83.33	88.00	80.00	0.6708
P_{ratio}(F44)	85.83	90.00	82.85	0.7193

positive rate (sensitivity) and false positive rate (1 – specificity) of a classification task. The curve passes through the point (0, 1) on the unit grid and a curve closer to this ideal point indicates the better discriminating ability of the system. The area A_Z under the ROC curve (AUC) is an index of the quantitative measure of the overall performance of a diagnosis system [38]. The values of AUC can be used to compare the performances of different methods in distinguishing positive and negative findings of breast tumors as well as the overall performance of a diagnostic system. The AUC values are calculated using software package SPSS (SPSS Inc., USA). The ROC curves in Figure 5 show the AUC values of GLCM features ($A_Z = 0.9380$), ratio of perimeters (P_{ratio}) ($A_Z = 0.8890$) and combined performance of GLCM and P_{ratio}($A_Z = 0.9444$).

Discussion

We have combined textural features and morphological features to improve the classification accuracy of diagnosing masses in breast ultrasound images. At first we have extracted features from the ROIs of the entire images in the database using textural as well as morphological methods separately as shown in Table 1. The observed accuracy

Table 2 Performances of the combined best sets of textural and morphological features for the entire database, using accuracy, sensitivity, specificity, and MCC as figures of merit

Combined features	Accuracy %	Sensitivity %	Specificity %	MCC
F08-F10,F42	79.16	80.00	78.57	0.5795
F11-F17,F42	85.83	84.00	87.14	0.7095
F18-F39,F42	90.83	86.00	94.28	0.8109
F08-F10,F43	83.33	86.00	81.43	0.6663
F11-F17,F43	88.33	88.00	88.57	0.7618
F18-F39,F43	93.33	94.00	92.85	0.8641
F08-F10,F44	84.16	86.00	82.86	0.6813
F11-F17,F44	91.66	90.00	92.85	0.8285
F18-F39,F44	95.83	96.00	95.71	0.9146

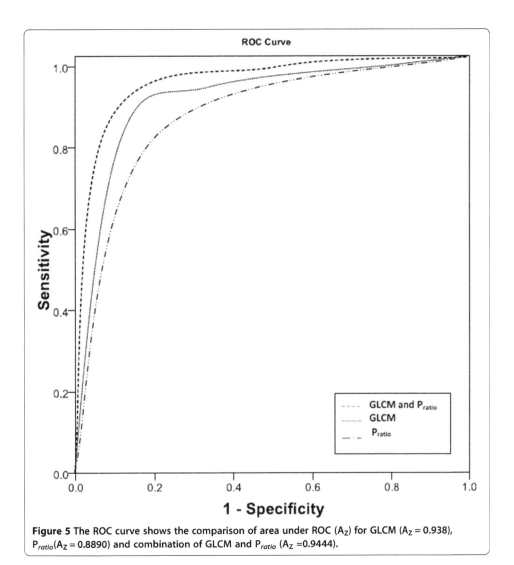

Figure 5 The ROC curve shows the comparison of area under ROC (A$_Z$) for GLCM (A$_Z$ = 0.938), P$_{ratio}$(A$_Z$ = 0.8890) and combination of GLCM and P$_{ratio}$ (A$_Z$ =0.9444).

values using the SVM classifier for textural features and morphological features are varied from 66.66% to 90.83% and 61.66% to 85.83% respectively. Texture analysis allows the detection of mathematical patterns in the gray-level distribution of the pixels. Textural features have been found to be efficient in classifying breast tumors in ultrasound images. Since the borders of benign tumors are smoother than the borders of malignant ones, breast tumors may be evaluated based on their morphological information [18]. The infiltrative nature of malignant tumors generate an irregular pattern of impedance discontinuities, which results irregular, spiculated or ill-defined boundary in breast ultrasound images. However, benign tumors have a more uniform growth with smooth, round, and well-defined boundaries [9].

Based on this, Wu et al. [17,18] combined textural and morphological features and achieved an A$_Z$ value of 0.9614. Furthermore, a sensitivity of 97.78% is achieved which means the system can detect malignant tumors with high probability in contrast with mammograms where the false negative rates are up to 20% [2]. Based on this, we have selected three best performing features from each textural and morphological category to form nine combined features.

As shown in Figure 6, the GLCM and P_{ratio} combination produced highest numerical values among the all combinations under comparison with accuracy, sensitivity, specificity and MCC (95.83%, 96%, 95.71% and 0.9146) respectively (Table 2). Moreover, we have achieved an A_Z value of 0.9444 with the combination of GLCM and P_{ratio}. The textural based features (F01-F39) are extracted through histogram, MRF, Tamura, GLRLN and GLCM from each segmented ROI of the 120 breast ultrasound images. The GLRLN is computed in four orientations $(0°, 45°90°135°)$ as suggested in [14]. The Gray Level Co-occurrence Matrix (GLCM) has been used to extract a total of twenty two features by considering the most appropriate direction $\theta = 45°$ and distance $d = 2$ as suggested in [14,39]. Besides, a quantization level of 32 is used in our experiment; although it is experimentally proved that the gray-level quantization does not improve or worsen the discrimination power of texture features but time consumption increases with the number of quantization levels [13].

The shape variation between benign and malignant tumors in an ultrasound image is an effective feature for classifying breast tumors [41,15]. Nineteen morphological features, used in [15] with 118 breast ultrasound images, yielded an A_Z value of 0.9087. The most common parameter to quantify tumor shape is the depth-to-width ratio [42], since benign cysts tend to be wider than deeper. An Aspect ratio [15] greater than 1 increases the probability of malignancy. The convex polygon technique is based on the determination of the convex hull; the smallest convex region that contains all points belonging to a given region shape [37]. Accordingly , the amount of irregularity in the contour increases the area difference between convex hull region and the tumor region,

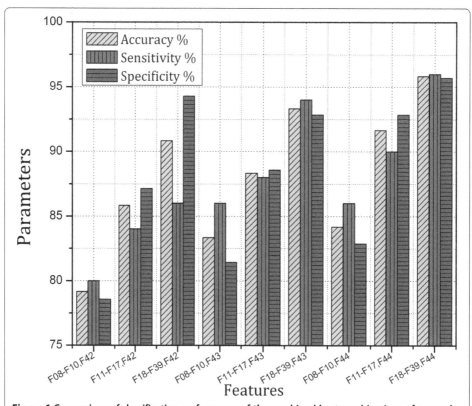

Figure 6 Comparison of classification performance of the combined best combinations of textural and morphological features, using accuracy, sensitivity, specificity, and MCC.

which corresponds to the level of malignancy. This characteristic can be quantified using two parameters: RS and NRV, using which, we have obtained accuracy values of 61.66% and 83.33% respectively. The length of the tumor perimeter is an important indicator for diagnosis [15]. As malignant tumors usually have irregular shapes, a large tumor perimeter indicates that a tumor is malignant. The circularity C, the ratio of square of the perimeter to the area, reflects the complexity of contours by producing higher values for irregular shapes. The ratio between the tumor perimeter and convex perimeter (P_{ratio}) [18] increases when the tumor shape is highly irregular. In our work, the accuracy values obtained by C and Pratio are 74.16% and 85.83% respectively.

The change in classification accuracy for different values of parameter γ is shown in Figure 7. The features for SVM are obtained through GLCM (θ = 45°, d = 2 and L = 32). The RBF kernel is used in SVM classifier, require appropriate values of C and γ for demonstrating optimum performance. We have set the C value (C = 100) as suggested in [18] and γ value is chosen (γ =0.2) by varying the value from 0.1 to 1 and observing the accuracy of discrimination as shown in Figure 7. The curves in Figure 5 compares the area A_Z produced by the GLCM (A_Z = 0.9388), P_{ratio} (A_Z = 0.8890) and the combination of these two (A_Z = 0.9444) which suggests that the combined performance of textural and morphological features increases the accuracy of diagnosis. Our experiment aims at assessing the individual and combined classification performance of textural and morphological features in breast ultrasound. However, for an automated breast CAD system, one cannot use all extracted features at the same time and it require an effective feature selection stage should be added.

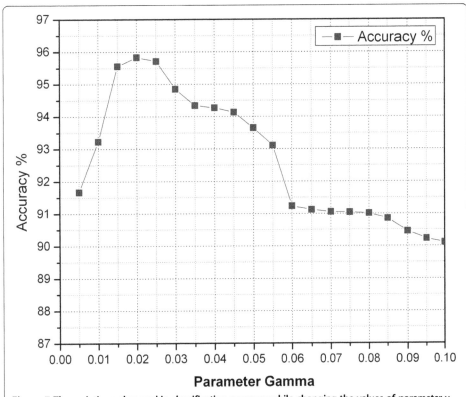

Figure 7 The variations observed in classification accuracy while changing the values of parameter γ between 0.1 to 1.

The classification performance depends on the selected feature set and also the size of the feature vector. Inadequate number of training samples for the finite number of training data leads to "curse of dimensionality" problem, which leads to degraded classification performance [43,44]. Introducing an efficient feature selection algorithm at this stage removes the irrelevant and redundant features and a new feature set is framed with low-dimensional dataset for effective classification [39,43]. This study suggests that an effective combination of textural and morphological features can increase the performance of CAD systems using breast ultrasound images.

Conclusion

In this work, we have evaluated the classification performance of combined textural and morphological features for the discrimination of breast masses in ultrasound images. The individual and combined results produced by textural and morphological features are analyzed using statistical parameters: accuracy, sensitivity, specificity, MCC and area under ROC curve. The results suggested that the classification accuracy of breast ultrasound CAD system increases with combined textural and morphological features.

Additional file

> **Additional file 1:** Detailed descriptions of features: Histogram(F01-F06), Tamura (F08-F10), GLRLM(F11-F17) and GLCM(F18-F39).

Competing interests
The authors declare that they have no competing interests.

Authors' contributions
Author KMP drafted this manuscript, conducted experiments using the datasets and analyzed the results. Author Dr PT suggested the methods used in this study and provided guidelines in drafting the manuscript. Author Dr RM offered technical support in constructing toolbox for experimental studies. All authors corrected and approved the manuscript.

Authors' information
Author KMP holds a Masters in Science, Masters in Philosophy degrees in Electronics. He also possesses Masters Degree in Computer Science and Engineering. Currently he works as Assistant Professor and Head of electronics and communication, K.S.Rangasamy college of arts and science, India.
Author PT holds PhD in Electronics and working as assistant professor in Electronics at Government arts college, Dharmapuri, India. He is also a research supervisor at Bharathiar University, Coimbatore, India.
Author RM holds PhD in Computer Science. He works as Associate Professor and Head of Computer Applications, K.S.Rangasamy college of arts and science, India. He is also a research supervisor at Periyar University, Salem, India.

Acknowledgements
We would like to acknowledge Dr T.S.A.Geertsma, MD, Head, Department of Radiology, Gelderse Vallei Hospital, Ede ,the Netherlands, for providing breast ultrasound images in various categories.

Author details
[1]Research & Development Centre, Bharathiar University, Coimbatore 641046, India. [2]Department of Electronics & Communication, K.S.R College of Arts & Science, Tiruchengode 637215, India. [3]Department of Electronics & Communication, Govt Arts College, Dharmapuri 636705, India. [4]Department of Computer Applications, K.S.R College of Arts & Science, Tiruchengode 637215, India.

References
1. Jemal A, Bray F, Center MM, Ferlay J, Ward E, Forman D (2011) Global cancer statistics. CA Cancer J Clin 61(2):69–90
2. Boyd NF, Guo H, Martin LJ, Sun L, Stone J, Fishell E, Yaffe MJ (2007) Mammographic density and the risk and detection of breast cancer. N Engl J Med 356(3):227–236

3.   Weigel S, Biesheuvel C, Berkemeyer S, Kugel H, Heindel W (2007) Digital mammography screening: how many breast cancers are additionally detected by bilateral ultrasound examination during assessment? Eur Radiol 23(3):684–691

4.   Zhou S, Shi J, Zhu J, Cai Y, Wang R (2013) Shearlet-based texture feature extraction for classification of breast tumor in ultrasound image.*Biomedical*. Signal Process Contr 8(6):688–696

5.   Sahiner B, Chan HP, Roubidoux MA, Hadjiiski LM, Helvie MA, Paramagul C, Blane C (2007) Malignant and Benign Breast Masses on 3D US Volumetric Images: Effect of Computer-aided Diagnosis on Radiologist Accuracy 1. Radiology 242(3):716–724

6.   Jalalian A, Mashohor SB, Mahmud HR, Saripan MIB, Ramli ARB, Karasfi B (2013) Computer-aided detection/diagnosis of breast cancer in mammography and ultrasound: a review. Clin Imaging 37(3):420–426

7.   Ikedo Y, Fukuoka D, Hara T, Fujita H, Takada E, Endo T, Morita T (2007) Development of a fully automatic scheme for detection of masses in whole breast ultrasound images. Med Phys 34(11):4378–4388

8.   Doi K (2009) Computer-aided diagnosis in medical imaging: achievements and challenges. In World Congress on Medical Physics and Biomedical Engineering, September 7–12, 2009, Munich, Germany (pp. 96–96) (2009, January). Springer Berlin Heidelberg.

9.   Pereira WCA, Alvarenga AV, Infantosi AFC, Macrini L, Pedreira CE (2010) A non-linear morphometric feature selection approach for breast tumor contour from ultrasonic images. Comput Biol Med 40(11):912–918

10. Li H, Wang Y, Liu KR, Lo SC, Freedman MT (2001) Computerized radiographic mass detection. I. Lesion site selection by morphological enhancement and contextual segmentation. Med Imaging, IEEE Trans 20(4):289–301

11. Prabusankarlal KM, Thirumoorthy P, Manavalan R (2014) Computer Aided Breast Cancer Diagnosis Techniques in Ultrasound: A Survey. J Med Imaging Health Inform 4(3):331–349

12. Huang YL, Chen DR (2005) Support vector machines in sonography: application to decision making in the diagnosis of breast cancer. Clin Imaging 29(3):179–184

13. Gómez W, Pereira WCA, Infantosi AFC (2012) Analysis of co-occurrence texture statistics as a function of gray-level quantization for classifying breast ultrasound. IEEE Trans Med Imaging 31(10):1889–1899

14. Radhakrishnan M, Kuttiannan T (2012) Comparative Analysis of Feature Extraction Methods for the Classification of Prostate Cancer from TRUS Medical Images. IJCSI Int J Comput Sci Issues 9(1):1694–0814

15. Huang YL, Chen DR, Jiang YR, Kuo SJ, Wu HK, Moon WK (2008) Computer-aided diagnosis using morphological features for classifying breast lesions on ultrasound. Ultrasound Obstet Gynecol 32(4):565–572

16. Alvarenga AV, Infantosi AFC, Pereira WCA, Azevedo CM (2010) Assessing the performance of morphological parameters in distinguishing breast tumors on ultrasound images. Med Eng Phys 32(1):49–56

17. Wu WJ, Moon WK (2008) Ultrasound breast tumor image computer-aided diagnosis with texture and morphological features. Acad Radiol 15(7):873–880

18. Wu WJ, Lin SW, Moon WK (2012) Combining support vector machine with genetic algorithm to classify ultrasound breast tumor images. Comput Med Imaging Graph 36(8):627–633

19. Alvarenga AV, Infantosi AFC, Pereira WC, Azevedo CM (2012) Assessing the combined performance of texture and morphological parameters in distinguishing breast tumors in ultrasound images. Med Phys 39(12):7350–7358

20. Ultrasoundcases [http://ultrasoundcases.info/category.aspx?cat=67] (Accessed May 2014).

21. Jia-Wei T, Chun-Ping N, Yan-Hui G, Heng-Da C, Xiang-Long T (2012) Effect of a Novel Segmentation Algorithm on Radiologists' Diagnosis of Breast Masses Using Ultrasound Imaging. Ultrasound Med Biol 38(1):119–127

22. Zhang J, Wang C, Cheng Y (2015). Comparison of Despeckle Filters for Breast Ultrasound Images. Circuits Syst Signal Process, 34(1):185-208

23. Lu K, Hall CS (2014). Automatic ultrasound image enhancement for 2D semi-automatic breast-lesion segmentation. In SPIE Medical Imaging(90351M-90351M). International Society for Optics and Photonics.

24. Buades A, Coll B, Morel JM (2005) A review of image denoising algorithms, with a new one. Multiscale Modeling Simulation 4(2):490–530

25. Wu J, Tang C (2014) Random-valued impulse noise removal using fuzzy weighted non-local means. SIViP 8(2):349–355

26. Zhan Y, Ding M, Wu L, Zhang X (2014) Nonlocal means method using weight refining for despeckling of ultrasound images. Signal Process 103:201–213

27. Salmon J (2010) On two parameters for denoising with non-local means. IEEE Signal Process Lett 17(3):269–272

28. Prabusankarlal KM, Thirumoorthy P, Manavalan R (2014) Combining Clustering, Morphology and Metaheuristic Optimization Technique for Segmentation of Breast Ultrasound Images to Detect Tumors. Int J Computer Appl 86:28–34

29. Li C, Zhou J, Kou P, Xiao J (2012) A novel chaotic particle swarm optimization based fuzzy clustering algorithm. Neurocomputing 83:98–109

30. Cheng HD, Shan J, Ju W, Guo Y, Zhang L (2010) Automated breast cancer detection and classification using ultrasound images: A survey. Pattern Recogn 43(1):299–317

31. Haralick RM, Shanmugam K, Dinstein IH. (1973) Textural features for image classification. IEEE Trans Syst Man Cybernetics, SMC-3(6):610-621

32. Schwartz W R, Pedrini H (2004) Texture classification based on spatial dependence features using co-occurrence matrices and Markov random fields. In: IEEE Int.Conf. Image Processing, 2004. (1) 239–242 (2004, October).

33. Tamura H, Mori S, Yamawaki T (1978) Textural features corresponding to visual perception. IEEE Trans Syst Man Cybernetics 8(6):460–473

34. Howarth P, Rüger S (2004)Evaluation of texture features for content-based image retrieval. In: Image and Video Retrieval (326–334). Springer Berlin Heidelberg.

35. Krishnan KR, Sudhakar R (2013) Automatic Classification of Liver Diseases from Ultrasound Images Using GLRLM Texture Features. In: Soft Computing Applications (611–624) Springer Berlin Heidelberg.

36. Al-Janobi A (2001) Performance evaluation of cross-diagonal texture matrix method of texture analysis. Pattern Recogn 34(1):171–180

37. Alvarenga AV, Pereira WC, Infantosi AFC, de Azevedo CM (2005).Classification of breast tumours on ultrasound images using morphometric parameters. In: IEEE Int. Workshop on Intelligent Signal Processing (206–210) (2005, September)

38. Huang YL, Wang KL, Chen DR (2006) Diagnosis of breast tumors with ultrasonic texture analysis using support vector machines. Neural Comput Appl 15(2):164–169

39. Thangavel K, Manavalan R (2014) Soft computing models based feature selection for TRUS prostate cancer image classification. Soft Comput 18(6):1165–1176

40. DeLong E R, DeLong D M, Clarke-Pearson D L (1988) Comparing the areas under two or more correlated receiver operating characteristic curves: a nonparametric approach. Biometrics 44(3):837–845

41. Chang RF, Wu WJ, Moon WK, Chen DR (2005) Automatic ultrasound segmentation and morphology based diagnosis of solid breast tumors. Breast Cancer Res Treat 89(2):179–185

42. Horsch K, Giger ML, Venta LA, Vyborny CJ (2002) Computerized diagnosis of breast lesions on ultrasound. Med Phys 29(2):157–164

43. James A, Dimitrijev S (2012) Ranked selection of nearest discriminating features. Human-Centric Comput Inform Sci 2(1):1–14

44. Ganesan K, Acharya U, Chua CK, Min LC, Abraham K, Ng K (2013) Computer-aided breast cancer detection using mammograms: a review. IEEE Rev Biomed Eng 6:77–98

13

Effects of blended e-Learning: a case study in higher education tax learning setting

Li-Tze Lee[1,2]* and Jason C Hung[1,2]

* Correspondence:
leelitze@ocu.edu.tw
[1]Department of Marketing and Supply Chain Management, Overseas Chinese University, 40721 No. 100, Chiao Kwang Rd., Taichung City, Taiwan, R.O.C
[2]Department of Information Technology, Overseas Chinese University, 40721 No. 100, Chiao Kwang Rd., Taichung City, Taiwan, R.O.C

Abstract

This article has two main objectives. First, we describe the design of an e-learning system for a University Income Tax Law course. Second, we analyze and explore learning results in terms of students' learning satisfaction and learning achievement. Learning achievement was examined by questions derived from the course content while learning satisfaction was analyzed based on an adaptation of the Technology Acceptance Model (TAM).

Results indicate that neither gender nor the school system affect students' e-learning system satisfaction. Since students' knowledge and exposure to computers are equal regardless of gender or educational background this reduces the significance of both these variables. Participating samples are divided into three groups: traditional, fully on-line and blended learning. We find, however, a statistically significant difference existed in learning achievement among groups. The blended learning group, combining on- line learning with paper-and-pencil testing, has the best learning achievement among the three groups.

Keywords: E-learning; Income Tax Law; Learning Achievement; TAM model

Introduction

It is known that e-learning as a widely accepted tool in many fields such as higher education, business and training [1]. The development of the Internet facilitates e-learning in the form of applications and reduces the boundaries to learning and compliments traditional teaching methods. Tax education, as part of a discipline in a higher education, receives little research attention for many years. However, tax knowledge, changed from time to time, is a life skill required by adults around the world. For example, to report personal income tax and know how to deduct your personal exemptions. Many prior studies focus on teaching methodology (e.g., [2,3]) or report characteristics of tax courses (e.g., [4]). Few studies address innovative approaches to implementing e-learning course in tax education. Craner and Lymer [4] indicate that taxation courses rarely use internet as instructional delivery method. Hite and Hasseldine [3] reinforce this point by arguing that continuing education for students and instructors should focus on creating effective learning environment using the internet for taxation courses. Therefore, this study implemented an e-learning web system on Income Tax Law subject in order to provide variety of learning environment and learning motivation. In addition, an experiment was conducted to assess student learning achievement as well as learning satisfaction.

Literature review

In the following sections, we present a short background about e-learning. In addition, we describe how short history about Technology Acceptance Model and its applications in prior studies. Third, we detail literatures about student learning achievement in an e-learning environment.

E-learning

E-learning relates to distance education facilitated through the use of electronic media such as the Internet, DVDs, CD-ROMs, videotapes, television or cellphones. E-learning brings tangible advantages in terms of accessibility to a learning environment that can be used anywhere and at anytime [5]. This approach to education is often characterized as improving learning efficiency while achieving cost reductions [1].

E-learning delivers information to end users via the Internet and is superior to traditional approaches in its capability to update, store, retrieve and share learning information. E-learning consists of three fundamental elements: (a) use of the internet for updating, retrieving, dispatching and sharing messages, (b) the availability of a standardized technology based platform that facilitates learning at a distance and (c) general concept learning instead of problem solving [6].

Henderson [7] states that E-learning brings a variety of benefits that include: (a) reduced costs, for example in traveling expenses, (b) students learn in a place of their own convenience, (c) student's define the pace of their learning and (d) institutions increase flexibility in their educational systems.

Blended learning refers to the integration of traditional classroom teaching with e-learning activities in order to enrich delivery in the learning environment [8,9]. Blended learning involves putting the major learning activities online while retaining traditional classroom teaching in a way that captures the best of face-to-face classroom teaching and online learning [8].

Jacob [10] explores benefits and barriers in blended learning in two US high schools and found that both students and parents' accept this kind of learning due to its efficiency; administrators and teachers thus increased the allocation of resources to blended learning. Vaughan [11] examines perceptions on blended learning in higher education and found that blended learning facilitated flexibility in learning times and increased individuals' responsibility for learning.

Technology acceptance model

The Technology Acceptance Model (TAM) explains the factors that underlie users' engagement with and use of technology [12]. The TAM explains and predicts technology acceptance in terms of two factors i.e., perceived usefulness and perceived ease-of-use.

TAM model has been widely used in many fields. In 2000, Lederer, Maupin, Sena, and Zhuang [13] conduct an e-mail survey sent to 163 participants to express their opinions about ease of use and usefulness of websites. The study employs ease of understanding and finding to estimate ease of use of websites while information quality in terms of revisiting websites to estimate usefulness. The study confirmed that TAM is a good instrument providing inclusive investigation for web designer, researcher, and manager to predict web users' preferences

In 2007, Kim and Chang [14] use TAM model to investigate users' perceptions about the design and operation of health information websites. Results from the structural equation method showed that characteristics were divided into three groups: factor impact perceived usefulness and perceived ease of use, factor impact only perceived ease of use, and not direct impact on either perceived usefulness and perceived ease of use. In health information websites, two key functional characteristics extended from original TAM are essential: 'usage support' and 'customization'

Recently, Polancic et al. [15] explore major factors which influence framework's popularity and success. Their research instrument revised from TAM and Seddon's information system. This study collected 389 questionnaires and analyzed data by using structural equation modeling. Their results maintained that two key factors, continues usage and perceived usefulness, have huge influence on success of frameworks and revise TAM provided a relationship between usage and successful of frameworks while usage brings financial benefits to the company.

Gender is an important issue when studying technology acceptance. Belenky et al. [16] state that learning methods are different by gender. Male learners tend to be independent learners or active learners while female learners tend to be group learners by building network connections when they study. To study the relationship between gender and technology acceptance, Ong and Lai [17] conducte a survey on 67 female and 89 male Science-based Industrial Park employees. They found that males are influenced by computer usefulness while females are influenced by computer self-efficacy and ease of use.

Smart and Cappel [18] conduct a study on student perceptions toward online learning in terms of leaner characteristic, course content, and learning context. They found that no significant differences in gender or business and non-business students but significant differences among fourth-year (senior) versus non-fourth-year (non-senior) students since fourth-year students have more computer experiences and positive technology attitudes toward learning than non-fourth-year students.

Lo and Hong [19] also examine learners' satisfaction toward e-learning experiences. Elements such as delivery method, content, system, and interaction were studied in terms of e-learning satisfaction while gender as a moderator factor. There are three hundred and twenty-two Malaysian public university students participated in this study. Research showed that delivery method, content, system, and interaction have significant impact on e-learning satisfaction and gender only impacts on interaction factor since male and female learn differently.

In 2012, González-Gómez, Guardiola, Rodríguez and Alonso [20] study gender issue in e-learning environment from survey on 1185 students from Universidad de Granada in Spain. Their results indicated that female learners have positive learning satisfaction than male learners and females concern about studying plan and use different learning channels to communicate with teachers.

Learning achievement

Learning achievement is an important factor when study e-learning. Al-Mutairi and Jordan [21] investigate student e-learning performance by involving 566 graduate students (353 female and 213 male) in the study. Factors such as gender, working student, status martial were investigated about student learning performance. Results revealed that female students' academic performance is better than their male counterparts and young students perform better than elder and non-national students. Lim and Morris [22] study learning outcome in the effects of learner and instruction characteristics under blended learning environment. However, they found that no gender effect on student learning outcome but age, prior e-learning experiences and study time are factors which can distinguish learning outcome.

In addition to gender issue, group learning difference has become an important issue on e-learning achievement. In 2004, Rovai and Jordan study sense of community on full time graduate students in higher education. Sixty eight students were divided into three groups: (a) traditional course with 26 enrolled (b) blended course with 28 enrolled, and (c) fully online course with 25 enrolled. Results found that blended learning course with attributes of learning-centered and active learning through cooperation and social construction produce a higher sense of community than either traditional or full online courses.

Additionally, Taradi et al. [23] investigate 121 second-year medical student learning outcome and satisfaction in acid-base physiology at the University of Zagreb Medical School. They found that in problem-based learning, blend web based group produces summative final grades than face-to-face group. El-Sofany et al. [24] propose a designed system with courses quizzes and for training and teaching. Sixty students have been randomly assigned to two groups: paper quiz and computer quiz groups. Results of their study found that computer group performs better and has positive attitudes toward computers used in their learning.

On the other hand, in 2010, Kanthawongs, Wongkaewpotong, and Daneshgar [25] compare learning outcomes among students in either non web-based or web-based enterprise resource planning (ERP) simulated classrooms. Experimental group involves students self-learned from prepared presentation slides in a web-based ERP simulated classroom while control group involves students study with peers and the teacher by using textbooks in a non web-based ERP simulated classroom. Results found that non web-based ERP simulated group produced higher achievement scores than web-based ERP simulated group.

Website establishment and instructions

Website design function and function instruction is presented in this chapter. The website homepage of this research is "http://ccw2.ocu.edu.tw/accounting/testt/". Membership is active once registration process is completed. This website can be divided into the user's interface and the administrator's interface; and, both interfaces can be differentiated as the following seven sections:

Website establishment

Software used in this research for designing the website is Dreamweaver CS4 because this software provides designers to create and manage website with its user-friendly interface (Figure 1).

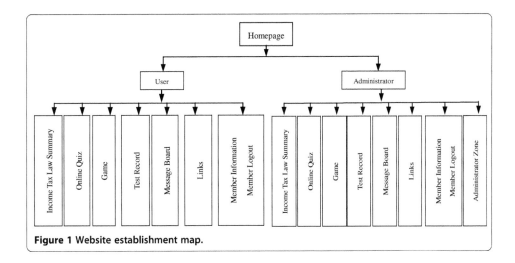

Figure 1 Website establishment map.

Income tax law

The course contents of Income Tax Law are separated into three chapters and transformed into website files. With one click, digital online learning is available right away (Figure 2).

Online quiz

Online learning quiz provides learners to access and test once they login to the system and without limitations of time or space. When learners complete online quizzes and click on "Done" button, the system will finish grading and provide the correct answer for each question automatically. If the answer is correct, the system will pop up a message of "You got it! 5 points". If the answer is incorrect, it will show "Wrong answer!" and provide the correct answer (Figure 3).

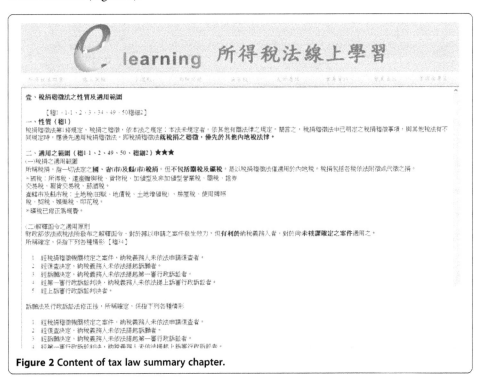

Figure 2 Content of tax law summary chapter.

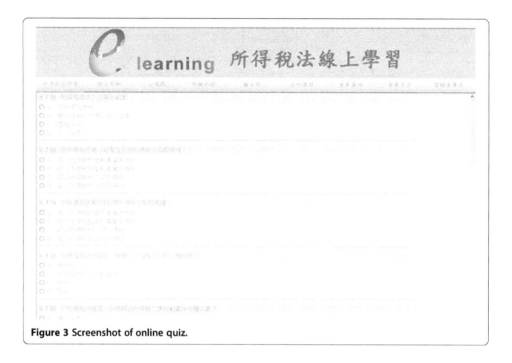

Figure 3 Screenshot of online quiz.

Game

The game, a coin catching activity, is designed to increase learning interest in this study. Three chapters can be selected according to learner's preference and multiple-choice questions are presented with four options: A, B, C, and D. The game will end when learners completed 20 questions. The final score will be showed on the game screen in the end of the game. Learners can check and review their learning progress after the game test (Figure 4).

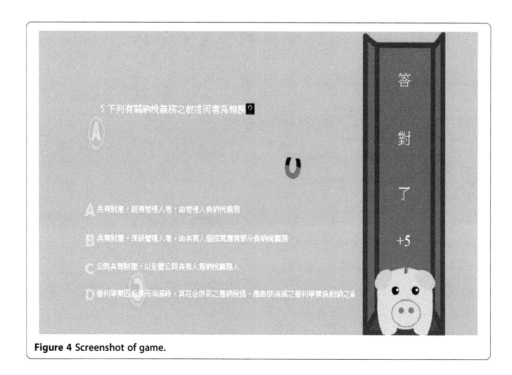

Figure 4 Screenshot of game.

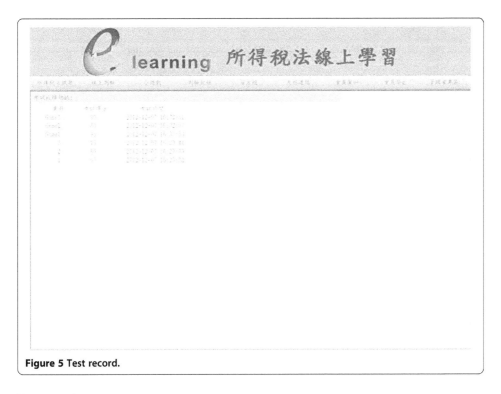

Figure 5 Test record.

Test record

When learners complete the courses and the online quizzes, they can click on "Test Record" to review their own study progress on the record page, where all the completed chapters, quiz scores and the time of quizzes are listed (Figure 5).

Administrator zone

The function of administrator zone is for examining the study progresses of learners and answering messages in a timely basis in order to achieve the goals of interactive tutorials and learning (Figures 6 and 7).

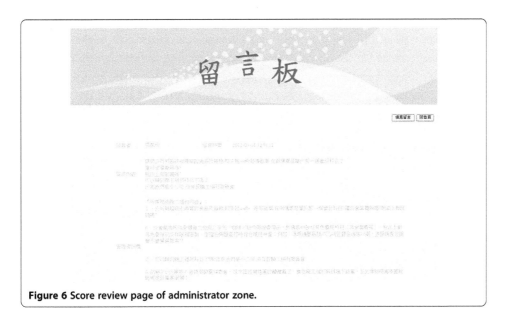

Figure 6 Score review page of administrator zone.

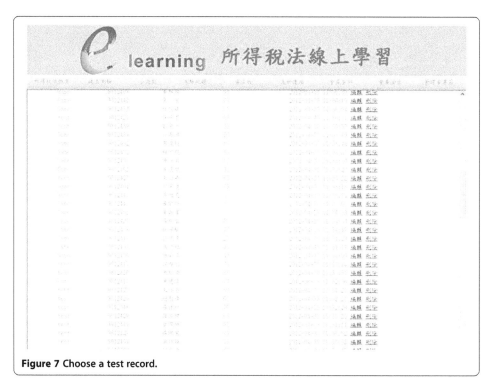

Figure 7 Choose a test record.

Data analysis

Sampling

There are 151 students majored in Accounting and Information participated in this study. The majority of sample subjects are females which consist 75.50% and males consist 24.50%. Regarding student classification, 54.97% are university and 45.03% are junior college. Students are randomly assigned to three groups (traditional, blended, or fully on-line) as shown in Table 1.

Research process

There are two main research objectives in this study. First, we describe the design of an e-learning system for a University Income Tax Law course. Second, we analyze and explore learning results in terms of students' learning satisfaction and learning achievement. It took us 3 months to implement the design of this e-learning platform by testing, editing, and revision to finish the first phase of this study.

Table 1 Demographic of student information

	Variable	N	Percentage
Gender	Male	37	24.50%
	Female	114	75.50%
Classification	University	83	54.97%
	Junior College	68	45.03%
Group	Traditional	52	46.36%
	Blended	46	23.18%
	Fullyon-line	53	30.46%

The second phase of this study is the evaluation of this system. Students' learning achievement and satisfaction were analyzed by a content test and a questionnaire adaptation of the Technology Acceptance Model (TAM). All students were randomly assigned into three groups: traditional, blended, and fully on-line groups. Among these three groups, traditional group studied and took tests with paper materials, blended group studied with digital online system but took tests with paper materials, and fully on-line group studied and took tests one digital online basis. The research procedure included three steps and two hours for the implementation. First, students were randomly assigned into groups and seated. After explaining the research procedures, they started to learn online or study with paper materials according to their groups. Third, after the learning period, students took either online tests or paper tests to measure their learning achievement and answered TAM questionnaires to measure their learning satisfaction.

Reliability and validity

A reliability analysis can be allotted into two components: stability and consistency. However, results may contain some errors; that is, the smaller the error, the higher reliability; on the contrary, the greater the error, the lower the reliability. This study uses reliability coefficient to measure the degree of the reliability. The greater the reliability coefficient, the higher the measured reliability is. Cronbach's alpha is to examine the reliability, and if the value greater than 0.7 it is considered as a high reliability; if the value is smaller than 0.35, the reliability is low [26]. In this study, TAM questionnaire reliability analysis was analyzed with 5 aspects. The result Cronbach's alpha value was 0.880; and, this indicates the reliability of this questionnaire is quite high.

Regarding validity, this questionnaire was created according to theory of related literatures and suggestions and modifications were obtained from discussions of three experts in this field. Therefore, this research should be provided with considerable face validity and adequate construct validity.

Result on TAM questionnaire

The factor of gender effect system usefulness, ease of use, attitude toward using, behavior intention, and the satisfaction of actual uses of the digital learning system was studied here. Through the independent sample T-test, the differences based on the gender were found in Question 1 and Question 3. The average score in Question 1 (3.9912) of female learners was higher than male learners' (3.7027). This shows that female learns believed that digital learning mode helps them to get familiar with the course content, compared to male learners. Also, the average score in Question 3 (3.8947) of female learns was higher than male learners' (3.6486). This indicates that female learners believed digital learning mode helps them to understand the course content, compared to male learners.

Secondly, this study discusses whether the system usefulness, ease of use, attitude toward using, behavior intention, and the satisfaction of actual use of digital learners to the digital learning system varied according to classification. Results from independent sample T-test show that Question 2, Question 4, Question 5, Question 6, Question 15, Question 18, Question 19, Question 23, and Question 24 differ according to classification. Interestingly, except for Question 19, junior college students have higher scores than university students. It may be that junior college students with younger age and having positive learning attitudes toward digital learning system than university students (Table 2).

Table 2 Independent sample T-test based on gender and classification

Factor	Question	Content	Gender	Classification
	Q1	I believe that this digital learning system helps me to be familiar with the course content	(2.3888) *	(0.8581)
	Q2	I believe that this digital learning system can improve my learning efficiency	(1.0700)	(1.6943) *
Usefulness	Q3	I believe that this digital learning system provides positive helps on the understanding of the course content	(1.9975) *	(1.5642)
	Q4	I believe that this digital learning system allows me to understand the course content easily	(1.9202)	(1.4564) *
	Q5	Overall, my evaluation to this digital learning system is positive	(1.2439)	(1.4327) *
	Q6	I think the operation of tax law digital study system is simple for me	(0.9671)	(2.9734) *
	Q7	I think browsing of tax law digital learning system is simple for me	0.5235	(1.2668)
Ease of use	Q8	I think the user interface of tax law digital learning system is simple for me	0.6192	(2.3010)
	Q9	I think tax law digital learning system is clear and easy to read for me	0.3980	(0.9599)
	Q10	Overall, I think using this system is easy	0.6116	(1.6266)
	Q11	I think tax law digital learning system is convenient	(0.0635)	(2.8388)
	Q12	I think tax law digital learning system is interesting	(1.3782)	(1.0306)
Attitude toward using	Q13	I think tax law digital learning system is helpful	(1.0559)	(0.1813)
	Q14	I would like to use this system for studying tax law	(0.3038)	(1.3859)
	Q15	Overall, my evaluation for this system is positive	(0.8562)	(1.9706)*
	Q16	I am willing to participate if there is a digital learning program	(1.1352)	(2.5256)
	Q17	I am willing to participate if there is a program designed with this model in the future	(0.6680)	(2.2812)
Behavioral intention to use	Q18	I will choose to study tax law with digital learning system if it is allowed in the future	(0.5865)	(0.7577) *
	Q19	I will keep studying tax law with digital learning system if it is allowed in the future	(0.8879)	0.1337 *
	Q20	Overall, I have a very high intention of using tax law digital learning system	(1.2976)	(1.6338)
	Q21	I will actually use digital study system if digital learning activity starts now	(1.4397)	0.1928
	Q22	I would like to participate some similar digital learning programs again	(0.2361)	(2.2162)
	Q23	I believe that participating digital learning activities will improve the learning efficiency	(2.2211)	(0.9289) *
Actual use	Q24	I like to participate digital learning activities because it can assist on traditional learning	(0.5103)	(0.7297) *
	Q25	I like to participate digital learning activities because it can replace traditional learning completely	(1.6214)	0.6560
	Q26	Overall, my evaluation of this system from my actual use experience is positive	(0.2670)	(1.3200)

Note: Significance is marked by stars: * $p< 0.05$ (2-tailed).

Table 3 Analysis of variance result on question 11

	Variance	SS	df	MS	F	Sig.
Q11	Between	5.7317	2	2.8658	4.8635	0.0090*
	Within	87.2087	148	0.5892		
	Total	92.9404	150			

Note: Significance is marked by stars: * $p< 0.05$ (2-tailed).

At last, this study investigated whether group impacts the system usefulness, ease of use, attitude toward using, behavior intention, and the satisfaction of actual use of digital learners to the digital learning system. Through single factor analysis of variance, Question 11, Question 15, Question 19 and Question 22 were found differ among groups. Question 11 states that "I think tax law digital learning system is convenient". Statistic significant differences were found that students in the traditional group believe that digital learning system is convenience than fully online students and students in the blend group believe that digital learning system is convenience than fully online students. Question 15 states that "Overall, my evaluation for this system is positive". Statistic significant differences were found that students in the traditional group have positive attitudes to digital learning system than fully online students. Question 19 states that "I will keep studying tax law with digital learning system if it is allowed in the future" were different according to their groups.

Statistic significant differences were found that students in the traditional group believe that they will use this system in the future than fully online students and the same in the blend group than fully online students. Question 22 states that "I would like to participate some similar digital learning programs again". A statistic significant difference was found that students in the blend group agree that they like to participate digital learning system than fully online students. Related results are stated in the following Tables 3, 4, 5 and 6.

Result on tax learning achievement

In addition to learning satisfaction, this study also examined learning achievement on this digital online learning system based on genders, classification, and groups. First, results on independent sample T-test indicated that no significant differences were found between genders (Sig. = 0.7098 > 0.05) or classifications (Sig. =0.2292 > 0.05); and, the related information are as shown in Table 7.

Next, the descriptive statistics of learning achievement based on group indicated that students in the blended group have the highest scores (74.6739), followed by the fully online group (67.7358), and the lowest is the traditional group (67.3077). The related data are as shown in Table 8.

Through one-way analysis of variance of learning achievement, a significant difference was found among groups (Sig. = 0.0255* < 0.05); and, the related information are as shown in Table 9.

Table 4 Analysis of variance result on question 15

	Variance	SS	df	MS	F	Sig.
Q15	Between	3.4448	2	1.7224	3.4659	0.0338*
	Within	73.5486	148	0.4970		
	Total	76.9934	150			

Note: Significance is marked by stars: * $p< 0.05$ (2-tailed).

Table 5 Analysis of variance result on question 19

	Variance	SS	df	MS	F	Sig.
Q19	Between	4.2053	2	2.1026	3.1907	0.0440*
	Within	97.5298	148	0.6590		
	Total	101.7351	150			

Note: Significance is marked by stars: * $p < 0.05$ (2-tailed).

Table 6 Analysis of variance result on question 22

	Variance	SS	df	MS	F	Sig.
Q22	Between	4.5597	2	2.2799	3.9732	0.0209*
	Within	84.9237	148	0.5738		
	Total	89.4834	150			

Note: Significance is marked by stars: * $p < 0.05$ (2-tailed).

Table 7 T test on tax learning achievement base on Gender and classification

	Variable	N	M	DS	T value	Sig.
Tax Learning Scores	Male	37	66.4865	14.6185	(1.5034)	0.7098
	Female	114	70.7456	15.0843		
	University	83	66.1446	13.3737	(3.3174)	0.2292
	Junior College	68	74.0441	15.8881		

Table 8 Statistic description on tax scores by group

	Group	N	M	SD	Min	Max
Tax Learning Scores	Traditional	52	67.3077	14.5677	35	100
	Blended	46	74.6739	16.8458	35	100
	Fully on-line	53	67.7358	12.9186	35	100

Table 9 One-way analysis of variance on tax learning achievement

Variance	SS	df	MS	F	Sig.
Between	1,640.1019	2	820.0509	3.7608	0.0255*
Within	32,271.4875	148	218.0506		
Total	33,911.5894	150			

Note: Significance is marked by stars: * $p < 0.05$ (2-tailed).

Table 10 LSD post Hoc comparison

	Group Comparison	MD	SE	Sig
Tax Learning Scores	Blended	7.3662	2.9889	0.0149*
	Traditional			
	Blended	6.9381	2.9756	0.0211*
	Fully on-line			

LSD post-hoc tests compare differences between groups. * $p < 0.05$ (2-tailed).

Compared with students in the traditional group, students in the blended group have better learning efficiency on tax law; and, the statistical significant difference was found (Sig. = 0.0149* < 0.05). In addition, compared with students in the fully online group, students in the blended group have better learning achievement on tax law; and, the statistical significant difference was found (Sig. = 0.0211* < 0.05). However, no significant difference was found between traditional and fully on-line groups; and, the related information are as shown in Table 10.

Conclusion and discussion

Conclusion

The research is to set up income tax law digital online learning system and discuss the learning satisfaction and learning efficiency. Learning satisfaction is analyzed through TAM questionnaire and learning efficiency is examined through contest test results. Study results showed that learning satisfaction on online digital learning does not affect by gender, classification, or group. In other words, learners regardless of gender (male or female), classification (junior college or university) or group (traditional, fully online, or blended) have similar learning satisfaction. It can imply that computer learning experiences and online training opportunity are similar in this study. Our result is similar to prior studies. For examples, Smart and Cappel's [18] found that gender o does not impact their learning satisfaction and Lo and Hong [19] also found that gender does not have a significant impact on e-learning satisfaction. Even no difference was found in on-line tax learning satisfaction between genders, females performed better than their male counterparts in tax learning achievement in this study. This result is consistent to Al-Mutairi's and Jordan [21] study that female students have better academic performance than male students.

In terms of student classification, the result is quite different from prior studies. Smart and Cappel [18] found older students with more computer experience and possess more positive attitudes with online learning. While Paechter et al. [27] study indicated that no difference was found among ages on online learning course achievement. Interestingly, in this study, students in junior college group have higher tax learning achievement than university group. Reasons may be that young students have more experiences exposing themselves to online learning and they are more concerned about their scores since it will affect their future schools option.

One of the important finding of this study is that students in blended learning group have the highest tax learning achievement scores than both fully-online and traditional groups. However, no difference was fond between fully-online and traditional groups. Corresponding to our findings, Rovai and Jordan [28] and Taradi, et. al's [23] identified that blended course students obtain better grades than traditional or fully online course.

Discussion

Income Tax law is a practical and important course to both college students and adults. The digital online learning system helps to provide a diverse learning environment. Even there is no difference on learning satisfaction in terms of gender, classification or group, a significant learning difference is found among groups. Blended learning group with online learning and paper test outperformed the other two groups which provide a perspective for teaching and learning practice.

Subjects and the scope of the research are suggested for future study. Student samples from both technical colleges and academic universities can be included as subjects to make the research more thorough. In addition, different disciplines are suggested to explore whether different subject areas can be one of factor to affect online learning satisfaction and efficiency. A longitudinal study with experimental period and learners background is suggest increasing research reliability and validity.

Competing interests

The authors declare that they have no competing interests.

Authors' contributions

The concept and the manuscript were made by LL, who carried out all the research design and performed the statistical analysis. JH participated in the website design and testing as well as literature revision. All authors read and approved the final manuscript.

References

1. Nicholson P (2007) A history of e-learning. In: Fernández-Manjón B et al (eds) Computers and Education: e-learning, from theory to practice. Springer, Springer Netherlands, pp 1–11
2. Hite P (1996) An experimental study of the effectiveness of group exams in an individual income tax class. Issues in Accounting Education 11(1):61–75
3. Hite P, Hasseldine J (2001) A primer on tax education in the United States of America. Accounting Education 10(1):3–13, doi: 10.1080/0963928011003473 4
4. Craner J, Lymer A (1999) Tax education in the UK: a survey of tax courses in undergraduate accounting degrees. Accounting Education 8(2):127–156, doi: 10.1080/096392899330973
5. Engelbrecht E (2005) Adapting to changing expectations: Post-graduate students' experience of an e-learning tax program. Computers & Education 45(2):217–229, doi:10.1016/j.compedu.2004.08.001
6. Rosenberg M (2001) E-Learning: Strategies for Delivering Knowledge in the Digital Age. McGraw Hill Companies, Columbus, OH
7. Henderson AJ (2003) The E-Learning Question and Answer Book: A Survival Guide for Trainers and Business Managers. AMACOM, New York, NY
8. Garnham C, Kaleta R (2002) Introduction to hybrid courses. Teaching with Technology Today 8(6):5
9. Singh H (2003) Building effective blended learning programs. Education Technology 43(6):51–54
10. Jacob AM (2011) Benefits and barriers to the hybridization of schools. Journal of Education Policy, Planning and Administration 1(1):61–82
11. Vaughan N (2007) Perspectives on blended learning in higher education. International Journal on E-Learning 6 (1):81–94
12. Davis FD (1989) Perceived usefulness, perceived ease of use, and user acceptance of information technologies. MIS Quarterly 13(3):319–340
13. Lederer AL, Maupin DJ, Sena MP, Zhuang Y (2000) The technology acceptance model the World Wide Web. Decision Support Systems 29(3):269–282
14. Kim D, Chang H (2007) Key functional characteristics in designing and operating health information websites for user satisfaction: An application of the extended technology acceptance model. International Journal of Medical Informatics 76:790–800, doi:10.1016/j.ijmedinf.2006.09.001
15. Polancic G, Hericko M, Rozman I (2010) An empirical examination of application frameworks success based on technology acceptance model. The Journal of Systems and Software 83:574–584, doi:10.1016/j.jss.2009.10.036
16. Belenky MF, Clinchy BM, Goldberger NR, Tarule JM (1997) Women's ways of knowing: The development of self, voice, and mind. Basic Books, New York, NY
17. Ong C, Lai H (2006) Gender differences in perceptions and relationships among dominants of e-learning acceptance. Computers in Human Behavior 22:816–829, doi:10.1016/j.chb.2004.03.006
18. Smart K, Cappel J (2006) Students Perceptions of Online Learning: A Comparative Study. Journal of Information Technology Education 5:201–219
19. Lo M, Hong TC (2011) Modeling user satisfaction in e-learning: A supplementary tool to enhance learning. Review of Business Research 11(2):128–133
20. González-Gómez F, Guardiola J, Rodríguez OM, Alonso MAM (2012) Gender differences in e-learning satisfaction. Computers & Education 58(2):283–290, doi:10.1016/j.compedu.2011.08.017
21. AL-Mutairi A, Jordan HM (2011) Factors affecting business students' performance in Arab Open University: The case of Kuwait. International Journal of Business and Management 6(5):146–156, doi:10.5539/ijbm.v6n5p146
22. Lim DH, Morris ML (2009) Learner and instructional factors influencing learning outcomes within a blended learning environment. Educational Technology & Society 12(4):282–293
23. Taradi SK, Taradi M, Radic K, Pokrajac N (2005) Blending problem-based learning with web technology positively impacts student learning outcomes in acid-base physiology. Advances in Physiology Education 29(1):35–39, doi:10.1152/advan.00026.2004
24. El-Sofany HF, Hasnah AM, ALJa'am JM, Ghaleb FFM, El-Seoud SA (2006) A web-based e-learning system experiment. International Journal of Computing & Information Sciences 4(1):22–29

25. Kanthawongs P, Wongkaewpotong O, Daneshgar F (2010) A comparative study of students' learning outcome in non web-based and web-based ERP-simulated classroom environments. International Journal of Business Research 10(3):130–136

26. Guielford JP (1965) Fundamental statistics in psychology and education, 4th edn. Mcgraw Hill Inc, New York

27. Paechter M, Maier B, Macher D (2010) Students' expectations of, and experiences in e-learning: Their relation to learning achievements and course satisfaction. Computers & Education 54(1):222–229, doi:10.1016/j.compedu.2009.08.005

28. Rovai AP, Jordan HM (2004) Blended learning and sense of community: A comparative analysis with traditional and fully online graduate courses. International Review of Research in Open and Distance Learning 5(2):1–13

14

Implementation of hybrid image fusion technique for feature enhancement in medical diagnosis

Jyoti Agarwal[1*] and Sarabjeet Singh Bedi[2]

* Correspondence:
agarwal200@gmail.com
[1]Department of Computer Science,
RIMT, Bareilly, Uttar Pradesh, India
Full list of author information is
available at the end of the article

Abstract

Image fusion is used to enhance the quality of images by combining two images of same scene obtained from different techniques. In medical diagnosis by combining the images obtained by Computed Tomography (CT) scan and Magnetic Resonance Imaging (MRI) we get more information and additional data from fused image. This paper presents a hybrid technique using curvelet and wavelet transform used in medical diagnosis. In this technique the image is segmented into bands using wavelet transform, the segmented image is then fused into sub bands using curvelet transform which breaks the bands into overlapping tiles and efficiently converting the curves in images using straight lines. These tiles are integrated together using inverse wavelet transform to produce a highly informative fused image. Wavelet based fusion extracts spatial details from high resolution bands but its limitation lies in the fusion of curved shapes. Therefore for better information and higher resolution on curved shapes we are blending wavelet transform with curvelet transform as we know that curvelet transform deals effectively with curves areas, corners and profiles. These two fusion techniques are extracted and then fused implementing hybrid image fusion algorithm, findings shows that fused image has minimum errors and present better quality results. The peak signal to noise ratio value for the hybrid method was higher in comparison to that of wavelet and curvelet transform fused images. Also we get improved statistics results in terms of Entropy, Peak signal to noise ratio, correlation coefficient, mutual information and edge association. This shows that the quality of fused image was better in case of hybrid method.

Keywords: Image fusion; Wavelet transform; Curvelet transform; Hybrid image fusion

Introduction

Fusion of two or more images of the same scene to form a single image is known as image fusion. Image fusion process combines the relevant information from two or more images into single image therefore the resultant fused image will be more informative and having important features from each image. Image fusion is important in many different image processing fields such as satellite imaging, remote sensing and medical imaging. Several fusion algorithms have been evolved such as pyramid based, wavelet based, curvelet based, HSI (Hue Saturation Intensity), color model, PCA (Principal Component Analysis) method. All of them lacks in one criteria or the other [1]. Fusion of medical images should be taken carefully as the whole diagnosis process depends on it. Medical images should be of high resolution with maximum possible details [2]. The medical images should represent all important characteristics of the organ to be imaged so the integrated image should present maximum possible details. Therefore our aim is to adopt the best method of image fusion so that the diagnosis should be accurate and perfect [3].

Wavelet method was supposed to be one of the most promising methods of image fusion due to its simplicity and ability to preserve the time and frequency details of the image to be fused. Wavelet Fusion transforms the images from spatial domain to wavelet domain. The wavelet domain represents the wavelet coefficient of the images [4,5]. The wavelet decomposition is performed by passing the image into series of low pass and high pass filters. In this method the input signal goes through two one digital filters. One of them performs high pass filtering and the other performs low pass filtering. The various filter bands are produced and each band producing images of different resolution levels and orientations. These sub bands are then combined using inverse wavelet transform [6-8].

The curvelet transform is used to represent the curved shapes. This transform represents edges better than wavelets. The fused image obtained yields higher details than the original image due to edge representation thereby preventing image denoising. It is based on the segmentation of the whole image into small overlapping tiles and then the ridgelet transform is applied to each tile [9]. The studies on curvelet fusion of MR and CT images shows that the application of curvelet transform in the fusion of MR and CT images is superior to the application of traditional wavelet transform. Segmentation approximates the curved lines by small straight lines [10]. Geetha et al. [11] suggested that the performance of algorithms can be improved by introducing the directional oriented multiresolution transforms such as steerable pyramids, contourlets etc., overlapping of tiles prevents edge effects. Bindu and Kumar [12] further evaluated the performance analysis of multi source (CT, PET and MRI images) fused medical images using multiresolution (combination of DWT and contourlet) transforms. While denoising of computer tomography images using curvelet transforms it has been found that the curvelet transform outperforms the wavelet transform in terms of signal to noise ratio [13,14].

Material and methods
CT and MRI images
CT and MRI scanned images of human brain are used as input images. The MRI scanned image of the same brain is given below by Figure 1(a). In MRI image, we observe the soft tissue like the membranes covering the brain can be clearly seen but the hard tissue like the skull bones cannot be clearly seen. The CT scanned image of the brain is given in Figure 1(b). In CT image hard tissue like the skull bone is clearly seen but the soft tissue like the membranes covering the brain are less visible. Therefore to get more information we combine CT and MRI scans. If we combine both the CT and MRI scanned images of the brain then we will get a resultant image in which both hard tissue like skull bones and the soft tissue like the membranes covering the brain can be clearly visible. The image addition can be used to combine both the CT and MRI scanned images.

Simulation tool/software used (MATLAB 7.1)
Proposed research work has been developed by using MATLAB ® for simulation of image fusion algorithms. This high performance language for technical computer,

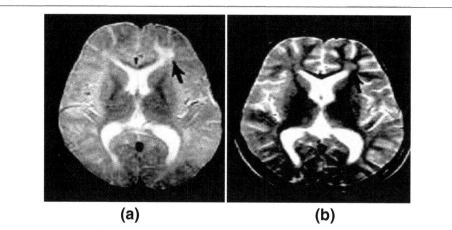

Figure 1 **Images of MRI and CT scan for wavelet and curvelet transforms. (a)** MRI image and **(b)** CT scan image of human brain.

integrates computation, visualization, and programming in an easy-to-use environment. One of the reasons of selecting MATLAB in this research is because it fits perfectly in the necessities of an image processing research due to its inherent characteristics. MATLAB basic data element is an array that does not require dimensioning. This is especially helpful to solve problems with matrix and vector formulations. And an image is nothing but a matrix or set of matrices which define the pixels value of the image, such a grey scale value in black and white images, and red, green and blue or Hue, Saturation and Intensity values in color images.

Image Processing Toolbox of MATLAB provides a comprehensive set of reference-standard algorithms and graphical tools for image processing such as analysis, image enhancement, feature detection, noise reduction and image registration etc.

Image processing toolbox supports a diverse set of image types, including high dynamic range, high resolution. Graphical tools explore an image, examine a region of pixels, adjust the contrast, create contours or histograms, and manipulate regions of interest (ROIs) Figure 2.

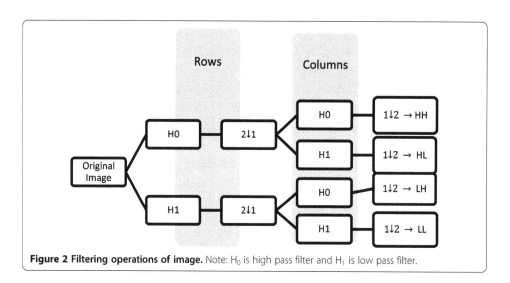

Figure 2 Filtering operations of image. Note: H_0 is high pass filter and H_1 is low pass filter.

Image fusion using wavelet transform

The block diagram of generic wavelet based image fusion technique is shown in the Figure 3. Wavelet transform is first performed on each source images, and then fused decision map is generated based on a set of fusion rules. The fused wavelet coefficient map can be constructed from the wavelet coefficients of the source images according to the fusion decision map. Finally the fused image is obtained by performing the inverse wavelet transform. From the above diagram, we can see that the fusion rules are playing a very important role during the fusion process. When constructing each wavelet coefficient for the fused image. We will have to determine which source image describes this coefficient better. This information will be kept in the fusion decision map. The fusion decision map has the same size as the original image [10]. This method considered the fact that there usually has high correlation among neighbouring pixels. In this research, we think objects carry the information of interest, each pixel or small neighboring pixels are just one part of an object.

Curvelet transform

The algorithm of the curvelet transform of an image P can be summarized in the following steps:

A) The image P is split up into three sub bands Δ1, Δ2 and P3 using the additive wavelet transforms [15].
B) Tiling is performed on the sub bands Δ1 and Δ2.
C) The discrete Ridgelet transform is performed on each tile of the sub bands Δ1 and Δ2.

The transform is performed in three steps:

1. Sub band filtering
2. Tiling
3. Ridgelet Transform

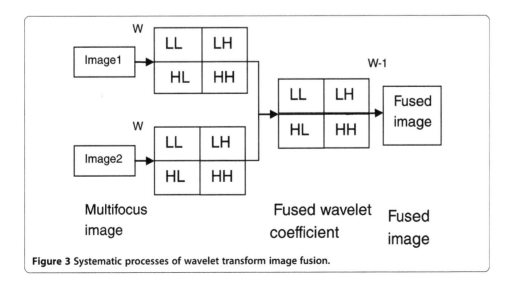

Figure 3 Systematic processes of wavelet transform image fusion.

Sub band filtering decomposes the image into various sub bands of different frequencies. Generally three sub bands are formed which is done by performing successive convolutions on image (Figure 4).

Tiling divides the image into overlapping tiles. These tiles are then used for transformation of curved lines into straight lines in the sub bands formed during sub band filtering. Tiling thus helps in handling curved edges.

Ridgelet transform is basically a 1-D wavelet transform applied on each tile. Ridgelet transform is viewed as a wavelet analysis in the Radon domain. This transform acts as shape detection of the objects in the image [16]. The ridgelet coefficients of an image f(×1, ×2) are represented by:

$$R_f(a, b, \theta) = \int_{-\infty}^{\infty} \int_{-\infty}^{\infty} \Psi_{a,b,\theta}(x_1, x_2) f(x_1, x_2) dx_1 dx_2 \qquad (1)$$

where

$$\Psi_{a,b,\theta}(x_1, x_2) = a^{-\frac{1}{2}} \Psi((x_1 \cos\theta + x_2 \sin\theta - b)/a) \qquad (2)$$

Is the ridgelet basic function for each a > 0 and $\theta \in [0,2\pi]$. This function is constant along with lines $X_1 \cos\theta + X_2 \sin\theta$ = constant.

The Radon transform for an object f is the collection of line integrals indexed by (θ, t) $\in [0, 2\pi] \times R$ and is given by:

$$R_f(\theta, t) = \int_{-\infty}^{\infty} \int_{-\infty}^{\infty} f(x_1, x_2 \delta(x_1 \cos\theta + x_2 \sin\theta - t) dx_1 dx_2) \qquad (3)$$

Thus, the ridgelet transform can be represented in terms of the Radon transform as follow:

$$R_f(a, b, \theta) = \int_{-\infty}^{\infty} R_f(\theta, t) a^{-\frac{1}{2}} \left(\frac{t-b}{a}\right) dt \qquad (4)$$

Hence, the ridgelet transform is the application of the 1-D wavelet transforms to the slices of the Radon transform where the angular variable θ is constant and it is varying. To make the ridgelet transform discrete, both the radon transform and the wavelet transform

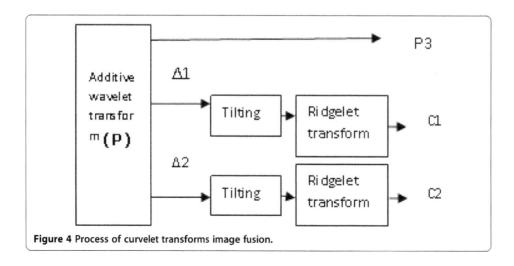

Figure 4 Process of curvelet transforms image fusion.

have to be discrete. Thus curvelet transform can be used to analyze dense structures in human body by visualising its shape, morphology of soft tissues and few other.

Hybrid image fusion technique

A single method of fusion may not be as efficient as it always lacks in one point or the other. Therefore their exists the need of developing a method which takes into consideration the advantages of various different fusion rules. Thus the hybrid image fusion is used. It performs processing of the image based upon the different fusion rules and then integrates these results together to obtain a single image. The results of various fusion techniques are extracted and then they are again fused by implementing a hybrid method presenting better quality results. A single method may not effectively result in removing the ringing artifacts and the noise in the source images. These inadequacies result in development of fusion rules which follow a hybrid algorithm and improve to great extent the visual quality of the image [17-19].

Therefore Hybrid Image fusion leads to minimum Mean Square Error Value and maximum Signal to Noise (S/N) Ratio value. The proposed work in this paper will describe the hybrid of two methods that is the wavelet based image fusion and the curvelet based image fusion.

Proposed work (hybrid of wavelet and curvelet fusion rules)

Curvelet based image fusion efficiently deals with the curved shapes, therefore its application in medical fields would result in better fusion results than obtained using wavelet transform alone. On the other hand wavelet transform works efficiently with multifocus, multispectral images as compared to any other fusion rule. It increases the frequency resolution of the image by decomposing it to various bands again and again till different frequencies and resolutions are obtained. Thus a hybrid of wavelet and curvelet would lead to better results that could be used for fusion of medical images (Figure 5).

A hybrid of wavelet and curvelet integrates various pixel level rules in a single fused image. Pixel based rules operates on individual pixels in the image but ignores some important details such as edges, boundaries of the image. Wavelet based rule alone may reduce the contrast in some images and cannot effectively remove the ringing effects and noise appearing in the source images. Curvelet method can work well with edges and boundaries and curve portions of the images using ridgelet transforms. In the hybrid method first the decomposition of the input images is done up to level N by passing the image through series of low and high pass filters. The low and high pass bands are then subjected to curvelet transform by decomposing it further into small tiles and then fused using wavelet transform and inverse wavelet transform to get full size images. This will take into account the drawbacks of wavelet and effectively remove it using curvelet transform and visual quality of the image is improved. Wavelet transform of an image up to level N till different resolution is obtained. This gives various frequency bands. Figure 3 shows the procedure of combining image 1 and image 2 into single fused wavelet coefficients.

These bands obtained are then passed through curvelet transform which segments it into various additive components each of which is subband of the image. These bands are then passed through tiling operation which divides the band to overlapping tiles.

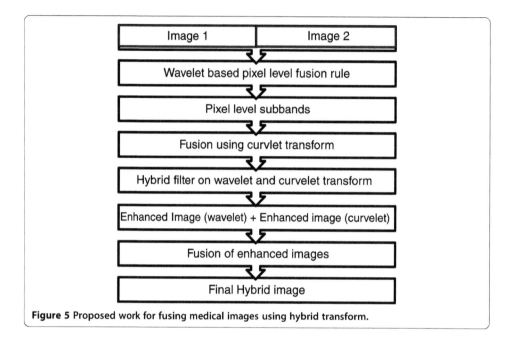

Figure 5 Proposed work for fusing medical images using hybrid transform.

The tiles are small in dimension to transform curved lines into small straight line and overlapping is done so as to avoid the edge effects. Tiling operation is performed after subband filtering of the filter bands. Finally these overlapped tiles are passes through ridgelet transform which is a kind of 1-D wavelet transform helps in wavelet transform in Radon Domain which helps in shape and edge detection (Figure 4) band obtained by wavelet transform. Now these fused bands after curvelet transform are fused again using Inverse wavelet Transform. The Inverse Wavelet Transform fuses together all the bands and result in a full size integrated image.

Performance parameters for determining the quality of fused Image

In the present work, we have used four performance measures to evaluate the performance of the wavelet, curvelet and hybrid fusion algorithms. MRI image is taken as the reference image in the calculation of performance metric values.

A. Entropy (H)

The Entropy (H) is the measure of information content in an image. The maximum value of entropy can be produced when each gray level of the whole range has the same frequency. If entropy of fused image is higher than parent image then it indicates that the fused image contains more information.

$$H = -\sum_{g=0}^{L-1} p(g) \log_2 p(q) \tag{5}$$

B. Correlation Coefficient (CC)

The correlation coefficient is the measure the closeness or similarity in small size structures between the original and the fused images. It can vary between -1 and $+1$. Values closer to $+1$ indicate that the reference and fused images are highly similar while the values closer to -1 indicate that the images are highly dissimilar.

$$CORR = \frac{2c_{rf}}{C_{r}+C_{f}} \qquad (6)$$

Where

$$Cr = \sum_{j=1}^{M} \sum_{j=1}^{N} I_r\,(i,\,j)^2 \qquad (7)$$

$$C_f = \sum_{j=1}^{M} \sum_{j=1}^{N} I_f(i,\,j)^2 \qquad (8)$$

$$C_{rf} = \sum_{i=1}^{M} \sum_{j=1}^{N} I_f(i,j)I_r(i,\,j) \qquad (9)$$

C. Root Mean Square Error (RMSE)

A commonly used reference based assessment metric is the RMSE. The RMSE will measure the difference between a reference image, R, and a fused image, F, RMSE is given by the following equation

$$RMSE = \sqrt{\frac{1}{MN} \sum_{n=1}^{M} \sum_{n=1}^{N} (R(m,n) - Fm,n))^2} \qquad (10)$$

where R(m, n) and F(m, n) are the reference (CT or MR) and fused images, respectively, and M and N are image dimensions. Smaller the value of the RMSE, better the performance of the fusion algorithm.

D. Peak Signal to Noise Ratio (PSNR)

PSNR is the ratio between the maximum possible power of a signal and the power of corrupting noise that affects the fidelity of its representation. The PSNR of the fusion result is defined as follows

$$PSNR = 10X \log \frac{(f_{max})2}{(RMSE)2} \qquad (11)$$

where f_{max} is the maximum gray scale value of the pixels in the fused image. Higher the value of the PSNR, better the performance of the fusion algorithm.

E. Mutual Information (MI)

Mutual information is the basic concept of measuring the statistical dependence between two random variables and the amount of information that one variable contains about the others. Mutual information here describes the similarity of the image intensity distributions of the corresponding image pair. Let A and B be two random variables with marginal probability distributions $p_A(a)$ and $p_B(B)$ and joint probability distribution $p_{AB}(a, b)$

$$I_{AB}(a,b) = \sum_{x,\,y} P_{AB}(a,b) \log \frac{P_{AB}\,(a,b)}{P_A(a)P_B(b)} \qquad (12)$$

Considering two input images A, B and a fused image F we can calculate the amount of information that F contains about A and B according to above equation

$$I_{FA}(f,a) = \sum_{x,\,y} P_{FA}(f,a) \log \frac{P_{FA}\,(f,a)}{P_F(f)P_A(a)} \qquad (13)$$

$$I_{FB}(f,b) = \sum\nolimits_{x,y} P_{FB}(f,b) \log \frac{P_{FB}(f,b)}{P_F(f)P_B(b)} \tag{14}$$

Thus the mutual information is given by

$$M_F^{AB} = I_{FA}(f,a) + I_{FB}(f,b) \tag{15}$$

F. Edge association

It is a measure of important visual information with the edge that is present in each pixel of an image. The visual to edge information association is well supported by HVS (Human Visual System) studies and is frequently used in compression systems and image analysis. The amount of edge information that is transferred from input images to the fused image can be obtained as

$$Q_F^{AB/F} = \frac{\sum_{x=1}^{M} \sum_{y=1}^{N} Q^{AF}(x,y) w^A(x,y) + Q^{BF}(x,y) w^B(x,y)}{\sum_{x=1}^{M} \sum_{y=1}^{N} (w^A(x,y) + w^B(x,y))} \tag{16}$$

Where Q^{AF}, Q^{BF} are edge preservation values and W^A, W^B are the corresponding weights.

Results

The hybrid image fusion has been performed using CT and MRI images. The quality of image obtained by hybrid technique has been verified using various criteria such as entropy, correlation coefficient, peak signal to noise ratio and root mean square error. The original input images and their corresponding fusion results using the proposed technique are depicted in detail. Wavelet and Curvelet transform are applied on the source images and then transform coefficients obtained are obtained for five different fusion methods.

Hybrid image fusion using GUI interface of MATLAB

Figure 6 shows the GUI user interface using MATLAB. This interface is created for the fusion of CT and MRI image using wavelet transform. Image 1(a) (CT image) and Image 1(b) (MRI image) is selected using database. Press to fuse icon is selected to obtain a fused image of CT and MRI image (Figure 7). Firstly fused image is obtained using wavelet transform image fusion technique, image obtained after fusion of two images i.e. CT and MRI image using wavelet transform is as shown in Figure 8, Table 1 shows the statistics results of various fusion methods i.e. wavelet transform, curvelet transformation is applied on CT and MRI images to obtain curvelet transform image, Final image obtained after fusion of CT and MRI images using curvelet transform is as shown in Figure 9. Further wavelet and curvelet image are then fused using hybrid transformation to obtain a better and more enhanced image. Now the fused image is having all the necessary details of CT image and MRI image. The quality of hybrid image (Figure 10) obtained using wavelet fusion transform and curvelet fusion transform is then evaluated on various performance parameters.

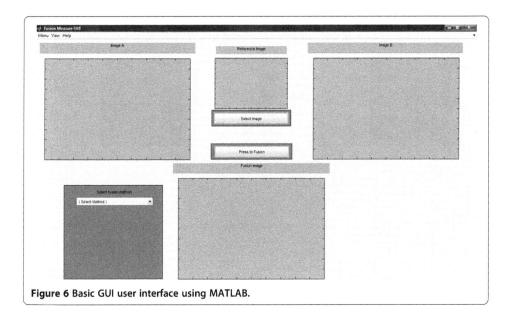

Figure 6 Basic GUI user interface using MATLAB.

Effect of fusion methods on entropy and root mean square error

Figure 11 shows the value of entropy with respect to fusion methods for wavelet, curvelet, hybrid and other image fusion methods. The value of entropy is maximum for Hybrid transform followed by curvelet transform and select maximum. The value of image fused by hybrid transform is better than that of curvelet and wavelet transform. Since entropy is a statistical measure of randomness that can be used to characterize the texture of the input image therefore the higher the value of entropy the better the texture of the image.

Figure 12 shows the variation of Root Mean Square Error value with that of fusion methods. As the value of root mean square error decreases the quality of image increase. The value of root mean square error for Hybrid transform as well as principal component analysis is minimum. Further the root mean square value for wavelet transform in maximum in comparison to that for curvelet and hybrid transform i.e. wavelet transform does not work well in comparison to that for curvelet and hybrid transform. Among all the three types of transforms the value obtained for hybrid transform are optimum.

Effect of fusion methods on peak signal to noise ratio and correlation coefficient

Figure 13 shows the peak signal to noise value for various fusion methods. The value of peak signal to noise ratio for hybrid transforms are maximum followed by Laplace Transform. Further while considering peak signal to noise ratio for different fusion methods it has been noticed that PSNR value are more for curvelet transform and principle component analysis whereas select minimum, select maximum and simple average does not behave well with reference to PSNR values for wavelet, curvelet and hybrid transform.

Figure 14 shows variation of correlation coefficient with fusion methods for fusion methods. The value of correlation coefficient for different fusions methods are maximum for wavelet transform followed by hybrid and curvelet transforms. Also the

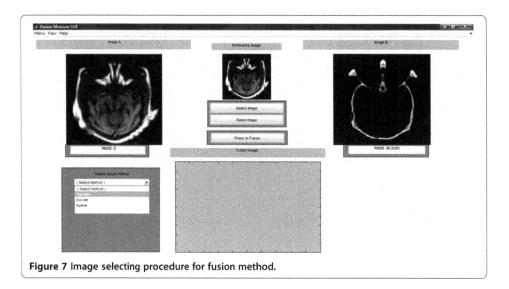

Figure 7 Image selecting procedure for fusion method.

values are maximum for principal component analysis whereas the values for select maximum and simple average are the least.

Effect of fusion methods on mutual index and edge association

Figure 15 shows the effect of fusion methods on mutual index. The value of mutual index is higher for hybid transform followed by select minimum and curvelet transform. This

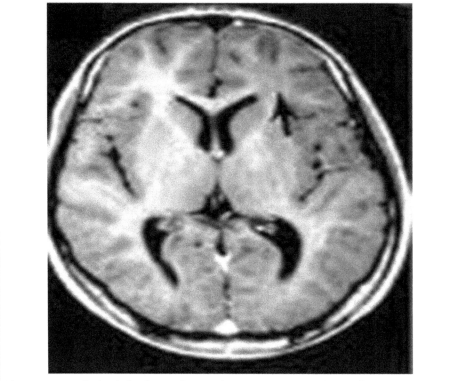

Figure 8 Image obtained after fusion of MRI and CT image using wavelet transform.

Table 1 Statistics results of various fusion methods

Fusion methods	Metrics					
	Entropy	RMSE	PSNR	CC	MI	Q$^{AB/F}$
Select maximum	6.63	4.248	29.56	0.61	5.23	0.55
Select minimum	2.89	15.23	23.25	0.67	6.92	0.74
Simple average	4.23	13.23	27.32	0.71	4.81	0.65
Principle component	6.34	3.421	36.12	0.88	5.89	0.79
Laplace transform	7.45	3.921	39.24	0.90	4.56	0.80
Wavelet transform	7.77	3.442	29.33	0.92	6.23	0.89
Curvelet transform	8.54	3.436	38.77	0.89	6.85	0.75
Hybrid transform	8.81	3.316	41.91	0.85	7.44	0.91

signifies that the information is uniformly shared between the two images and the resulting image is having better characteristics than the individual images obtained from wavelet and curvelet transforms.

Figure 16 shows the effect of fusion methods on edge association methods. The value of edge association is higher for hybrid transform followed by wavelet transform, Laplace transform and principle component method. This represents that the visual information in the pixels of hybrid fused image is more than that of the other fusion methods.

From the above analysis it has been concluded that hybrid transform works well with all the fusion methods also the value of testing parameters are optimum for hybrid transform

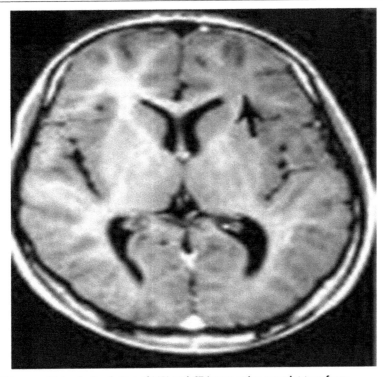

Figure 9 Image obtained after fusion of MRI and CT image using curvelet transform.

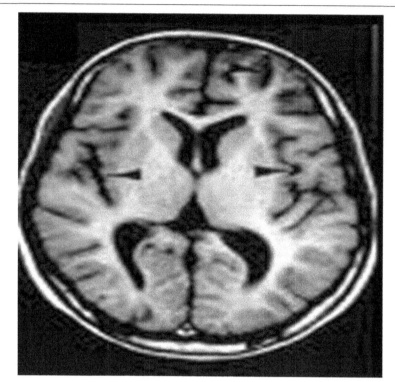

Figure 10 Hybrid image obtained after fusion of wavelet and curvelet transform.

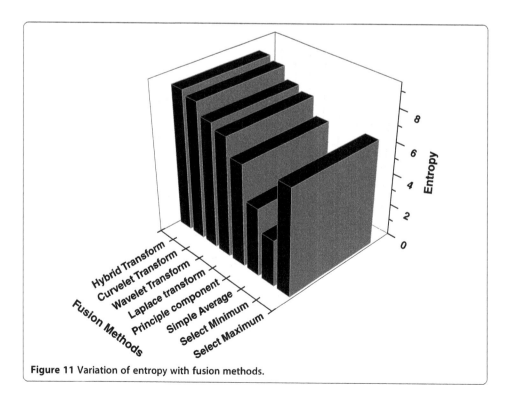

Figure 11 Variation of entropy with fusion methods.

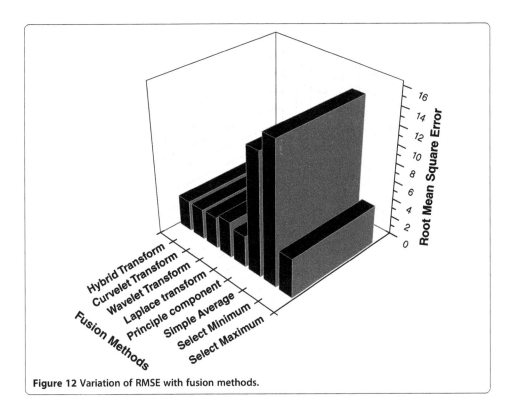

Figure 12 Variation of RMSE with fusion methods.

as visualization is clear and image is more intact by the combination of the two transform methods i.e. wavelet and curvelet transforms. Furthermore the proposed hybrid fusion scheme in this research work compensates all the short comings of wavelet and curvelet transform. It also removes the ringing effect and produced smooth corners and edges in the fused image. From the image quality assessment tables, it is clear that the proposed fusion

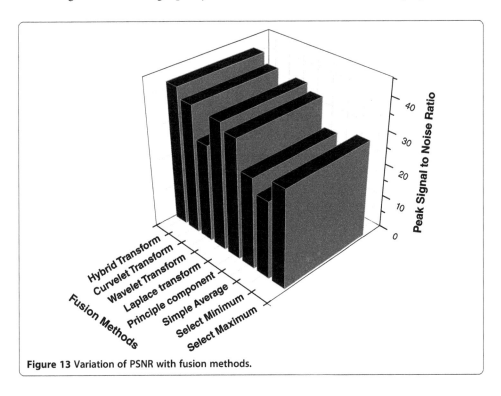

Figure 13 Variation of PSNR with fusion methods.

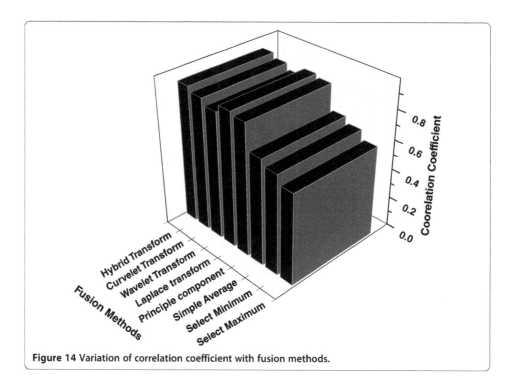

Figure 14 Variation of correlation coefficient with fusion methods.

technique outperforms other methods based on performance evaluation criteria's i.e. Entropy, Correlation Coefficient, Peak signal to noise ratio, Root mean square error, Mutual index and Edge information. The fusion methods also focuses on the fact the finally obtained image is much clearer and contains more information in comparison to the other existing fusion methods.

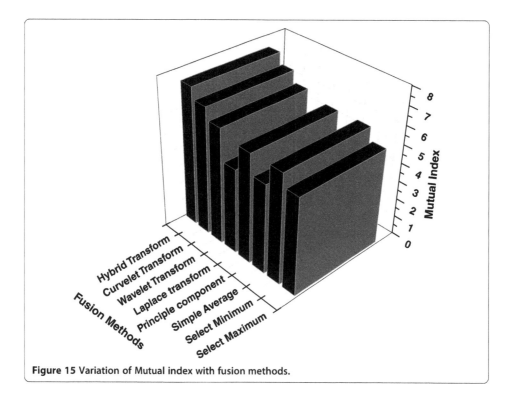

Figure 15 Variation of Mutual index with fusion methods.

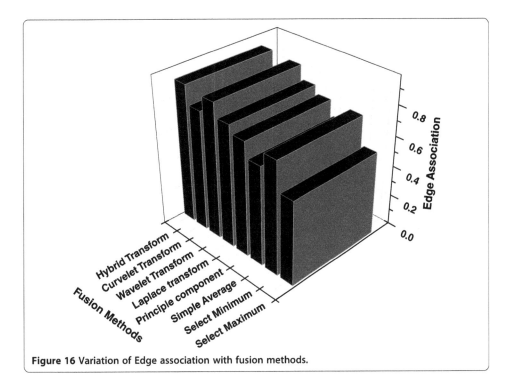

Figure 16 Variation of Edge association with fusion methods.

Conclusion

In this research work, attention was drawn towards the current trend of the use of multi-resolution image fusion techniques such as wavelet transform and curvelet transform. An efficient image fusion technique has been proposed here which is formed by combining the features of both wavelet and curvelet image fusion algorithms. In our proposed technique of image fusion we get more enhanced image and work well for edges, corners and helps in minimization of the localized errors. The high pass filter mask enhances the edges whereas averaging filter mask helps in removing noise by taking mean of grey values surrounding the centre pixel of the window. The response to image fusion is found to have higher values of Entropy, Peak signal to noise ratio, correlation coefficient, mutual index and edge association. The root mean square error also gets reduced. Finally the smoothness parameter should be taken relatively high value to decrease the slope of the filter function reducing the oscillations of the filter response function in the time domain.

Thus the two different modality images are fused using the various fusion rules based on the Wavelet, Curvelet and hybrid transforms. Moreover the difference in performance for these transforms is clearly exhibited using six performance measures. It is observed that, fusion methodology based on the Curvelet transform has given curved visual details better than those given by the Wavelet fusion algorithm. The fused image obtained using hybrid transform contains more useful information than the fused image using wavelet or curvelet transform. The proposed technique compensates all the shortcomings of either wavelet or curvelet transform method of fusion. Thus enabling the radiologists to locate the imperfections accurately, making the treatment easier and perfect.

From the various image quality assessment table and graphs, it has been clear that the proposed fusion technique outperforms other methods in terms of entropy, correlation coefficient, peak signal to noise ratio, root mean square error, mutal index information and edge association.

Competing interests

The authors declare that they have no competing interests.

Authors' contributions

JA carried out the studies on hybrid image fusion technique for feature enhancement using CT and MRI techniques, designed the hybrid fusion algorithm carried out simulation experiments using MATLAB coding and drafted the manuscript. SSB provided full guidance and support and designed the MATLAB framework to carry out the experiments. He also guided in drafting the manuscript for important technical content and finally approved the manuscript to be published. Both the authors read and approved the final manuscript.

Authors' information

Jyoti Agarwal has graduated in Computer Science and Engineering from SRMSCET, Bareilly and completed post graduation in Computer Science from NITTR Chandigarh. Currently she is working as an assistant professor in Computer Science and Engineering Department of RIMT, Bareilly, India. Her research interests lie in the area of Network security, Brain computer interface and Image fusion and enhancement techniques.

Dr. S.S. Bedi is the Assistant professor for the department of Computer Science and Engineering of MJP Rohilkhand University. He received the PhD degree in Networking and Information Sciences from IIIT, Allahabad. He has very strong background in the area of information security and parallel and distributed computing. He has guided number of post graduate and doctorate thesis.

Author details

[1]Department of Computer Science, RIMT, Bareilly, Uttar Pradesh, India. [2]Department of Computer Science, MJP Rohilkhand University, Bareilly, India.

References

1. K P Soman, K I Ramachandran (2005) Insight into Wavelets from Theory to Practice, 2nd edn. PHI Learning Pvt. Ltd, New Delhi -110001, India
2. Ping YL, Sheng LB, Hua ZD (2007) Novel image fusion algorithm with novel performance evaluation method. Syst Eng Electron 29:509–513
3. Sahu DK, Parsai MP (2012) Different image fusion techniques – a critical review. Int J Modern Eng Res 2:4298–4301
4. Hall D, Llinas J (1997) An introduction to multisensory data fusion. Proc IEEE 85:6–23
5. Wu H, Xing Y (2010) Pixel – based image fusion using wavelet transform for SPOT and ETM + Image. IEEE Trans 19:6744–6789
6. Kirchgeorg M, Prokop M (1998) Increasing spiral CT benefits with post processing applications. Eur J Radiol 28:39–54
7. Tan Y, Shi Y, Tan KC (2010) A multi-modality medical image fusion algorithm based on wavelet transforms. Adv Swarm Intell 6146:627–633
8. Godse DA, Bormane DS (2011) Wavelet based image fusion using pixel based maximum selection rule. Int J Eng Sci Technol 3:5572–5577
9. Chandana M, Amutha S, Kumar N (2011) A hybrid multi-focus medical image fusion based on wavelet transform. Int J Res Rev Comput Sci 2:1187–1192
10. Ali FE, El-Dokany IM, Saad AA, Abd El-Samie FES (2008) Curvelet fusion of MR and CT images. Prog Electromagnetics Res C 3:215–224
11. Geetha G, Raja Mohammad S, Murthy YSSR (2012) Multifocus image fusion using multiresolution approach with bilateral gradient based sharpness criterion. J Comput Sci Inf Technol 10:103–115
12. Bindu CH, Prasad KS (2012) Performance analysis of multi source fused medical images using multiresolution transforms. Int J Adv Comput Sci Appl 3(10):54–62
13. Sivakumar R (2007) Denoising of computer tomography images using curvelet transform. ARPN J Eng Appl Sci 2 (1):21–26
14. Stark JL, Candes E, Donoho DL (2002) The curvelet transform for image denoising. IEEE Trans Image Process 11(6):670–684
15. Chao Z, Zhang K, Li YJ (2004) An image fusion algorithm using wavelet transform. Chin J Electron 32:750–753
16. Choi M, Kim RY, Kim MG (2004) The curvelet transform for image fusion. Int Soc Photo Grammetry Remote Sensing 35:59–64
17. Tsai IC, Huang YL, Kuo KH (2012) Left ventricular myocardium segmentation on arterial phase of multi-detector row computed tomography. Comput Med Imaging Graph 36:25–37
18. Zhan GQ, Guo BL (2006) Fusion of multi sensor images based on the curvelet transforms. J Optoelectronics Laser 17:1123–1127
19. Bedi SS, Agarwal J, Agarwal P (2013) Image fusion techniques and quality assessment parameters for clinical diagnosis: a review. Int J Adv Res Comput Commun Eng 2:1153–1157

15

Social design feedback: evaluations with users in online ad-hoc groups

Asbjørn Følstad[1*], Kasper Hornbæk[2] and Pål Ulleberg[3]

* Correspondence: asf@sintef.no
[1]SINTEF, Pb124 Blindern, 0314 Oslo, Norway
Full list of author information is available at the end of the article

Abstract

Social design feedback is a novel approach to usability evaluation where user participants are asked to comment on designs asynchronously in online ad-hoc groups. Two key features of this approach are that (1) it supports interaction between user participants and development team representatives and (2) user participants can see and respond to other participants' comments. Two design cases, involving 250 user participants, were studied to explore the output of social design feedback and investigate the effect of the two key features of this approach. Of all the design feedback, 17% was rated highly useful, and 21% contained change suggestions. The presence of an active moderator, representing the development team and interacting with the user participants, increased the usefulness of the design feedback. The opportunity to see and respond to others' design feedback had a minor effect on the kind of design feedback provided, but no effect on usefulness. Based on the findings, we offer advice on how to implement social design feedback and suggest future research.

Keywords: Human-computer interaction; Social design feedback; Usability evaluation; Online user involvement

Introduction

Involving users in usability evaluation is valuable when designing information and communication technology (ICT). Traditionally, evaluation with users has been conducted face-to-face with methods such as usability testing, participatory evaluation and post-experience interviews [1]. Increasingly, however, online evaluation methods are more used.

Online evaluation methods include (a) methods that require user participants and development team representatives to be present synchronously and (b) methods that require user participants to contribute asynchronously. Synchronous evaluation methods comprise, among others, moderated remote usability testing [2] and online focus groups [3]. Asynchronous evaluation methods include online questionnaires [4], unmoderated remote usability testing [5], and involvement of online user communities in design and development [6].

The established asynchronous online evaluation methods have inherent benefits and limitations. Questionnaires and unmoderated remote usability testing allow for relatively easy access to participants as participation does not require long-term engagement. However, these methods restrict interaction between the development team and the user participants, barring the development team from asking participants to clarify or elaborate their contributions. The involvement of online user communities enables interaction between the development team and user participants, for example in user forums or as part of beta testing [7]. As the establishment of active online user communities requires dedicated and long-term efforts, these typically are not available to a development project.

The popular uptake of social internet solutions, often referred to as social media [8], supports new opportunities for gathering design feedback online. In particular, designs at any level of maturity may be presented online for groups of colleagues, peers, clients or users to contribute design feedback, by way of comments and discussion threads. Available services for such design feedback include Notable [9] and ConceptShare [10].

We term this emerging approach *social design* feedback, as it exploits social internet solutions. By this term we mean asynchronous feedback in ad-hoc online groups. Compared to other methods for asynchronous evaluation with users, social design feedback has two key features: (1) There may be interaction between user participants and development team representatives and (2) the user participants can see and respond to other participants' contributions. No pre-existing online user community is required, since participants for social design feedback can be recruited in the same manner as for online surveys or unmoderated usability testing and the feedback is gathered in ad-hoc groups.

Our knowledge of social design feedback as an approach to usability evaluation is limited. Little is known concerning what level of usefulness to expect from the output of social design feedback, and the qualitative characteristics of this output is not sufficiently explored. Furthermore, we have no knowledge on the effect of the key characteristics of social design feedback. This lack in knowledge is critical if the Human–Computer Interaction (HCI) community is to judge the relevance of this approach and develop it further as an HCI evaluation method.

We present a study on social design feedback that investigates the output of social design feedback and the effect of the two key features of this method on output quality.

The contribution of the study is to increase our understanding of social design feedback as an approach to usability evaluation. The study contributes an exploration of the usefulness of the output from social design feedback in terms of its relevance and ability to inspire subsequent design work, as well as the qualitative characteristics of this output in terms of users' concerns and change suggestions. Furthermore, the effects of the key features of this novel approach to usability evaluation are examined. In particular, we examine how the interaction between study participants and an active moderator, as well as the participants' direct view of each other's contributions, affect the usefulness and qualitative characteristics of the evaluation output. The study is of particular interest for HCI researchers and practitioners concerned with new ways of conducting usability evaluations.

Background
Design feedback in evaluations with users

Involving users in evaluations may generate two types of output: *Interaction data* and *design feedback*. Interaction data are data from the users' interaction with a system such as observational data, system logs, and data from think-aloud protocols. Design feedback are data on users' reflections concerning an interactive system, such as comments on experiential issues [11], considerations on the system's suitability for its context of use [12], predictions of usability issues [13], and suggestions on design improvements [14]. Design feedback may address any aspect of a design, such as visual layout, interaction design, content categories, and technical or performance issues [13].

Methods that generate interaction data are well exemplified by usability testing, the most commonly used method for involving users in evaluation when designing ICT [15,16]. It should, however, be noted that usability testing also may involve design feedback, in particular through the application of post-test questionnaires or interviews [17].

Evaluation methods that may be used to gather design feedback include enquiry methods (for example workshop evaluations [18], focus groups [19], and questionnaire methods [20]), but also usability testing methods that allow users to contribute their reflections on the evaluated designs (for example cooperative usability testing [21]) and inspection methods supporting users as inspectors (for example pluralistic walkthrough [22] and group-based expert walkthrough [23]). It has been suggested that evaluation methods used to gather design feedback should provide substantial guidance and support so as to enable users inexperienced with usability evaluation to generate useful feedback [23].

In current usability evaluation practice, users are often asked for design feedback. In a recent survey, involving 112 participants reporting on their latest usability test [24], 80% reported having asked test participants for their opinion on usability problems (64%), redesign suggestions (48%), and/or other issues (28%).

Social design feedback, which is our approach to gathering design feedback, has only sporadically been studied in the field of HCI. Hagen and Robertson [25] discussed user participation through social technologies. Apart from this, we are aware of three empirical studies of evaluation methods resembling social design feedback, all concerning the use of online forums for usability evaluation.

Smilowitz, Darnell and Benson [26] and Bruun, Gull, Hofmeister, and Stage [27] compared online forums for usability evaluation to usability testing and individual self-report of usability problems. Self-reports were gathered as part of beta testing [26], remote asynchronous usability testing [27], and diary reports [27]. In both studies, the online forum approach was found to identify fewer usability problems than did the usability test. However, none of the studies were set up to exploit the opportunity for increased numbers of user participants in online forum evaluations, as the number of participants in the forum conditions were the same as in the usability test conditions.

Cowley and Radford-Davenport [14] compared evaluations in online forums to evaluations in focus groups with respect to design suggestions and participant conversations. They found that the online forum evaluations generated more design suggestions, but that the focus group evaluations to a greater degree induced conversations that could lead to unexpected findings.

None of the three studies considered design feedback as encompassing both usability problems and change suggestions. Smilowitz et al. and Bruun et al. studied evaluation output in terms of usability problems only, whereas Cowley and Radford-Davenport studied the output in terms of design suggestions. Only one of the studies [14] concerned the usefulness of the users' design feedback, by including an analysis of the feasibility of the resulting design suggestions. None of the studies included more than one case, something that may represent a threat to the external validity [28] of the studies' conclusions.

The three studies provided only limited insight in the effect of the two key features of social design feedback. The effect of interaction between user participants and development team representatives was not investigated in any of the studies. The effect of allowing user participants to access each other's comments could have been investigated in two of the studies [26,27] as these compared methods for individual self-reporting of problems to forum methods. However, as the compared methods differed on several features, the findings from these comparisons cannot be directly attributed to whether or not user participants were allowed to access each other's comments.

Current solutions for social design feedback

Emerging solutions for social design feedback follow one of two approaches. One approach is to enable feedback on a visual presentation of a user interface by adding comments as annotations in a separate visual layer, as for example Notable [9], Notebox [29], Cage [30], and ConceptShare [10]. All contributed annotations are visualised on-screen. This allows all participants to see the feedback that has already been given, but also serves to limit the number of contributions that may be handled due to the on-screen clutter resulting from large numbers of annotations. Some solutions, including ConceptShare, Cage and Notable, support discussion threads associated with the annotations.

Another approach is to enable feedback as comments in an adjacent discussion thread without on-screen annotations, such as the Open Web Lab, OWELA [31] and the RECORD online Living Lab [32]. All contributions are available to all participants for reading and commenting. This approach allows larger amounts of feedback as the discussion thread avoids the problem of on-screen clutter that may result from large numbers of comments added as annotations directly to the visual presentation. However, the lack of on-screen annotations may make it more difficult for participants to get an overview of all comments addressing a given element in the visual presentation.

Assessing the output of social design feedback

Within the field of HCI, usability evaluation output is typically assessed on *thoroughness* and *validity* [33]; that is, the proportion of real usability problems that are identified in the evaluation and the proportion of problem predictions that actually correspond to real usability problems (as opposed to false positives). This approach to assessment, however, is hardly viable when assessing output from social design feedback; partly because such output may include more than just usability problem predictions, in particular positive feedback and change suggestions, and partly because the thoroughness and validity assessments require a *comparison criterion* [33], a comprehensive set of real usability problems against which the evaluation output can be assessed. Such comparison criteria are typically established through usability testing, something that is not possible for ideas and early concepts which are important objects of evaluation in social design feedback.

Another approach to the assessment usability evaluation output is to assess its impact on the subsequent design process [12,13,34]. This approach, however, requires access to the development team at a later stage in the design process. Furthermore, this approach may be vulnerable to spurious effects caused by conditions in the design process not related to the evaluation, for example, management decisions to prioritise a particular area of functionality in subsequent development.

For the purpose of our study of social design feedback, a viable approach to the assessment of usability evaluation output may be that of Følstad and Knutsen [35]. They presented a study where an online survey tool was used to collect design feedback from more than 200 user participants across four student design cases. They assessed the design feedback using two approaches: (a) The feedback was rated on usefulness by the involved student designers, and (b) the feedback was categorised according to its qualitative characteristics – *positive, negative, constructive*; constructive feedback included suggestions on needed design changes. About one-third of the design feedback was rated as useful. The feedback categorised as *constructive* was judged by the student designers as more useful that the other feedback. Negative feedback was judged as slightly more useful than positive feedback, which was not judged as useful at all. In follow-up interviews, the student designers were concerned with the lack of detail in the design feedback and suggested online dialogue between the participants as a means to improve the level of detail in the feedback.

A strength of the analysis scheme suggested by Følstad and Knutsen [35] is that it supports analysis of design feedback in the context of usability evaluations. In particular, *usefulness* may be seen as an early measure of the possible impact of design feedback; design feedback that is not seen as useful will not have any impact on the subsequent design process and, conversely, design feedback seen as useful is likely to have an impact if this is feasible within the practical constraints of the design process. Likewise, the qualitative characteristics *negative* and *constructive* correspond to key outputs of a usability evaluation: usability problems and change suggestions. Though other schemes for analysing data from online social interaction exist, such as the one presented by Agichtein, Castillo, Donato, Gionis, and Mishne [36], the scheme of Følstad and Knutsen is used in this study as it has been developed particularly for the context of usability evaluations.

The effect of the key features of social design feedback

Though the effect of the two key features of social design feedback has not been sufficiently studied within the field of HCI, research from other fields may provide some indications of the effects to be expected.

The effect of interaction between user participants and development team representatives

Social design feedback supports interaction between user participants and development team representatives. For the user participants, such interaction will serve as feedback on their contributions from the development team. Research on online social networks indicates that visible feedback, in particular others' comments, increases the motivation to make future contributions [37-40]. In the field of online learning communities, moderators' comments and summaries have been found to strengthen collaboration [41]. Likewise, in the field of online political debate, it has been found that the presence of an active moderator may increase the quality of the debate [42].

For the development team representatives, interaction with user participants will serve as an opportunity to acknowledge good feedback, ask follow-up questions, and provide direction for future comments. User participants are likely to have an imperfect understanding of the kind of design feedback that is expected from them. Consequently, the feedback from the development team representatives may have an *uncertainty reducing function* [43], clarifying what kinds of contributions are relevant to and appreciated by the development team. Such clarification may be valuable for improving the usefulness of the user contributions gathered in social design feedback.

The effect of access to other participants' contributions

In social design feedback, user participants are given immediate access to other participants' contributions to enable participants to build on each other's contributions. The literature on electronic brainstorming provides relevant insight concerning this feature of social design feedback. Studies on electronic brainstorming indicate that access to others' contributions may have a *synergy* effect; that is, ideas from one participant may trigger new ideas in others [44]. Synergy seems to be dependent on there being a sufficiently high number of participants in the group – DeRosa, Smith and Hantula [45] suggested more than eight – as well as sufficient time for each participant to take advantage of the potential synergy from others' ideas [44]. Consequently, access to others' contributions may be expected to have a beneficial effect on the output of social design feedback if the number of participants is sufficiently high and the participants spend enough time to be able to use each other's contributions as a basis for their own feedback.

Access to others' contributions may also invoke the detrimental effect of *social loafing* [46]; that is, the tendency of individuals to perform worse when part of a group than on their own. Research on electronic brainstorming suggests that social loafing is reduced if participants are clearly identifiable as individuals by the use of nicknames or pseudonyms [47], as they were in the setup for social design feedback in this study.

Summary: needed knowledge on social design feedback

The presented background shows three aspects of social design feedback for which we need new knowledge.

Firstly, we need knowledge concerning the output to be expected from social design feedback, in particular for studies exploiting the potential of an online medium to involve large numbers of users. Knowledge is needed both on the usefulness of such output and on its qualitative characteristics.

Secondly, we need knowledge concerning the interaction between development team representatives and user participants, a key feature of social design feedback. No studies have previously addressed the effect of such interaction. However, studies from other fields indicate that such interaction may be beneficial.

Thirdly, we need knowledge concerning the effect of user participants' access to other's comments, the second key feature of social design feedback. No studies have previously studied this effect systematically. However, studies on online brainstorming indicate that access to other's contributions may lead to beneficial synergy.

Research questions

Our research questions are formulated so as to address each of the three knowledge needs summarized above.

RQ1: What is the usefulness and qualitative characteristics of social design feedback?

Following Følstad and Knutsen [35], we wanted to explore the output of social design feedback in terms of its usefulness and qualitative characteristics. The exploration should provide insight in the potential downstream value of the output from social design feedback. Furthermore, it should provide a more comprehensive exploration of the qualitative characteristics of such output than what has been provided in previous studies [14,26,27]. It was seen as important to conduct this exploration with a sufficiently high number of participants so as to take advantage of the capacity for large scale user involvement in social design feedback.

RQ2: How does the active participation of a moderator affect the output of social design feedback?

Social design feedback allows two-way interaction between user participants and development team representatives. Our study focused, for reasons discussed in the Method section below, on the possible interaction between user participants and a moderator serving as the recipient of feedback to the development team. On the basis of earlier work on uncertainty reduction [43], we hypothesised that moderator feedback on user participants' comments would increase the usefulness in the design feedback. Furthermore, we hypothesised that moderator feedback would increase the proportion of suggestions for change or redesign in the design feedback, as constructive user feedback previously has been found to be closely associated with high-usefulness comments [35].

RQ3: How does access to others' contributions affect the output of social design feedback?

Access to other participants' contributions can lead to synergy, as is seen in research on electronic brainstorming [44]. Consequently, we hypothesised that giving user participants' access to others' contributions would increase the usefulness of their design feedback. We also hypothesised that this increase in usefulness would be associated with an increase in the proportion of suggestions for change or redesign in the design feedback. However, such synergy may depend on multiple factors, for example on the participants spending enough time on others' feedback [48].

Method

To study the usefulness and qualitative characteristics of the output of social design feedback we explored such output in two ICT design cases (RQ1). In both cases, the participants contributed design feedback as free text comments in an online environment. All comments were displayed in discussion threads adjacent to the visual representation of the design. The environment did not support annotations in the visual representation thereby avoiding problems with visual clutter.

To allow conclusions on the effects of the key features of social design feedback (RQ2 and RQ3), each case was designed as a 2 × 2 factorial experiment where the participants were randomly assigned to one of four conditions (see Table 1). This design also allowed us to check for interaction effects between these two features, though no such effects were hypothesised.

The purpose of conducting our study in two cases was to generalize and challenge our findings. Our research design, however, does not support conclusions about differences

Table 1 Overview of the experimental conditions

		Direct view of other participants comments' prior to own comment	
		Yes	No
Moderator providing feedback on participants' comments	Yes	Condition 1	Condition 2
	No	Condition 3	Condition 4

between the two cases. Rather, we assumed that the two cases would yield the same experimental findings.

Cases

The cases were from different sectors: football (Case 1) and telecommunications (Case 2). Furthermore, the cases were in different design phases with designs of different levels of maturity: a running prototype website and a non-functional visualisation of a competing user interface design (Case 1), and pre-prototype concepts presented through simple storyboards (Case 2). For both cases, the purpose of the design feedback was to guide subsequent design and development. The purpose of selecting cases that differed on multiple characteristics was to study social design feedback in different contexts, thereby checking for the potential threat to external validity due to only using one particular study setting [28]; conducting the same experiment in two different contexts allowed us to challenge the findings of one case with reference to the findings of the other.

Case 1 was an early running prototype of a blog feed aggregator for a Norwegian premier league football club (see Figure 1). Its purpose was to provide team supporters one place to be updated on blogs concerning the team. The study commenced on the day of the launch of the prototype. The participants were asked to provide feedback on (a) the running prototype and (b) a visual presentation of an alternative user interface for the blog aggregator.

Case 2 was about novel concepts for social text-based communication on mobile devices, designed at the Oslo School of Architecture and Design. The concepts were presented as story-boards outlined as cartoon strips. The design feedback was meant to support prioritising concepts and subsequent design work. See Figure 2 for an example concept from Case 2.

Setup for social design feedback

The online environment for social design feedback consisted of a set of webpages, each structured as a frameset with four frames containing (a) instructions, (b) a free text comment field and a discussion thread, (c) the object of feedback, and (d) buttons to navigate between feedback topics. Figure 3 shows an example webpage.

The instruction frame was placed horizontally at the top of the webpage. The instructions were intended to be short and precise, while allowing room for discussion and reflection. In the feedback topic in Figure 3, the instructions read: "The look and functions of the blog portal. Currently there is a lot of text on the blog portal. The content is presented under headings indicating its origin. Do you have suggestions on how the blog portal should look in the future? Ideas on functionality? Thoughts on how the blog portal should be tied to other webpages, for example, football club webpage and Facebook?"

Figure 1 Home-page of the prototype web site evaluated in Case 1.

The comment field and the discussion thread were placed vertically at one side of the screen; the comment field above the discussion thread, and the thread sorted chronologically with the newest comment on top. Each comment in the threads included the contributor's nickname and a timestamp. Commenting on others' comments was available as a "reply" function associated with each comment in the thread. When commented on, a participant received an e-mail notification with a description of the reply and a link to access the relevant feedback topic.

The object of feedback was presented in the frame next to the comment field and discussion thread. When the object of feedback was a website (parts of Case 1), the participants could navigate the website while retaining the frames containing the instructions, comment field, and discussion thread. In parts of both cases, the objects of feedback were presented as images.

Figure 2 Example concept from Case 2. E-mail in places. (Concept developed by Jon Olav Eikenes, Theo Tveterås, and Lars Martin Vedeler at the Oslo School of Design and Architecture. Permission granted).

Figure 3 Example webpage for social design feedback. Instructions in the top frame **(a)**, comment field and discussion thread to the left **(b)**, the object of feedback, the prototype webpage of Case 1, to the right **(c)**, and buttons to navigate between feedback topics below the discussion thread **(d)**.

The navigation buttons, *next* and *previous*, were located immediately below the discussion thread. The participants could move between feedback topics at will.

Case 1 included five feedback topics; Case 2 included six. The feedback topics concerned different functionalities and design suggestions and were selected in co-operation with the case owners. All participants were shown the feedback topics in the same order and asked to contribute feedback for at least three of the topics. The participants were allowed to move on to the next topic even if they had not contributed feedback to the current one.

We were aware that the setup for social design feedback would be unfamiliar to the study participants, and consequently included explanatory texts for guidance and support in the invitation and recruitment process as well as for each feedback topic. The participants were explained that their feedback was meant to advise future design. They were also, for each discussion thread, asked to provide feedback in a manner consistent with this purpose; for example, to provide their "impression of the design," what they perceive to be "good / bad" in the design, or to "suggest changes." In particular, change suggestions and problems ("bad" in the design) were meant to trigger useful feedback.

Participant recruitment

In Case 1, invitations were included in an electronic newsletter to the football club supporters. In Case 2, participants were invited from a national market research panel provided they reported that they used e-mail on their mobile phones several times a week or more. The recruitment strategy allowed us to get user participants experienced with similar solutions.

Upon accepting the invitation, the participants clicked a link taking them to the social design feedback solution where they entered background data, including a nickname and an e-mail address for notifications, and were given instructions. No one participated in more than one case.

As compensation for their time, all participants entered a lottery with a prize worth about $300. The participants' chances in the lottery were not dependent on the content of the participants' comments. Participant fallout was calculated as the proportion of participants entering a nickname and e-mail address but not providing any design feedback. The fallout rate was 22% in Case 2 (unavailable for Case 1). We assume that the fallout rate was mainly due to the novelty of this kind of data collection and that some participants upon registration found that they did not want to participate because of the study setup. Indeed, the setup was duly described in the study invitation, but some participants may have overlooked this information.

Data collection and analysis – to explore the output of social design feedback (RQ1)

The study data consisted of the comments made in the environment for social design feedback, as well as the participant background data. To explore the output of social design feedback (RQ1), the comments were analysed in terms of their *usefulness* and *qualitative characteristics*, following Følstad and Knutsen [35]. This choice was made as the analysis scheme used by these authors has been developed particularly to analyse online design feedback.

The usefulness of the comments as input to a design process was rated by two independent analysts. Both analysts rated all participant comments to check inter-rater agreement. This rating was assumed to require special training in user-centred design, as judgments on the usefulness of design feedback require experience and understanding of the design process. One of the analysts had been working as a concept designer in an IT development company for three years. The other (the first author of this paper) had been working as a researcher on user-centred design in IT for ten years.

None of the analysts was responsible for the designs in any of the two cases, but one (the first author of this paper) had served as moderator in the two cases. Their distance to the design process allowed the design feedback to be rated without being affected by spurious idiosyncrasies in the two design processes, as, for example, could happen if a development team representative were to rate design feedback corresponding to design ideas previously suggested by this representative but for some reason not being pursued in the current design. Avoidance of such idiosyncrasies is arguably beneficial to the reliability of the rating. However, insufficient understanding of the designs could compromise the validity of the rating. Consequently, prior to the ratings, both analysts familiarised themselves thoroughly with the designs at hand.

Usefulness scores were calculated as the average of the analysts' ratings on two scales: *Relevance* and *Inspiration*. *Relevance* was defined as "the comment directly concerns a key part of the solution or its context of use"; *Inspiration* was defined as whether "the comment is suited to contribute to a change in the design." The two scales were motivated by Amabile's [49] work on creativity assessment, where the main components of creativity are held to be relevance and novelty.

Both aspects of usefulness were rated on scales from 0 to 10, the latter being the best. For a comment to receive a *Relevance* score above 5, it should be judged as suited to provide new insight. For it to receive an *Inspiration* score above 5, it should be judged to build the idea further, not just motivate the removal of something that does not work. Inter-rater agreement *r* ranged from 0.65–0.83 for the two scales across the two cases. The correlation *r* between *Relevance* and *Inspiration* ranged between 0.84–0.90.

The rating was conducted blind; that is, no information was provided during analysis on the conditions which the comments belonged to. This was done to avoid possible biases associated with expectations related to the different conditions. However, as one of the raters was also the moderator of the cases, this rater might remember which comments belonged to which condition. To check this possible source of bias, an additional set of usefulness analyses was run with the usefulness scores obtained only from the other analyst. These additional analyses showed the same pattern as the analyses using the average usefulness scores. The *Usefulness* scores obtained by the other analyst were only found to be significantly affected (p < .05) by the *Moderator* conditions in both cases, but not affected by the *Direct view* conditions in any of the cases. Thus, we can rule out the possibility that the analysis of usefulness was biased by analyst expectations.

The qualitative characteristics of the comments were coded by two independent analysts. As this was not expected to require special training in HCI, the analysis was done by two student assistants who received initial training and piloting. Both analysts rated all participant comments to check inter-rater agreement.

The comments were coded on:

- *Negative/problem* (yes/no). Comments expressing a general negative attitude to the function or solutions manifested in the design and/or identifying a particular problem with the same function or solution. (Inter-rater agreement: Cohen's kappa = 0.87 indicating almost perfect agreement [50]).
- *Suggestions* (yes/no). Comments explicitly suggesting a change or redesign to the function or solution manifested in the design (Inter-rater agreement: Cohen's kappa = 0.76 indicating substantial agreement [50]).

Negative/Problem was initially treated as two distinct characteristics during coding, but merged because the analysts expressing difficulties differentiating between *negative* and *problem*, something that also was reflected in lower inter-rater agreement for these initial characteristics (Cohen's kappa 0.68 and 0.55, respectively).

Comments containing content corresponding to a coding category, for example a *suggestion*, were coded *yes* for this category. All other comments were coded *no*. The exception to this coding system was the initial coding category *negative*, which was coded as positive, neutral, or negative, upon which *negative* was recoded as *yes*, and *positive* and *neutral* were recoded as *no*. In the case of disagreement between the raters, only those comments coded *yes* by both raters were counted within a given category.

A comment could potentially be coded as both *Negative/Problem* and *Suggestion*. Such overlap did not have implications for the subsequent analyses, as the different codes were never included in the same analysis.

The comments were also coded on other characteristics. These were *references to similar solutions, references to other participants, information on the intended context of use,* and *comments on good details in the design.* The first three of these were not included in the following analysis, as each of them covered less than 10% in any of the cases. The last of these was not included as the inter-rater agreement for this characteristic was too low.

All coding of the comment characteristics was conducted blind. None of the analysts were aware of which conditions the different comments were made in. This was done to control for possible biases associated with analyst expectations.

Experimental conditions - to investigate the effect of the two key features of social design feedback (RQ2 and RQ3)

For each case, RQ2 and RQ3 were investigated by implementing the four experimental conditions of Table 1 as four instances of the online environment. After being presented to the study instructions, the participants were randomly directed to one of the four conditions by a JavaScript. The participants were not aware of there being different conditions.

Moderator feedback

In Conditions 1 and 2, a moderator provided feedback on the participants' comments. Using a moderator as the main point of interaction between the user participants and the development team made it practically possible to conduct and analyse the interaction in a systematic manner, this being a necessary condition for the experimental setup. The moderator gave feedback as comments in the discussion thread, clearly specifying the nickname of the user participant being addressed. The moderator feedback was phrased as praise/thank you, enquiries for more detail, or requests for others to offer their viewpoint. More than two-thirds of the participants in the moderated conditions received moderator feedback on one or more of their comments. In Conditions 3 and 4, no such moderator comments were given. Examples of moderator feedback are given in Table 2.

Direct view of others' comments

In Conditions 1 and 3, the participants could see the discussion thread with the other participants' comments before making a comment. In Conditions 2 and 4, the participants could see a given discussion thread only after having made a root comment, a *root comment* being understood as a participant's first comment for a particular feedback topic. As all participants were allowed to contribute more than one comment in any thread, the participants in Conditions 2 and 4 could reply to other participants' comments if they made a root comment to get to see the thread. The direct view of other participants' comments was meant to allow participants in Conditions 1 and 3 to benefit from synergy with the other participants' comments when making their root comment in the thread. Participants in Conditions 2 and 4 were not allowed such a potential benefit of synergy when making their root comment for any feedback topic. To check that participants' in Conditions 2 and 4 did not make bogus root comments just to get access to other participants' comments, we particularly reviewed the participant comments to detect such bogus statements.

Table 2 Examples of moderator feedback

Moderator feedback types	Example feedback case 1	Example feedback case 2
Praise/thank you	Hi **@nemezizz**. Thanks for your good feedback on the blog portal. (AsbjornF – partly responsible for the study :-)	Really like your rich reflections on the function for delayed sending of e-mail, **@idieh**. Free choice of time for sending, and that it should distract from "send" (as in "send now"). Thanks! (AsbjornF – partly responsible for the study :-)
Enquiry for more detail	Good feedback on the blog portal, **@csandoy**. Would be great to get to know more on what you think of the new blog portal suggestion vs. the existing portal, and why? (AsbjornF – partly responsible for the study :-)	Thanks for your enthusiastic feedback on the function for delayed sending of e-mail, **@Lisa**. Would be great to get some examples on how you would use this. Is it possible to ask you for a couple of these? (AsbjornF – partly responsible for the study :-)
Request others to offer their viewpoint	Hi **@Anon1**. Thanks for telling us that we need more pictures. Anybody else having an opinion on this? (AsbjornF – partly responsible for the study :-)	Some of you, e.g. **@bestorp**, suggest automatic zoom. I definitely see the point, but I wonder if one easily gets a kind of key-hole effect where you see too little of a long message. [...] What do all of you think about this? (AsbjornF – partly responsible for the study :-)

Results

Initial analyses

In total, 250 participants took part in the study and provided one or more comments; 86 participants in Case 1 (35% females; mean age = 29 years, $SD = 13$ years) and 164 participants in Case 2 (32% females; mean age = 28 years, $SD = 5$ years). The mean number of comments per participant was 3.0 in Case 1 ($SD = 1.6$) and 4.7 in Case 2 ($SD = 2.0$). No participant provided more than 13 comments.

The participants provided 1036 comments across the two cases. Of these comments, 19 were discarded for being unintelligible or the same comment submitted twice by the same participant. The remaining 1017 comments were analysed; 980 of these were root comments, whereas 37 were follow-ups. As a *root comment* is understood as a participant's first comment for a particular feedback topic, a participant could have as many as five or six root comments depending on the number of feedback topics in the case.

The moderator contributed a total of 103 comments across the two cases. Details of the distribution of participant and moderator comments are given in Table 3.

Only a small proportion of the participant comments were follow-ups. This was surprising to us and will be treated further in the Discussion section. Because of this lack of follow-up comments, the subsequent analyses include only the participants' root comments. We have done this to simplify interpretation, as the low number of follow-up comments (37) makes it difficult to draw general conclusions on the nature of such comments.

The usefulness and qualitative characteristics of the comments (RQ1)

The usefulness of the participant comments was skewed towards the lower end of the scale. In Case 1, only 17.1% of the comments received usefulness scores above 5, and in Case 2, only 17.0% were above 5; this means that 167 of the 980 comments were judged as potentially giving new insight and/or being suited to build the design further. Details are presented in Table 4.

Example comments for different levels of usefulness, as well as different characteristics, are presented in Table 5. All comments are from Case 2, from the feedback topic on the concept presented in Figure 2. The instruction for the topic was as follows: "Suggestion 2: E-mail in places. If the recipient has GPS on the phone you can send e-mails that are only received when the recipient is where you want the message to be read; as in the example in the cartoon below. How would you use such a function? What should we think of when developing this function further?"

The effect of Moderator (RQ2) and Direct view of others' contributions (RQ3)

The effects of an active moderator and direct view of other participants' contributions were analysed by using data on comment *Usefulness*, as well as the comment characteristics

Table 3 Distribution of participants and comments across the cases

	Case 1 (n = 86)	Case 2 (n = 164)	Total (n = 250)
Participant root comments	246	734	980
Participant follow-up comments	8	29	37
Moderator comments	42	61	103

Table 4 Distribution of usefulness scores

	Usefulness 0–2.50		Usefulness 2.51–5.00		Usefulness 5.01–7.50		Usefulness 7.51–10		All comments	
	Count	%	Count	%	Count	%	Count	%	Count	%
Case 1	112	46%	92	37%	41	17%	1	0%	246	100%
Case 2	330	45%	279	38%	103	14%	22	3%	734	100%

Negative/Problem and *Suggestion* as dependent variables in two-way ANOVAs, based on the 2 × 2 factorial experimental design.

The ANOVAs were carried out on the level of individual participants. The dependent variables were calculated as follows:

- Individual scores on *Usefulness* were calculated as the proportion of a participant's comments with usefulness score above 5. This approach to individual scoring, instead of, for example, using the mean of the usefulness ratings for an individual participant's comments, was chosen to clearly differentiate between highly useful comments and other comments. In the case that a larger proportion of the comments had received high usefulness scores, we would have chosen the mean of the usefulness ratings. However, to check whether the analysis would have yielded a different result if we had chosen a different calculation, we also replicated our analyses using *mean usefulness rating* (as outlined above) and *number of usefulness ratings above 5* (a measure which disregards the number of low-usefulness scores provided by an individual).
- Individual scores on *Negative/Problem* and *Suggestion* were calculated as the proportion of a participant's comments being coded as *Negative/Problem* and *Suggestion* respectively.

Descriptive analyses

To provide an initial overview of the findings, prior to presenting the results from the ANOVAs, we present mean scores for *Usefulness*, *Negative/Problem*, and *Suggestion* as bar charts for each of the two independent variables (*Moderator* and *Direct view*). This mode of presentation, where the independent variables are seen independently, is justified as no interaction effects were observed in the ANOVAs (to be presented below).

The mean scores for the dependent variables in the *Moderator* and *No Moderator* conditions are presented in Figure 4. We see that in both cases, *Moderator* is associated with higher scores on *Usefulness* and *Suggestion*. However, this difference only approached significance in Case 1. Also, *Moderator* is associated with lower scores for *Negative/Problem*, but these differences are not statistically significant in either of the cases. The results indicate that *Moderator* had a positive effect on the usefulness of the comments, as well as the participants' tendency to contribute suggestions. However, the presence of a moderator did not have a positive effect on the participants' tendency to contribute negative- / problem-oriented comments.

In the same manner, the mean scores for the dependent variables for *Direct view* and *No Direct view* are presented in Figure 5. There seems to be no common pattern across the two cases for *Usefulness* and *Suggestion*. The scores for *Negative/Problem* are higher for the *Direct view* condition in both cases, though this difference was statistically

Table 5 Example participant comments, Case 2

Usefulness rating	Qualitative characteristic	Example comments
0 - 3	Negative/Problem	John turning off the GPS may have catastrophic consequences.
	Suggestion	NA
	Both	NA
	Neither	This is perfect. It is much easier than having notes or similar lying around to remember things.
4.5 - 5.5	Negative/Problem	I would not use this kind of function. It is a type of function that limits the freedom of people to move about as they wish, and as Anonymous2 writes, this assumes that the recipient is moving in a "given pattern" …
	Suggestion	If this is to be interesting, the recipient needs to be updated on whether the message is read or not.
	Both	A bit too 1984, except that it is Linda who sees you and not big brother. I would not use this function and would turn it off if it was default. If you absolutely need this, it would be good if it could (if possible) find its position by way of mobile signals, this would save battery capacity dramatically. (Think HTC Hero does this if the GPS is turned off and one uses the map, with a 5–800 meter error margin, but still).
	Neither	This is a function I would use for road descriptions and meeting information.
7 - 10	Negative/Problem	Everything is wrong with this functionality. First the GPS reception is poor in the pocket or in the purse. Second, this will drain the phone battery empty even faster. Third, I doubt that John finds it nice that Linda can do 24/7 surveillance on him. All in all GPS on the phone is a double-edged sword in a world where it seems as if the EU data directorate may be accepted (use all your influence and VOTE AGAINST). This can be useful for Taxi drivers and couriers etc. as a working tool but involves too much surveillance for my liking.
	Suggestion	Would be a cool function that can be used for a lot of useful things. To limit misuse the user should choose who are allowed to do this, for example persons in the contact list, anybody who wants, just some contacts, block some contacts, etc. And for it to work everywhere it needs to use a radius that is bigger than the exact shop door, maybe 50–100 meters from the chosen point.
	Both	I find this superfluous. It should be designed to fit better for people not familiar with the area, rather than people living nearby and therefore knowing where the closest grocery store is. Maybe a kind of a GPS showing guests or visitors where they should go from the nearest bus stop to the party they are to visit.
	Neither	NA

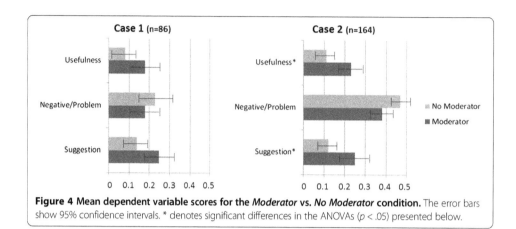

Figure 4 Mean dependent variable scores for the *Moderator* vs. *No Moderator* condition. The error bars show 95% confidence intervals. * denotes significant differences in the ANOVAs ($p < .05$) presented below.

significant only in Case 2. The results indicate that *Direct view* had a positive effect on the participants' tendency to contribute negative/problem-oriented comments, whereas there was no such effect on either the usefulness of the comments or the participants' tendency to contribute suggestions.

Moderator and *Direct view* clearly had different effects on the participants' feedback. Whereas the presence of a moderator increased usefulness and the participants' tendency to contribute suggestions, a direct view of other participants' comments increased the participants' tendency to contribute negative or problem-oriented comments.

The effect of Moderator and Direct view on Usefulness

The effects of *Moderator* and *Direct view* on the dependent variable *Usefulness* were analysed in two-way ANOVAs, one ANOVA for each case. In Case 2, *Usefulness* was significantly higher in the *Moderator* conditions than in the *No Moderator* conditions. In Case 1, we also found a difference in *Usefulness* between the *Moderator* and *No Moderator* conditions, but here it only approached significance ($p = .05$).

Usefulness was not affected by *Direct view* in either of the cases. No interaction effect between *Moderator* and *Direct view* was found. See Table 6 for details.

The square root of the effect size ω^2 is comparable to r [51]. Following Cohen's rules of thumb [52], the effect sizes associated with *Moderator* were small; the effect sizes associated with *Direct view* and the interaction term were negligible.

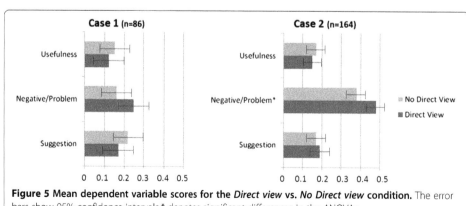

Figure 5 Mean dependent variable scores for the *Direct view* vs. *No Direct view* condition. The error bars show 95% confidence intervals.* denotes significant differences in the ANOVAs.

Table 6 The effect of *Moderator* and *Direct view* on *Usefulness*; results from two-way ANOVAs

| Independent variables | Usefulness | | | | | |
| | Case 1 | | | Case 2 | | |
	$F(1,82)$	p	ω^2	$F(1,160)$	p	ω^2
Moderator	3.87	.05	.02	9.25	<.01	.02
Direct view	.21	.65	.00	.09	.77	.00
Interaction	.00	.97	.00	.05	.82	.00

We replicated the ANOVAs with two alternative measures for usefulness, *mean usefulness rating* and *number of usefulness ratings above 5*, to check that our choice of usefulness score did not unduly impact our analysis. The results of these analyses paralleled those of Table 6. We found no effect of *Direct view* in either of the cases for either of the two alternative scores. We found a significant effect of *Moderator* in Case 2 for both the alternative scores. Furthermore, the effect of *Moderator* approached significance in Case 1 for *number of usefulness ratings above 5* ($p = .08$). For *mean usefulness rating*, however, the effect of *Moderator* was not significant ($p = 0.17$).

The effect of Moderator and Direct view on Negative/Problem and Suggestion

The effect of *Moderator* and *Direct view* on the dependent variables *Negative/Problem* and *Suggestion* were also analysed in two-way ANOVAs. Two ANOVAs, one for each dependent variable, were run for each case.

For *Negative/Problem*, the cases were not consistent concerning the findings. In Case 1, *Negative/Problem* was not significantly affected either by *Moderator* or *Direct view*. In Case 2, *Negative/Problem* was reduced in the *Moderator* condition, the reduction bordering significance ($p = .05$), and significantly increased in the *Direct view* condition. That is, in Case 2 when a moderator was present, the participants generated a smaller proportion of comments containing dislikes or concerns, whereas when they had immediate access to the other participants' contributions, the participants generated a larger proportion of such comments. No interaction effect was observed between *Moderator* and *Direct view*. See Table 7 for details.

The same kind of inconsistency between the cases was not found for *Suggestion*. *Suggestion* was higher for the *Moderator* conditions than the non-Moderator conditions in both cases, but the difference was significant only in Case 2. In Case 1, this difference only bordered significance ($p = .07$). *Suggestion* was not affected by *Direct view* in either of the cases. No interaction effect was observed between *Moderator* and *Direct view*. See Table 8 for details.

Table 7 The effect of *Moderator* and *Direct view* on *Negative/Problem*; results from two-way ANOVAs

| Independent variable | Negative/problem | | | | | |
| | Case 1 | | | Case 2 | | |
	$F(1,82)$	p	ω^2	$F(1,160)$	p	ω^2
Moderator	.94	.34	.00	3.85	.05	.01
Direct view	1.73	.19	.00	5.25	<.05	.01
Interaction	1.54	.22	.00	.98	.32	.00

Table 8 The effect of *Moderator* and *Direct view* on *Suggestion*; results from two-way ANOVAs

Independent variable	Suggestion					
	Case 1			Case 2		
	$F(1,82)$	p	ω^2	$F(1,160)$	p	ω^2
Moderator	3.28	.07	.01	11.93	<.01	.03
Direct view	.53	.47	.00	.64	.43	.00
Interaction	.15	.33	.00	.50	.48	.00

Non-parametric replications of the findings

Due to the fairly low proportion of comments scoring above 5 on *Usefulness*, the data for the *Usefulness* score used in the analyses did not follow a normal distribution. This is a violation of the assumptions of ANOVA. ANOVA has been found to be robust against such violations as long as the experimental groups are of equal size [51]. Even so, we found it desirable to conduct non-parametric tests of all group differences as an additional verification of our findings.

For all three dependent variables we conducted Mann–Whitney U tests for the effect of *Moderator* and *Direct view* respectively. We conducted two sets of these tests, one for each case. The output of the tests followed almost exactly the pattern of the ANOVAs. All significant differences observed in the ANOVAs were also found in the Mann–Whitney U tests. Furthermore, the Mann–Whitney U tests showed non-significance for all non-significant differences observed in the ANOVAs; the only exception was that the Case 2 analysis for *Negative/Problem*, which only bordered significance in the ANOVA ($p = .05$), was found to be significant in the Mann–Whitney U test ($p < .05$).

Discussion

The two cases have provided insights into the kind of output that social design feedback may give (RQ1), as well as the effect of the key features of social design feedback (RQ2 and RQ3). These insights have theoretical implications and help advise about the practical implementation of social design feedback.

The usefulness and qualitative characteristics of the output of social design feedback (RQ1)

The output of social design feedback was explored in terms of its usefulness and qualitative characteristics. Across the two cases, 167 comments (17%) received usefulness scores above 5, indicating that they provided new insights and/or concerned how to build the idea further. Furthermore, 201 comments (21%) contained change suggestions which have previously been found to be the most useful type of design feedback [35]. The user participants also provided 395 (41%) comments containing negative issues or perceived problems. Social design feedback clearly can generate useful output. We find the user participants to be able to generate feedback holding characteristics corresponding to what is expected of the output from a usability evaluation, in particular, usability problems and redesign suggestions.

However, showing that the output of social design feedback can be useful is only half the story. The output of social design feedback can also be littered with comments of low usefulness. Across the two cases, 813 comments received usefulness scores of 5 or below; that is, four-fifths of the comments did not provide new insight or make constructive input suited to drive the design process. Also, nearly half the comments contained neither suggestions nor participant concerns. An important challenge concerning social design feedback will be to increase the proportion of useful comments or to effectively filter out comments that are not useful in the subsequent development process.

The high frequency of comments not useful to subsequent development indicates that the majority of the participants were not able to comply with the intended purpose of their participation; that is, to provide feedback that could serve to drive the design process. This lack of compliance may be due to a lack in the participants' understanding of the intended purpose of social design feedback. The importance of sufficient guidance and support for user participants providing design feedback in usability evaluation have previously been accentuated [23]. We sought to provide such guidance and support by explaining the purpose of the study in the invitation and recruitment process, as well as in the descriptions for each feedback topic. Possibly, however, the social design feedback method may require even more in the way of guidance and support for the user participants that what was provided in our instantiation of the method.

The effect of an active moderator (RQ2)

An active moderator clearly affected the participants' contributions. Participants in the *Moderator* conditions received higher usefulness scores on their comments and provided more comments including suggestions for change or redesign. The hypothesis for RQ2 is supported, though the effect of an active moderator only approached significance in Case 1. As an active moderator both improves usefulness scores and causes more suggestions to be made, it seems reasonable to speculate that an active moderator improves the usefulness of design feedback in particular by guiding the participants to provide more constructive feedback, that is, more suggestions. This interpretation reverberates findings on the beneficial effect of moderators from online learning communities, where moderator summaries have been found to enhance collaboration [41], and online political debate where the beneficial effect of moderators have been attributed to their ability to focus the discussion [42].

It is fascinating that the beneficial effect of an active moderator was found even though we only analysed the participants' root comments. The analysed participant comments were affected only by the moderator's comments made previously in response to other participants, not by moderator responses to their own comments. Consequently, the effect of an active moderator is clearly not limited to the interaction between each individual participant and the moderator.

The beneficial effect of an active moderator may be explained by its potential *uncertainty reducing function* [43]. That is, the potential of the moderator's comments to guide the user participants towards providing comments in line with the goal of the design feedback as seen from the moderator's perspective. As the moderator's comments contain praise for useful participant comments, enquiry for more detail, and requests for others to offer their viewpoint, these comments may clarify to the participants what is expected from their participation.

However, an active moderator may also serve as a motivational factor for the participants. We know that others' comments may increase participants' motivation to make future contributions [37-40]. In this light, moderator comments may motivate not only those that are commented on, but possibly also other participants seeing that the design feedback is actually being read and acted upon by its recipients.

Though our hypothesis for RQ2 was supported, we observed a non-hypothesised difference in the effect of an active moderator on the two qualitative characteristics of the design feedback, *Suggestion* and *Negative/Problem*. The moderator was associated with higher scores on *Suggestion* and lower scores on *Negative/Problem*, though these differences were not significant for three of the four analyses. This unexpected finding may suggest that an active moderator does not trigger participants' tendency to provide negative feedback or unfiltered voicing of concerns. It may, possibly, be speculated that an active moderator can help the participants transform their negative feedback or concerns into suggestions. If so, this could help explain the beneficial effect of an active moderator. However, as this finding was both unexpected and only partially underpinned by statistically significant differences, it should not be regarded as valid knowledge. Nonetheless, it may serve as inspiration for future research on the causes for the effect of an active moderator.

The effect of seeing other participants' comments (RQ3)

Seeing other participants' comments prior to making one's root comment did not have a significant effect on either the usefulness of the participants' comments or on the participants' tendency to provide suggestions. This was contrary to our hypotheses for RQ3.

The number of participants in each condition was sufficiently high to allow for the synergy predicted on the basis of research on electronic brainstorming. However, we did not control for the time spent by the participants on the study. Most likely the participants spent some time reading others' comments in the study, given the effect of an active moderator, but we do not know whether the time spent was sufficient for synergy. Possibly, seeing others' contributions would have had a positive effect, given that we had introduced mechanisms or constraints to make sure that the participants spent enough time to utilise each other's contributions fully.

Seeing other participants' comments, however, had a positive effect on *Negative/Problem* in one of the cases. That is, the participants in the *Direct view* conditions contributed more negative and/or problem-oriented feedback than did those of the *No Direct* view conditions. It may be speculated that whereas participants in the *Moderator* conditions to a greater degree utilised the guidance provided by the moderator comments to adjust their contributions, and hence provided more constructive feedback, the participants in the *Direct view* conditions to a greater degree were left with the other participants' comments to adjust their contributions, which did not provide the needed guidance. However, no interaction effect was observed between *Moderator* and *Direct view* even though such an interaction may be inferred from the above speculation.

Differences between the cases?

RQ2 and RQ3 were investigated through an experimental design conducted within two cases. Our inclusion of two cases was done to generalize and challenge our findings, our expectation being that the two cases would yield the same empirical findings.

How, then, should we understand the differences observed between the cases? In particular, none of the findings in Case 1 were significant at $p > 0.5$, though the pattern of the findings in Case 1 was similar to the pattern of the findings in Case 2 (as can been seen, for example, in Figures 4 and 5).

Our interpretation is that these differences between the cases are likely due to the difference in the number of participants in each case and, consequently, differences in statistical power. As the main effects were small size only, the sample size in Case 1 was insufficient to achieve adequate statistical power. A sample size of 86 in a two-way ANOVA is only sufficient to observe medium to large size effects given a statistical power ($1-\beta$ error probability) of .80, according to the statistical software G*Power 3.1.5 [53]. We assume, therefore, that given a larger sample size in Case 1, the differences between the cases concerning statistically significant findings would have been substantially reduced, if not eliminated altogether. In hindsight, it would have been beneficial to include a larger number of participants in Case 1. However, this was judged as impractical at the time of the study due to time-constraints in the recruitment process.

Advice on the practical implementation of social design feedback

As we have seen, social design feedback elicits a substantial amount of useful feedback for early concepts, visual prototypes, and implemented applications. However, social design feedback also allows user participants to make contributions with low usefulness. Therefore, the successful implementation of social design feedback depends on our ability to either reduce the proportion of low usefulness feedback or to filter out low usefulness comments. Our findings motivate advice on how to reduce the proportion of low usefulness comments. In the following, we summarise three key learning points on the practical application of social design feedback:

- Clearly explain the purpose of the social design feedback to your participants. The participants are likely to be inexperienced in providing such feedback and, consequently, need guidance. Make sure to explain that you want feedback useful for subsequent design activities, in particular, suggestions for changes and redesign.
- Guide your participants by being responsive to participant comments. Comments from development team representatives, such as a moderator, will help the participants understand what kind of feedback you want. Since the participants are affected by moderator comments made to previous participants, it will be particularly important to moderate early in the feedback session in order to establish a norm for what constitutes useful feedback.
- Pay attention to participant motivation. Participants should belong to the main user groups of the solution under development, potentially improving participant motivation. Being responsive to participant comments and commenting on how the participant comments are useful to the design process should also improve participant motivation.

Limitations

The main limitation of this study is that we were not able to generate substantial interaction between participants and development team representatives. Thereby, some of the conclusions may be limited to social design feedback without such interaction.

The setup for the social design feedback supported asynchronous interaction between participants and moderators. Whenever a participant or a moderator was mentioned in a comment, a notification e-mail was sent to the mentioned person. In total, the moderator made 166 comments to the participants. However, only 37 follow-up comments were made by the participants. This volume of follow-ups was smaller than we had hoped.

This limitation may, in particular, be relevant to findings about the effect of seeing other participants' contributions prior to making one's root comment. The lack of support for the hypothesised effect of *Direct view* may be a consequence of a lack of substantial interaction between the participants, assuming an interaction effect between *Direct view* and the level of interaction.

The participants' limited interaction with each other or the study moderator is, however, not an indication that the social context of the study did not matter. On the contrary, the effect of an active moderator indicates that the participants, at least to some extent, paid attention to other's comments in the discussion thread. This point is particularly demonstrated as the analysis included only the participants root comments on any feedback topic; meaning that for a moderator's comments to have an effect, this had to be caused by the participants reading the moderator's comments on other participants' contributions. Thus, we hold that the studies were social in the sense that the participants were aware of, and to some degree related to, each other's comments.

How to increase participant interaction will be an important issue in future research on social design feedback, as we assume that increased interaction also will increase the level of detail in the feedback and thus its value in the subsequent design process.

Conclusions and future work

The present study provides new knowledge on the benefits and limitations of social design feedback. However, important future research remains to be done before we have sufficient knowledge about this approach to evaluations with users. We find the following three knowledge areas particularly relevant.

First, we need knowledge on how to improve the interaction between participants and development team representatives in social design feedback. Two strands of research may be relevant for this purpose: (a) research on the effect of the design and layout of the environment for social design feedback and (b) research on process improvements, such as improvements in the instructions to participants as well as in the moderator activity.

Second, we need knowledge on how to filter out low-usefulness comments. Given that we are not able to avoid getting low-usefulness comments we need reliable approaches to easily filter out such comments. Two strands of research may be relevant: (a) research on automatic content analysis for automatic filtering and (b) research on social filtering where the participants themselves are allowed to vote up and down other participants' contributions.

Third, it will be relevant to study individual differences in feedback usefulness. Given the large volumes of low-usefulness comments, filtering participants on individual differences may be a possible way to improve the ratio of high-usefulness feedback. Furthermore, as some participants may be more prone to engage in interaction with other participants in a social design feedback study, filtering participants on their tendency to engage socially online may provide a possible way to improve the interaction between participants.

Social design feedback is a novel approach to getting design feedback during the design of IT and may complement existing approaches to collecting design feedback. For HCI practitioners, social design feedback represents an opportunity to use the internet to gather design feedback. For HCI researchers, social design feedback may be seen as an exciting new field of method development.

Competing interests
The authors declare that they have no competing interests.

Authors' contributions
AF conceived of the study and its design, conducted the data collection and analyses, and drafted the manuscript. KH participated in the design of the study and in drafting the manuscript. PU participated in the analyses. All authors read and approved the final manuscript.

Acknowledgements
The presented study was conducted as part of the research projects RECORD and SociaLL, supported by the Norwegian Research Council VERDIKT program and the NordForsk LILAN program respectively. The study forms part of a doctoral thesis to be submitted to the Department of Psychology, University of Oslo.

Author details
[1]SINTEF, Pb124 Blindern, 0314 Oslo, Norway. [2]Department of Computing, University of Copenhagen, Njalsgade 128, 2300 Copenhagen, Denmark. [3]Department of Psychology, University of Oslo, Forskningsveien 3B, 0373 Oslo, Norway.

References
1. Maguire M (2001) Methods to support human-centred design. Int J Hum Comput Stud 55:587–634
2. Hammontree M, Weiler P, Nayak N (1994) Remote usability testing. Interactions 1:21–25
3. Thomset-Scott BC (2006) Web site usability with remote users. J Libr Adm 45:517–547
4. Ozok AA (2008) Survey design and implementation in HCI. In: Sears A, Jacko JA (eds) The human-computer interaction handbook, 2nd edn. Lawrence Erlbaum Associates, New York, pp 1151–1170
5. Bruun A, Stage J (2012) The effect of task assignments and instruction types on remote asynchronous usability testing. In: Konstan JA, Chi EH, Höök K (eds) Proceedings of the SIGCHI conference on human factors in computing systems, CHI '12. ACM Press, New York, pp 2117–2126
6. Holmström H, Henfridsson O (2006) Improving package software through online community knowledge. Scand J Inf Syst 18:3–36
7. Hess J, Offenberg S, Pipek V (2008) Community driven development as participation? Involving user communities in a software design process. In: Simonsen J, Robertson T (eds) Proceedings of the Tenth Anniversary Conference on Participatory Design 2008. ACM Press, New York, pp 31–40
8. Kaplan AM, Haenlein M (2010) Users of the world, unite! The challenges and opportunities of social media. Bus Horiz 53:59–68
9. Notable http://notableapp.com
10. ConseptShare http://conceptshare.com
11. Law ELC, Roto V, Hassenzahl M, Vermeeren APOS, Kort J (2009) Understanding, scoping and defining user experience: a survey approach. In: Olsen DR Jr, Arthur RB, Hinckley K, Morris MR, Hudson S, Greenberg S (eds) Proceedings of the SIGCHI conference on human factors in computing systems, CHI '09. ACM Press, New York, pp 719–728
12. Følstad A (2007) Work-domain experts as evaluators: usability inspection of domain-specific work-support systems. Int J Hum Comput Interact 22:217–245
13. Følstad A, Hornbæk K (2010) Work-domain knowledge in usability evaluation: experiences with cooperative usability testing. J Syst Softw 83:2019–2030
14. Cowley JA, Radford-Davenport J (2011) Qualitative data differences between a focus group and online forum hosting a usability design review: a case study. In: Proceedings of the Human Factors and

Ergonomics Society 55th annual meeting, HFES 2011. Human Factors and Ergonomics Society, Santa Monica, pp 1356–1360

15. Vredenburg K, Mao J, Smith PW, Carey T (2002) A survey of user-centered design practice. In: Wixon D (ed) Proceedings of CHI '02. ACM Press, New York, pp 471–478

16. Bark I, Følstad A, Gulliksen J (2005) Use and usefulness of HCI methods: results from an exploratory survey among Nordic HCI practitioners. In: McEwan T, Gulliksen J, Benyon D (eds) People and computers XIX - the bigger picture: Proceedings of HCI 2005. Springer-Verlag, London, pp 200–217

17. Rubin J, Chisnell D (2008) Handbook of usability testing: how to plan, design and conduct effective tests, 2nd edn. Wiley Publishing, Indianapolis

18. Hertzum M (1999) User testing in industry: a case study of laboratory, workshop, and field tests. In: Kobsa A, Stephanidis C (eds) Proceedings of the 5th ERCIM workshop on user interfaces for all. Dagstuhl, Germany

19. Hertzum M, Andersen HHK, Andersen V, Hansen CB (2002) Trust in information sources: Seeking information from people, documents, and virtual agents. Interact Comput 14:575–599

20. Tullis T, Albert B (2008) Measuring the user experience. Morgan Kaufmann, Boston

21. Frøkjær E, Hornbæk K (2005) Cooperative usability testing: complementing usability tests with user-supported interpretation sessions. In: van der Veer G, Gale C (eds) Proceedings of CHI '05. Extended Abstracts on Human Factors in Computing Systems. ACM Press, New York, pp 1383–1386

22. Bias RG (1994) The pluralistic usability walkthrough: coordinated empathies. In: Nielsen J, Mack R (eds) Usability inspection methods. Wiley, New York, pp 63–76

23. Følstad A (2007) Group-based expert walkthrough. In: Scapin D, Law E (eds) R3UEMs: Review, Report and Refine Usability Evaluation Methods. Proceedings of the 3. COST294-MAUSE international workshop. R3UEMs, Athens

24. Følstad A, Law ELC, Hornbæk K (2012) Analysis in practical usability evaluation: a survey study. In: Konstan JA, Chi EH, Höök K (eds) Proceedings of the SIGCHI conference on human factors in computing systems, CHI '12. ACM Press, New York, pp 2127–2136

25. Hagen P, Robertson T (2010) Social technologies: Challenges and opportunities for participation. In: Robertson T, Bødker K, Bratteteig T, Loi D (eds) Proceedings of the biennial participatory design conference, PDC '10. ACM Press, New York, pp 31–40

26. Smilowitz ED, Darnell MJ, Benson AE (1994) Are we overlooking some usability testing methods? A comparison of lab, beta, and forum tests. Behav Inf Technol 13:183–190

27. Bruun A, Gull P, Hofmeister L, Stage J (2009) Let your users do the testing: a comparison of three remote asynchronous usability testing methods. In: Hickley K, Morris MR, Hudson S, Greenberg S (eds) Proceedings of the SIGCHI conference on human factors in computing systems, CHI '09. ACM Press, New York, pp 1619–1628

28. Shadish WR, Cook TD, Campbell DT (2002) Experimental and quasi-experimental designs for generalized causal inference. Houghton Mifflin, Boston

29. Notebox http://noteboxapp.com

30. Cage http://cageapp.com

31. Owela http://owela.fi

32. RECORD online Living Lab http://livinglab.origo.no

33. Hartson HR, Andre TS, Williges RC (2001) Criteria for evaluating usability evaluation methods. Int J Hum Comput Interact 13:373–410

34. John BE, Marks SJ (1997) Tracking the effectiveness of usability evaluation methods. Behav Inf Technol 16:188–202

35. Følstad A, Knutsen J (2010) Online user feedback in early phases of the design process: lessons learnt from four design cases. Advances in Human-Computer Interaction. doi:10.1155/2010/956918

36. Agichtein E, Castillo C, Donato D, Gionis A, Mishne G (2008) Finding high-quality content in social media. In: Najorc M, Broder A, Chacrabarti S (eds) Proceedings of the 2008 international conference on web search and data mining. ACM Press, New York, pp 183–194

37. Lampe C, Johnston E (2005) Follow the (Slash) dot: effects of feedback on new members in an online community. In: Pandergast M, Schmidt K, Mark G, Ackerman M (eds) Proceedings of GROUP '05. ACM Press, New York, pp 11–20

38. Brzozowski MJ, Sandholm T, Hogg T (2009) Effects of feedback and peer pressure on contributions to enterprise social media. In: Teasley S, Havn E, Prinz W, Lutters W (eds) Proceedings of GROUP '09. ACM Press, New York, pp 61–70

39. Lüders M, Følstad A, Waldal E (2013) Expectations and experiences with MyLabourParty: From right to know to right to participate? J Comput Mediat Commun (in press)

40. Burke M, Marlow C, Lento T (2009) Feed me: motivating newcomer contribution in social network sites. In: Olsen DR Jr, Arthur RB, Hinckley K, Morris MR, Hudson S, Greenberg S (eds) Proceedings of the SIGCHI conference on human factors in computing systems, CHI '09. ACM Press, New York, pp 945–954

41. Kienle A, Ritterskamp C (2007) Facilitating asynchronous discussions in learning communities: the impact of moderation strategies. Behav Inf Technol 26:73–80

42. Stomer-Galley J, Wichowski A (2011) Political discussion online. In: Consalvo M, Ess C (eds) The handbook of internet studies. Wiley-Blackwell, Chichester

43. Ashford SJ, Cummings LL (1983) Feedback as an individual resource: personal strategies of creating information. Organ Behav Hum Perform 32:370–398

44. Dennis AR, Valacich JS (1993) Computer brainstorms: more heads are better than one. J Appl Psychol 78:531–537

45. DeRosa DM, Smith CL, Hantula DA (2007) The medium matters: mining the long-promised merit of group interaction in creative idea generation tasks in a meta-analysis of the electronic group brainstorming literature. Comput Human Behav 23:1549–1581

46. Karau SJ, Williams KD (1993) Social loafing: a meta-analytic review and theoretical integration. J Pers Soc Psychol 65:681–706

47. Jung JJH, Schneider C, Valacich JS (2005) The Influence of real-time identifiability and evaluability performance feedback on group electronic brainstorming performance. In: Proceedings of the Hawaii international conference on system sciences, HICSS '05. IEEE, Los Alamitos. doi:10.1109/HICSS.2005.566

48. Dennis AR, Pinsonneault A, Hilmer KM, Barki H, Galupe B, Huber MW, Bellavance F (2005) Patterns in electronic brainstorming. International Journal of eCollaboration 1:38–57

49. Amabile TM (1996) Creativity in context. Westview Press, Boulder

50. Landis JR, Koch GG (1977) The measurement of observer agreement for categorical data. Biometrics 33:159–174

51. Field A (2009) Discovering statistics using SPSS. Sage, London

52. Cohen J (1992) A power primer. Psychol Bull 112:155–159

53. G*Power 3 http://www.psycho.uni-duesseldorf.de/abteilungen/aap/gpower3

16

WordBricks: a virtual language lab inspired by Scratch environment and dependency grammars

Maxim Mozgovoy* and Roman Efimov

* Correspondence:
mozgovoy@u-aizu.ac.jp
University of Aizu, Tsuruga,
Ikki-machi, Aizu-Wakamatsu,
Fukushima, Japan

Abstract

This paper explains design decisions forming a foundation of WordBricks — an intelligent computer-assisted language learning environment, recently initiated at our institution. WordBricks is intended to serve as a "virtual language lab" that supports open experiments with natural language constructions. Being based on dependency grammars, this instrument illustrates the use of modern natural language processing technologies in language learning. The latest prototypes of WordBricks also show how dependency-styled constructions can be represented in a more natural sequential form that facilitates easier user interaction.

Keywords: Computer-assisted language learning, Natural language processing, Dependency grammar

Introduction[a]

The use of computer-assisted language learning (CALL) instruments is now widespread and well recognized both by language teachers and language learners. Past decades brought more powerful and accessible computers and numerous CALL software packages; the level of technological awareness among teachers has also increased greatly. At this point, it seems natural that researchers are often more focused on the integration of existing technologies into language curricula and the development of well-balanced teaching methods that combine theory, technology, and pedagogy, rather than on purely technological advancements for CALL systems [1].

However, popular CALL systems still rarely incorporate modern achievements of natural language processing technologies. For example, language learning software packages, recently reviewed in PC Magazine [2], at best provide the following capabilities: lessons with multimedia content, word-based memory games, online tutoring, and pronunciation training. Some systems were characterized as being brilliantly designed, nicely organized (as a combination of traditional lessons, word drills, scenario-based lessons/dialogues, etc.), or based on innovative educational concepts, such as involving a learner into a real text translation project. Undoubtedly, these features are beneficial for a language learner, but in most cases they do not make use of recent research advancements (probably, the only exception is high-quality speech recognition).

The lack of intelligence in CALL systems is a well-known problem, clearly formulated at least as early as in 1992 [3]. It has been suggested that a hypothetical intelligent CALL (ICALL) system can be based on both technical (natural language processing, speech recognition, feedback generation) and theoretical (pedagogy, cognitive science) advancements. The review of ICALL instruments conducted in 2002 identified at least 40 systems that use artificial intelligence (AI) technologies to a certain extent [4]. The same paper admits that many capabilities of ICALL systems cannot be reliably addressed with state-of-the-art technologies. This is a likely reason for a low interest in AI technologies for CALL today. As noted in [5], "the development of systems using NLP technology is not on the agenda of most CALL experts, and interdisciplinary research projects integrating computational linguists and foreign language teachers remain very rare".

Examples of ICALL systems provided in [4] and [5] show that AI technologies are most commonly used for grammar checking, textual feedback generation, and automatic speech recognition. Still, these technologies rarely address one of the major flaws of today's CALL systems, lying in their strictly limited interactivity. Typically a student accesses learning materials in the same way as in case of traditional books and audiotapes, while having little or no ways to *experiment* with language. One can note a contrast between CALL instruments and educational software, available for natural sciences, such as physics or chemistry. For these subjects, in addition to browsing multimedia learning materials, a student can often perform numerous experiments in a "virtual lab" (such as, for example, The Virtual Physical Laboratory [6] and The ChemCollective [7]).

Theoretically, numerous language learning activities might benefit from students' unrestricted experimentation (checking the applicability of a certain construction in a certain context, finding the best translation for the given phrase, exploring word morphology and the rules of verb government). In practice, many of these options are still too challenging for today's speech and language processing technologies. Given these limitations, one might consider an alternative approach: instead of fulfilling pedagogical aims with immature technology, it makes sense to try to implement scenarios that are technologically doable, and still have pedagogical value.

The idea of a "virtual language lab" based on established natural language processing technologies is the starting point of a project recently initiated at our institution. In this paper, we will introduce this project, and discuss its expected advantages and drawbacks as well as possible research directions. The first version of our software will be English language-based, but in this paper we will also use examples from other languages to illustrate certain grammatical phenomena.

The basic concept of "Word Bricks"

We decided to devote our project to one specific type of language learning activities: to the process of constructing grammatically correct phrases. A student with initial vocabulary and some knowledge of grammar rules might want to practice them by creating simple sentences. At this stage, it is important to make sure that the sentences are built properly, and if not, the student gets necessary feedback. By creating sentences, the student in the simplest case can test hypotheses about the correctness of certain constructions. In more advanced scenario, the feedback might include hints on the proper use of words and word combinations. For example:

- A student can check whether a certain word is appropriate in a certain context. Suppose the student knows that one can *ride a horse*, but can one *ride a car*?
- A student can find the correct word form for the given syntactical context. In English, the verb form depends on the subject's person, so the student has to choose between the base form of the verb and the 3rd person singular form. For other languages these rules can be more complicated. For example, Russian verbs are conjugated according to the subject's person and number in the present tense, but to the subject's gender and number in the past tense.
- A student can find correct prepositions and/or grammatical cases for the given context. For example, in Finnish some verbs require that the object noun is always set into a certain form (so the verb "governs" the noun). This verb / noun form list has to be memorized.

The idea of incorporating a grammar checker into CALL software is not new. Such an automated feedback generation system was implemented, e.g., in Robo-Sensei Japanese tutoring system [8]. However, today's grammar checkers are not very helpful in open experiments with language constructions. As noted in [5], grammar checkers are usually aimed at native speakers, and do not provide sufficient feedback for language learners. One possible way to solve this problem is to restrict user input. This approach is implemented in Robo-Sensei: the system asks the student to answer a specific question, and then compares the response with an "answer schema" that specifies the pattern of the expected correct response.

We believe that free experiments with language constructions are possible without traditional grammar checking technologies. Consider the following analogy. A programmer, working with traditional programming languages, has to write plaintext code that is translated into low-level machine instructions. It is a job of a compiler or interpreter to parse the code, and to identify possible syntactic errors. Unlike them, *visual programming systems*, often used for teaching programming to kids, store programs in graphical flowcharts (see, e.g., Flowol [9]), thus eliminating the need of parsing and error checking. One can draw a flowchart that corresponds to a wrong algorithm, but the flowchart itself cannot be "syntactically incorrect", since the visual editor allows no illegal links between the elements.

In a sense, flowcharts represent "parsed" programs, stored in the form that directly reflects their syntactic and semantic structure. Natural language sentences also can be represented in a parsed tree-like form with *phrase-structure* grammars or *dependency grammars* [10]. Our idea is to let the students compose *parsed* sentences directly instead of traditional writing.

General design of the system

Currently, we are developing the system with the following image in mind. A student is given a number of "word bricks" that represent single words. The student can connect individual bricks to form phrases and sentences. Every brick has typed incoming and outgoing "connectors", ensuring that only grammatically correct links are possible.

We believe that dependency links are easy to understand, since they connect words of a sentence directly, and do not require additional non-word bricks, as in case of phrase-structure links. The dependency link from the word A to the word B can be informally explained as a question that contains A, and has B as an answer. For example, in the phrase *he likes apples* there is a dependency link from *likes* to *he*, since it is possible to construct a question *who likes apples?*, having *he* as an answer. This idea is illustrated in the Figure 1 that shows the parse tree of the phrase *Tomorrow we go to Tokyo*.

At this point it is important to note that the Figure 1 shows just a possible visualization of a parse tree, displaying a number of word bricks, connected with directed arrows. However, this is not the only way to draw a parse tree, and we will return to this question later.

From basic bricks to typed bricks

Let us recall that one of our aims is to restrict possible connections, so the student cannot produce ungrammatical sentences. The formalism of dependency grammars allows specifying the type of word-word relationship, such as verb-subject, verb-object, noun-modifier, and so on. If we know the type of this relationship, we can decide which restrictions should be applied in the given case.

Perhaps, the development of such word linking constraints for each relationship type is the most challenging part of our project. These rules vary greatly from language to language, and might require morphological or even semantic information about the words to be linked. We will not discuss here all possible types of grammatical relationships and all kinds of challenges that arise in the task of linking constraints declaration, let us consider several examples for the sake of illustration.

Noun-adjective link

In English, we can establish a link between any noun and any adjective (answering the *which?*-question). In Russian and Spanish this noun-adjective link can be established only if the adjective agrees in number and gender with the noun:

libro rojo *(red book)*
libros rojos *(red books)*

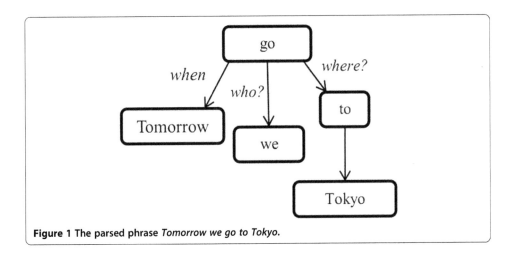

Figure 1 The parsed phrase *Tomorrow we go to Tokyo*.

rosa roja *(red rose)*
rosas rojas *(red roses)*

Verb-object link

In English, normally any noun or pronoun in objective case can be used as an object of a verb:

I like cars.
I like her. *('her' is an objective case of 'she')*

In Russian, we need to know whether the object represents something alive. For animate things the word form of the object is identical to the genitive case form, while for inanimate things the nominative case form should be used.

Verb government

The examples above describe general grammatical rules that hold for wide classes of word pairs. However, there are also verb-object relationships that depend on particular verbs. For example, the verb *to buy* can be used with an indirect object *place-of-purchase* with the preposition *in*:

I buy fish in a shop.

This fact is not as trivial as it might seem: in Finnish language one buys something *from* a shop (and this is expressed without any prepositions; the corresponding form of the word *shop* is used instead). So the choice of prepositions and word forms of verb objects is not obvious. It might depend on a particular verb, such as *to buy*.

Semantics-driven links

The discussed above link types can be used to ensure grammatical correctness of phrases. However, they do not prevent improper word use. Consider the following example. In English, one can *break the cup* and *break the law*. The student, familiar with English, might try to reproduce the same pattern in Russian, but this is incorrect: in Russian it is impossible to use the same verb in these two distinct contexts.

We believe this problem can be addressed with additional constraints on word types, as suggested in [11], though we did not decide yet whether we are going to implement this functionality, as it requires considerable amount of work. The idea is to introduce a hierarchy of word categories. By employing it, we can specify that one can break only breakable things, drive only drivable things, and so on. Several such ontologies are already available and can be used (see, for instance, the system of WordNet categories [12]).

Visualizing word bricks

In the first prototype of our system we have implemented a straightforward user interface: the students can arrange word bricks in the main window and connect them with lines to obtain graphs, similar to the one shown in the Figure 1. While this kind of visualization is the most natural way to show dependency trees, the process of drawing such diagrams hardly can be considered as the most intuitive way to build sentences. By drawing dependency trees, the students understand the tree-like structure of sentences, but such knowledge is beyond the curriculum of most language courses.

This problem has forced us to start designing an alternative visualization system for dependency trees, which would provide a more natural way for students to build sentences. The main source of inspiration for this work is the Scratch programming language learning environment [13]. In Scratch, the programs are created by connecting blocks, containing conventional elements of a programming language, such as assignments, input / output statements, branching and looping constructions. The blocks are shaped like jigsaw puzzle pieces, so it is impossible to create a syntactically incorrect program. For example, an IF-THEN-ELSE block contains three slots that have to be filled: the Boolean conditional expression, the THEN branch, and the ELSE branch (see the Figure 2). Unfortunately, natural language constructions are much more complex than the elements of a programming language, and our first attempts to formalize them in form of jigsaw puzzle parts are far from being complete.

Such a puzzle-styled representation has one more important advantage: it provides a natural way to formalize word order rules (Figure 3). In the standard visualization of dependency trees (Figure 1) there is no means to specify the correct word order. However, it is unclear how puzzle parts can be effectively used in languages with relaxed word order.

Pros and cons

In the previous sections we have outlined specific techniques for addressing particular language phenomena. Now let us discuss the potential advantages and drawbacks of our "virtual language lab", affecting its pedagogical value.

At present, we see the following positive sides of our approach:

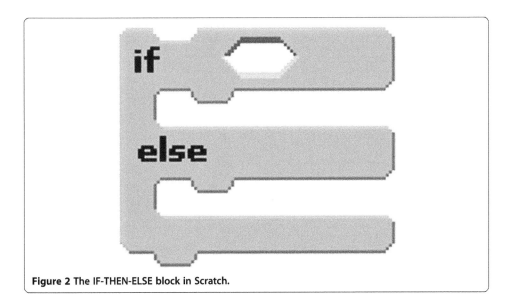

Figure 2 The IF-THEN-ELSE block in Scratch.

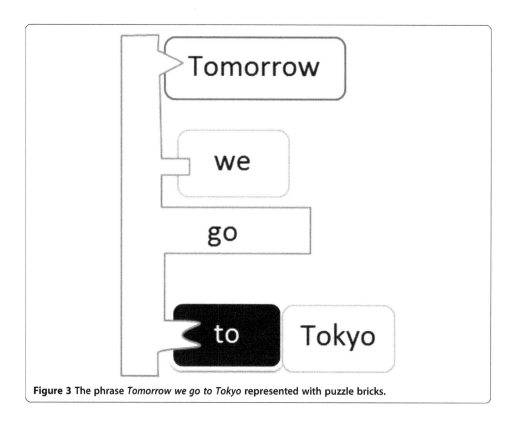

Figure 3 The phrase *Tomorrow we go to Tokyo* represented with puzzle bricks.

Supporting "virtual labs" in language learning. As mentioned above, the idea of open experimentation is supported in numerous educational software projects. However, in computer-assisted language learning this "virtual lab" approach is clearly underrepresented.

Formalized explanations. Typed word bricks provide a natural way to explain such language phenomena, as morphology, homonymy, cases and prepositions, verb government, and proper word use. Students can see how the choice of a word form affects brick type; how subjects and objects are linked to verbs, and so on.

Understanding underlying structures. Parse trees show the structure of sentences, thus contributing to deeper understanding of grammar rules and word-linking principles.

Contextualized assistance. Since the system knows internal structure of phrases, being constructed by students, it can provide numerous context-dependent hints. For example, it can automatically select the proper verb form for the given subject-verb word pair; it can provide a list of prepositions and grammatical cases, used with the given verb; it can display a list of breakable things used with the verb *to break* or a list of drivable things used with the verb *to drive*, and so on.

Our approach has also disadvantages, whose impact can be evaluated only in real-life experiments:

Unnatural constructions. Lucien Tesnière, who pioneered dependency grammars, distinguished the concepts of *words* as syntactic elements and of *nuclei* as complex elements carrying the same role as words [14]. For example, both the word *sees* and the word combination *will have been* seeing correspond to single nuclei. In a sense, "will have been seeing" is logically a single word, syntactically made up of separate tokens.

Dependency trees provide a convenient and natural way to link nuclei, but the situation becomes less obvious for the words inside a single nucleus. What kind of links connect the words *will*, *have*, *been*, and *seeing*? There are many such confusing sentence elements: complex objects that consist of and-, or-, or comma-separated elements; quotations; prepositions and articles; proper names; punctuation marks. Researchers have developed consistent guidelines that assist constructing dependency trees (see, e.g., Stanford typed dependencies manual [15]), but the need of knowing these technicalities is an unnecessary burden for a language learner. One may argue that even the parsed representation itself is a burden, so these complications with word linking rules make the system impractical.

Dependency grammars were also criticized for little support of word ordering rules. There are attempts to address this defect (see, e.g., [16]), but currently it is unclear how to incorporate word ordering into our system in a natural, pedagogically sound way. The situation can be partially remedied by the system of jigsaw puzzle blocks that can incorporate complete nuclei and word order rules, but it is much harder to design a complete set of such blocks than to employ traditional parse trees.

Limitations of error prevention system. The proposed system is not bullet-proof. By design, it analyzes local contexts of words only, so it cannot detect errors that appear at paragraph level. For example, the system is generally unable to detect improper article use (except simple cases with precise phrase-level rules, such as "do not use articles with people's names"). The system is also unable to detect semantic errors, when the sentence is grammatically correct, but the meaning is wrong.

Technical difficulties. The complete set of word-linking rules, described in Section IV, is most probably too large for manual implementation. For the proof-of-concept system, we plan to limit ourselves with a small vocabulary, and to declare rules manually. However, for a full-sized system we will need to learn rules automatically from treebank data.[b] Currently, it is hard to estimate how challenging this process is.

Conclusion

In this paper we have outlined basic design ideas of WordBricks — a new virtual language lab project, recently initiated at the University of Aizu. We are trying to implement a tool for open experimentation with language constructions. Such ICALL instruments are still very rare today.

Throughout the paper, we have seen how various linguistic phenomena, such as word agreement, verb government, cases and prepositions can be handled, and how dependency parse trees can be used by students to construct phrases and sentences. We believe that such a visual representation of sentence structure is helpful for deeper understanding of human language grammar rules.

This year we are planning to conduct first experiments in a real classroom environment and to make grounded conclusions about the feasibility of our approach. We are aware of potential limitations and drawbacks, but many of them are caused with objective complications of human language, and there is no way to overcome them completely.

Endnotes

[a] This paper is based on: M. Mozgovoy. Towards WordBricks — a Virtual Language Lab for Computer-Assisted Language Learning. *The 2nd Int'l Workshop on Advances in Semantic Information Retrieval*, Wroclaw, Poland, 2012, p. 251-254.

[b] A *treebank* is the collection of manually parsed sentences.

Competing interests

The authors declare that they have no competing interests.

Authors' contributions

MM created initial design of the WordBricks system, which allows the users to create sentences in form of dependency parse trees. RE is the main developer of the same system in the form of Scratch blocks, which should be a simpler choice for the users not familiar with dependency parsing. All authors read and approved the final manuscript.

References

1. Garrett N (2009) Computer-assisted language learning trends and issues revisited: integrating innovation. The Modern Language Journal 93:719–740
2. Duffy J The best language-learning software. PC Magazine, April 12, 2012. URL: http://www.pcmag.com/article2/0,2817,2381904,00.asp
3. Swartz M, Yazdani M (1992) Intelligent tutoring systems for foreign language learning. Springer Verlag
4. Gamper J, Knapp J, Gamper J, Knapp J (2002) A review of intelligent CALL systems. Computer Assisted Language Learning 15(4):329–342
5. Amaral L, Meurers D (2011) On using intelligent computer-assisted language learning in real-life foreign language teaching and learning. ReCALL 23(1):4–24
6. The Virtual Physical Laboratory, URL: http://www.colpus.me.uk/vplabd/
7. The Chemistry Collective, URL: http://chemcollective.org/
8. Nagata N (2009) Robo-Sensei's NLP-based error detection and feedback generation. Calico Journal 26(3):562–579
9. Flowol, URL: http://www.flowol.com
10. Rambow O, Joshi A (1997) A formal look at dependency grammars and phrase-structure grammars, with special consideration of word-order phenomena. Recent Trends in Meaning-Text Theory 39:167–190
11. Mozgovoy M, Kakkonen T (2009) An Approach to Building a Multilingual Translation Dictionary that Contains Case, Prepositional and Ontological Information. In: (ed) Proc. of the 12th Int'l Conf. on Humans and Computers, pp 135–139
12. Vossen P et al (1998) The EuroWordNet Base Concepts and Top Ontology. Technical report 1998-TR-004, Centre National de la Recherche Scientifique, France
13. Silver J, Silverman B, Kafai Y (2009) Scratch: programming for all. Communications of the ACM 52(11):60–67
14. Kahane S (1996) If HPSG were a dependency grammar.... In: (ed) Proc. of the 3rd TALN Conf, pp 45–49
15. de Marneffe M-C, Manning C (2008) Stanford Typed Dependencies Manual. Stanford University
16. Duchier D, Debusmann R (2001) Topological Dependency Trees: A Constraint-Based Account of Linear Precedence. In: (ed) *Proc. of the 39th Annual Meeting on Association for Computational Linguistics.* pp 180–187

17

Image contour based on context aware in complex wavelet domain

Nguyen Thanh Binh

Correspondence:
ntbinh@hcmut.edu.vn
Faculty of Computer Science and
Engineering, Ho Chi Minh City
University of Technology, Ho Chi
Minh, Vietnam

Abstract

Active contours are used in the image processing application including edge detection, shape modeling, medical image-analysis, detectable object boundaries, etc. Shape is one of the important features for describing an object of interest. Even though it is easy to understand the concept of 2D shape, it is very difficult to represent, define and describe it. In this paper, we propose a new method to implement an active contour model using Daubechies complex wavelet transform combined with B-Spline based on context aware. To show the superiority of the proposed method, we have compared the results with other recent methods such as the method based on simple discrete wavelet transform, Daubechies complex wavelet transform and Daubechies complex wavelet transform combined with B-Spline.

Keywords: Daubechies complex wavelet transform; Context-awareness; Active contour

Introduction

Contours are used extensively in image processing applications. Active contours can be classified according to several different criteria. One of the classifications is based on the flexibility of the active contour and is proposed in a slightly modified form by Jain [1]. The active contour models can be accordingly partitioned in two classes: free form of active contour models and limited form of active contour models.

The free form of active contour models constrained by local continuity and smoothness constraints [2–7]. Its limit uses a priori information about the geometrical shape directly. This information is available in the form of a sketch or a parameter vector that encodes the shape of interest. The geometric shape of the contour is adjusted by varying the parameters [8–13]. They cannot take any arbitrary shapes.

The snake has found wide acceptance and has proven extremely useful in the applications for medical analysis, feature tracking in the video sequences, three-dimensional object recognition [14], and stereo matching [15]. To take active contour, there are many methods to take it.

In the past, many algorithms have been built to find object contour. The dual-tree Complex Wavelet Transform (DTCWT) was proposed by Kingsbury [16]. In DTCWT, he used two trees of real filters for the real and imaginary parts of the wavelet coefficients. Recently, Bharath [17] has presented a framework for the construction of steerable complex wavelet.

This transform also avoids the shortcomings of discrete wavelet transform, but it uses a non-separable and highly redundant implementation. The redundancy of this transform is even higher than that of DTCWT.

In the entire complex transforms above, use of real filters make them not a true complex wavelet transform and due to the presence of redundancy, they are computationally costly. Lawton [18] and Lina [19] used an approximate shift-invariant Daubechies complex wavelet transform for avoiding redundancy and providing phase information. Shensa [20] and Ansari [21] use Lagrange filters, Akansu [22] uses binomial filters. Shen [22] used the Daubechies filter roots. Goodman [23] considered them as the roots of a Laurent polynomial. Temme [24] described the asymptotic of the roots in terms of a representation of the incomplete beta function. Almost of that method related Daubechies filters.

The wavelet transform for contour has serious disadvantages, such as shift-sensitivity [25] and poor directionality [26]. Several researchers have provided solutions for minimizing these disadvantages. Some of them have suggested the other method such as: local binary fitting [27, 28], local region descriptors [29], local region [30], local region based [31], local intensity clustering method. There exist some drawbacks with local regions. In [32], the problem is how to define the degree of overlap.

The local region based method has two drawbacks: (i) the Dirac functional is restricted to a neighborhood around the zero level set. (ii) Region descriptors only based on regions mean information without considering region variance [33].

Use of complex-valued wavelet can minimize these disadvantages. The DCWT uses complex filters and can be made symmetric, thus leading to symmetric DCWT, and it is more useful for image contour.

In this paper, we propose a new method to implement an active contour model using Daubechies complex wavelet transform combined with B-Spline based on context-aware (DCWTBCA). To show the superiority of the proposed method, we have compared the results with the other recent methods such as the method based on simple discrete wavelet transform (DWT), Daubechies complex wavelet transform (DCWT) and Daubechies complex wavelet transform combined with B-Spline (DCWTB). The rest of the paper is organized as follows: in section 2, we described the basic concepts of Daubechies complex wavelet transform. Details of the proposed algorithm have been given in section 3. In section 4, the results of the proposed method for contour have been shown and compared with other methods. Finally in section 5, we presented our conclusions.

Background

In this section, we present the theory related to the work such as: Complex Daubechies Wavelet and advantages of B-Spline for Snakes.

Construction of complex Daubechies wavelet

The basic equation of multiresolution theory [34-37,38] is the scaling equation:

$$\varphi(x) = 2\sum_{k} a_k \,\varphi(2x-k) \qquad\qquad (2.1)$$

where, a_k are the coefficients. The a_k can be real as well as complex valued and $\sum a_k = 1$. Daubechies wavelet bases $\{\psi_{j,k}(t)\}$ in one dimension are defined through the above scaling function and multiresolution analysis of $L_2(R)$ [37].

For $\varphi(x)$ to be Daubechies scaling function the following conditions must be satisfied [39, 40]:

(i) *Compactness of the support of φ*: It requires that φ (and consequently ψ) has a compact support inside the interval $[-J, J+1]$ for the integer J, that is, $a_k \neq 0$ for $k = -J, -J+1,...., J, J+1$

(ii) *Orthogonality of the $\varphi(x-k)$*: This condition defines in a large sense the Daubechies wavelets. Defining the polynomial

$$F(z) = \sum_{n=-J}^{J+1} a_n z^n, \quad with \, F(1) = 1, |z| = 1 \tag{2.2}$$

where z is on the unit circle, the orthonormality of the set $\{\varphi_{0,k}(x), k \in Z\}$ can be stated through the following identity

$$P(z) - P(-z) = z \tag{2.3}$$

where the polynomial P(z) is defined as

$$P(z) = zF(z)\overline{F(z)} \tag{2.4}$$

(iii) *Accuracy of the approximation*: To maximize the regularity of the functions generated by the scaling function φ, we require the vanishing of the first J moments of the wavelet in terms of the polynomial Eq. (2.2)

$$F'(-1) = F''(-1) = ... = F^{(J)}(-1) = 0 \tag{2.5}$$

(iv) *Symmetry*: This condition amounts to have $a_k = a_{1-k}$ and can be written as

$$F(z) = zF(z^{-1}) \tag{2.6}$$

As anticipated by Lawton [18], only complex-valued solutions of φ and ψ, under the four constraints above, can exist and for even J only. The first solutions (from $J = 0$ to $J = 8$) were described in [32] by using the parameterized solutions of Eq. (2.3), (2.5) and (2.6). The solutions have also been investigated in the spirit of the original Daubechies approach, i.e. by inspection of the roots of a so-called "valid polynomial" that satisfies Eq. (2.4). Such a polynomial is defined as

$$P_J(z) = \left(\frac{1+z}{2}\right)^{2J+2} p_J(z^{-1}) \tag{2.7}$$

where

$$p_J(z) = \sum_{j=0}^{2J} r_j(z+1)^{2J-j}(z-1)^j$$

with

$$\begin{cases} r_{2j} = (-1)^j 2^{-2J} \binom{2J+1}{j}, & j = 0, 1, ..., J \\ r_{2j+1} = 0 \end{cases} \tag{2.8}$$

Straightforward algebra shows that $P_J(z)$ does satisfy Eq. (2.3).

The *2J* roots of $p_J(z)$ display obvious symmetries: the conjugate and the inverse of a root are also roots; furthermore, no root is of unit modulus. If we denote by x_k *(k = 1,2,.......J)*, the roots inside the unit circle *(|x_k| < 1)* then

$$p_J(z) = \prod_{k=1}^{J}\left(\frac{z-x_k}{1-x_k}\right) \times \prod_{k=1}^{J}\left(\frac{z-\bar{x}_k^{-1}}{1-\bar{x}_k^{-1}}\right) \tag{2.9}$$

and the low-pass filter *F(z)* can be written as:

$$F(z) = \left(\frac{1+z}{2}\right)^{1+J} p(z^{-1}) \tag{}$$

With

$$p(z) = \prod_{m\in R}\left(\frac{z-x_m}{1-x_m}\right)\prod_{n\in R'}\left(\frac{z-\bar{x}_n^{-1}}{1-\bar{x}_n^{-1}}\right) \tag{2.10}$$

where *R, R'* are two arbitrary subsets of *{1, 2, 3,...,J}*. The spectral factorization of $P(z) = zF(z)\bar{F}(z)$ implies $p_J(z) = z^J p(z^{-1})p(\bar{z})$ which leads to the following constraint on *R* and *R'*:

$$k \in R \Leftrightarrow k \notin R' \tag{2.11}$$

This selection of root fulfills the conditions (i), (ii) and (iii). The addition of the symmetry condition (iv) defines a subset of solutions of Eq. (2.11). It corresponds to the constraint

$$k \in R \Leftrightarrow J - k + 1 \in R' \quad and \, k \notin R'$$

For any even value of *J*, this defines a subset of $2^{J/2}$ complex solution in the original set of "Daubechies wavelets". A complex conjugate of a solution is also a solution.

Properties of Daubechies complex wavelet
Daubechies Complex Wavelet has important properties [26, 39]:

(i) *Symmetry and linear phase property*:
   The nonlinear phase distortion was precluded by the linear phase response of the filter. It keeps the shape of the signal. This is very important in image processing.
(ii) *Relationships between real and imaginary components of the scaling and the wavelet functions.*
(iii) *Multiscale edge Information*

With Daubechies complex wavelet transforms, we can act as local edge detectors. In here, the imaginary components represent strong edges, and the real components represent only some of the stronger edges.

Advantages of B-Spline for snakes

In computer graphics, there are two splines which usually used: B-Splines and Bezier Splines. However, B-Splines have two advantages over Bezier Splines [41]: the number of control points can be set independently to the degree of a B-Spline polynomial and B-Splines allow local control over the shape of a Spline curve. From the advantages above of B-Splines, we choose B-Splines for our proposed method.

The important of constructing a snake is convenient to choose a set of control points on the image than to connect the point with straight lines. The B-Spline basis for snakes on the following:

(i) B-splines are piecewise polynomial that makes them very flexible.

(ii) B-splines can be make smooth curve.

(iii) B-splines preserve the shape that a spline has the same shape as its control polygon or more precisely.

Advantages of DCWT for active contour

In the past, many algorithms have been built to process image by DWT. DWT has three serious disadvantages [26]: shift sensitivity, poor directionality and lack of phase information. We can use DCWT to reduce these disadvantages. On the basis of Daubechies complex wavelet, we have the following advantages for the active contour:

(i) Symmetric and linear phase property of DCWT can keeps the shape of the signal and carries strong edge information. The linear phase response of the filter precludes the nonlinear phase distortion and keeps the shape of the signal and it reduces the misleading and deformed shape of objects.

(ii) DCWT can act as the local edge detectors. The imaginary and real components represent strong edges. This helps in preserving the edges and implementation of edge-sensitive contour methods.

(iii) DCWT has reduced shift sensitivity. DCWT reconstructs all local shifts and orientations in the same manner. So, it is clear that it can quickly find the boundary of objects.

The proposed method for image contour

This section describes the proposed method for contour objects. The term 'context-aware' [42] refers to context as locations, identities of nearby people and objects, and changes to those objects.

Most of previous definitions of context are available in literature [43] that context-aware looks at who's, where's, when's and what's of entities and uses this information to determine why the situation is occurring. Here, our definition of context is:

"Context is any information that can be used to characterize the situation of an image such as: pixel, noise, strong edge, and weak edge in a medical image that is considered relevant to the interaction between pixels and pixels, including noise, weak and strong edge themselves."

In image processing, if a piece of information can be used to characterize the situation of a participant in an interaction, then that information is context. Contextual information can be stored in feature maps on themselves. Contextual information is collected over a large part of the image. These maps can encode high-level semantic features or low-level image features. The low-level features are image gradients, texture descriptors and shape descriptors information [42, 44].

The proposed algorithm is of three steps: preprocessing of images, Daubechies complex wavelet filter bank and context- aware closed contour with boundary information. The goal of the second step is to detect the dominant edge points so that the resulting image will be composed of textures separated by the edges. We use Daubechies complex wavelet transform for edge detection that can act as the local edge detectors. The imaginary components of complex wavelet coefficients represent strong edges. Using a threshold parameter weak edges is wiped out. It works as a structure preserving noise removal process as well. Since we need to find the coordinates of the edges after this process, we use contour lines for that purpose since they provide closed edge curves which will ease the process when computing in the wavelet domain. Here, we use B-Spline contour lines. Steps of the proposed method are as follows in Fig. 1:

Firstly, preprocessing of images. The collected images are scale normalized to 256×256 pixel, 512×512 pixel dimensions in order to reduce complexity.

Secondly, Daubechies complex wavelet filter bank. For Daubechies complex filter bank computation in the proposed method, Daubechies decomposition proceeds through two main periods: reconstruction of the signal from the coefficients and energy formulation to define strong point.

Finally, context- aware closed contour with boundary information. Here, we use B-Spline contour lines, which covers the object.

Reconstruction of the signal from the coefficients

According to the multi-resolution analysis with tensor product bases, an image f(x, y) is projected onto some "approximation" spaces generated by the dyadic translations of the scaled function φ(x) and φ(y) (at the resolution scale jmax of the original image). If we denote the complex projection coefficients by

$$c_{x,y}^{j_{max}} = h_{x,y}^{j_{max}} + i g_{x,y}^{j_{max}} \tag{3.1}$$

then we can estimate $h_{x,y}^{j_{max}}$ and $g_{x,y}^{j_{max}}$ with the following steps of the iterative procedure:

1. Start from the usual approximation:

$$h_{x,y}^{j_{max}} = I(x,y) \tag{3.2}$$

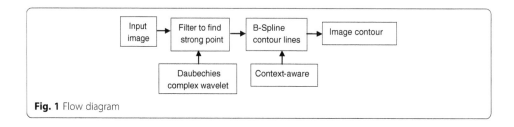

Fig. 1 Flow diagram

2. Evaluate $h_{x,y}^{j_{\max}+1}$ using a one-level synthesis operation with the real part of the inverse symmetric Daubechies wavelet kernel only.

3. Make a one-level complex wavelet transform. The result is a quite accurate estimation of the real and imaginary parts of the projection coefficient $c_{x,y}^{j_{\max}}$. In the first approximation,

$$h_{x,y}^{j_{\max}} \cong I(x,y) \tag{3.3}$$

and $g_{x,y}^{j_{\max}}$ is proportional to the Laplacian of the $f(x, y)$.

A N-level wavelet transform W can be represented as

$$\left\{c_{x,y}^{j_{\max}}\right\} \xrightarrow{W} \left\{c_{x,y}^{j_{\max}-N}, \quad d_{x,y}^{j_{\max}-N}, \quad \dots \quad d_{x,y}^{j_{\max}-1}\right\} \tag{3.4}$$

where the quantities $d_{x,y}^{j_{\max}-k}$ represent the set of coefficients for the three wavelet sectors. The complex scaling wavelet coefficients $c_{x,y}^{j_{\max}-N}$ result from the nested actions of the complex low-pass filter.

To solve the snake problem numerically, we express its cubic Spline solution using the standard B-Spline expansion

$$s^*(x) = \sum_{k \in Z} c(k)\beta^3(x-k) \tag{3.5}$$

where $c(k)$ are the B-Spline coefficients, and the generating function is the cubic B-Spline given by

$$\beta^3(x) = \begin{cases} 2/3 + |x|^3/2 - x^2, & 0 \le |x| < 1 \\ (2-|x|)^3/6, & 1 \le |x| < 2 \\ 0, & 2 \le |x| \end{cases} \tag{3.6}$$

Using the basic convolution and differentiation rules of Splines [45], we obtain the explicit formula

$$\zeta(s) = \sum_{k \in Z} V\left(k, \left(b_1^3 * c\right)(k)\right) + \lambda \sum_{k \in Z} \left(b_1^3 * d^{(2)} * c\right)(k)\left(d^{(2)} * c\right)(k) \tag{3.7}$$

where $*$ denotes the discrete convolution operator and the kernels b13(discrete cubic B-spline) and d(2) (second difference) are defined by their z-transform as follows [45]:

$$B_1^3(z) = (z + 4 + z^{-1})/6 \text{ and } D^{(2)}(z) = z - 2 + z^{-1} \tag{3.8}$$

We have now replaced the integral in the second term by a sum, which is much more computationally tractable. The task is then to minimize Eq. (3.7), which is typically achieved by differentiation with respect to c(k).

The Spline snake Eq. (3.5) has as many degrees of freedom (B-Spline coefficients) as there are discrete contour points, i.e., one per integer grid point. In Eq. (3.7), if λ is sufficiently small, then the Spline will interpolate exactly. Conversely, the use of larger values of λ will have the effect of stiffening the Spline and smoothing out the discontinuities of the unconstrained contour curve f(x). It is also necessary to mention that λ can eventually be dropped by using a variable size knot spacing, which still assures smoothness.

The argument is essentially the same for more general curves in the plane, which are described using two Splines instead of one. Specifically, we represent a general B-Spline snake as follows:

$$s_h(t) = \left(s_x(t), s_y(t)\right) = \sum_{k \in Z} c(k).\beta^n\left(\frac{t}{h} - k\right) \qquad 0 \leq t \leq t_{max} = hN \qquad (3.9)$$

where sx(t) and sy(t) are the x and y Spline components, respectively; these are both parameterized by the curvilinear variable. The exact value of tmax, which marks the end of the curve, is dictated by the desired resolution of the final discrete curve; by convention, we do only render the curve points for t integer. This 2D Spline snake is characterized by its vector-sequence of B-Spline coefficients c(k) = (cx(k), cy(k)). Note that there are only N = tmax/h primary coefficient vectors, each corresponding to a Spline knot on the curve; the other coefficient values are deduced using some prescribed boundary conditions. Clearly, if we specify N, the above automatically defines the knot spacing h and therefore the smoothness constraint for the curve.

Assuming a curve representation by M = tmax discrete points, we obtain h = M/N. The freedom of the Spline curve has been reduced by the same amount, resulting in a smoothing and stiffening of the curve. Increasing the number N of node points will reduce the knot spacing, and consequently it will reduce the smoothing effect of the curve.

Energy formulation

The external potential function is typically given by a smoothed version of the gradient of the input data [45, 46]

$$g(x, y) = \sqrt{\left(\frac{\partial}{\partial x}\varphi * f\right)^2 + \left(\frac{\partial}{\partial y}\varphi * f\right)^2} \qquad (3.10)$$

where f denotes the input image and φ is a smoothing kernel; for example, a Gaussian. Our cost function is the summation of the gradient (external force) over the path of the curve s(x) sampled at M consecutive points

$$\xi(c(k)) = \sum_{i=0}^{M-1} -g(s(i)) \qquad (3.11)$$

For the cost function to be a good approximation of the curvilinear integral, we typically select M sufficiently large so that the curve points are connected (i.e., within a distance of one pixel of each other). However, we note that the exact value of M is not critical; a less dense sampling may be used to increase optimization speed. The negative sign in Eq. (3.11) is used because we employ a minimization technique for the optimization.

The problem consists in evaluating Eq. (3.9) at M discrete points. Such an evaluation is necessary for the computation of the energy function Eq. (3.11) and for the display of the curve (where M may typically be chosen larger). Therefore, the continuous variable t is replaced by a discrete variable i, $0 \leq i < M$. The value of M and the number N of given node point directly determines the knot spacing h. The discrete B-spline snake with N node points and curve points is given as

$$s(i) = \sum_{k \in Z} c(k).\beta^n\left(\frac{i}{h} - k\right), \qquad h = \frac{M}{N} \tag{3.12}$$

Below, we present two different ways for fast curve rendering by digital filtering.

(i) Interpolation: The most straightforward way is interpolation. The B-Spline function is evaluated at every position (i/h - k) multiplied by the corresponding B-Spline coefficient and summation. B-Splines are of compact support, and therefore, the summing needs only to be carried out over a subset of all coefficients. To interpolate the curve at a point i, only the coefficients c(k)

$$\left[\frac{i}{h} - \frac{n+1}{2}\right] \le k \le \left[\frac{i}{h} + \frac{n+1}{2}\right] \tag{3.13}$$

need to be included in the sum ([.] denotes integer truncation).

The main computational drawback of this procedure is that the function Eq. (3.6) needs to be evaluated for each term in the sum.

(ii) Digital Filtering: The above described algorithm works for any combination of values of M and N. If we can impose M such that h is an integer value, a much more efficient algorithm can be described. In general, this requirement is easily met, it is not critical and can be loosely chosen. The simplification is based on a convolution property for B-Splines [45]. It states that any Spline of degree n and knot spacing h (integer) can be represented as the convolution of n + 1 moving average filters of size h followed by a Spline of knot spacing one. Hence, three successive steps can obtain the curve points:

- Up-sampling of the B-Spline coefficients;
- Averaging by (n + 1) moving average filters of size h;
- Filtering by a unit B-Spline kernel of degree n.

This algorithm can be implemented with as few as two multiplications and two additions per node point plus (2n) additions per computed contour coordinate. Generally, it is faster and also at least a factor of two better than the Oslo knot insertion algorithm commonly used in the computer graphics.

Border conditions

Appropriate boundary conditions are necessary for the computation of Eq. (3.9) and Eq. (3.10) [45]. In the following, we distinguish the cases of a close snake and an open snake.

(i) *Close Snake Curve*: For a set of node points *n(k)*, *k = 0,1,...., N-1* we require that *n(N) = n(0)* and *n(-1) = n(N-1)*. The corresponding boundary conditions are periodic. The extended signal $n_s(k)$ of infinite length can be described as

$$n_s(k) = n(k \bmod N) \tag{3.14}$$

(ii) *Open Snake Curve*: Different choices can be implemented for the open snake such as mirror or anti-mirror boundary conditions. In this application, the anti-mirror conditions with a pivot at the boundary value are the most suitable choice because they allow us to lock the end points of the curve.

These anti-mirror conditions are such that

$$(n(k_0 + k) - n(k_0)) = (n(k_0) - n(k_0 - k)) \tag{3.15}$$

where k0 ∈ {0, N-1}. Since the extended signal has a center of anti-symmetry at the boundary value, this value will be preserved exactly whenever the filter applied is symmetric, which turns out to be the case here. However, a new boundary value cannot be defined as the lookup of an existing signal value, which makes the implementation slightly more complicated.

From Fig. 2 and many cases of the other image tests, we observed that the proposed method accurately detects contour.

Experiments and results

To demonstrate the validity of the proposed method, we have tested on many images. We have compared the results with the other recent methods such as the method based on simple discrete wavelet transform (DWT), and the Daubechies complex wavelet transform (DCWT), the Daubechies complex wavelet transform combined with B-Spline (DCWTB) and the proposed method using the Daubechies complex wavelet transform combined with B-spline based on context aware. These methods were implemented on our matlab program and comparison has been made on the same images and on the similar scale. In our approach, we have taken dataset images for testing. This data set has 600 images. The proposed method was tested on different cases.

(a)

(b)

(c)

(d)

Fig. 2 Result of the proposed method with Lena's face image. (**a**) Lena original image (**b**) Selected Lena face. (**c**) Lena face at 200 iterations (**d**) Lena face at 300 iterations

To test our algorithm, many images of different sizes have been used. We compare the proposed method on two cases: strong objects and weak objects. The strong object is defined as an object whose boundaries are clear and the weak object is defined as an object whose boundaries are blurred. We have experimented on several images and here we report on some selected images.

As shown in Fig. 3, for the Cameraman image, we select an object. In this case, the object is Cameraman body (strong object) as Fig. 3(b). The results of DWT, DCWT and DWTB method are shown in Fig. 3(c), (d) and (e). The result of the proposed method is shown in Fig. 3(f). Here it can be observed that the result in Fig. 3(f) is better than the result in Fig. 3(c), (d), (e) at the same number of iterations (600 iterations).

Fig. 3 Performance of the proposed method on Cameraman image, compared to the DWT based method with the strong objects. (**a**) Cameraman original image. (**b**) Selected Cameraman body. (**c**) With DWT method at 600 iterations (**d**) With DCWT method at 600 iterations. (**e**) With DWTB method at 600 iterations (**f**) With proposed method at 600 iterations

Similarly, as shown in Fig. 4, for the Lena image, we select an object. In this case, the object is Lena's hat (strong object) as Fig. 4(b). The results of DWT, DCWT and DWTB method are shown in Fig. 4(c), (d) and (e). The result of the proposed method is shown in Fig. 4(f). Here it can be observed that the result in Fig. 4(f) is better than the result in Fig. 4(c), (d), (e) at the same number of iterations (400 iterations).

We tested the proposed method on a set of several images and compared with the other methods. From Figs. 3, 4 and many other tests, we observed that, in the case of strong objects, the proposed method is better than the other methods.

Fig. 4 Performance of the proposed method on Lena image compared to the DWT based method with the strong objects. (**a**) Lena original image (**b**) Selected Lena hat. (**c**) With DWT method at 400 iterations (**d**) With DCWT method at 400 iterations (**e**) With DWTB method at 400 iterations (**f**) With proposed method at 400 iterations

We now apply the proposed method with the weak objects cases. The weak objects are the objects with less clear boundaries. The important edge site is blurred in the object; therefore, the boundaries become obscure, thereby misleading the curve deforming. Weak objects have less clear boundaries, the extraction of weak object is not easy work. As a result, weak object could not be extracted precisely.

In Fig. 5, we select the Cameraman body (weak object) image as Fig. 5(b). The Fig. 5(a) is Cameraman original image. Heavy blur and noise has been added in this image to make the object weak. The results of DWT, DCWT and DWTB method are shown in Fig. 5(c), (d) and (e). The result of the proposed method is shown in Fig. 5(f). Here it

Fig. 5 Performance of the proposed method on Cameraman image compared to the DWT based method with the weak objects (blurred and noisy). (**a**) Cameraman original image (**b**) Selected Cameraman Body (**c**) With DWT method at 600 iterations (**d**) With DCWT method at 600 iterations (**e**) With DWTB method at 600 iterations (**f**) With proposed method at 600 iterations

can be observed that the result in Fig. 5(f) is better than the result in Fig. 5(c), (d), (e) at the same number of iterations (600 iterations). In contour classification, the goal is to assign an object into one of a set of predefined set of contour classes. The classification is performed by using a subset of the sub-band energies that are measured to produce a feature vector that describes the contour.

Figure 6 also compares the proposed algorithm with other methods on an image that comprises the object with weak edge (blurred image). The results shown in Fig. 6(f) is better than the results shown in Fig. 6(c), (d) and (e) at the same number of 450

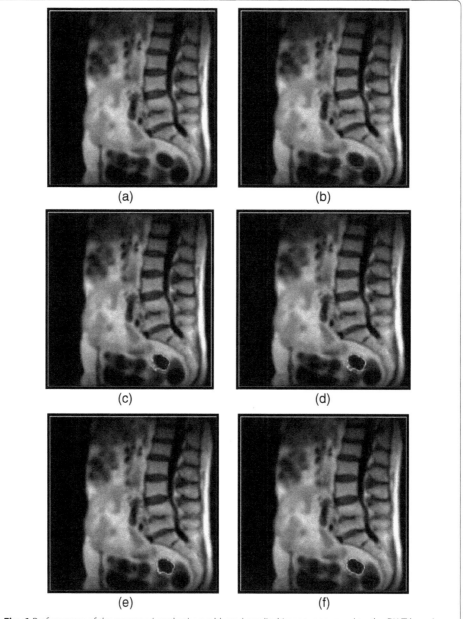

Fig. 6 Performance of the proposed method on a blurred medical image, compared to the DWT based method with the weak objects. (**a**) Image original (**b**) Selected weak object (**c**) With DWT method at 450 iterations (**d**) With DCWT method at 450 iterations (**e**) With DWTB method at 450 iterations (**f**) With proposed method at 450 iterations

iterations. Therefore, we can say that the performance of the proposed method is better than other methods in case of weak objects.

To sum up, from all the above experiments and many other experiments, we observe that the performance of the proposed method is better than the DWT based method in the both cases: weak objects and strong objects. However, in the case of weak objects, they have less clear boundaries, the extraction of weak object is not easy work.

The symmetry and linear phase property is one of the reasons why the Daubechies complex wavelet performs better than other methods. The proposed method keeps the shape of the signal and carries strong edge information. It prevents the deformation of object boundaries. Therefore, it is helpful to find edges of an object in image. On the other hand, DCWT has reduced shift sensitivity. As the contour moves through space, the reconstruction using real valued discrete wavelet transform coefficients changes erratically, while complex wavelet transform reconstructs all local shifts and orientations in the same manner. Therefore, it is clear that it can quickly find boundaries of an object.

Conclusions

In this paper, the image contour model with Daubechies complex wavelet transform combined with B-Spline based on context-aware is proposed. The proposed technique allows estimating the contour location of a target object along an image. The contribution in the use of Daubechies complex wavelet transform for image was discussed. Mathematical basis of the Daubechies complex wavelet transform and B-Spline proved that image features based on the wavelet transform coefficients can be used very efficiently for image contour classification.

From the results shown in the above section, we see that the proposed method performs better in case of both strong and weak objects. The proposed method can be applied on any modality of images. However, in the case of weak objects, the proposed method finds approximate boundaries. Therefore, if the quality of the image is very bad due to heavy noise or heavy blur, etc., then the estimation ability is reduced because of the effect to edge the object. To avoid this problem, we can reduce noise and blur before applying the proposed method. In the future work, the method is going to be compared with some other methods to evaluate its results in different cases and the complexity of them.

Competing interests
The authors declare that they have no competing interests.

Authors' information
Nguyen Thanh Binh received the Bachelor of Engineering degree from Ho Chi Minh City University of Technology, Vietnam, the Master's degree and Ph.D degree in computer science from University of Allahabad, India. Now, he is a lecturer at Faculty of Computer Science and Engineering, Ho Chi Minh city University of Technology- Vietnam National University in Ho Chi Minh City. His research interests include recognition, image processing, multimedia information systems, decision support system, time series data.

Acknowledgment
The author is grateful to the valuable guidance provided by Dr. Ashish Khare, Department of Electronics and Communication, University of Allahabad, India.

References

1. Jain AK, Zhong Y, Lakshmanan S (1996) Object Matching Using Deformable Templates. IEEE Transactions on Pattern Analysis and Machine Intelligence 18(3):267–278
2. Kass M, Witkin A, Terzopoulos D (1988) Snakes: Active contour models, International Journal of Computer Vision, 1(4):321–331, ISSN 0920-5691. http://link.springer.com/article/10.1007/BF00133570
3. Szekely G, Kelemen A, Brechbuhler C, Gerig G (1996) Segmentation of 2-D and 3-D objects from MRI volume data using constrained elastic deformations of flexible Fourier contour and surface models. Med Image Anal 1(1):19–34
4. Lewis FL, Gurel A, Bogdan S, Doganalp A, Pastravanu OC, Wong YY, Yuen PC, Tong CS (1998) Segmented snake for contour detection. Pattern Recogn 31(11):1669–1679
5. Gunn SR, Nixon MS (1998) Global and local active contours for head boundary extraction. Int J Comput Vis 30(1):43–54
6. Garrido A, Blanca DL (1998) Physically-based active shape models: initialization and optimization. Pattern Recogn 31(8):1003–1017
7. Blake A, Isard M (1998) "Active contours", Springer
8. Chuang JH (1996) A potential-based approach for shape matching and recognition. Pattern Recogn 29(3):463–470
9. Chakraborty A, Staib LH, Duncan JS (1994) Deformable boundary finding influenced by region homogeneity, Proceedings of IEEE Computer Society conference on Computer Vision and Pattern Recognition (CVPR), pp. 624–627
10. Cootes TF, Taylor CJ, Cooper DH, Graham J (1995) Active shape models-their training and application. Comput Vis Image Underst 61(1):38–59
11. Yuille AL, Cohen DS, Hallinan PW (1989) Feature extraction from faces using deformable templates, Proceedings of IEEE Computer Society Conference on Computer Vision and Pattern Recognition, pp. 104–109
12. Amit Y, Grenander U, Piccioni M (1991) Structural image restoration through deformable templates. J Am Stat Assoc 86(414):376–387
13. Lakshmanan S, Grimmer D (1996) A deformable template approach to detecting straight edges in radar images. IEEE Transactions on Pattern Analysis and Machine Intelligence 18(4):438–442
14. Wang JY, Cohen FS (1994) Part II: 3-D object recognition and shape estimation from image contours using B-splines, shape invariant matching, and neural networks, IEEE Transactions on Pattern Analysis and Machine Intelligence, vol. 16, no. 1, pp. 13–23
15. Menet S, Marc PS, Medioni G (1990) B-snakes: Implementation and application to stereo, Image Understanding Workshop, pp. 720–726
16. Kingsbury NG (1999) Image processing with complex wavelets, Philosophical Transactions of Royal Society London. Ser A 357:2543–2560
17. Bharath AA, Ng J (2005) A Steerable Complex Wavelet Construction and Its Application to Image Denoising, IEEE Transactions on Image Processing, vol. 14, no. 7, pp. 948–959
18. Lawton W (1993) Applications of complex valued wavelet transform in sub band decomposition. IEEE Trans Signal Process 41(12):3566–3568
19. Lina JM, Mayrand M (1995) Complex Daubechies Wavelets. Journal of Applied and Computational Harmonic Analysis 2:219–229
20. Shensa MJ (1992) The discrete wavelet transform: wedding the á trous and Mallat algorithms. IEEE Trans Signal Process 40(10):2464–2482
21. Ansari R, Guillemot C, Kaiser JF (1991) Wavelet construction using Lagrange halfband filters. IEEE Transactions on Circuits and Systems 38(9):1116–1118
22. Akansu AN, Haddad RA, Caglar H (1993) The binomial QMF-wavelet transform for multiresolution signal decomposition. IEEE Trans Signal Process 41(1):13–19
23. Shen J, Strang G (1996) The zeros of the Daubechies polynomials. Proc Am Math Soc 124:3819–3833
24. Goodman TNT, Micchelli CA, Rodriguez G, Seatzu S (1997) Spectral factorization of Laurent polynomials. Adv Comput Math 7(4):429–454
25. Candes EJ (1998) Ridgelets: Theory and Applications, PhD thesis, Stanford University. http://statweb.stanford.edu/~candes/papers/Thesis.ps.gz
26. Khare A, Tiwary US (2006) Symmetric Daubechies Complex Wavelet Transform and its application to Denoising and Deblurring. WSEAS Transactions on signal processing 2(5):738–745
27. Li C, Kao C, Gore JC, Ding Z (2008) Minimization of Region-Scalable Fitting Energy for Image Segmentation. IEEE Trans Image Process 17:1940–1949
28. Li C, Kao C, Gore J, Ding Z (2007), Implicit Active Contours Driven by Local Binary Fitting Energy, IEEE Conference on Computer Vision and Pattern Recognition, pp 1–7, ISSN:1063-6919 http://ieeexplore.ieee.org/xpl/login.jsp?tp=&arnumber=4270039&url=http%3A%2F%2Fieeexplore.ieee.org%2Fxpls%2Fabs_all.jsp%3Farnumber%3D4270039
29. Darolti C, Mertins A, Bodensteiner C, Hofmann U (2008) Local Region Descriptors for Active Contours Evolution. IEEE Trans Image Process 17:2275–2288
30. Brox T, Cremers D (2009) On Local Region Models and a Statistical Interpretation of the Piecewise SmoothMumford-Shah Functional. Int J Comput Vis 84:184–193
31. Lankton S, Tannenbaum A (2008) Localizing Region-Based Active Contours. IEEE Trans Image Process 17:2029–2039
32. Lawton WM (1991) Necessary and sufficient conditions for constructing orthonormal wavelet bases. J Math Phys 32(1):57–61
33. Li C, Huang R, Ding Z, Gatenby C, Metaxas D, Gore JC (2011) A Level Set Method for Image Segmentation in the Presence of Intensity Inhomogeneity with Application to MRI. IEEE Trans Image Process 20:2007–2016
34. Strang G (1992) The optimal coefficients in Daubechies wavelets. Physical D: Nonlinear phenomena 60:239–244
35. Lina JM, Mayrand M (1993) Parameterizations for Daubechies wavelets. Phys Rev E 48:4160–4163
36. Smith H (1998) A parametrix construction for wave equations with C1, coefficients. Ann Inst Fourier 48(3):797–835
37. Daubechies I (1992) Ten Lectures on Wavelets. Society for Industrial and Applied Mathematics, Philadelphia, PA
38. Temme NM (1997) Asymptotics and numerics of zeros of polynomials that are related to Daubechies wavelets. Appl Comput Harmon Anal 4(4):414–428

39. Lina JM (1997) Image processing with complex Daubechies wavelets. Journal of Mathematical Imaging and Vision 7(3):211–223
40. Clonda D, Lina JM, Goulard B (2004) Complex Daubechies wavelets: Properties and statistical image modeling. Signal Process 84(1):1–23
41. Hearn D (1997) Computer Graphics C Version, Pearson publishing, Second edition, ISBN-10: 817758765X
42. Huaizu Jiang, Jingdong Wang, Zejian Yuan, Tie Liu, Nanning Zheng, Shipeng Li. Automatic Salient Object Segmentation Based on Context and Shape Prior. British Machine Vision Conference, pp 1–12 (2011)
43. Abowd G, Dey A, Brown P, Davies N, Smith M, Steggles P (1999) Towards a Better Understanding of Context and Context-Awareness. Lect Notes Comput Sci 1707:304–307
44. Schilit B, Theimer M (1994) Disseminating Active Map Information to Mobile Hosts. IEEE Netw 8:22–32
45. Brigger P, Hoeg J, Unser M (2000) B-spline snakes: a flexible tool for parametric contour detection. IEEE Trans Image Process 9(9):1484–1496
46. Xu C, Prince JL, (1998), Snakes shapes and gradient vector flow, IEEE Transactions on Image Processing, vol. 7, Issue 3, pp. 359–369, ISSN:1057-7149. http://ieeexplore.ieee.org/xpl/login.jsp?tp=&arnumber=661186&url=http%3A%2F%2Fieeexplore.ieee.org%2Fxpls%2Fabs_all.jsp%3Farnumber%3D661186

Permissions

All chapters in this book were first published in HCIS, by Springer; hereby published with permission under the Creative Commons Attribution License or equivalent. Every chapter published in this book has been scrutinized by our experts. Their significance has been extensively debated. The topics covered herein carry significant findings which will fuel the growth of the discipline. They may even be implemented as practical applications or may be referred to as a beginning point for another development.

The contributors of this book come from diverse backgrounds, making this book a truly international effort. This book will bring forth new frontiers with its revolutionizing research information and detailed analysis of the nascent developments around the world.

We would like to thank all the contributing authors for lending their expertise to make the book truly unique. They have played a crucial role in the development of this book. Without their invaluable contributions this book wouldn't have been possible. They have made vital efforts to compile up to date information on the varied aspects of this subject to make this book a valuable addition to the collection of many professionals and students.

This book was conceptualized with the vision of imparting up-to-date information and advanced data in this field. To ensure the same, a matchless editorial board was set up. Every individual on the board went through rigorous rounds of assessment to prove their worth. After which they invested a large part of their time researching and compiling the most relevant data for our readers.

The editorial board has been involved in producing this book since its inception. They have spent rigorous hours researching and exploring the diverse topics which have resulted in the successful publishing of this book. They have passed on their knowledge of decades through this book. To expedite this challenging task, the publisher supported the team at every step. A small team of assistant editors was also appointed to further simplify the editing procedure and attain best results for the readers.

Apart from the editorial board, the designing team has also invested a significant amount of their time in understanding the subject and creating the most relevant covers. They scrutinized every image to scout for the most suitable representation of the subject and create an appropriate cover for the book.

The publishing team has been an ardent support to the editorial, designing and production team. Their endless efforts to recruit the best for this project, has resulted in the accomplishment of this book. They are a veteran in the field of academics and their pool of knowledge is as vast as their experience in printing. Their expertise and guidance has proved useful at every step. Their uncompromising quality standards have made this book an exceptional effort. Their encouragement from time to time has been an inspiration for everyone.

The publisher and the editorial board hope that this book will prove to be a valuable piece of knowledge for researchers, students, practitioners and scholars across the globe.

List of Contributors

Naseem Ibrahim
Department of Mathematics and Computer Science, Albany State University, Georgia, USA

Mubarak Mohammad
Department of Computer Science and Software Engineering, Concordia University, Montreal, Canada

Vangalur Alagar
Department of Computer Science and Software Engineering, Concordia University, Montreal, Canada

Varun Gupta
Uttarakhand Technical University, Dehradun, Uttarakhand, India

Durg Singh Chauhan
Uttarakhand Technical University, Dehradun, Uttarakhand, India

Kamlesh Dutta
Department of CSE, National Institute of Technology, Hamirpur, India

Juan C Augusto
Middlesex University, London, UK

Vic Callaghan
University of Essex, Colchester, UK

Diane Cook
Washington State University, Pullman, USA

Achilles Kameas
Hellenic Open University, Patras, Greece

Ichiro Satoh
National Institute of Informatics, Tokyo, Japan

Arjulie John Berena
National Institute of Informatics, Tokyo, Japan

Sila Chunwijitra
The Graduate University for Advanced Studies, Tokyo, Japan

Hitoshi Okada
National Institute of Informatics, Tokyo, Japan

Haruki Ueno
National Institute of Informatics, Tokyo, Japan

KP Krishna Kumar
Equal contributors Department of Computer Science and Information Systems, BITS-Pilani, Hyderabad Campus, Jawahar Nagar, Hyderabad, India

G Geethakumari
Equal contributors Department of Computer Science and Information Systems, BITS-Pilani, Hyderabad Campus, Jawahar Nagar, Hyderabad, India

Hyunduk Kim
Department of Convergence, Daegu Gyeongbuk Institute of Science & Technology (DGIST), 50-1 Sang-Ri, Hyeongpung-Myeon, Dalseong-Gun, 711-873 Daegu, South Korea

Sang-Heon Lee
Department of Convergence, Daegu Gyeongbuk Institute of Science & Technology (DGIST), 50-1 Sang-Ri, Hyeongpung-Myeon, Dalseong-Gun, 711-873 Daegu, South Korea

Myoung-Kyu Sohn
Department of Convergence, Daegu Gyeongbuk Institute of Science & Technology (DGIST), 50-1 Sang-Ri, Hyeongpung-Myeon, Dalseong-Gun, 711-873 Daegu, South Korea

Dong-Ju Kim
Department of Convergence, Daegu Gyeongbuk Institute of Science & Technology (DGIST), 50-1 Sang-Ri, Hyeongpung-Myeon, Dalseong-Gun, 711-873 Daegu, South Korea

Alex Pappachen James
School of Engineering, Nazarbayev University, Astana, Kazakhstan
Enview R&D Labs, Thiruvananthapuram, India

Bincy Mathews
Enview R&D Labs, Thiruvananthapuram, India

Sherin Sugathan
Enview R&D Labs, Thiruvananthapuram, India

Dileep Kumar Raveendran
Department of Computational Biology and Bioinformatics, University of Kerala, Trivandrum, India

Mohammad Isam Malkawi
Jordan University of Science and Technology, Irbid 21410, Jordan

Vijayalakshmi Saravanan
WINCORE Lab, Ryerson University, Toronto, Canada

Kothari Dwarkadas Pralhaddas
WINCORE Lab, Ryerson University, Toronto, Canada

Dwarkadas Pralhaddas Kothari
I.I.T. Delhi, India

Isaac Woungang
WINCORE Lab, Ryerson University, Toronto, Canada

Geeta U Navalyal
Department of Computer Science & Engg, KLE Dr. M.S.S
CET, Udyambag, Belgaum, India

Rahul D Gavas
Department of Computer Science & Engg, KLE Dr. M.S.S
CET, Udyambag, Belgaum, India

Konstantinos Chorianopoulos
Department of Informatics, Ionian University, 7 Tsirigoti
square, Corfu 49100, Greece

Kadayanallur Mahadevan Prabusankarlal
Research & Development Centre, Bharathiar University,
Coimbatore 641046, India
Department of Electronics & Communication, K.S.R
College of Arts & Science, Tiruchengode 637215, India

Palanisamy Thirumoorthy
Department of Electronics & Communication, Govt Arts
College, Dharmapuri 636705, India

Radhakrishnan Manavalan
Department of Computer Applications, K.S.R College of
Arts & Science, Tiruchengode 637215, India

Li-Tze Lee
Department of Marketing and Supply Chain Management,
Overseas Chinese University, 40721 No. 100, Chiao
Kwang Rd., Taichung City, Taiwan, R.O.C
Department of Information Technology, Overseas Chinese
University, 40721 No. 100, Chiao Kwang Rd., Taichung
City, Taiwan, R.O.C

Jason C Hung
Department of Marketing and Supply Chain Management,
Overseas Chinese University, 40721 No. 100, Chiao
Kwang Rd., Taichung City, Taiwan, R.O.C
Department of Information Technology, Overseas Chinese
University, 40721 No. 100, Chiao Kwang Rd., Taichung
City, Taiwan, R.O.C

Jyoti Agarwal
Department of Computer Science, RIMT, Bareilly, Uttar
Pradesh, India

Sarabjeet Singh Bedi
Department of Computer Science, MJP Rohilkhand
University, Bareilly, India

Asbjørn Følstad
SINTEF, Pb124 Blindern, 0314 Oslo, Norway

Kasper Hornbæk
Department of Computing, University of Copenhagen,
Njalsgade 128, 2300 Copenhagen, Denmark

Pål Ulleberg
Department of Psychology, University of Oslo,
Forskningsveien 3B, 0373 Oslo, Norway

Maxim Mozgovoy
University of Aizu, Tsuruga, Ikki-machi, Aizu-Wakamatsu,
Fukushima, Japan

Roman Efimov
University of Aizu, Tsuruga, Ikki-machi, Aizu-Wakamatsu,
Fukushima, Japan

Nguyen Thanh Binh
Faculty of Computer Science and Engineering, Ho Chi
Minh City University of Technology, Ho Chi Minh,
Vietnam

Printed in the USA
CPSIA information can be obtained
at www.ICGtesting.com
JSHW051428221024
72173JS00006B/1406